Class Actions in Context

Class Actions in Context

How Culture, Economics and Politics Shape Collective Litigation

Edited by

Deborah R. Hensler

Stanford Law School, USA

Christopher Hodges

Centre for Socio-Legal Studies and Wolfson College, Oxford, UK

Ianika Tzankova

University of Tilburg, the Netherlands

Edward Elgar
PUBLISHING

Cheltenham, UK • Northampton, MA, USA

Published by
Edward Elgar Publishing Limited
The Lypiatts
15 Lansdown Road
Cheltenham
Glos GL50 2JA
UK

Edward Elgar Publishing, Inc.
William Pratt House
9 Dewey Court
Northampton
Massachusetts 01060
USA

A catalogue record for this book
is available from the British Library

Library of Congress Control Number: 2015959653

This book is available electronically in the **Elgar**online
Law subject collection
DOI 10.4337/9781783470440

MIX
Paper from responsible sources
FSC® C013056
FSC www.fsc.org

ISBN 978 1 78347 043 3 (cased)
ISBN 978 1 78347 044 0 (eBook)

Typeset by Columns Design XML Ltd, Reading
Printed and bound in Great Britain by TJ International Ltd, Padstow, Cornwall

Contents

Contributors

Agustin Barroilhet is Assistant Professor at the University of Chile Law School. He received his JSM at Stanford Law School and is currently pursuing a doctoral degree at Georgetown University Law School.

Camille Cameron is the Dean and Weldon Professor of Law at the Schulich School of Law at Dalhousie University in Halifax, Canada. Prior to joining Dalhousie, Prof. Cameron was Dean of Law at the University of Windsor, Ontario and on the faculty of law at the University of Melbourne, Australia. Her research and teaching focus on civil justice administration and reform, including class actions.

Naomi Creutzfeldt is an ESRC Research Fellow at the Centre for Socio-Legal Studies, Oxford University, England. Dr. Creutzfeldt's research has focused on European civil justice systems and alternative dispute resolution.

Manuel A. Gómez is Associate Professor of Law and Associate Dean of International & Graduate Studies at Florida International University College of Law (United States). Prof. Gomez's research and teaching focuses on comparative civil procedure, complex litigation, international arbitration, law and society, and alternative dispute resolution.

Axel Halfmeier is Professor of Civil Law, Comparative Law and International Private and Procedural Law at Leuphana University Lüneburg (Germany). His research focuses on the enforcement of law in a global setting. In 2009, he was the lead author of the evaluation of the KapMuG ("model case proceeding") that was commissioned by the German Ministry of Justice.

Deborah R. Hensler is the Judge John W. Ford Professor of Dispute Resolution and Associate Dean for Graduate Studies at Stanford Law School (United States), and holds a personal chair in Empirical Studies on Mass Claims Resolution at Tilburg University (Netherlands). Prof. Hensler's research and teaching focuses on complex litigation, including mass torts and class actions. Prior to joining Stanford, she was the director of the RAND Institute for Civil Justice.

Christopher Hodges is Professor of Justice Systems, Fellow of Wolfson College, and Head of the Swiss Re/CMS Research Programme on Civil Justice Systems at the Centre for Socio-Legal Studies, University of Oxford, England.

Kuo-Chang Huang is a member of Taiwan's national congress. At the time he conducted his case studies he was a researcher at Institutum Iurisprudentiae, Academia Sinica and Professor at National Cheng-Chi University in Taiwan. He was the principal investigator of the first nationwide study on access to justice in Taiwan.

Jasminka Kalajdzic is Associate Professor of Law, University of Windsor, Ontario, Canada. Prof. Kalajdzic teaches and writes in the areas of access to justice and class actions. In 2011 she was appointed to the five-member Class Proceedings Committee, which provides funding to class action plaintiffs in Ontario. She is also a member of the Advisory Committee for the Law Commission of Ontario's Class Action Project.

Alon Klement is a Professor at the Buchman Faculty of Law, Tel-Aviv University, Israel. He writes on civil procedure, law and economics and law and social norms. His articles on class actions have been cited numerous times by the Supreme Court of Israel.

Byron Stier is Associate Dean for Research and Professor of Law at Southwestern Law School, Los Angeles, California. He teaches and writes about mass torts and complex litigation and is the founding editor of the mass tort litigation blog, http://lawprofessors.typepad.com/mass_tort_litigation/.

Elizabeth Thornburg is the Richard R. Lee Endowed Professor of Law and Senior Associate Dean for Academic Affairs, SMU Dedman School of Law, Dallas, Texas. Prof. Thornburg teaches and writes in the areas of civil procedure, comparative procedure, online dispute resolution and the intersection of law and culture.

Ianika Tzankova holds the Chair in Mass Claims Dispute Resolution at Tilburg University, the Netherlands and was a Fulbright Visiting Scholar at Stanford in 2012. She was a member of a commission that conducted a fundamental review of Dutch civil procedure law for the Netherlands Ministry of Justice in 2001–2006. She has authored numerous articles on the unique Dutch procedure for resolving mass claims.

Stefaan Voet is an Associate Professor of Law at the University of Leuven (Belgium) and a Visiting Professor at the University of Hasselt. He was a visiting scholar at the University of Houston Law Center

(2010) and Stanford Law School (2014), and a visiting lecturer at various US law schools. He focuses on civil procedure, complex litigation, ADR, ODR and litigation costs.

Acknowledgements

The research reported here could not have been conducted without the cooperation of judges, other public officials, lawyers and other representatives of corporations, NGOs and individual parties in the litigation that was investigated, most of whom preferred to remain anonymous. We gratefully acknowledge their willingness to give of their time and to share their knowledge, experience and perspectives.

The collaborative effort that produced this book was initiated by a series of international conferences on the globalization of class actions, co-sponsored by Stanford Law School and the Oxford Centre for Socio-Legal Studies, from 2007–2011. We gratefully acknowledge the support of all those who contributed to funding these conferences, especially the American Academy of Political and Social Sciences, Stanford Law School and the Oxford Centre for Socio-Legal Studies, which provided the lead grants for the 2007 conference, and Australian National University, Florida International University Law School and Tilburg University, which helped fund the subsequent international conferences. Deborah Hensler and Ianika Tzankova thank the Private Law Department of Tilburg University and the Royal Academy of Science of the Netherlands for supporting their collaborative research on the Dutch collective settlement procedure which initiated the empirical research program. The organization of the research team was facilitated by the American Law & Society Association's International Research Collaborative program. All of the authors gratefully acknowledge the support of their home institutions for their research and writing and for enabling the group to convene in various parts of the world to share their findings. The authors also thank Inge Pullens for her assistance editing the final manuscript.

Abbreviations

ACT	Aliança de Controle do Tabagismo (consumer protection group)
ADESF	Assocação de Defensa da Saúde do Fumante (Association for the Defense of the Health of Smokers)
ALGA	ALGA Technology Corporation
ANADEUS	Asociación Nacional de Usuarios de la Seguridad Social (National Association of Users of the Social Security Services)
ANVISA	Agência Nacional dta Vigilância Sanitária (National Health Surveillance Agency)
ASIC	Australian Securities and Investment Commission
ASR	Automatic Speech Recognition
BAT	British American Tobacco
BP	British Petroleum
BUNPIG	Buncefield Property Insurance Group
CA	Competent Authority
CAA	Clean Air Act
CAL	Israeli Class Action Law
CCCTB	Comitê Coordenador do Controle do Tabagismo no Brasil (anti-smoking advocacy group)
CERCLA	Comprehensive Environmental Response Compensation and Liability Act
CFAs	conditional fee agreements
Charter (The)	Canadian Charter of Rights and Freedoms
CMC	Case Management Conference
COMAH	Control of Major Accident Hazards Regulations 1999
CPP	Canada Pension Plan
DRAM	dynamic random access memory
EA	Environmental Agency

EPA	Environmental Protection Agency
EPS	earnings per share
FCAA	Federal Court of Australia Act 1976
FRCP	Federal Rules of Civil Procedure
Fund (The)	Ontario's Class Proceedings Fund
GAAP	Generally Accepted Accounting Principles
GLO	Group Litigation Order
HOSL	Hertfordshire Oil Storage Limited
HSE	Health and Safety Executive
IDEC	Instituto Brasileiro de Defesa do Consumidor (consumer protection group)
IHLS	independent high-level switch
ILF	International Litigation Funding Partners Pte Ltd
IMF	Australian litigation funder
IPO	initial public offering
ISA	Israeli Securities Authority
KapMuG	Kapitalanleger-Musterverfahrensgesetz (Capital Market Investors' Model Proceedings Act)
KYEC	King Yuan Electronics Company
LDCs	Language Development Companies
L&H	Lernout & Hauspie Speech Products
MBOA	Modernization of Benefits and Obligations Act
MDL	Multi-District Litigation
MI	Metropolis-Intercom
MIIB	Buncefield Major Incident Investigation Board
MTBE	Methyl Tertiary Butyl Ether
NCSL	National Conference of State Legislatures
NHTSA	National Highway Traffic Safety Administration
NIS	New Israeli Shekels
NTD	New Taiwan Dollars
NYSE	New York Stock Exchange
OSC	Ontario Securities Commission
PMI	Philip Morris Brasil Industria e Comercio Ltda. (subsidiary of Philip Morris International)

Proposition 65	Safe Drinking Water and Toxic Enforcement Act
PSCs	Plaintiff Steering Committees
R$	Brazilian Reals
SEC	Securities and Exchange Commission
SERNAC	Servicio Nacional del Consumidor (public administrative agency in charge of protecting Chilean consumers)
SFIPC	Securities and Fortunes Investors Protection Center
SIFTP	Securities Investors and Fortunes Trader Protection Act
SOP	Statement of Position
SST	Soporte servicio técnico (technical support service)
TARP	Trouble Asset Relief Program
TASE	Tel Aviv Stock Exchange
TCC	Technology and Construction Court
TCCP	Taiwan Code of Civil Procedure
TWSE	Taiwan Stock Exchange
USTs	underground storage tanks
VEB	Vereniging van Effectenbezitters (Association of Smaller Investors in the Netherlands)
VTR	Chilean cable television company
WCAM	Wet Collectieve Afwikkeling Massaschade (Dutch Collective Mass Claims Settlement Act)

PART I

Introduction

1. The global landscape of collective litigation

Deborah R. Hensler

INTRODUCTION

Over the past several decades, the class action—a representative legal procedure in which some person or organization comes forward to litigate on behalf of a group or group interest—has spread worldwide. Some form of representative collective litigation procedure is now recognized by more than three dozen national jurisdictions (see Table 1.1). The procedure goes by different formal names in different parts of the world—for example 'collective action', 'collective redress', 'popular action'—but is often referred to informally as a class action in recognition of its resemblance to the American class action. Although previously regarded strictly as a common law procedure, the class action has now been integrated into civil law regimes in Asia, Europe and South America, and 21 of the 25 largest economies in the world have adopted a class action procedure to date, most in the last 20 years. As a result of the 2013 European Union Recommendation on Collective Redress,[1] more European countries can be expected to join this list in the near future.

Many jurisdictions provide for class actions by statute. In some jurisdictions that do not have such statutes but have Constitutions or statutes that grant collective rights—for example, for protection of consumers, the environment or national heritage—judges have permitted representative collective litigation to claim those rights. In the United States (US), federal and state rules of civil procedure provide for class actions.

[1] Commission Recommendation of 11 June 2013 on common principles for injunctive and compensatory collective redress mechanisms in the member states concerning violations of rights granted under Union Law (2013/396/EU) available at http://eur-lex.europa.eu/legal-content/EN/TXT/?uri=OJ:JOL_2013_201_R_NS0013.

The spread of class actions globally is an example of what have come to be called 'legal transplants' (Watson, 1974). The term refers to a legal institution, doctrine, rule or practice that after arising in one country is adopted in one or more other countries (Graziadei, 2006). An extensive literature on legal transplants sees them as a sub-set of public policies that have diffused across jurisdictions, sometimes as a result of external pressure and sometimes in response to perceived domestic needs (Dobbins, Simmons & Garrett, 2007).

To date, there has been no systematic analysis of the factors motivating the spread of class actions beyond the US, but one of the most important seems to be the increased frequency of mass claims. With the rise of multinational and national corporations whose success depends on their ability to market goods and services to vast populations, the chance of mass injuries resulting from negligence or violations of private contractual terms or public law or other unknown causes has increased markedly. Mineral resource extraction and distribution and electric power generation—all marks of a modern economy—have also been sources of mass injuries and environmental damage. Analysts have speculated that as societies modernize, popular expectations of redress in such instances increase, as events that were once viewed as chance occurrences or ordained by deities are increasingly attributed to human behaviors. Consistent with this observation, legal doctrine in many countries now holds private and public institutions accountable for violating legal standards—for example, by manufacturing and selling defective products, failing to accurately disclose financial information to shareholders, colluding on price with other manufacturers or service providers, and damaging the environment. Accountability is often although not always tied to a responsibility to redress losses. As a result of these economic, cultural and legal changes when many individuals or organizations suffer personal injury, property damage or financial harm allegedly as a result of another party's improper behavior, it is now common for a large number of similar claims ('mass claims') to appear (Hensler, 2013).

Typically designed to handle single claims on a case-by-case basis, neither private dispute resolution institutions nor public courts are well-equipped to handle a sudden deluge of claims arising from an untoward event or information disclosure. To many, the similarity of law and facts that characterizes mass claims suggests that some sort of group treatment might be attractive. The class action procedure is one such approach. Others include private and public administrative programs that permit quick processing of individual claims according to a well-specified protocol; group litigation procedures; and ad hoc management strategies that identify certain aspects of claims that can be resolved on a

Table 1.1 Countries that have adopted a class action procedure for one or more types of legal claims

NORTH AMERICA	CENTRAL & SOUTH AMERICA	EUROPE & THE MIDDLE EAST	AFRICA	ASIA & AUSTRALASIA
Canada	Argentina	Belgium	South Africa	Australia
Mexico	Bolivia	Bulgaria		China
United States	Brazil	Denmark		Indonesia
	Chile	England		Japan
	Colombia	Finland		South Korea
	Costa Rica	France		Taiwan
	Ecuador	Israel		Thailand
	Panama	Italy		
	Peru	Lithuania		
	Uruguay	Netherlands		
	Venezuela	Norway		
		Poland		
		Portugal		
		Spain		
		Sweden		

group-wide basis. What distinguishes all of these latter procedures from a class action is that they all preserve—at least as a formal matter—the ability of claimants to pursue redress on an individual basis and the ability of potential payers to contest their responsibility for such redress on an individual basis.

Administrative schemes adopted to resolve mass claims typically sort claims into groups—for example, by type of injury or amount of financial loss—and apply the same treatment to all the claims within each group, ignoring possible individual differences. This is sometimes termed a 'compensation matrix'. These types of schemes have been adopted by governments to forestall or minimize litigation and by private corporations, both on a voluntary basis and as a result of a negotiated settlement of lawsuits (Feinberg, 2012).

Group litigation procedures permit a judge or other dispute resolution official to apply decisions on common issues—for example, jurisdictional competence or admissibility of evidence—to all of the claims in a group while preserving final decisions on the merits for individual claim resolution. Sometimes the resolution of common issues leads to voluntary group settlements by the parties. England, Germany and the US are three national jurisdictions that have formally adopted such procedures (Hodges, 2001; Hensler, 2014).

Informal ad hoc strategies allow a judge or other dispute resolution officer to identify circumstantial aspects of claims that make group treatment advantageous without impairing claimants' ability to proceed individually. Often termed 'case management', this approach took hold in US courts more than two decades ago, in part in response to mass litigation, and was endorsed by English jurists in the late 1990s. Civil law judges have long had the authority to shape the course of civil lawsuits but many are said to be reluctant to engage in the close direction of lawsuits that is typical of managerial judges in the US and England.

In contrast to administrative programs, group litigation procedures and informal case management, in a class action the class members' interests are represented by one or a few individuals or organizations that they may have had no role in selecting. Typically, the class members' claims are not formally before the court (hence the term, 'absent parties' to apply to class members), but the decision of the court will significantly affect their claims. (In formal terms, the outcome is *res judicata*.) Because this is such a radical departure from modern legal norms, most jurisdictions that permit class actions specify the circumstances in which a class action may proceed, require a judge to 'certify' that the dispute fits these circumstances and require either that potential class members be notified that they can join the litigation if they wish or that they can decline to participate. Many jurisdictions' class action statutes or rules also include other provisions intended to protect the interests of class members, including their right to a fair adjudicatory process ('due process').

Although many recently legislated class action procedures were adopted to deal with instances of mass claims, there are other situations in which legislatures or judiciaries have deemed collective litigation appropriate. For example, many Latin American jurisdictions provide for class actions to protect indivisible collective interests (variously called 'diffuse' or 'popular' interests), such as environmental quality. Unlike class actions that aggregate individual claims for redress, these actions typically seek declaratory or injunctive relief, not monetary damages. In some instances, the indivisible interest is that of a specific group, for example, an indigenous community in the environs of resource extraction; in others, it is the public at large. The modern form of the US class action rule provides for both collective interest claims (although this term is rarely used in US procedural law) and aggregated monetary claims.

The class action statutes and rules adopted around the world in recent years differ in several important respects. In some jurisdictions, the rule is trans-substantive, meaning class actions may be pursued in virtually every circumstance in which an individual claim could be brought. For example, in Australia, Canada, the Netherlands and the US, investors may bring class actions for violation of securities law, businesses and consumers may bring class actions for violation of anti-trust (competition) statutes, consumers may bring class actions for violation of consumer protection statutes, and citizens may bring suits for violation of their constitutional rights. Israel's procedure is not trans-substantive but permits class actions for many causes of action, including, among others, consumer, securities, banking, antitrust, environmental, employment and discrimination claims.

In other jurisdictions, class actions may be used exclusively for consumer protection (for example, Belgium, France and Japan) or shareholder claims (for example, South Korea) or anti-trust (competition) claims (for example, the United Kingdom), or in more limited fact-specific circumstances. Some jurisdictions first adopted a class action procedure to address a particular situation but then extended it to apply to other mass claim situations. For example, the Netherlands' collective settlement procedure (which permits claimants and defendants to jointly petition a court to approve a global 'opt-out' settlement that they have negotiated) was adopted initially to assist in a large-scale settlement of DES pharmaceutical product defect claims but has since been used to resolve securities, investment product and insolvency litigation. Israel enacted multiple statutes for different types of substantive claims that permitted class actions, before it adopted a more general class action statute.

Another important distinction among class action procedures is who has standing to represent the class. In common law jurisdictions with class action procedures, any class member may come forward to represent the class, provided that party meets certain requirements intended to assure that the representative will adequately represent the interests of all class members. In many civil law jurisdictions, standing is limited to one or a few associations that have been declared eligible to represent a class or to special purpose foundations established to bring the action. In a few jurisdictions, only a government official may bring certain types of class actions. In all EU member states, whether based on civil law or common law, standing is permitted for defined public and private entities.

In some jurisdictions, everyone who meets the class definition must come forward and affirmatively state that they wish to be part of the action ('opt in') in order to realize its benefits. In other jurisdictions, everyone who meets the class definition is considered a class member unless they formally declare that they do not want to be part of the action ('opt out'). (In a few jurisdictions, the court may decide whether a class action should proceed on an opt-out or opt-in basis.) In both sorts of class actions, the outcome of the suit binds all of the class members, meaning that they are not free to individually litigate the issues that were decided (or settled) in the class litigation. In jurisdictions where standing to bring a collective action is limited to an association, the decision may formally bind only that association or that association's members.

Finally, in some jurisdictions, class actions may only deliver declaratory or injunctive relief (even when class members are seeking monetary compensation), while in others, class actions may yield declaratory or injunctive relief or money damages (or all three). In jurisdictions where class members cannot obtain monetary damages, if the court issues a declaratory judgment holding that the defendant has violated the law, class members seeking monetary redress must file individual follow-on lawsuits to pursue those claims.

Taken together, these (and other) provisions of class action procedures determine how often class action lawsuits will be filed, by whom and under what circumstances. However, class actions do not operate independently of other features of civil litigation regimes. Rules on how the costs of litigation are allocated between plaintiffs and defendants, and how lawyers may be paid have a significant impact on individuals' and organizations' willingness to serve as class representatives. Most jurisdictions other than the US impose a 'loser-pays' rule on all civil litigation including class actions (Hodges, Vogenauer and Tulibacka, 2010). In ordinary litigation this means that if plaintiffs lose they must pay the defendants' costs (and vice versa). This substantially increases the risk of litigating. In a class action, it is the representative plaintiff who bears the risk of adverse costs. In a jurisdiction that permits individual class members to serve as class representatives, there may be no class member who is willing to take this risk. But cost shifting does not only deter individual class members. In a jurisdiction that limits standing to associations and other non-profit organizations, there may be few that have the resources to take on this risk. Even public officials who have standing to bring class actions have to calculate the risk of proceeding against the background of budgetary constraints. In some jurisdictions, private or public funding mechanisms have emerged to mitigate the adverse cost risk for representative plaintiffs.

Most class actions are more complex than ordinary civil lawsuits and hence more expensive to prosecute and defend. If professional rules forbid lawyers to charge speculative or contingent fees (that is, 'no win, no pay' or a fee amount linked to the amount obtained by plaintiffs) there may be few class members who can afford to hire lawyers. But even where professional rules permit speculative fees, there may be few lawyers who can assume the risk of having to cover their own expenses if defendants prevail. In some jurisdictions, legal aid or legal expenses insurance may help parties overcome these financial obstacles. In still others, third-party litigation financers help pay for the litigation in exchange for a share of any monetary remedies.

Substantive and procedural rules that apply to all litigation, class and non-class alike, also determine the attractiveness of bringing class actions. If pleading standards are very strict or evidence hard to obtain, the risk-benefit calculus for parties and lawyers considering bringing class actions will be more negative than if pleading standards are relatively relaxed and document discovery readily available. If the expected value of damages is large—for example, because of statutory treble damages, compounded statutory interest rules or the availability of exemplary or punitive damages—the risk-benefit calculus will be more positive. In the US, arbitration clauses agreed to prior to a dispute arising (for example, in consumer contracts) frequently forbid any form of collective dispute resolution.

No jurisdiction consistently reports the number of class actions filed in its courts annually or the distribution of class action lawsuits by the substantive type of claim. The available evidence suggests that class actions account for a small percentage of all civil lawsuits in the jurisdictions that permit them. In many jurisdictions, there have been just a few class action lawsuits filed to date, perhaps as a result of the obstacles to successful class litigation identified above. In the US, thousands of complaints seeking class certification have been filed in recent decades but fragmentary evidence suggests that only a small fraction of these move forward in the form of class actions (Hensler, forthcoming).

CLASS ACTION CONTROVERSIES

In virtually every jurisdiction in which a class action procedure has been formally proposed, there has been vigorous controversy about the virtues and vices of class actions. And in many jurisdictions that have adopted class actions, controversies over rules and practices persist long after their adoption. The intensity and nature of controversy over class actions vary within and among jurisdictions, reflecting national politics and temporal circumstances.

Debates over the adoption of class actions implicate many different beliefs and values. Historical commitments to individual dispute resolution lead to skepticism about the consequences of aggregating claims whatever the approach. Does treating claims en masse lead to more efficient dispute resolution, or does it simply introduce new sources of litigation expense and delay? If aggregation does reduce the cost of claiming, will it encourage frivolous claims, needlessly increasing the burden on court resources and imposing an inappropriate financial burden on defendants that will ultimately be passed on to consumers? Conversely, does aggregation open the courthouse to parties with legitimate claims that they cannot afford to litigate individually, and help ensure that defendants properly internalize the external impact of their behavior—that is, the costs they impose on others—when making decisions?

For those who are open to considering aggregating claims under some circumstances, representative class actions raise further questions. How can class members' interests in substantive and procedural due process be assured when they are represented by just one or a few individuals or an association that the class members played no role in selecting? How can defendants' interests be protected when they face a mass of claimants, rather than individuals? How should courts deal with conflicts of interest that may arise among class members? Is it possible to fashion rules and practices that minimize the principal-agent problems that arise when an attorney represents a large group of claimants, none of whom can effectively monitor the lawyer's behavior? Are there holistic answers to these questions about representative litigation, or do the answers differ, depending on the type of substantive claim, suggesting that representative procedures might be appropriate in some circumstances, but not others? Finally, are the issues presented by representative class actions unique to the representative device or are they inherent to all aggregated procedures?

In most jurisdictions, these controversies have proceeded without reference to empirical evidence. The absence of empirical data to test assertions of critics and proponents of class actions is not unique to this debate; in most jurisdictions, collecting and analyzing empirical data to support policy making regarding civil litigation is a relatively new phenomenon. In the absence of such data, claims regarding the frequency of class actions, the ratio of meritorious to non-meritorious suits, and the outcomes of class actions and other collective procedures have not been subject to testing.

There is also a lack of qualitative evidence about the circumstances that give rise to class actions and other forms of mass litigation, the people and organizations that play a role in shaping litigation, the ways in which formal law and informal practices influence legal strategy and the variety of ways in which litigation is resolved. When critics and supporters of class actions refer to actual cases, they often exaggerate their apparent good and bad points, and rarely discuss the context in which the cases arose: the events leading up to the litigation and the events that may have swirled around it and determined its progress and outcomes. Advocates' stories about lawsuits exaggerate either their (seemingly) positive or (seemingly) negative aspects, erasing complexities that might make judgments about the lawsuits' ultimate value more difficult to reach or more ambivalent. The lack of qualitative data leads to debate that focuses on high theory and ignores the social reality on the ground—the 'law on the books' rather than the 'law in action'. Without such data, policy makers run the risk of making decisions that seem wise from a theoretical perspective but are likely to produce unanticipated consequences when implemented in the real world.

FILLING THE QUALITATIVE EMPIRICAL GAP

The globalization of class actions and other collective litigation procedures has created an opportunity to learn more about how class actions operate on the ground in different legal regimes, with different legal cultures, rules and practices, and in different political contexts. This book is a first step in that direction. It is the product of a global collaboration that brought together 14 scholars from different parts of the world to conduct qualitative research on recent class or mass litigation in their own or another country.

The method the collaborators selected for their research is the method of choice for qualitative social research. Known as the 'case study' method, it has deep roots in sociological inquiry, but has also been adopted by historians, political scientists and management analysts. It has been used by scholars to investigate the evolution of international crises, the adoption of economic and social policies, and the implementation of business decisions (George & Bennett, 2005; Yin, 2013). In recent years, it has also been used to investigate civil litigation (Green, 1996; Hensler et al., 2000; Schuck, 1987; Sobol, 1991). The approach is animated by the belief that understanding social phenomena requires intensive investigation of examples of the phenomenon (the 'cases') in the context in which they occur. Sometimes the cases are nations or local communities;

sometimes they are policies or programs. In research on litigation, the cases are frequently legal disputes or lawsuits.

The case study method relies heavily on close reading of documentary evidence and on interviews with key informants. For this reason, case study research projects almost always investigate only a small number of cases. The representative sampling techniques that are common to large-scale data collection are inapposite to such 'small-N' studies. As a result, both the selection of cases for investigation and the selection of interviewees is purposive rather than random. Because each interviewee is likely to have a different perspective on the process under investigation, the researcher uses a semi-structured interview protocol rather than a standardized questionnaire to guide the interview. Depending on the nature of the questions asked, some of the data collected may be quantitative, but most will be qualitative. The product of the case study approach is a 'thick description' of what happened and why, including the roles different actors played in the program or process under investigation. Over the past several decades, comparative legal scholars have made extensive use of the case study method.

In this project, the case studies for investigation were large-scale litigations that were resolved in class actions, group litigation or aggregated procedures. Each of the project collaborators selected one or more lawsuits (or a related 'family' of lawsuits) that he or she thought would provide insights into the inception, evolution and resolution of mass litigation within that jurisdiction's contemporary legal regime. The substantive legal claims underlying the litigation included employment wage claims, property damage claims arising from catastrophic accidents and environmental contamination, consumer protection, shareholder and other investment claims, and civil rights claims (Table 1.2). This diversity of substantive claims was dictated primarily by differences in the law that permitted or facilitated certain types of claims but not others in the chosen jurisdictions, and secondarily by the researchers' individual interests and expertise and their access to informants. Despite the lack of standardization regarding case selection, securities (shareholder) claims dominated.

At the start of the project, the collaborators agreed on a common interview protocol. The interviews covered the factual circumstances that gave rise to the litigation; the relevant substantive and procedural law; key court decisions; litigation strategy; the roles of judges, parties, legal representatives of parties and civil society; claim characteristics; legal outcomes including damages (if any); and litigation financing. Because, in

Table 1.2 Type of legal claims investigated, by jurisdiction

Country	Number of cases	Type of claims
Australia	2	Securities
Belgium	1	Securities
Brazil	1	Consumer
Canada	2	Securities & civil rights
Chile	2	Consumer
England	1	Catastrophic property damage
Germany	1	Securities
Israel	1	Securities
Netherlands	2	Securities & insurance
Taiwan	2	Employment & securities
United States	4	Product defect, catastrophic property damage, environmental contamination & securities

many jurisdictions, the collective litigation procedures used were relatively new, the interviews also covered respondents' views of how the procedures' characteristics affected the litigation and its outcomes. All of the interviews were conducted on a confidential basis, although some interviewees volunteered that they would be pleased to be identified. In addition to interviews, the researchers drew on court documents and media reports of the litigation.

Each of the jurisdictions in which the research took place has a different structure for addressing mass claims. Table 1.3 summarizes the characteristics of the procedures that were in place at the time of the case study research. Australia, Canada and the US have similar (but not identical) class action procedures and each has used the class action procedure for at least a decade. Israel's more recently adopted class action procedure resembles these in many respects. Brazil and Chile's class action regimes rely more on public prosecution than the regimes in the first three countries. Taiwan's class action regime provides for class actions prosecuted by associations and, in securities cases, a quasi-public agency. The Netherlands has two class action regimes, one that permits a class to litigate, with remedies limited to declaratory or injunctive relief,

Table 1.3 Summary of collective procedures' features at the time of the case study research

Country	Type of procedure	Scope	Standing	Opt-out/Opt-in	Remedies	Funding	Funding issues
Australia	Class action	Trans-substantive	Class members	Opt-out. When third- party funding is provided, class is opt-in	Money, injunctive or declaratory relief	Class counsel 'no win, no pay' fees/ third-party funding	Cost shifting. No equitable fund doctrine to ensure class members share costs
Belgium		Criminal cases with private claims. Criminal prosecutor develops case, but may be assisted by legal counsel for civil claimants	Victims Associations	Opt-in	Money, injunctive or declaratory relief	Hourly rate, contingency fee, lump sum	Cost shifting
Brazil	Class action	Consumer cases	Governmental agencies and consumer associations	n/a	Money, injunctive or declaratory relief	Membership fees and donations	Cost shifting risk abrogated for consumer cases
Canada	Class action	Trans-substantive	Class members	Opt-out	Money, injunctive or declaratory relief	Class counsel contingency fee/ public fund subsidized by successful class action damages	Cost shifting

Chile	Class action	Consumer cases	Public consumer protection agency Associations	Formally opt-out but individually represented parties can join class	Injunctive relief/ contractual pecuniary damages	Contingency fees/ court awarded fees/legal costs and public budget	Cost shifting
England	Group litigation procedure (GLO). Judicial case management may eliminate need for GLO order	Trans-substantive	Multiple plaintiffs	Opt-in	Money, injunctive or declaratory relief	Legal aid, legal expenses insurance, 'no win, no pay' fee; third-party funding	Cost shifting
Germany	Group litigation procedure (KapMuG)	Capital market cases	Multiple plaintiffs	One case selected for 'model proceeding'; other cases register and are bound by liability decision	Liability decision applies to all cases registered for proceeding. If liability is found claimants may pursue damages individually	Legal expenses insurance	Cost shifting
Israel	Class action	Multiple causes of action	Class members, associations, certain public agencies	Opt-out	Money, injunctive or declaratory relief	Class counsel. Some public funding	Discretionary cost shifting
Netherlands	Collective action	Trans-substantive	Ad hoc or pre-existing special purpose foundation or association	n/a	Injunctive or declaratory relief	Legal aid funding, legal expense insurance, membership fees	Cost shifting
Netherlands	Collective settlement (WCAM)	Trans-substantive	Special purpose foundation or pre-existing association	Opt-out	Monetary compensation and other financial relief	Legal aid funding, legal expense insurance, membership fees	Consensual settlement eliminates adverse cost risks

Country	Type of procedure	Scope	Standing	Opt-out/Opt-in	Remedies	Funding	Funding issues
Taiwan	Class action	Labor, securities	Association or quasi-public entity	Opt-in	Monetary, injunctive or declaratory relief	Public funding, association membership fees	Cost shifting
United States	Class action	Trans-substantive	Class member	Opt-out	Money, injunctive or declaratory relief	Judge awards fees as a percentage of fund or on an hourly fee plus premium basis ('lodestar')	No cost shifting in most cases. Equitable fund doctrine eliminates free riding
United States	Group litigation procedure (MDL)	Trans-substantive	Parties	n/a	Money, injunctive or declaratory relief	Individually retained lawyers on contingent fees, third-party funding	MDL judges may order additional fees for lead counsel. No cost shifting

and one that permits class treatment of a negotiated settlement for money damages, with judicial approval. England, Germany and the US all have formal group litigation procedures. In the US, the group litigation procedure is sometimes used in conjunction with a class action. England had not adopted a class action procedure at the time of the study and, over time, judicial case management had come to be regarded as preferable to the formal group litigation procedure that was adopted in the 1990s. Germany has adopted a formal group litigation procedure for investor claims; its judges are said to be uncomfortable engaging in the close judicial case management that is characteristic of US and English judges. Belgium had not adopted a class action procedure at the time of the study; there, civil claims proceeded as 'piggy back' additions to criminal proceedings.

The case studies were conducted between 2010 and 2015. As the research progressed, the collaborators shared their preliminary observations in writing and in person. Early in the process, all were struck by the extent to which certain themes emerged among the cases, despite differences in substantive law, procedural rules, legal regime and national politics. In all of the cases the collaborators investigated, cultural factors played an important role in encouraging litigation and shaping the litigation process and outcomes. 'Culture' has been variously defined by social scientists but generally comprises the ideas, norms and values that are transmitted to and shape the behavior of members of a particular society at a particular time. In the case of litigation, these ideas, norms and values were transmitted by many actors and institutions but particularly by mass media, which often drove litigation forward and led to the delivery of compensation to self-perceived victims, even when the formal law did not require such compensation.

A second theme cutting across all cases was the importance of legal financing rules. The aphorism 'money makes the world go round' applies to litigation worldwide. The availability of legal financing enables litigation and in its absence, litigation generally fails. Although the importance of financing may seem obvious, it is often neglected in statutory decision-making and rule-making pertaining to class actions and other collective litigation procedures. Countries that adopt new collective litigation procedures rarely adopt different legal financing rules to accommodate the new forms of litigation. In some instances, this has stymied use of the new procedures. However, in others, the advent of collective litigation has incentivized new forms of legal financing, an example of how legal procedural developments can impact other dimensions of a legal regime.

A third theme was the importance of public legal actors to the development and outcomes of what is ostensibly private legal action. In the cases the researcher investigated, public actors sometimes facilitated and sometimes hindered private litigation. Sometimes the private litigation was caught up in larger political debates of the day. The public-private law distinction that is so central to legal theory and has been at the core of the debate over class actions in many jurisdictions was less easy to discern 'on the ground'.

As they proceeded with their research, the collaborators attempted to test these cross-cutting observations against their data. By holding up their individual case study research to these over-arching themes, the researchers hoped that the ultimate product of the project would be more than simply a collection of individual case studies. Ultimately the themes became the organizing structure of this book.

ORGANIZATION OF THE BOOK

Most of the book is devoted to the case studies. With one exception, each case study reports on litigation within a single country; the exception is a chapter reporting on a transnational litigation that took place both in the US and the Netherlands. Some chapters report on a single case and some on two cases.

Rather than organizing the chapters by geographic locale or by type of legal regime or some other legal variable, the book groups the chapters by theme. Part II focuses on cultural factors that shape collective litigation; Part III on the economic enablers of collective litigation; and Part IV on the public dimension of private collective litigation. Each of these Parts begins with a chapter that introduces the theme, summarizes the case study results in that Part and analyzes how those cases illustrate the theme. Part V synthesizes the descriptive data and analysis in the preceding chapters and discusses their implications for public policy-making and scholarship.

Readers interested in the 'big picture' of collective litigation might read only the introductory chapters in each Part and the conclusion, and perhaps dip into one or two case study chapters to get a better sense of the materials the authors of these chapters drew upon. Readers interested in learning more about a particular jurisdiction or a particular type of litigation might focus on those chapters most relevant to their interests. Law faculty who assign the book for classes on private law, complex litigation or comparative law might wish to assign different chapters to different students as a basis for in-class discussion on comparative procedure.

The authors, of course, hope that you will read the entire volume.

REFERENCES

Frank Dobbins, Beth Simmons & Geoffrey Garrett, *The Global Diffusion of Public Policies: Social Construction, Coercion, Competition, or Learning?* (2007) 33 Annual Review of Sociology 449

Kenneth Feinberg, *Who Gets What? Fair Compensation After Tragedy and Financial Upheaval* (Perseus Books 2012)

Alexander George & Andrew Bennett, *Case Studies and Theory Development in the Social Sciences* (MIT Press 2005)

Michele Graziadei, Comparative Law as the Study of Legal Transplants, in Mathias Reimann & Reinhard Zimmermann (eds.), *The Oxford Handbook of Comparative Law* (Oxford University Press 2006)

Michael Green, *Bendectin and Birth Defects: The Challenge of Mass Toxic Substances Litigation* (University of Pennsylvania Press 1996)

Deborah Hensler et al., *Class Action Dilemmas: Pursuing Public Goals for Private Gain* (RAND 2002)

Deborah Hensler, The Socio-Economics of Mass Torts: What We Know, Don't Know and Should Know, in Jennifer Arlen (ed.), *Research Handbook on the Economics of Torts* (Edward Elgar 2013)

Deborah Hensler, Justice for the Masses? Aggregate Litigation and Its Alternatives, in Judith Resnik & Linda Greenhouse (eds.), *The Invention of Courts*, Daedalus 143:3, Summer 2014 (MIT Press)

Deborah Hensler, Can Private Class Actions Enforce Marketplace Regulations? Do They? Should They?, in Francesca Bignami & David Waring (eds.), *Comparative Law and Regulation: National, International and Transnational Perspectives* (Edward Elgar forthcoming)

Christopher Hodges, *Multi-Party Actions* (Oxford University Press 2001)

Christopher Hodges, Stefan Vogenauer & Magdalena Tulibacka (eds.), *The Costs and Funding of Civil Litigation: A Comparative Approach* (Hart 2010)

Peter Schuck, *Agent Orange on Trial: Mass Toxic Disasters in the Courts* (Belknap Press 1987)

Richard Sobol, *Bending the Law: The Story of the Dalkon Shield Bankruptcy* (University of Chicago Press 1991)

Alan Watson, *Legal Transplants: An Approach to Comparative Law* (University Press of Virginia 1974)

Robert Yin, *Case Study Research: Design and Method, 5th edition* (Sage 2013)

PART II

Culture

2. The culture of collective litigation: A comparative analysis

Byron Stier and Ianika Tzankova

INTRODUCTION

Social scientists define culture differently but generally the term refers to norms, customs and practices of a particular community at a particular point in time. The relationship of culture to collective litigation may be considered from various perspectives. Different norms regarding the proper role of litigation in a society, for example, may lead to different rules about who should pay, and how much, for bringing a dispute to court. Different norms about the proper role of government relative to private parties, including corporations, may lead to different views on whether private litigation should strictly serve compensatory purposes—'redress'—or should supplement public enforcement activities. Legal financing rules and perspectives on the role of public versus private enforcement may in turn explain rules facilitating or inhibiting collective litigation. (Parts III and IV of this book deal with these aspects of collective litigation.)

A cultural analyst might investigate the ways in which national legal culture has shaped the adoption or design of collective litigation procedures. This chapter takes a different approach to culture. Instead of discussing national legal cultures or analyzing the cultural differences between jurisdictions in relation to collective litigation, we examine *the culture of collective litigation itself* as we see it emerging from case studies from four jurisdictions: Brazil, Taiwan, the United States (US) and the Netherlands. Despite cultural differences between these and other countries discussed later in this book, similar behavior patterns and acts emerge with regard to collective litigation.[1] Before we proceed with what

[1] Although our analysis is primarily based on the six case studies discussed in this chapter, where appropriate we will refer also to some of the case studies discussed in other chapters of this book.

we define as different facets of the culture of collective litigation, we provide brief summaries of the case studies discussed in this Part.

OVERVIEW OF THE CASE STUDIES

The first case study in this section (Chapter 3) describes the Brazilian tobacco litigation brought by the Associação de Defensa da Saúde do Fumante (ADESF) against Souza Cruz Corporation and Philip Morris Brasil Industria e Comercio Ltda. Lawyers Mario Albanese and Luiz Carlos Martins Mônaco and doctor José Rosemberg founded the ADESF for the purpose of bringing a collective tobacco suit. Other consumer protection organizations joined them later. Albanese and Mônaco had served as legal counsel to the Comitê Coordenador do Controle do Tabagismo no Brasil (CCCTB), an anti-smoking advocacy group; Rosemberg also served on the CCCTB and was a member of the State Nicotine Dependency Commission (Commissão Estadual de Tabagismo). Albanese's father had passed away from smoking-related coronary disease; Rosemberg had researched issues concerning nicotine dependency and public health since 1975, and was awarded a Tobacco and Health medal by the World Health Organization.

The case was filed in the Nineteenth Civil Court of Sao Paulo, sought compensatory damages and moral damages (for emotional distress) for those affected by cigarettes, and also aimed to alter cigarette manufacturers' advertisements. In 2004, the Court found that Souza Cruz and Philip Morris had engaged in misleading advertising with regard to the chemicals in cigarettes and the addictiveness of nicotine. The Court held that as a result of their cigarette purchases, induced by the companies' advertising, consumers had incurred compensable financial losses. It ordered the tobacco corporations to pay cigarette smokers (apparently throughout Brazil) both compensatory and moral damages, and to re-label tobacco products so as to highlight health and safety issues. In addition, the defendants were ordered to pay all procedural costs, as well as the plaintiffs' attorneys' fees. On appeal, however, the Tribunal de Justiça do Estado de São Paulo reversed the trial court's decision. On remand, the trial court found that the defendants had not undertaken illegal conduct and dismissed the complaint. While the litigation did not succeed for the plaintiffs, the extensive media attention promoted the anti-tobacco movement within Brazil and surrounding countries, and brought pressure against governmental entities to regulate tobacco products more closely—pressure which continues today.

Chapter 4 discusses two Taiwanese case studies. The first case study involves a wage-and-hour class action seeking unpaid interest for separately mediated overtime pay, brought by the Parking-Lots Attendant Union against the Parking-Lots Bureau of the Taipei Municipal Government. The class action, which was brought on behalf of 777 union members, sought recovery for small amounts for each union member, but was also part of a larger ongoing conflict between the labor union and the government agency. Indeed, the long-term battle between the labor union and the government, rather than the small dollar amounts at issue, may have prompted the union leaders to pursue the litigation. The class action, vigorously led by the union leaders, ended with a victory for the labor union. But the government subsequently fired the three union leaders who initiated and led the action.

The second Taiwanese case study discusses litigation originating in the initial public offering (IPO) of the King Yuan Electronics Company (KYEC) in 2001. Shortly after the IPO, the value of the shares dropped dramatically. The company was accused of making false financial disclosures to the market in connection with the IPO. In Taiwan, the Securities and Fortunes Investors Protection Center (SFIPC) generally files securities class actions following a government decision to pursue criminal prosecution of the alleged wrongdoer. SFIPC is a publicly funded private entity closely supervised by the Taiwan SEC. Unlike the labor union in the previous case, SFIPC receives sufficient financial support to file follow-on securities class actions. In the case of KYEC, the prosecutor decided not to seek criminal charges. However, media coverage of a favorable verdict in a contemporaneous lawsuit brought by a single private investor, ALGA Technology Corporation, against KYEC and its chairman spurred SFIPC to file two separate class actions. SFIPC brought one case against KYEC and its chairman, general manager, and financial manager, and in the other case, sought recovery from Capital Securities and the two accountants who certified KYEC's financial reports. The Taiwan High Court subsequently reversed the District Court decision in favor of investor ALGA, and the Taiwan Supreme Court dismissed ALGA's appeal. Taiwan courts thereafter also dismissed both class actions initiated by SFIPC.

Chapter 5 presents two case studies from the US. The first case study discusses the Toyota unintended acceleration litigation. In 2009, the media repeatedly played a recording of an emergency phone call from several people in a Toyota automobile frantically reporting that their car was accelerating uncontrollably; subsequently, the car crashed and all occupants died. Other reports of uncontrolled acceleration in Toyota automobiles soon appeared and were spotlighted by the media. In the ensuing months, the National Highway Traffic Safety Administration (NHTSA) worked with Toyota to investigate the reports of uncontrolled acceleration. The US Congress held hearings at which the CEO of Toyota testified. Toyota recalled millions of automobiles. Ultimately, a 2011 NHTSA report found no problems with the electronic throttle control in Toyota automobiles that could result in unintended acceleration, and instead pointed to driver pedal misapplication, or in extremely rare instances, to pedal entrapment by a floor mat or slow-returning accelerator pedals. However, in July 2013, a federal court granted final approval to a $1 billion class settlement for Toyota owners seeking payment for reduced vehicle resale value because of the risk of unintended acceleration. In addition, in the fall of 2013, an Oklahoma jury delivered a verdict in favor of the families of two women who died in a crash, and Toyota thereafter entered intensive settlement negotiations of remaining cases alleging personal injuries from unintended acceleration.

The second case study in Chapter 5 addresses the Gulf Coast Claims Facility. In 2009, a fire on the Deepwater Horizon oil rig resulted in nearly five million barrels of oil pouring into the Gulf of Mexico. In response, President Obama arranged for BP to create a $20 billion claims fund to compensate Gulf coast fishermen and businesses that lost income from the ecological disaster. Noted claims fund administrator Kenneth Feinberg oversaw the fund, which distributed more than $6 billion to more than 169,000 claimants, before being supplanted by a class settlement initially estimated to be $7.8 billion, which was the product of parallel litigation by other claimants in federal court. BP subsequently claimed that its class settlement costs far exceeded initial estimates because the class settlement administrator in the class action provided impermissible payouts, but the Fifth Circuit Court of Appeals rejected BP's arguments.

Finally, Chapter 6 presents a Dutch case study describing the rise and fall of Dutch life insurance company Vie d'Or in 1993, long before the start of the global financial crisis in 2008. The bankruptcy of Vie d'Or left 11,000 policyholders without a life insurance policy. Normally in such circumstances the Dutch insurance industry would collectively devise a solution to prevent the bankruptcy of a fellow insurance company or at least to minimize the losses of its policyholders. However, the founders of Vie d'Or were viewed by the close-knit insurance industry as opportunistic outsiders. As a result, the industry did not come forward to save the company or the policyholders. Instead, pursuant to a new class action law that was introduced in 1994, a special purpose foundation—the Vie d'Or Foundation—was established to bring a collective action against the Dutch financial regulator, for failure to properly monitor the insurance company, the Dutch State (as the financial back-up and alleged overseer of the financial regulator) and the private accountant and actuaries of Vie d'Or to obtain compensation for the policyholders. The policyholders initially distrusted the Board of the Foundation because it was appointed by the financial regulator, but the Foundation's board members proved to be faithful agents of the policyholders. In the initial stage of the litigation, the Foundation met with some success, but a Supreme Court ruling subsequently made it very difficult to bring the action to a successful end. After years of litigation, the case was ultimately settled in 2008 as a result of political pressure from the government and an unexpected offer of the insurance industry to voluntarily contribute to a settlement fund. The protracted litigation and personal drama of the policyholders, some of whom had meanwhile died, was damaging for the image of the industry. Moreover, the litigation resulted in a regulatory action imposed on the Dutch insurance industry aimed at preventing a second bankruptcy drama of a life insurance company.

THE CULTURE OF COLLECTIVE LITIGATION

Our analysis of the culture of collective litigation in these and other cases we studied identified three common themes:

(1) Collective litigation and cultural power relationships. As depicted in popular culture representations of mass litigation, collective litigation highlights and challenges existing societal power structures. Indeed, collective litigation must contend with a traditional judicial culture wary of the use of procedural power in mass litigation. Collective litigation may create new networks of social power and help drive social change.

(2) The role of the media. Collective litigation draws mass media interest, and mass media explore the basis of the dispute and press governmental entities to investigate, prosecute and reform. Media publicize potential claims, assisting collective litigation, but also sometimes leading to unmeritorious claims. Sometimes media coverage of a crisis is the main trigger for a collective action. Mass media also communicate to the public the litigants' own accounts of the potentially ongoing crisis and evaluation of the conduct at issue prior to and during the crisis. The role and involvement of the media brings an additional dimension to the interactions of the

various actors involved in the collective litigation and requires special attention from all concerned.

(3) The prevalence of agency issues in class and group litigation. Various case studies show that in collective litigation, in contrast to ordinary individual litigation, what we call the 'human element' often determines the course and outcome of a collective action. It is the people who make the case and they can make or break the action. The outsized role of individuals in collective litigation is often associated with common law jurisdictions that view entrepreneurial class action lawyers as private attorneys general. But individuals also play an important role in jurisdictions that assign class representation to non-profit associations. The importance of the human element is often overlooked in the latter, where trust in organizational values prevails and the absence of agency problems is frequently assumed when it should not be.

Below, we discuss each of these themes in greater detail. Following our analysis of themes derived from our case studies, we explore future paths for managing collective redress that may involve more explicit attention to crisis management among lawyers and judges, as well as the use of claims funds or claim resolution schemes and facilities as an expression of cultural connectedness.

Collective Litigation and Cultural Power Relationships

Collective litigation reflects and shapes cultural power relationships. Cultural or social change may spawn mass disputes as established power structures are challenged. Collective litigation may reveal widespread social friction and disjunction in cultural power relationships. Collective litigation can also create new social networks that reorganize social power, potentially disturbing existing power relationships and facilitating change. Once initiated, collective litigation must also contend with cultural resistance within the judiciary to mass methods of claim resolution, from judges who favor traditional one-on-one methods of dispute resolution. More generally, collective litigation may seek to empower individuals against concentrated corporate or governmental power. We identified three different types of power relationships that shape collective litigation:

(1) individual plaintiffs versus big corporations;
(2) individuals or regulated industries versus public regulators or the State; and

(3) long-standing associations or institutionalized plaintiffs versus ad hoc associations or individuals acting as private attorneys general.

Individuals versus big corporations

The extent to which collective litigation reveals and unsettles existing power relationships is frequently shown in popular culture representations of collective litigation. For example, the films *A Civil Action* and *Erin Brockovich* both pit dispersed, injured plaintiffs, and the small law firms representing them, against corporate power and the well-heeled large corporate law firms representing the corporate defendants accused of wrongdoing.[2] Although specific procedures may vary within and between countries, collective litigation empowers individuals in their common pursuit of redress against larger corporate entities. At the same time, in jurisdictions where collective litigation has only recently emerged, it poses challenges to the plaintiffs' firms that are unaccustomed to the burdens of such litigation, and requires judges to adapt old procedures and fashion new ones to wrestle with the efficiency and fairness issues it raises.[3]

The Brazilian tobacco litigation is an example of a global movement by advocacy organizations from legislative and public awareness efforts to litigation. In 1995, four months after the Associação de Defensa da Saúde do Fumante (ADESF) was founded, ADESF brought a lawsuit against Souza Cruz Corporation and Philip Morris Do Brasil Industria e Comercio Ltda., seeking to have the defendants pay compensatory and moral damages to all persons suffering losses from cigarette smoking. In addition, the lawsuit sought stringent regulations on tobacco advertising. Consumer groups ACT (Aliança de Controle do Tabagismo) and IDEC (Instituto Brasileiro de Defesa do Consumidor) joined the litigation as well, while also expanding their public anti-tobacco education campaign. In addition, at least 14 lawyers and four law firms formed an informal network and assisted ADESF, and a Medical-Scientific Council that included more than 40 persons also provided assistance, sharing the financial burden of the litigation. The various entities connected to the

---

2 *A Civil Action* (Paramount Pictures 1998); *Erin Brockovich* (Jersey Films 2000). For other films depicting mass litigation and the ways in which it challenges power structures, see also *Class Action* (Twentieth Century Fox 1991); *The Insider* (Touchstone Pictures 1999); *Michael Clayton* (Castle Rock Entertainment 2007); and *Runaway Jury* (Regency Enterprises 2003).

3 *See* Chapters 13 and 15 (discussing case studies from the United Kingdom and Germany).

litigation also became active in coordinated political and public relations activity against tobacco.

In contrast to the plaintiffs, Souza Cruz and Philip Morris Brasil were well-funded and well-organized entities with formidable legal counsel. With more than a 60 percent tobacco market share in Brazil, Souza Cruz manufactures 80 billion cigarettes a year and is a subsidiary of British American Tobacco, whose global reach extends to more than 180 countries. Philip Morris Brasil is a subsidiary of Philip Morris International, the world's largest global tobacco company. Souza Cruz's counsel included corporate law firms from Rio de Janeiro and São Paulo, and Philip Morris Brasil's law firm was one of the largest in the country. Although the litigation was ultimately unsuccessful for the plaintiffs and two of the men who initially spearheaded the litigation died in 2005 and 2011, respectively, ADESF lived on, uniting a variety of individuals and groups from different settings to propel further efforts at tobacco regulation.[4]

Individuals or regulated industries versus regulators or the State

While the Brazilian case highlights the struggle of individuals and non-profit organizations against multi-national corporations, the Taiwanese labor class action is a story of individuals taking on the State. In Taiwan, a small-claims class action procedure was used by parking-lot attendants to pursue claims against a governmental entity for the interest due on past unpaid wages calculating overtime based on a background salary that includes both regular wages and monthly bonuses. For decades, Taiwan suppressed unionization of workers, and parking-lot attendants only unionized in 1997, after a three-year struggle. Following unionization, the governmental Parking-Lots Bureau attempted to penetrate the Parking-Lots Attendant Union and undercut its leadership, and also sought to use private companies to outsource the tasks of parking-lot attendants, but the Union asserted its interests by becoming politically active. Beginning in 1999, the Parking-Lots Bureau agreed to pay the parking-lot attendants a monthly bonus. Subsequently, the parking-lot attendants claimed that their overtime pay should be calculated based on a monthly wage that included the monthly bonus. In 2002, management

---

[4] Cases described elsewhere in this book also illustrate the entangling of collective litigation with politics and the challenges litigation can pose to societal power. For example, the MTBE litigation in the United States (Chapter 16) may be seen as resulting from a prior political battle in which oil companies lobbied for the use of MTBE as an additive, and farmers lobbied for greater use of ethanol, with the oil companies prevailing in Congress.

agreed to do so, and afterwards the Parking-Lots Bureau agreed to pay back pay for bonuses, but the question of interest on back pay remained unclear. Three female parking-lot attendants, all of whom were on the executive board of the Union, filed suit against the Parking-Lots Bureau, seeking interest for parking-lot attendants that generally amounted to less than NTD 6,000 (Taiwan New Dollar), or $200 per claimant. The plaintiffs prevailed in the trial court. On appeal, the Taiwan High Court found for the parking-lot attendants, but also held certain claims to be time-barred; the Taiwan Supreme Court dismissed the Parking-Lots Bureau's further appeal. Following the victory for the parking-lot attendants, the Parking-Lots Bureau demanded that the three executive directors of the Union, who had initiated the lawsuit, resign their union leadership positions, and support the private-contractor policy and lower working conditions and benefits for the Union. After rejecting the Parking-Lots Bureau's demands, the three Union executive directors were fired by the Parking-Lots Bureau for absence from work during the law suits, and their subsequent court lawsuit to reinstate their positions was unsuccessful.

The second Taiwanese case study illustrates the power relationship between a regulated company (KYEC) and SFIPC, which, although a private entity, is publicly funded and closely supervised by the Taiwanese SEC. SFIPC has the financial resources and power to engage in extensive litigation. In some circumstances, the utility and societal value of the litigation against the defending company might be questioned. SFIPC filed two securities class actions against KYEC, forcing the company to spend resources to defend itself, but Taiwan courts subsequently dismissed both actions and related appeals.

The Dutch Vie d'Or litigation illustrates the power relationships between the State and the regulator on the one hand and the regulated insurance industry and insurance policyholders on the other. The insurance industry and policyholders alleged that the regulator could have prevented the bankruptcy of Vie d'Or. Ultimately, however, the courts held that the State could not be held liable for the losses of the policyholders and that the regulator had a large margin of discretion to act. The industry found itself in a position where it was in their interest to contribute voluntarily to a settlement fund to compensate the policyholders. Although from a formal perspective the success of the litigation was very limited, as a result of the litigation the regulator put in place a stronger regulatory framework that included the establishment of a general fund by the industry to cover policyholders' losses should a life insurance company become bankrupt in the future. Moreover, although the Supreme Court's decision in Vie d'Or made it extremely difficult to hold a regulator liable for the results of failed regulatory supervision, the Dutch legislature essentially overturned the holding by enacting a new law in 2012 that stipulates explicitly that the financial regulator may be held liable albeit only in extreme circumstances.[5] The power relationship between the regulator and the policyholders was also reflected by the regulator's desire to keep control over the actions of the Board of the Foundation once it decided to start an action against the regulator and the Dutch State.[6]

Long-standing associations versus ad hoc drivers of collective litigation
In many civil law jurisdictions, associations such as consumer protection and investor protection associations have long advocated on behalf of their members' interests. But in Vie d'Or, an ad hoc association had to be established to represent the interests of the policyholders. For internal policy reasons, none of the existing long-standing consumer associations was willing to come forward to play this role. The Vie d'Or experience suggests a drawback of legislation—common in many civil law jurisdictions—that grants standing to act in collective actions exclusively to long-standing associations or so called 'designated entities'.

The Role of the Media

Because of mass litigation's relevance to large numbers of persons, it garners extensive mass media attention. Mass media may affect the development of mass litigation in numerous ways that may have the effect of supporting the plaintiffs' litigation against the defendant. Prior to the inception of litigation, the media may investigate possible misconduct and pressure regulatory and legislative entities; sometimes the plaintiffs' counsel may suggest or encourage such coverage and investigation. In reporting the results of investigations and related allegations and disseminating information about product risks, the media also

---

[5] Effective 1 July 2012 Article 1:25d of the Dutch Financial Supervision Act (Wet financieel toezicht) stipulates that the two Dutch financial regulators, the AFM and DNB, cannot be held liable for damages resulting from improper supervision, unless the improper supervision is attributable to intent or gross negligence.

[6] Other cases we studied also show how litigation can upset the normal role of government institutions. For example, in the Canadian litigation over same-sex spouses' right to retroactive pension benefits (Chapter 11), class action plaintiffs won these benefits as a result of the Court's decision, even though the Canadian legislature had yet to enact a statute granting such rights.

publicizes (inadvertently or not) potential claims, attracting the interest of the claimants and the plaintiffs' attorneys and ultimately expanding the scale of litigation.[7] In addition, the media can aid the functioning of class actions by disseminating class notices and claims fund information to the claimants. Moreover, the plaintiffs' counsel may be aided by public outreach efforts by non-profit entities active in the area relevant to the litigation. In countries where there is no official court register of group or collective actions, media coverage is the only way for the public or interested parties to follow pending litigation. The skill of the plaintiff's lawyer or law firm in developing and managing a strategy in opposition to the defendant's own media efforts may be known among the other plaintiffs' counsel and be part of a professional reputation, cultivated in part through media coverage, that leads the other plaintiffs' counsel to defer to such lawyers when it comes to the selection of lawyers to lead litigation. In some jurisdictions, however, lawyers may be precluded by ethical rules from using mass media to communicate the facts of a litigation, which may be considered client solicitation and therefore an ethical violation.

Media engagement with litigation has several drawbacks. Media attention to claimed product malfunction can cause immediate reduction of resale value for products, regardless of the truth of the underlying claims, as may have occurred in the Toyota case study. At the extreme, media attention to potential safety threats may cause public panic and widespread emotional distress, even though the underlying claims are subsequently rejected as unsubstantiated. In addition, while media attention to litigation can appropriately inform persons of their likely meritorious claims, media attention may also draw fraudulent claimants as appears to have occurred in the BP oil spill case.

Mass media coverage shapes the defendants' strategic decisions and conduct in mass litigation. Initially, the defendants may need to find a way to respond to an immediate crisis in a way that preserves their reputation without excessively curtailing their ability to respond to regulatory demands and likely future litigation. As the facts surrounding injury claims emerge, the defendants may face a choice between vigorously contesting their liability and voluntarily offering compensation or seeking a consensual settlement. Often, a potentially favorable reputational strategy of taking responsibility for harm caused sharply conflicts with the optimal legal strategy of taking responsibility only for harm that

---

7 The Dexia case from the Netherlands offers an example of collective litigation that was triggered by a TV show: *see* Tzankova, 2012, pp. 577–578.

the plaintiffs could show was caused by the defendants' products or conduct and for which the defendants were legally liable.

In the Toyota unintended acceleration litigation in the US, mass media provided far-reaching coverage of a fatal crash involving an off-duty police officer where the vehicle's occupants claimed during an emotional emergency phone call from the car that the car was accelerating uncontrollably. That media attention galvanized inquiries by the National Highway Traffic Safety Administration (NHTSA), which led to several recalls of millions of cars, and hearings before the US Congress, where Toyota CEO Akio Toyoda testified and apologized for his company's actions, conceding that an emphasis on growth may have supplanted product safety at Toyota. Following the media coverage, Toyota owners across the country filed hundreds of lawsuits against Toyota. Some claimants were suspected of falsely claiming unintended acceleration in their cars. In one case where such questions were raised, a driver stopped his car and refused emergency phone operator requests to put the car into neutral, but then stopped the car when police rode beside him. Although subsequent reports by NHTSA and the National Academy of Sciences rejected the central claims of problems with Toyota's electronic throttle system, Toyota elected to settle a class action, for more than $1 billion, of Toyota owners seeking to recoup economic losses from lowered resale value of the automobiles stemming from public concern about Toyota safety. Ironically, these diminished value claims may have had legal merit even though the objective evidence did not support the public's safety concerns.

The Vie d'Or litigation also was ultimately settled partly as a result of ongoing negative publicity for the insurance industry. Unlike the Toyota case, where there is substantial question about the allegations of product design defects, there is little question that the Vie d'Or founders violated insurance regulations. But with them no longer on the scene and the company bankrupt, there was a concern that the subscribers would never be able to secure compensation for their losses. In this instance, media attention essentially drove the government to force the insurance industry to pick up the pieces when they had no legal obligation to do so.

After the BP oil spill in the Gulf of Mexico, the US Coast Guard named BP a 'responsible party' under the Oil Pollution Act of 1990, resulting in BP being strictly liable for economic losses to those affected by the spill; in the absence of gross negligence, such losses were statutorily limited to $75 million. The facts surrounding the oil rig explosion and resulting spill would ultimately be the subject of an extensive public investigation. But shortly after the accident, and long before the investigation reached its conclusion that the explosion and spill were the result of regulatory and safety lapses by government and industry, BP's CEO met with President Obama in the White House and agreed to create a $20 billion fund to pay claims stemming from the oil spill. BP's agreement to create such a fund was likely motivated not only by its legal responsibility under the Oil Pollution Act of 1990, but also by its desire to generate goodwill and preserve public image, and avoid difficulties in obtaining future regulatory approvals for drilling in the US. By establishing a fund, BP would have an opportunity to forestall or at least reduce the amount of civil litigation for property damage that was sure to follow. President Obama announced the fund while discussing the Gulf Oil spill in his first Oval Office address, carried to the country on television and the internet. Ultimately, Kenneth Feinberg—widely renowned as the administrator of the Congressionally authorized 9/11 Victims' Compensation Fund—was appointed claims administrator of the Gulf Coast Claims Facility, replacing BP's initial claims administration process, which had involved 35 offices across the Gulf and 1,300 claims adjusters. To avoid inconsistency, Feinberg centralized claim decision-making. Recognized as a master of public relations, Feinberg traveled to town hall meetings throughout the Gulf, explaining the claims procedure and extolling its virtues, by comparison to litigation. Local and national media extensively covered these meetings. Following extensive media coverage of the claims fund, the Gulf Coast Claims Facility received numerous fraudulent claims, based on altered and fake documents, as well as apparent misrepresentations. Suspected fraudulent claims were referred to a private fraud-investigation company, and more than 10,000 claims were deemed suspicious, with several thousand claims referred to the US Justice Department for prosecution. Before being supplanted by an estimated $7.8 billion class settlement, the Gulf Coast Claims Facility disbursed more than $6 billion to the claimants.

The Brazilian tobacco litigation presented a confluence of the media, mass litigation and social advocacy. Two lawyers and a doctor who had been involved in tobacco control efforts founded the consumer organization ADESF, specifically to bring tobacco litigation against two major tobacco companies. Their efforts were then aided by certain media outlets and other consumer protection groups who also undertook a public anti-tobacco campaign, leading to both public and political support for the litigation. Perhaps in part as a result, the trial court initially found that the defendants Souza Cruz and Philip Morris had engaged in misleading and abusive advertising in not providing consumers with information on the chemical ingredients in cigarettes, and deceiving consumers about negative health effects and addictiveness of nicotine, and ordered the defendants to indemnify the smokers represented by ADESF. Following the ruling, ADESF distributed press releases and aggressively engaged the media, which attracted the attention of consumer advocates in several other Latin American countries to their litigation strategy. Although the court's decision was reversed on appeal in 2008 and the complaint was subsequently dismissed, the undertaking furthered goals of media attention and public and political support for tobacco control.

In the King Yuan Electronics Company securities litigation in Taiwan, media attention to the company's share price collapse propelled the litigation. When KYEC lowered its earnings outlook by 97 percent, major Taiwanese newspapers raised questions about whether the company had previously deliberately concealed material information. Subsequently, the Taiwan Stock Exchange investigated KYEC's actions and issued a demerit to KYEC for misconduct in its earnings forecasts. Thereafter, one corporate investor sued KYEC and its chairman, and obtained a verdict of more than NTD 18 million. Media widely covered that verdict, which was particularly notable for it being achieved by a single private civil litigant where the government had not filed securities criminal charges, and two securities class actions were then filed against KYEC. After several years of litigation, KYEC later prevailed in appeals of the actions to multiple courts, including the Taiwan Supreme Court.[8]

The Prevalence of Agency Issues in Class and Group Litigation

Who should have standing in class or collective actions is probably one of the most debated topics among policy makers. The topic has been on the agenda of the European Commission for years. The status of the

---

[8] The use of media by lawyers is reflected in other case studies as well. For example, in the Canadian Atlas securities litigation in Canada (Chapter 11), plaintiffs' lawyers advertised in a national newspaper for an Atlas unit-purchaser in the primary market. A retired lawyer who fit the requirements responded to the ad, and subsequently agreed to serve as class representative. In contrast, in the Belgian L&H securities fraud litigation (Chapter 14), the lawyers were barred from recruiting clients though the media by professional ethics rules, despite efforts by the Brussels Bar Association to ease such restrictions. A different use of media is illustrated by the transnational litigation against Royal Dutch Shell (Chapter 8). In the settlement class procedure that resolved the non-US dimension of the litigation, lawyers needed to conduct a world-wide notice campaign that extended to 96 countries beyond the European Union, and used announcements in mass media, among other modes of communication, for this purpose.

European discussions is to be found in the Recommendation on principles on collective redress of the European Commission.[9] In brief, the Recommendation rejects the common law model where an individual can act as a representative of the group and recommends granting standing to act in collective actions to public entities, pre-approved non-profit associations, so-called designated entities and to ad hoc certified or ad hoc court approved non-profit entities.[10]

Generally speaking, there are four basic models with respect to standing in collective actions. There is the entrepreneurial lawyer, the private attorney general who, by advancing his own interest, allegedly also serves the best interest of the group.[11] The Toyota case study illustrates this model. Although people might have different views about the societal utility of the approximately $1 billion settlement that was achieved for the Toyota drivers, the private attorney general—in the form of class counsel—achieved a significant recovery for the class. A substantial body of law-and-economics-oriented literature addresses agency problems surrounding the concept of the profit-driven entrepreneurial lawyer acting as private attorney general. Some social scientists have also examined the dynamics and evaluated real or perceived agency problems in class actions in the US. In the common law academic literature, proposals have been put forward and implemented on the basis of such studies to improve the alignment of interests between class and class counsel in class action litigation.

Less academic and legislative attention has been given to whether similar or different agency issues also arise for other types of agents when they play a key role in collective litigation. In many jurisdictions that rely on two other types of agents—governmental agencies or longstanding non-profit organizations—to bring class actions it is assumed that the latter will naturally act vigorously and unselfishly in the best interest of the entire group.[12] Indeed, sometimes that is the case, as the Taiwanese case studies illustrate. Here, the agent was the union, a

---

[9] http://eur-lex.europa.eu/legal-content/EN/TXT/PDF/?uri=CELEX:32013H0396&from=EN.

[10] *See* also the ELI Statement on collective redress with comments on the Recommendation: http://www.europeanlawinstitute.eu/fileadmin/user_upload/p_eli/Projects/S-5-2014_Statement_on_Collective_Redress_and_Competition_Damages_Claims.pdf.

[11] For a discussion of the agency issues surrounding the concept of the private attorney general, *see* Chapter 9; Coffee, 1983; Tzankova & Kortmann, 2010.

[12] For a critical reflection *see* Tzankova & Hensler, 2013, pp. 103–105.

longstanding non-profit association and the (semi-)public SFIPC (the Taiwanese securities follow-on class action). However, the course of action of the latter demonstrates again other issues that a governmental agent involvement invokes: governmental agencies have their own institutional agendas and motives to proceed in a certain fashion[13] and here that meant that the unlimited availability of financial (public) resources for the litigation supported an action that it knew beforehand might be unsuccessful and would therefore have questionable public utility.

Finally, there is a fourth model that we might think of as standing in between the previous groups: the ad hoc approved or certified non-profit entity established exclusively to litigate on a specific issue. The Brazilian and the Dutch case studies illustrate that model. In the Netherlands and Brazil, the ad hoc associations fought fiercely and faced the many challenges of the litigation with a lot of creativity. In the end, the Vie d'Or Foundation managed to obtain a reasonable compensation for the group it represented, despite a discouraging Supreme Court ruling. Although they did not prevail in the instant litigation, the stamina of the three Brazilian anti-tobacco musketeers promoted the anti-tobacco movement not only within Brazil, but also in surrounding countries, and encouraged governmental entities to engage in structural measures against tobacco products.

Foundation board members like the ones in Vie d'Or may be difficult to find today: they seem to be exponents of a different era. The same seems to be true for the three Brazilian musketeers, of whom only one is still alive. The efforts of the individuals behind the associations in the case studies are intriguing and remarkable: the Brazilian lawyers Mario Albanese and Luiz Carlos Martins Mônaco and doctor José Rosemberg who took the anti-tobacco action as a personal mission; the three Taiwanese (female) labor union leaders who got fired after they vigorously and successfully protected the interests of their fellow union members; and finally, the Vie d'Or Foundation Board whose members had no personal interest in the matter at all, but who, once appointed 'on the job', saw it as their public duty to serve the policyholders and help them recover their pension plans, even if that meant fighting a 13-year war with the Dutch financial regulator and the Dutch State. The Vie d'Or Board served the interests of the group despite the fact that they were appointed by the regulator. Impressive individuals and strong personalities made a difference in those case stories.

---

[13] As is the case with respect to Chilean SERNAC, discussed in Chapter 17.

At the same time, this observation is also alarming. If individuals make the difference in a case, what happens in the absence of such individuals or when the defendants try to influence their conduct by all means? Would the Taiwanese union leaders or their successors have acted as vigorously as they did, knowing what the consequences of their actions would be for them personally? And can one realistically trust that, as in Vie d'Or, there will always be individuals who will unselfishly lead the ad hoc association to a final resolution? The dilemma that the organizational model faces is that on the one hand, ad hoc associations are needed to provide checks and balances for the proper role of long-standing organizations in collective actions, but on the other hand, how does one ensure that the ad hoc associations remain faithful agents to the class, especially when they have been set up by the defendants or by commercially operating individuals or entities?[14]

The case studies suggest that if the ad hoc associations or private actors had not initiated the respective actions, those actions may not have been initiated in the first place. That would have been the case in the Dutch collective action and the Taiwanese securities litigation. This reveals an under-appreciated agency complication[15] and illustrates the risk one runs when standing to act in collective actions is granted exclusively to long-standing associations. Does that mean that ad hoc approved entities are the answer to agency problems in collective litigation? Probably not (Tzankova & Hensler, 2013, 103–105).

What the case studies demonstrate is that agency problems do not disappear when we eliminate private entrepreneurial lawyers from class litigation and that public entities, long-standing associations or ad hoc approved entities each present their own agency problems, although perhaps of a different sort.

The case studies suggest that legislators, and especially the ones operating within civil law jurisdictions, need to improve their understanding of the agency complications that might arise in the context of

---

[14] For a discussion of a Dutch initiative laid down in a so-called Claim Code, *see* Tzankova & Hensler, 2013, pp. 103–104.

[15] The Dexia case study revealed yet another facet of the institutional agency problem: long-standing associations might prefer not to get involved in a specific collective action because of conflicting interests within the group of consumers. *See* Tzankova & Hensler, 2013, pp. 104–105.

collective redress when governmental, long-standing associations or designated entities and ad hoc approved entities serve as agents of the group.[16]

POTENTIAL FUTURE PATHS FOR MANAGING COLLECTIVE REDRESS

The case studies in this section suggest several possible emerging trends for the management of collective litigation and mass harm that require further study and attention:

(1) crisis management and the law;
(2) judicial case management and court interaction with the media; and
(3) the creation of claims funds as an expression of cultural protection or solidarity.

These approaches offer additional possibilities for accommodating and shaping longstanding collective-litigation themes of cultural power relationships, the influence of the media and agency relationships.

The Growth of Crisis Management in Law

Large corporations that are potential defendants in class actions and other forms of mass litigation are usually well aware of the importance and the role of the media and have well-developed public relations departments

[16] While scholars have given less attention to the functioning of non-profit associations than private attorneys general as agents in class or collective litigation, we were able to find an empirical study of US class actions in the late 1970s and early 1980s that found that public interest organizations were more faithful agents for class members than private attorneys: *see* Garth, Nagel & Plager, 1988. The study found that long-standing public interest advocacy organizations were better positioned to identify and investigate the issues that play a role in the lives of their constituencies, which influenced their litigation and settlement negotiation strategies, including the remedies they sought. Moreover, public interest organizations sometimes had procedural advantages in US class actions. For example, they were able to survive challenges on adequacy of representation because they had a large reservoir of members to act as adequate class representatives. On the other hand, such organizations were often dependent on public agencies for financial support and sometimes for political support, introducing a different kind of agency complication. However, this study is outdated and its relevance somewhat limited.

as well as outside public relations consultants. Law firms that represent these corporations have been slower to develop such functions. Although many lawyers have been involved in helping clients manage crises, the growth of mass media attention for mass injuries and the governmental inquiries and litigation that frequently follow, have heightened the need for such efforts. However, legal academics have paid little attention to crisis management. In contrast, schools of business, public policy and communications have long studied and taught crisis management. A program on crisis management for lawyers could draw on multiple disciplines, including management, leadership, communications and public relations, and also include topics specific to legal practice, such as ethical obligations, client counseling, interaction with the media, negotiation strategies and alternative dispute resolution design.

Given the evident need for crisis management among defendant corporations increasingly facing mass claims stemming from, for example, large-scale industrial or mass-marketed products, defense law firms have in recent years developed formal crisis-management practices. Numerous large law firms based in the US, some of which have global reach, have recently created formal crisis-management practice groups, and European law firms may also be moving toward creating such crisis-management groups.

In assembling crisis management groups, global defense firms benefit from their large structure, with specialized departments covering numerous areas of procedural and substantive law, with both a national and international reach. Such groups highlight their ability to provide a rapid and continuous response to legal emergencies that counsels and represents clients in connection with communications to the media, governmental organizations, insurance companies, employees, investors and potential claimants, utilizing expertise in public relations and crisis communications. In particular, such groups formulate responses with close attention to ongoing factual investigations, the possibility of extensive liability, the need to preserve corporate reputation and goodwill, and especially where juries may be involved, the desire to shape the public perception of possible wrongdoing. Lawyers within these practice groups bring prior expertise involving class actions and mass litigation, as well as environmental, tort, product liability, criminal, securities, antitrust, intellectual property, international trade and privacy law.

Moreover, crisis-management groups sometimes feature lawyers who previously worked in a governmental setting, and who may be particularly adept at managing both governmental and media inquiries. In addition to offering to assist with ongoing crises, such groups also offer to work with clients in advance, to prevent such crises, through compliance with regulations and environmental law, analysis of potential litigation exposure and insurance, and preparation of advance emergency plans. Firms also promote their ability to use attorney-client privilege in connection with internal investigations. Global firms may promote their ability to handle cross-national crises, and tout their multinational offices and their established networks of local counsel and multinational experts. In addition to geographical reach, the depth of staffing at such large firms offers the ability to simultaneously manage litigation and inquiries implicating various substantive areas.

Adjudicating in Crisis: Case Management and Interacting with the Media

Judicial case management

The role of the courts in the adjudication of mass claim disputes is often underappreciated by policy makers when preparing class action legislation (Tzankova, 2014). The tendency is to focus on issues such as who should have standing to act, selection criteria for lead representatives and their counsel, the formation of the group (opt-in or opt-out) or notice requirements, and to assume that the courts will naturally have the expertise and know-how to respond when called upon to adjudicate a mass dispute and apply the statutory framework. Interpreting statutes and developing case law is what courts do. There may be a perception among the judiciary[17] that mass disputes are nothing extraordinary and do not require different attitudes, competencies or skill sets from a judge. The reality is, however, that judicial case management and active judges are essential for the adequate handling of mass disputes that strikes a balance between due process requirements and efficient resolution. In fact, an active judge who is directing and communicating with the parties could be much more effective in the adjudication of a mass dispute, without any form of a statutory class action framework,[18] than a judge who

[17] During the consultation stage of the Dutch Draft Proposal on collective damages actions, the response of the Counsel for the Judiciary, the administrative body that directs the judiciary and determines the courts' budgets, was that class actions are just like any other civil dispute and do not require special attention or specialization. But the Dutch Association of Judges, the traditional professional organization of the judiciary, did not share that view.

[18] An example of this is the handling of the Buncefield litigation (Chapter 15).

strictly follows the applicable statutory class action provision and turns a blind eye to litigation dynamics and the specific needs of a case.

From the case studies discussed in this section, only the US litigation offers a distinct example of judicial case management.[19] In the Toyota unintended acceleration litigation, Judge Selna actively managed the federal multidistrict litigation, which involved hundreds of lawsuits. In addition to ruling on unsettled theories such as economic injury from loss of value in vehicles, and limiting the scope of the US litigation with regard to foreign claimants, Judge Selna also issued orders addressing the particular challenges of bilingual discovery involving witnesses and documents from Japan and the US, oversaw wide-reaching electronic discovery and coordinated case management with parallel proceedings in state courts.

Indeed, in the US there is a long-standing and extensive experience with the management of mass litigation. Over the years, trial and error have demonstrated which judicial case management styles work in certain cases, what might raise issues and where improvements are welcome. That has led the US Federal Judicial Center to publish the Manual for Complex Litigation that is now in its fifth edition.[20] The Manual is a collection of best practices for the handling of complex litigation, including but not limited to class actions, based on judicial experience. Judges are not obliged to follow the Manual and ultimately it is at their discretion how to handle a case at hand, but the Manual does offer guidance and a menu with options to choose from or to adjust when judges are faced with a particular complex litigation challenge. The Manual recognizes that the handling of class actions and the like is not 'business as usual' and requires a different approach, if not different competencies and skill sets, from the judiciary. Policymakers considering the introduction of a new statutory class action regime should try to apportion equal attention to its implementation and the role of the judiciary in order to facilitate an adequate adjudication of mass disputes. Scholars could contribute to that process by facilitating the collection of existing best practices and approaches across jurisdictions.[21]

The courts and the media

Governments are often called upon to respond to crises. When public safety may be jeopardized in a crisis, governments frequently call upon

---

19 Another example, discussed in Chapter 15, is again the Buncefield case.

20 Available at http://www.fjc.gov.

21 For an account of a related project supported by The Hague Institute for Global Justice, *see* Tzankova, forthcoming 2016.

the police and military to manage crises. After the BP oil spill in the Gulf of Mexico in 2010, the US Coast Guard swiftly designated BP a 'responsible party' under the Oil Pollution Act of 1990, and after a meeting with BP in the White House, President Barack Obama announced in his first Oval Office address a $20 billion BP claims fund for Gulf-area fishermen and businesses that suffered losses stemming from the oil spill.

Notwithstanding government's executive involvement with the media and crisis management, the judiciary has generally refrained from involvement with the media.[22] The courts' reluctance to become involved in actively managing the media in connection with pending litigation may stem from the courts' traditionally passive role in responding to discrete disputes brought to the courts. In addition, the courts and general entities generally lack the profit incentive that private counsel have in learning to actively manage the media as part of their private practice. Moreover, the judiciary may believe that communication with the media may compromise the judicial equanimity that is viewed as essential to neutrality: media communication may tempt blindfolded Lady Justice to remove her blindfold.

In the US, however, the role of the judge has become more active in recent decades. Courts have monitored institutional reforms of various types and imported case management techniques and alternative dispute resolution, especially to complex litigation. The modern transferee judge in a federal multidistrict litigation not only moves hundreds or thousands of cases through pre-trial discovery, but frequently, with the assistance of a special master, coordinates discovery and trial dates with state judges managing related state litigation throughout the country. Communication with the parties of the litigation or third parties, including when appropriate with the media, has become more and more a part of what a case-managing judge should do. Since 2006, the US Supreme Court has posted transcripts of the day's oral arguments on the Court's website, and beginning in 2010, the Court began weekly posting of audio recordings of oral arguments on the Court's webpage. In the United Kingdom (Moran, 2013) and the Netherlands,[23] as well as in other European Union countries, the courts have realized that the media cannot be banned from

---

[22] The German Telekom case presents a remarkable and rare example of the judiciary seeking assistance from the media to communicate with parties and the legislature about the inadequacy of the existing procedural regime to deal with mass claims. *See* Chapter 13.

[23] Illustrative is the example of the climate change verdict of the Hague District Court in a collective action initiated by sustainability foundation

the courtrooms and can be helpful in improving the image of the profession. As a consequence, European courts began utilizing designated staff to proactively communicate with the media about cases of interest, and to develop policy and strategies for communication with journalists and the use of the media.[24] Because of their societal impact, mass disputes are cases in which the media has great interest. In our opinion, the trends with respect to the role of the media for practitioners and judges also justify the expansion of academic courses or practical training on class and collective litigation to include crisis management and the role of the media.

Culture and Claims Funds

Mass harm poses various challenges to the use of individual litigation, including the burden placed on the courts to manage so many cases, thereby delaying access to justice, and the economic disincentives to bringing individual lawsuits for claimants with small value claims. Societies have found different ways, in and out of court, to deal with such challenges. One of those is claims funds. A claims fund is a designated amount of money set aside for paying persons or entities who have suffered a physical or economic injury, as determined by guidelines for claim eligibility and recovery (Hensler, 2005, 1430 n.3; Hensler, 1995, 1616; McGovern, 2005; Tzankova, forthcoming 2016). Claims funds may be publicly established by statute and taxpayer subsidized, or created by private entities, either as a result of litigation, as in class-action settlements or bankruptcy trusts, or voluntarily without litigation. Academics argue that the origin of a claims fund influences its acceptance and perceived legitimacy by the group (McGovern, 2005, 1367). An example of a public claims fund is the 9/11 Victim Compensation Fund, which was created by US federal statute and was funded by general tax revenue to compensate victims of the September 11, 2001 attacks on the

---

Urgenda: http://www.nytimes.com/2015/06/25/science/ruling-says-netherlands-must-reduce-greenhouse-gas-emissions.html?_r=0. The reading of the verdict by the Court was recorded and made available to interested parties who posted it on the internet with English subtitles: http://www.urgenda.nl/en/. The Court posted the ruling on its website in Dutch and in English: http://uitspraken.rechtspraak.nl/inziendocument?id=ECLI:NL:RBDHA:2015:7196&keyword=urgenda.

[24] *See* the report of the European Network of Councils for the Judiciary (ENCJ), *Justice, Society and the Media, report 2011/2012*, available at http://www.encj.eu/images/stories/pdf/GA/Dublin/encj_report_justice_society_media_def.pdf.

World Trade Center. An earlier example of such a public claims fund in the US is the Black Lung Program, which was funded by a tax on industry and provided compensation to miners diagnosed with black lung disease. In contrast, the settlement fund that was created after the Vie d'Or litigation was a private claims fund: the accountants, actuaries and the Association of Insurers contributed to it. The Gulf Coast Claims Facility assembled following the BP Deepwater Horizon Gulf oil spill displayed certain traits of both public and private claims funds, and therefore might be considered to be a quasi-public claims fund (Stier, 2011). Like a private fund, the Gulf Coast Claims Facility was funded by a private entity, BP, and provided a route for BP to avoid future litigation by settling potential claims. But like a public fund, the Gulf Coast Claims Facility received the government's imprimatur via President Obama's public announcement of the fund and his statement that the fund's payments would be fair and that the fund would be independent of BP. Subsequently the Gulf Coast Claims Facility was superseded by a fund established to settle a federal class action.

The presence of various types of claims funds—public, private and quasi-public—offers various alternatives for the resolution of mass claims, especially but not exclusively in relation to the address under corporate social responsibility standards of environmental damages caused by multinationals in jurisdictions where a class action regime is absent or where the rule of law is less well developed. But certain claims funds may be subject to criticism based on concern about the lack of independence of the claims administrators or the fund distribution criteria, as well as the lack of meaningful, informed consent by the settling claimants, yielding further worry that the culpable defendants may escape liability, without paying adequate compensation or being appropriately deterred. For example, the plaintiffs' counsel challenged in court the independence of claims administrator Kenneth Feinberg of the Gulf Coast Claims Facility, in light of his pay having been determined by BP and subsequently renegotiated between himself and BP. While the plaintiffs' attorneys may themselves have had an economic interest generally in criticizing the Gulf Coast Claims Facility, which obtained releases from claimants who might otherwise have pursued litigation with the services of the plaintiffs' counsel, the federal multidistrict court ruled in favor of the plaintiffs' counsel, and found that 'Mr. Feinberg and the GCCF cannot be considered "neutral" or "totally independent of BP"'.[25]

[25] *In re* Oil Spill by the Oil Rig 'Deepwater Horizon' in the Gulf of Mexico, on 20 April 2010, MDL No. 2179, slip op. at 11 (E.D. La. Feb. 2, 2011),

Furthermore, the claimants to the Gulf Coast Claims Facility were able to obtain payments and release their claims without being represented by an attorney, raising questions about fully informed consent, though the Facility did obtain the assistance of the Mississippi Center for Justice to provide pro bono legal assistance to interested claimants. The design of optimal procedures for claims funds merits further study and academic attention.

Another aspect of claims funds deserving further attention is the extent to which claims funds are generated in response to, and seek to assuage, cultural injury. When harm is sufficiently widespread within a particular group to be perceived as harming a shared cultural identity, members of that group may respond outside traditional court-related routes to ensure that justice is accomplished in remedying the wrong. The experience of widely shared cultural injury may be facilitated by mass media attention and dissemination of news and emotional video or audio about the event. If cultural injury has occurred to a discrete group, a charitable private claims fund may appear.[26] Mass dispute resolution and claims funds may then serve as a vehicle for cultural preservation and healing. Cultural connectedness can also lead to group cohesiveness in accepting a settlement or electing not to pursue formal litigation in light of charitable payments. In Vie d'Or, where the claims resolution process lasted for 14 years, the person who administered the Foundation over the years acquired substantial authority, as he was the main point of reference for the claimants. Over time, he became the face of the Foundation, the person to whom they directed administrative questions. Although technically mundane, often such questions related to life-changing events (births, deaths, divorce, change of address, retirement and so on) of great significance to the claimants. Through interactions with him and each other, the claimants were ultimately transformed into a little community bound by more than just the financial loss they had in common.

---

available at http://www.laed.uscourts.gov/OilSpill/Orders/222011OrderonRecDoc912.pdf.

[26] The Dutch Vie d'Or case study in Chapter 6 raises the possibility that voluntary contributions may be based in part on a collective identity that is commercial. Here, the Association of Insurers elected to contribute € 6.5 million to a settlement fund to assist policyholders of bankrupt Vie d'Or, even though Vie d'Or was not a member of the Association. The settlement totaled € 45 million and also included contributions from reserved funds from the bankruptcy, as well as the accountants and actuaries involved; in addition, the Insurance Regulator agreed to cover the Foundation's costs and expenses, thereby allowing settlement funds to pass completely to policyholders. The settlement was subsequently approved under the Dutch Act on Collective Settlements.

In the US, the yearning to heal a cultural injury, sometimes based on shared group loyalty, may have underpinned multiple claims funds. For example, following a shooting by a mentally ill student at Virginia Tech University in 2007, numerous charitable donors created an $8 million Hokie Memorial Spirit Fund for victims, named after the school mascot. Discussing his administration of the Virginia Tech fund, Kenneth Feinberg stated that 'the importance of this communitarian feeling cannot be overstated', and noted that few recipients of the charitable fund subsequently brought suit against the school (Feinberg, 2012). If cultural injury has occurred to a politically significant group, the government may become involved in creating a fund. According to Feinberg, the 9/11 Victim Compensation Fund, which was passed by Congress less than two weeks after the World Trade Center fell, was a collective response to a national tragedy:

> Staggered by this foreign attack on American shores, Congress quickly enacted a generous, publicly funded compensation program as proof positive that Americans stood together, a single community ready to help one another in our collective hour of need.

By expressing both solidarity and caring, Feinberg opined that the 9/11 Victim Compensation Fund 'helped the nation cope with tragedy' (Feinberg, 2012, 57).

With the media widely disseminating news of the spill and images of oil pouring into the ocean, in his first Oval Office address, President Barrack Obama announced the creation of a $20 billion claims fund by BP to compensate those in the Gulf. BP had agreed to the fund after meeting with President Obama in the White House. In introducing the fund to the country, President Obama highlighted the fund's prevention of ongoing destruction of the culture of the Gulf, which might be irreversible if businesses were forced to wait for litigated settlements, stating:

> [F]or generations, men and women who call this region home have made their living on the water … The sadness and anger they feel is not just about the money they've lost. It's about a wrenching anxiety that their way of life may be lost. I refuse to let that happen.[27]

[27] The White House, Office of Press Secretary, Remarks of the President to the Nation on the BP Oil Spill (15 June 2010).

Although Feinberg himself has frequently asserted that the claims funds he has directed remain exceedingly rare and non-precedential,[28] such funds have continued to be created in the US in recent years. Recently, Feinberg has become involved in a $5 million claims fund charitably donated for victims of an Aurora, Illinois movie theater mass shooting, an $11 million charitable claims fund for the 2012 school shooting at Sandy Hook Elementary School in Connecticut, and the $60 million One Fund Boston, which was politically created, but charitably funded, for victims of the 2013 Boston Marathon bombing. Growing access to images and video from social media and the internet may strengthen the bonds of community, empathy and solidarity that push forward both charitable and political claims funds. Today and increasingly in future years, people may find it unsurprising that an acquaintance, connected through social media and the internet, is personally involved in the news stories that a decade ago were displayed only on television news, and the desire to give aid may be correspondingly greater. The use of charitable claims funds in such situations may serve not only to distribute much-needed funds to victims, but also to express care and concern within a community, and to facilitate the community's healing after a traumatic mass injury.

REFERENCES

John Coffee, *Rescuing the Private Attorney General: Why the Model of the Lawyer as Bounty Hunter is Not Working*, (1983) 42 Maryland Law Review 215

Kenneth Feinberg, *Who Gets What: Fair Compensation After Tragedy and Financial Upheaval* (PublicAffairs Books 2012)

Bryant Garth, Ilene Nagel & Jay Plager, *The Institution of the Private Attorney General: Perspectives from an Empirical Study of Class Action Litigation*, (1988) 61 Southern California Law Review 353

Deborah Hensler, *A Glass Half Full, A Glass Half Empty: The Use of Alternative Dispute Resolution in Mass Personal Injury Litigation*, (1995) 73 Texas Law Review 1587

Deborah Hensler, *Alternative Courts? Litigation-Induced Claims Resolution Facilities*, (2005) 57 Stanford Law Review 1429

---

[28] In contrast to the 9/11 Victim Compensation Fund, no politically or charitably organized claims fund arose after the 1995 Oklahoma City terrorist federal-building bombing by Timothy McVeigh that resulted in the deaths of more than 160 people and injured more than 600. Nor was there a fund after the 1993 World Trade Center terrorist bombing that killed six people and injured more than 1,000 others.

Francis McGovern, *The What and Why of Claims Resolution Facilities*, (2005) 57 Stanford Law Review 1361

Leslie Moran, Managing the "Critical Interdependencies" of the Media and Judiciary in the United Kingdom, in Mike Asimow, Kathryn Brown & David Ray Papke (eds.), *Law and Popular Culture: International Perspectives* (Cambridge Scholars Publishing 2014)

Byron Stier, *The Gulf Coast Claims Facility as Quasi-Public Fund: Transparency and Independence in Claim Administrator Compensation*, (2011) 30 Mississippi College Law Review 255

Ianika Tzankova, *Funding of Mass Disputes: Lessons from the Netherlands*, (2012) 8 Journal of Law, Economics & Policy 549

Ianika Tzankova, *Case Management: The Stepchild of Mass Claim Dispute Resolution*, (2014) 19 Uniform Law Review 329

Ianika Tzankova, From Transnational Principles to European Rules of Civil Procedure: Reflections on the Potential of Case Management for the Resolution of Mass Disputes, in Hans Micklitz (ed.), *The Transformation of Enforcement in Europe* (Hart Publishing, forthcoming 2016)

Ianika Tzankova & Deborah Hensler, Collective Settlements in the Netherlands: Some Empirical Observations, in Christopher Hodges & Astrid Stadler (eds.), *Resolving Mass Disputes* (Edward Elgar Publishing 2013)

Ianika Tzankova & Jeroen Kortmann, *Remedies for Consumers of Financial Services: Collective Redress and Improvement of Class Representation*, European Journal of Consumer Law/Revue Européenne de Droit de la Consommation (Larcier 2010)

3. Smoke signals from the south: The unanticipated effects of an 'unsuccessful' litigation on Brazil's anti-tobacco war[1]

Manuel A. Gómez

INTRODUCTION

Class action lawyers tend to view litigation as the only vehicle through which their clients can obtain full satisfaction for their grievances. Court judgments, which may include monetary or injunctive relief, almost always constitute the sole objective in a litigation-centered strategy. As a result, once the lawyers have obtained a favorable judgment for their clients, they tend to assume that they have won the war. While this might be true in the ordinary run of cases, sometimes litigation is just one of several battles to be fought in a multifaceted war to obtain redress. This is the case for many claims based on alleged injuries stemming from defective products. Consumer products are subject to government regulation and industry standards regarding their manufacturing, commercialization and distribution. They are also the subjects of media attention, which in turn shapes public opinion. All of these may become the sites of

[1] This chapter is drawn from interview data and documentary evidence including court records, news reports and scholarly publications related to tobacco litigation in Brazil, and especially the Souza Cruz case. The interviews were conducted in Miami, São Paulo and Rio de Janeiro between 2010 and 2012 with key informants that included lawyers, their clients and third parties. I am indebted to them for their time and disposition to help me understand the intricacies of the dispute, which this chapter describes. I am grateful to Larissa Clare Pochmann Da Silva for her superb assistance in obtaining court records, securing interviews and other information about the Souza Cruz case, and sharing with me her expertise about collective litigation and procedural law in Brazil.

conflict. As a result, the outcome of litigation—albeit important—is not necessarily what determines the overall success or failure of an effort to obtain redress or deter harmful behavior. Sometimes, a party may lose in court but still succeed in advancing their goals. That is precisely what occurred in the case study presented in the following pages. The litigation was filed in 1995 in the courts of São Paulo in Brazil by representatives of the Association for the Defense of the Health of Smokers (Assocação de Defensa da Saúde do Fumante, or ADESF) against Brazilian tobacco manufacturers Souza Cruz and Philip Morris. Several rulings, most of them against the plaintiffs, have been handed down in the course of this 20-year litigation, but the Souza Cruz case still lingers in Brazilian courts.

The Souza Cruz litigation has been part of a broad anti-tobacco campaign. Since the initial filing, the litigation acquired notoriety and a symbolic meaning that helped mobilize political actors, the media and the general public. Following the legal strategy that had served the industry well for decades, tobacco defendants concentrated all their efforts on defeating ADESF only on the judicial front. The plaintiffs, on the other hand, acted on different fronts, including mobilizing the general public and government officials, which in turn helped their lobbying efforts toward a more stringent regulation of the industry. The Souza Cruz litigation thus became a valuable device for the plaintiffs to achieve their goals beyond the possibility of a favorable judgment.

TOBACCO LITIGATION HEADS SOUTH

Litigation against tobacco manufacturers has a long and convoluted history that spans more than 60 years and involves multiple judicial proceedings in nearly every continent. The cases to which the academic literature has devoted most of its attention are the ones litigated in the United States (Rabin, 1992, 2001a, 2001b, 2008), the United Kingdom (Sirabionian, 2005) and a handful of other jurisdictions (Daynard, 2000).

By comparison, legal scholars have paid very little attention to anti-tobacco litigation in South America (Flores, 2006, 96), despite the importance of the tobacco industry in the region. Policy debates on tobacco control have become increasingly lively during the last decade, and there has been a surge of lawsuits filed against tobacco manufacturers in several Latin American countries, including Argentina, Brazil, Colombia, Mexico and Venezuela. This chapter helps to fill that gap by focusing on the development of anti-tobacco litigation in Brazil, through a case study of a lawsuit brought by ADESF against the Souza

Cruz Corporation and Philip Morris Brasil Industria e Comercio Ltda. in the state courts of São Paulo. ADESF is a private consumer association, established in 1995, with the main purpose of pursuing legal claims against tobacco manufacturers on behalf of smokers. The Souza Cruz Corporation is the Brazilian subsidiary of the multinational conglomerate British American Tobacco (BAT). Further, Philip Morris Brasil Industria e Comercio Ltda. is a subsidiary of Philip Morris International (PMI), the largest tobacco manufacturer in the world.

Focusing on Brazil is important for at least three reasons:

(1) the economic importance of the tobacco industry in that country and Brazil's preeminent position in the global tobacco market;
(2) unlike in some other Latin American countries, tobacco-control policies have gained prominence on the agenda of the Brazilian government during the last twenty years; and
(3) the surge in anti-tobacco litigation in Brazilian courts during the last decade.

The latter has been motivated by the expansion of consumer protection mechanisms enabled by the enactment of special legislation, the adoption of procedural vehicles for mass claims (Gómez, 2012) and the emergence of consumer protection associations like ADESF that have taken the lead in the various judicial battles against large tobacco manufacturers in Brazilian courts.

Industry-wise, Brazil is the second largest producer of tobacco in the world and the largest exporter of tobacco leaves (World Health Organization, 2009). Although the Brazilian tobacco industry only employs around 2.2 million people (3.2 percent of the country's work force), it is nonetheless important and financially attractive. Tobacco yields a very high net return for farmers and other investors, and its unique marketability guarantees the purchase of the country's entire tobacco production, which may not be the case for other crops. Moreover, several state governments 'depend heavily on revenues raised from the value added tax on tobacco', and the Brazilian federal government also obtains significant fiscal benefits from tobacco products, which 'are considered luxury goods and have a heavy tax burden' (Food and Agricultural Organization of the United Nations, 2003).

Notwithstanding these incentives, during the last two decades the Brazilian government has led various efforts to thwart the domestic consumption of cigarettes. The government has accomplished this through a number of policies, which have ranged from the adoption of special anti-tobacco legislation to stringent fiscal measures. Recently there has been praise for the Brazilian anti-tobacco policies due to their success in contributing to dramatic reductions in the smoking rate in that country over the last decade (Levy et al., 2012). These policies have also been credited for placing Brazil at the forefront of the fight against tobacco companies in the region (World Health Organization, 2009).

Another important facet in the war against big tobacco consists of a series of lawsuits filed by public and private parties against multinational cigarette manufacturers in Brazilian courts and elsewhere. Brazilian parties have not limited themselves to seeking remedies in their own courts, but also have stretched their battle into foreign courts. One example is the lawsuit filed on behalf the state of São Paulo against various manufacturers and distributors of tobacco products in United States courts. In this action, the state of São Paulo joined other Latin American governments in seeking 'to recover medical expenses they claimed to have incurred for decades in treating the health problems resulting from their citizens' consumption of the tobacco company defendants' tobacco products' (*State of São Paulo v. Am. Tobacco Co.*, 2007). Although this lawsuit was later dismissed on grounds of remoteness, it had an important symbolic meaning for those engaged in the global war against big tobacco. The fact that the plaintiffs in these cases were foreign governments gave anti-tobacco activists confidence that their cause had finally garnered support from public officials, so activists in turn increased the political pressure back home.

In Brazil alone, by mid-2012 there were almost 300 tobacco-related cases pending in federal and state courts. Of these, all but ten were filed as individual lawsuits, with the smaller subset comprising collective actions based on alleged violations of the Consumer Defense Code. Table 3.1 shows the number and status of the pending cases by 2012.

Table 3.1 Tobacco litigation in Brazil

Pending cases	Individual lawsuits	Collective lawsuits	Decided in favor of plaintiff	Decision pending on appeal	Reversed on appeal
296	286	10	40	13	27

THE LANDSCAPE OF CONSUMER COLLECTIVE LITIGATION IN BRAZIL

Until recently, the scholarly literature on comparative civil procedure generally referred to Brazil as one of the few civil law jurisdictions—and noticeably the only in Latin America—that featured a procedural device similar to US style class actions. Such landscape is rapidly changing as the number of countries that allow collective or representative litigation is on the rise.

Collective proceedings have been a possibility in Brazil since at least 1934, when the Constitution allowed the challenge of statutory acts deemed to affect the public interest through an *actio popularis* ('popular action'). Slightly more than 20 years later, in 1965, Brazil further developed the catalogue of remedies against illegal acts deemed harmful to the general interest of society, including the environment, the cultural heritage and other rights belonging to society as a whole, through the passage of the Popular Legal Action Act. In 1985, the Popular Civil Legal Action Act authorized class actions. A new Constitution approved in 1988 consolidated the importance of consumer protection by declaring it an active obligation of state organs.

The capstone of this regime was the passage of the Consumer Defense Code in 1990. The Consumer Defense Code materialized the Constitutional mandate by establishing a detailed collective litigation platform that included both substantive and procedural provisions, thus placing Brazil at the helm of consumer class actions in Latin America (Londoño Toro, 2002; Pellegrini Grinover, 2004). Although consumer class actions were already a possibility prior to the passage of the Consumer Defense Code, this statute incorporated certain key provisions regarding res judicata, notice and standing, which made the filing of class actions more attractive in Brazil.

Furthermore, the Consumer Defense Code introduced an important distinction between diffuse, collective and individual-homogeneous rights. Both diffuse and collective rights were conceived as 'trans-individual and indivisible' (Gómez, 2012). Their main difference was that the former affects the rights of an indeterminate group of people (that is, the general public, all consumers, all children) or the general interest of society, such as the protection of the environment; and the latter the rights of a specific 'group, category or class determined by common elements of law, or a pre-existing legal relationship', as would occur, for instance, when a group of consumers transact with the same service provider and sustain an injury as a result (Gidi, 2003). On the other hand, 'individual-homogeneous rights were defined as subjective rights but of common origin or cause' (Gómez, 2012). As a result, a large number of claims for the protection of such rights could be consolidated into a single action for the sake of efficient disposition.

Even though the Consumer Defense Code governs both the individual and collective dimensions of the relationship between consumer and provider, its provisions regarding the collective realm were very important (Gidi, 2003). Some of the most salient were:

(1) the adoption of a strict liability rule;
(2) the shifting of the burden of proof to the defendant;
(3) the exemption from court fees for plaintiffs; and
(4) the possibility of allowing the consolidation of several claims in a single litigation by piercing the defendant's corporate veil.

Notwithstanding other important features, the most significant achievement of the Consumer Defense Code regime was the extension of the res judicata effects of any decision rendered by a class action judge, to the general population (*erga omnes* effect) and to potential members of the plaintiff group, class or category (Gómez, 2012). As a result, any new suit arising out of the same claims previously decided by the class action judge would be barred. Interestingly, the Consumer Defense Code also included an exception that allowed individual class members to pursue a separate action in case the class complaint was defeated.

The establishment of a class action regime in Brazil was welcomed by consumer protection advocates, but feared by many in the corporate sector, including obviously the tobacco industry. Some thought that the incentives created by these legislative changes would mobilize hordes of would-be plaintiffs and provoke a litigation surge in Brazilian courts. Tobacco manufacturers were particularly concerned that the plaintiff bar in the United States and elsewhere would lend their support and expertise gained from litigating tobacco cases for almost three decades, and encourage a new wave of tobacco litigation in South America. Given the then-current state of affairs, Brazil seemed like an obvious place for this to happen. Despite these concerns, foreign plaintiff lawyers neither supported nor became involved in the anti-tobacco collective litigation movement in Brazil, nor did these types of cases immediately erupt all over the country's courts. It took almost five years for the first tobacco collective lawsuit to be filed in Brazilian courts, and the case filed by ADESF against Souza Cruz and Philip Morris in 1995 was among the first.[2]

THE SOUZA CRUZ LITIGATION

Consumer Associations as Plaintiff: Standing, Financing and the Network-Based Litigation Strategy

Mario Albanese, Luiz Carlos Martins Mônaco and José Rosemberg established ADESF in February of 1995 with the sole purpose of bringing legal actions against cigarette manufacturers in Brazil. Pursuant to Brazilian law, class action lawsuits can only be brought on behalf of the federal government, States, Municipalities, the Federal District, the Public Prosecutor (Ministério Público) or a Consumer Association.

Merely four months after being established, ADESF's representatives filed a lawsuit in the Nineteenth Civil Court of São Paulo (19a Vara Civel do Foro Central de São Paulo) against Souza Cruz, S.A. and Philip Morris Do Brasil, S.A. Through this action, ADESF sought to force the defendant corporations to pay civil damages (both compensatory and 'moral' damages[3]) to all those affected by cigarette smoking, and also to impose stringent regulations on cigarette manufacturers regarding their advertising practices. Although some of the allegations mentioned in the complaint had a broad impact on the general population, the action was

---

[2] *ADESF v. Souza Cruz and Philip Morris* was the third collective action to be filed against tobacco manufacturers in Brazil. The Office of the Public Prosecutor (Ministério Público) of the Federal District, and the Association of Exploited Consumers of the Federal District (Associação dos Consumidores Explorados do Distrito Federal, or ACODF), respectively, filed the first two collective lawsuits against tobacco manufacturers, in the courts of Rio de Janeiro. The Ministério Público action sought an injunction and monetary damages (diffuse moral damages) against Cruz, Ogilvy do Brasil Comunicação Ltda. and Conspiração Filmes Entretenimento Ltda., based on an alleged fraudulent advertisement of tobacco products. The second collective suit, filed against Cabo Friense Indústria, Comércio de Cigarros Ltda., sought to enjoin the defendant from manufacturing and selling tobacco products in the whole country. The Ministério Público action was granted in part and dismissed in part in 2007, and the ACODF action was entirely dismissed in 2006. *See* Menezes Homsi, 2008, 11.

[3] In civil law jurisdictions, moral damages play a role similar to pain and suffering and other non-monetary damages in common law jurisdictions, but they may also have a punitive dimension, akin to US-style punitive damages.

based on the protection of the individual-homogeneous rights of a specific category of consumers: current and former cigarette smokers domiciled in the state of Sao Paulo.

Article 82 of the Consumer Defense Code requires consumer associations willing to act as plaintiffs to have been established for at least one year prior to commencing any litigation. The rationale for this rule is to deter the opportunistic formation of an association with the single purpose of pursuing a specific lawsuit, and more generally to deter the rise of a litigation-prone industry in Brazil. That same provision, however, also contains an exception that gives judges a certain degree of discretion to waive this requirement, should they find an association to have a manifest social interest. Waiver is also possible when the alleged harm is of such gravity that it justifies a newly formed association to pursue judicial remedies, or when the rights to be protected by the court are found to be particularly important.

One of the first challenges brought by defendants in the Souza Cruz litigation was precisely geared to attack ADESF's non-compliance with the one-year requirement, and ADESF's standing to bring legal action against defendants. After a prolonged battle to decide this preliminary issue, which lasted several years and included multiple motions and tactical delays, the highest appellate court in Brazil, the Superior Tribunal de Justiça, ruled for ADESF on the basis that protecting the health of smokers was an important goal, and that an association like ADESF played a key role in ensuring their effective defense. The case was then allowed to move forward.

The Souza Cruz lawsuit marked the entry of ADESF in the war against tobacco companies and a shift in the strategy of Brazilian anti-tobacco advocates who began focusing on judicial actions instead of just political lobbying and public awareness campaigns. It was, however, not the first time Albanese, Mônaco and Rosemberg had waged war against the industry, for all of them had spent years as anti-tobacco activists. In the particular case of Albanese, he took the fight against tobacco companies very personally after losing his father to a smoking-related coronary disease in the late 1950s. Before founding ADESF, he and Mônaco—the only lawyers of the group—had served as legal counsel to the Comitê Coordenador do Controle do Tabagismo no Brasil (CCCTB), an anti-smoking advocacy group. Rosemberg, a doctor and a medical researcher by training, also served on the CCCTB and was a member of the State Nicotine Dependency Commission (Commissão Estadual de Tabagismo). Rosemberg had been studying and publishing scholarly works on nicotine dependency and public health issues since at least 1975. His 1979 book about the effects of nicotine dependency on health was the first scientific publication about this problem in Brazil (Rosemberg, 1987). Because of his contribution to the field, Rosemberg was the first Latin American to be awarded the prestigious medal Tobacco and Health by the World Health Organization. Rosemberg died in 2005 and Mônaco in 2011, leaving Albanese as the only surviving founder of ADESF and its main leader.

At the time of ADESF's incorporation, the Brazilian government had already begun a crusade against tobacco manufacturers that had met with a moderate degree of success. The entry of ADESF and other consumer associations into the picture, however, helped galvanize public and government support, and revealed collective litigation as a viable alternative. Despite the widespread sympathy and public enthusiasm in favor of the anti-tobacco campaign, ADESF has not relied on any outside financial support. ADESF's members have been the sole backers of all its activities, and a number of friends and selected media outlets have helped them on a pro bono basis. Other consumer protection groups such as ACT (Aliança de Controle do Tabagismo) and IDEC (Instituto Brasileiro de Defesa do Consumidor) have also lent their expertise and resources in the battle against Souza Cruz and Philip Morris, both by joining the litigation and intensifying their public anti-tobacco campaign. Nonetheless, ADESF still carries the heaviest burden as the main plaintiff.

On its website, ADESF mentions a roster of at least 14 lawyers and four affiliated law firms, in addition to a Medical-Scientific Council of more than 40 individuals. However, hardly any of these people work at the organization on a full-time basis. Most of them are employed elsewhere—some by private industry, others by the government—and only lend a portion of their time to assist ADESF in pursuing its litigation against tobacco manufacturers, or to advance the ongoing anti-tobacco campaign led by the organization. ADESF operates from a modest office in São Paulo, with one or two staff members who provide daily support to Albanese. It is perhaps because of this that the tobacco industry has rarely seen ADESF as a threat or taken it seriously. Nonetheless, from the standpoint of ADESF, the fact that some of its supporters are also employed elsewhere—in some cases by government agencies, the healthcare sector, other consumer associations and even private industry—is advantageous and not necessarily detrimental.

The connections between these people and other influential actors and even with decision-makers that might have an effect on ADESF's cause are very important. In this sense, ADESF can be viewed more as a hub that connects different stakeholders engaged in anti-tobacco activism, than as a monolithic closed-door organization. And while this network configuration may have led to certain inefficiencies, such as increasing the risk of duplicative efforts, a lack of a centralized decision-making, and difficulties in coordinating an overall strategy, it has also broadened the reach of ADESF by engaging groups of independent stakeholders who might not have the capacity or willingness to pursue litigation independently. ADESF's extensive network has become an effective political and public relations campaign, which might have also influenced the few favorable decisions in their legal case.

The lack of a permanent structure and a robust financial platform has also imposed certain constraints on ADESF, whose limited resources are almost entirely devoted to the Souza Cruz litigation. The fact that Brazilian law waives all judicial fees and related court costs to plaintiff organizations such as ADESF, and exempts them from the general fee-shifting rule in case of dismissal, is no trivial incentive. Nonetheless, ADESF cannot afford expensive representation or to expand its litigation strategy beyond the state of São Paulo and perhaps a few other Brazilian jurisdictions such as Santa Catarina and Minas Gerais, where ADESF appears to have affiliates.

Big Tobacco and their Litigation Strategy in Brazil

Defendant corporations do not enjoy any of the procedural benefits afforded by the Consumer Defense Code to consumer associations. Moreover, they face some additional procedural hurdles such as bearing the burden of proof and not being able to shift the costs to the other party, even if they prevail in the litigation. On the other hand, defendant companies are significantly wealthier and much more sophisticated than ADESF or any other similar group in Brazil.

Souza Cruz, for instance, is a subsidiary of British American Tobacco (BAT), one of the largest conglomerates in the world, with a presence in more than 180 countries. Souza Cruz manufactures around 80 billion cigarettes per year and has a share of more than 60 percent of the Brazilian market. The company's legal team includes leading corporate and litigation firms from Rio de Janeiro and São Paulo, such as Veirano Advogados and Lopes Muniz Advogados. The other defendant, Philip Morris Do Brasil, S.A., is part of the American conglomerate Philip Morris International (PMI), the largest tobacco company in the world, by global market share—although a distant second in Brazil. Philip Morris has retained São Paulo-based Mattos Muriel Kestener Advogados, which is also one of the largest law firms in the country.

Though each co-defendant has retained their own legal team, they work in close coordination with each other and also with BAT and PMI's global army of lawyers, led by American law firms with significant experience and expertise in defending tobacco lawsuits, such as Shook, Hardy and Bacon. These firms have entire practice groups devoted to preparing, organizing and carrying out a comprehensive defense strategy for tobacco companies, both in and out of court. The decades of experience attained by these law firms in defending tobacco cases worldwide have enabled them to develop a sophisticated platform for the exchange of information regarding tobacco cases litigated in many jurisdictions. It is common for these firms to host regular meetings and conferences so that members of their global legal teams can update each other and coordinate their case management strategies. Experts and other consultants are frequently invited to attend these meetings and provide their input. Because of the multifaceted nature of the war against big tobacco, defense law firms also work in tandem with groups of lobbyists, media relations' experts and political consultants.

Counsel for Souza Cruz and Philip Morris seem to have relied on the same litigation strategy used by defendant corporations during the first wave of tobacco litigation in the United States. Their stance was to devote all necessary resources to aggressively litigate every single case and to treat them individually. As one tobacco lawyer put it during an interview: 'Litigation is the only thing that we don't package or deal with in bulks. Each case has its own life. Regardless of how little or big a case is, we keep it separate from others, so each case rises and dies alone.'

Defense counsel obviously coordinated their cases, but for internal purposes only, as court proceedings were held separately. Settlement was always out of the question. 'The idea was to send a strong signal that the company would not admit any wrongdoing or settle with anyone', an experienced tobacco defense lawyer pointed out. Although litigation became increasingly expensive for cigarette manufacturers, their overall strategy was to drag plaintiffs through prolonged court battles hoping to both exhaust them and their clients, and to deplete their resources before they were able to obtain any recovery. The strategy worked well for decades in the United States, causing tobacco claims to dwindle and helping the industry to remain undefeated on the litigation front (Rabin, 1992, 857; Henderson & Twerski, 2010, 72). It was not until the 1990s, after two prior unsuccessful litigation waves that American tobacco plaintiffs began prevailing in court as a result of a combination of exogenous and endogenous factors specific to the United States, and some even obtained substantial recoveries (Henderson & Twerski, 2010, 76).

Notwithstanding setbacks to their strategy in the United States, when anti-tobacco lawsuits began being filed in Brazilian courts, defense counsel was confident that their no-settlement, aggressive litigation strategy would scare off any potential plaintiffs with relative ease. Brazilian defense counsel's prediction was that the lack of a financially robust plaintiff bar in Brazil would pose immensurable difficulties to anyone willing to bring a lawsuit against their clients. Defense counsel also observed that although the Consumer Defense Code provisions appeared to be generally pro-plaintiff, there were some inherent obstacles and deficiencies in the system. For example, under the standing rules of the Consumer Defense Code, only a small list of entities—public agencies and a few private associations—were allowed to bring suit on behalf of allegedly affected consumers. Most if not all of these public agencies were either understaffed or overcommitted, which significantly decreased their chances of becoming engaged in a protracted litigation against big multinationals.

With regard to consumer associations, the only ones that existed were also understaffed; none had set tobacco control as part of their agenda, and they all lacked the necessary resources to pursue an expensive court battle. Finally, the Office of the Public Prosecutor, which was another potential source of concern, had not expressed any interest in spear-heading any litigation against cigarette manufacturers.

First Round for ADESF, but Not for Long

Against all predictions, ADESF was not only able to bring a collective claim against big tobacco manufacturers, but also survived a fierce challenge to their standing to bring a suit raised by the co-defendants. ADESF was also able to sustain an aggressive court battle with help from a small army of lawyers and eventually other consumer associations. As mentioned earlier, the court used its discretion to apply an exception to the one-year constitution requirement, thus allowing the case to move forward. Public notice was given according to the provisions of the Consumer Defense Code, so anyone interested could join the litigation; and the Office of the Public Prosecutor was notified of the proceedings so it could intervene on behalf of the state. Conciliation was attempted to no avail, and the co-defendants proceeded to answer the complaint, denying any form of liability.

On 7 April 2004, the Nineteenth Civil Court of São Paulo handed down a final decision on the merits in favor of the plaintiff. That point marked the culmination of eight years of litigation, during which the defendants filed a number of appeals, writs of mandamus, actions for annulment of decisions, and brought motions for disqualification against at least two magistrates. The parties also engaged in rounds of expert testimony on the harmful effects of nicotine and the purported impact of the cigarette advertisement campaign on consumers during the last 20 years. The court battle had also spilled over to the media, which helped ADESF garner a significant amount of popular and political support.

In a detailed decision, the trial judge found the co-defendants Souza Cruz and Philip Morris to have engaged in misleading and abusive advertising by failing to inform consumers about the chemical components of cigarettes and by deceiving them about the pernicious effects and addictive properties of nicotine. The judge also established that consumers had suffered a financial loss as a result of their compulsion to continue buying cigarettes, which the co-defendants were not able to disprove. The discussion in the judge's decision about the co-defendants' inability to produce evidence was particularly intriguing given that the court had already said that its ruling would be strictly based on the interpretation of legal provisions and not on evidence produced by the parties, as allowed by Article 330 of the Code of Civil Procedure. This would later be the main argument for reversing the trial court's decision on appeal.

The alleged conduct of the co-defendants, the court said, was in direct breach of several provisions of the Consumer Defense Code including Articles 7, 9, 12 and 31. As a result, the court found Souza Cruz and Philip Morris liable, and ordered them to indemnify all cigarette smokers represented by ADESF. Although the court did not expressly define the criteria for class membership, it implied that the beneficiaries were all those individuals who had purchased and consumed tobacco products manufactured and distributed by the co-defendants throughout the Brazilian territory.

Co-defendants were also ordered to re-label all tobacco products distributed by them throughout Brazil, in compliance with Law No. 9294 of 15 July 1996 and with the National Consumer Relations Policy. The new labeling, the court established, should include:

> correct, clear, precise, ostensible information in the Portuguese language on the characteristics, qualities, quantity, composition, origin, among other data, as well as on the risks that such products offer to the health and safety of the consumers.

These changes had to be implemented within 60 days of the court's ruling, or the co-defendants would have to pay a daily fine of R$100,000 (Brazilian Reals), as per Article 461 of the Code of Civil Procedure.

The court ordered the co-defendants to pay both compensatory and moral damages. The amount of the former was left to be determined during the award calculation stage, upon the production of expert evidence about the specific extent of the harm sustained by the victims. Regarding moral damages, the court ruled that the co-defendants should pay R$1,000 per person for each year during which they had smoked cigarettes manufactured or distributed by the co-defendants. This amount, the court added, had to be adjusted for inflation plus interest at a rate of 1 percent per month from the date of the ruling until a total payment was effectively made. Such moral damages, the court stated, were not only intended to compensate the victims for an affront to their emotional distress, suffering or grief, as these types of damages generally do. The court viewed these damages as having a punitive purpose, writing that they would 'suffice to discourage defendants from disregarding this decision or from taking other actions of the same kind'.

Finally, the court ordered the co-defendants to bear all court costs, in addition to:

> provable procedural and extra-procedural expenses related to the action, as well as attorneys' fees (...) set at R$100,000 by equity, taking into account the complexity of the action filed and its lengthy evidentiary stage, as well as the time spent by the professionals that have acted in the proceeding.

Naturally, ADESF received the court ruling with great excitement. The ruling was also followed by numerous press releases, an aggressive media campaign and public appearances by ADESF representatives. Other consumer advocacy groups felt encouraged and decided to join the anti-tobacco crusade more actively. Government agencies were also incentivized to increase their efforts to further restrict the use of tobacco products in Brazil. More importantly, consumer protection and anti-tobacco advocates from several Latin American countries turned their attention to the Souza Cruz litigation and began talking about the possibility of replicating it in their own countries.

A Reversal of Fortune for ADESF and the Arrival of Other Consumer Associations

Far from accepting defeat, Souza Cruz and Philip Morris instructed their lawyers to appeal the adverse first instance ruling. Although their main objective was obviously to seek reversal, they were particularly keen to suppress the flurry of negative publicity generated by ADESF and other anti-tobacco activists in the aftermath of the decision. On appeal, co-defendant Philip Morris challenged the trial court's ruling on the basis that it had allegedly decided on matters not included in the prayer for relief.

Philip Morris also asserted that several due process violations had allegedly been committed by the trial judge, and insisted on ADESF's lack of standing. The appellants argued against the appropriateness of using collective proceedings in a case where, in their view, the individual issues predominated over collective issues. In their motion to support the appeal, co-defendant Souza Cruz presented the argument that plaintiffs were well aware of the inherent risks associated with smoking, and that defendants should not be held liable for any harm suffered as a result. Alternatively, the co-defendant Souza Cruz requested that the class be limited only to those residents of the state of São Paulo who had become ill as a direct result of smoking. Moreover, Souza Cruz requested that moral damages should be reevaluated and limited according to the individual circumstances of each victim.

At some point during the appeal, another consumer association, IDEC, asked to be added as a plaintiff in the case. Established in 1987, IDEC is perhaps the largest and best-organized consumer association in Brazil. Its involvement in the fight against cigarette manufacturers was the result of a natural progression in a trail of cases that spanned from financial claims to defective products to drugs, food and services. Unlike ADESF, IDEC is formally affiliated to the leading global advocacy groups such as Consumers International and has a more robust organizational platform. Even though the co-defendants Souza Cruz and Philip Morris were opposed to IDEC's joinder, the Office of the Public Prosecutor (Procuradoria Geral de Justiça) recommended that the court allow it, which the judge ended up rejecting because of its tardiness. The judge ruled that IDEC had filed its petition too late, and that admitting it would be detrimental to its own position in the process, for it would not have the same opportunities afforded to the other parties involved. However, IDEC was later allowed to join the lawsuit.

On 12 November 2008, the Tribunal de Justiça do Estado de São Paulo, acting as a court of appeal, found for the appellants and annulled the first instance ruling. The main reasons given had to do with the lower court's decision to exclude any factual evidence produced by the co-defendants, and the fact that the court should have (but did not) limited its analysis only to 'matters of law' (*a questão de merito de direito*). The Tribunal de Justiça also agreed with the appellants with respect to the *extra petita*, and deemed it moot to continue examining the other allegations.

Right after this decision, on 3 December 2008, Souza Cruz counterattacked by suing the National Health Surveillance Agency (Agência Nacional de Vigilância Sanitária, or ANVISA) in another court, asking to enjoin said agency from regulating cigarette advertisement.

In 2009, the *ADESF v. Souza Cruz* case was remanded to the lower court and IDEC refiled its request to join the plaintiff's case; another consumer organization, ACT, also sought to join the litigation. On 16 May 2011, a new decision on the merits was proffered. After examining and weighing all the evidence produced by the parties, and following a decision handed down by the Superior Tribunal de Justiça in 2010, which had exonerated big tobacco companies from liability, the new trial judge declared that the tobacco manufacturers had not engaged in faulty behavior and dismissed the complaint.

Later that year, on 4 October 2011, another collective lawsuit pending against Souza Cruz since 2007 was also dismissed. This case, brought by the Office of the Public Prosecutor of São Paulo was based on similar allegations to the ones presented by ADESF. Many other—mostly individual—lawsuits filed by former or current smokers throughout the country were also rejected.

The absolute turn-around of the 16 May 2011 decision on remand was an important setback for plaintiffs who unsurprisingly filed an appeal that took the court four years to decide. Finally, on 28 January 2015, the Tribunal de Justiça de São Paulo confirmed the dismissal of the claim, thus precluding plaintiffs from obtaining any judicial redress from big tobacco in the foreseeable future.

LOSING THE BATTLE, BUT WINNING THE WAR? ENTREPRENEURIAL LAWYERING AND MULTI-PRONGED STRATEGIES AGAINST BIG TOBACCO

The string of defeats suffered by ADESF and other plaintiffs during the last few years might suggest that the anti-tobacco war in Brazil is a lost cause. The fact that no one has been able to obtain a favorable final judgment or any form of monetary compensation from a tobacco manufacturer is certainly disheartening for those who put all their faith in litigation. ADESF and other organizations, however, do not see it that way. To them, litigation is just one of many strands in a long-term war against cigarette manufacturers. In the aftermath of their first court victory, ADESF representatives realized that litigation had an enormous value outside of the judiciary, regardless of any favorable judgment.

The court case helped ADESF gain notoriety and support from other organizations such as ACT and IDEC. More importantly, it also helped the anti-tobacco cause reach a much broader audience, and placed significant pressure on government agencies such as ANVISA, and the

Office of the Public Prosecutor, to act more decisively. Evidence of this can be found in the several administrative and court proceedings initiated by the aforementioned entities. Even after the reversal of fortune suffered by ADESF with the annulment of the trial court's ruling, external support from private and public agencies continued to increase. The Brazilian government intensified its campaign against Souza Cruz and Philip Morris by way of judicial and non-judicial means. In turn, foreign governments and consumer protection advocates from neighboring countries became encouraged and opened new fronts against tobacco in their own jurisdictions.

While it is true that big tobacco companies are virtually undefeated in Brazilian courts, they have been forced to defend themselves on multiple fronts against a myriad of opponents, at a very high cost. Anti-tobacco activists such as ADESF have learned to value litigation, not only because of its potential for helping them get redress through a judicial decision. More importantly, litigation has served them symbolically to garner sympathy and support, which has often translated into more effective out-of-court strategies that include mass media campaigns and regulatory actions. Although it is hard to measure with precision the impact of the Souza Cruz case on the war against cigarette manufacturers in Brazil, those with knowledge and familiarity of the issues on both sides of the table agree about its extraordinary significance and trend setting value in the fight against big tobacco.

Whereas cigarette manufacturers became known by their unbending anti-settlement stance since the first wave of litigation in the United States, the strategy taken by ADESF in the Souza Cruz litigation may define how plaintiffs situate themselves in the anti-tobacco war. Consumer protection organizations, NGOs and other actors who do not have the infrastructure, resources or organizational strength to compete with the often-powerful defendants might use litigation not only because of its intrinsic value, but also because of its potential in helping them raise awareness, garner public and governmental support for their cause, and for enabling the use of other strategies.

REFERENCES

Federative Republic of Brazil, Código de Defensa do Consumidor, Lei No. 8.078, de 11 de Setembro de 1990 (Consumer Protection Code), available at http://www.planalto.gov.br/ccivil_03/leis/L8078.htm

Federative Republic of Brazil, Constituição da República dos Estados Unidos do Brasil, de 16 de Julho de 1934 (1934 Constitution), available at http://www.planalto.gov.br/ccivil_03/Constituicao/Constituicao34.htm

Federative Republic of Brazil, Lei da Ação Popular, Lei No. 4.717, de 29 de Junho de 1965 (Popular Action Act), available at http://www.planalto.gov.br/ccivil_03/leis/L4717.htm

Federative Republic of Brazil, Lei da Açao Civil Publica, Lei No. 7.347, de 24 de Julho de 1985 (Civil Public Action Act), available at http://www.planalto.gov.br/ccivil_03/Leis/L7347orig.htm.

Federative Republic of Brazil, Constituição da República Federativa do Brasil de 1988 (1988 Constitution) Article 5, available at http://www.planalto.gov.br/ccivil_03/Constituicao/ConstituicaoCompilado.htm

Richard Daynard et al., *Tobacco Litigation Worldwide*, (2000) British Medical Journal 320

M.L. Flores et al., *Litigation in Argentina: Challenging the Tobacco Industry*, (April 2006) 15 Tobacco Control 90

Food and Agricultural Organization of the United Nations, Tobacco in Brazil, in *Issues in the Global Tobacco Economy: Selected Case Studies* (FAO/UN, 2003), available at ftp://ftp.fao.org/docrep/fao/006/y4997e/

Edith Friedler, *Moral Damages in Mexican Law: A Comparative Approach*, (1986) 8 Loyola of Los Angeles International and Comparative Law Review 235

Antonio Gidi, *Class Actions in Brazil: A Model for Civil Law Countries*, (2003) 51 American Journal of Comparative Law 311

Manuel A. Gómez, *Will The Birds Stay South? The Rise of Class Actions and Other Forms of Group Litigation Across Latin America*, (2012) 43 University of Miami Inter-American Law Review 481

James Henderson & Aaron Twerski, *Reaching Equilibrium in Tobacco Litigation*, (2010) 62 South Carolina Law Review 67

David Levy, Liz Maria de Almeida & Andre Szklo, *The Brazil SimSmoke Policy Simulation Model: The Effect of Strong Tobacco Control Policies on Smoking Prevalence and Smoking-Attributable Deaths in a Middle Income Nation*, PLoS Med 9(11): e1001336, (2012)

Beatriz Londoño Toro, *Análisis de las estadísticas sobre acciones populares y derechos colectivos*, (2002) 29 Revista Tutela, Acciones Populares y de Cumplimiento 1211

Clarissa Menezes Homsi, *Pesquisa Sobre Acões Judiciais Indenizatórias Promovidas Contra A Indústria do Tabaco*, Aliança de Controle do Tabagismo, 2008

Ada Pellegrini Grinover, Hacia Un Sistema Iberoamericano de Tutela de Intereses Transindividuales, in Antonio Gidi & Eduardo Ferrer Mac-Gregor (eds.), *La Tutela De Los Derechos Difusos, Colectivos e Individuales Homogéneos* (Editorial Porrúa 2004)

Robert Rabin, *A Sociolegal History of the Tobacco Tort Litigation*, (1992) 44 Stanford Law Review 853

Robert Rabin, Institutional and Historical Perspectives on Tobacco Tort Liability, in Robert Rabin & Stephen Sugarman (eds.), *Smoking Policy: Law, Politics, And Culture* (Oxford University Press 1993)

Robert Rabin, The Third Wave of Tobacco Tort Litigation, in Robert Rabin & Stephen Sugarman (eds.), *Regulating Tobacco* (Oxford University Press 2001)

Robert Rabin, *The Tobacco Litigation: A Tentative Assessment*, (2001) 51 DePaul Law Review 331

Robert Rabin, *Tobacco Control Strategies: Past Efficacy and Future Promise*, (2008) 41 Loyola of Los Angeles Law Review 1721

José Rosemberg, *Tabagismo, Sério Problema de Saúde Pública*, 2nd ed., (1987) ALMED Editora e Livraria Ltda

Keith Rosenn, *Civil Procedure in Brazil*, (1986) 34 American Journal of Comparative Law 487

Andrei Sirabionian, *Why Tobacco Litigation has not been Successful in the United Kingdom*, (2005) 25 Northwestern Journal of International Law & Business 485

State of São Paulo of the Federative Republic of Brazil v. American Tobacco Company, 919 A.2d 1116 (Del. 2007)

Tribunal de Justiça de São Paulo, Apelaçao Civel com Revisão, No. 479 713-4/8-00, Philip Morris Brasil SA, Philip Morris Marketing S/A, 12 November 2008

World Health Organization, (2009) 87 Bulletin of the World Health Organization 805–884

4. Using associations as a vehicle for class action: The case of Taiwan

Kuo-Chang Huang

1. INTRODUCTION

Taiwan, as a civil law country, owes the origin of its civil procedure to the German system. Most of the articles of the first modern Taiwan Code of Civil Procedure (TCCP) are virtually literal translations of the German Code of Civil Procedure of 1877.[1] As a result, traditionally the concept of a class action was foreign to the Taiwan civil justice system. While under the influence of Japanese civil procedure, TCCP has long provided a '*representative suit*' device through which a litigant can receive an explicit delegation from another party who shares common interests in the subject matter in dispute to sue or be sued on the latter's behalf. The application of such device is limited in practice and has never been considered as performing the modern function of a class action.

The concept of a class action was formally introduced by the Consumer Protection Act of 1994, which provides that a certified consumer protection association can bring a lawsuit to seek damages from a business provided that 20 or more consumers delegate their rights against such business to the consumer protection association.[2] This provision establishes the basic model of the modern class action in Taiwan.

The newly established procedure has four features. First, it overcomes the traditional dogma inherited from the German way of thinking that a party cannot delegate its right to sue to a third party who does not share a common cause of action. Second, however, in order to prevent undesirable solicitation of litigation, the nature of the third party is tightly controlled.[3] As a matter of general principle, only a certified public interest association may be delegated to litigate on behalf of the real

[1] For a literal English translation of this Code, *see* Huang & Thurston, 2006.
[2] *See* Article 50 of Consumer Protection Act.
[3] *See* Article 49 of Consumer Protection Act.

parties in interest. This feature is similar to the European principle of standing in class actions (Tzankova, chapter 6, this volume) Third, the delegation must be explicitly made and evidenced in writing. The concept that any member falling within the scope of a specified class is represented by a self-appointed litigant unless she opts out, is not recognized in Taiwan. Finally, the law explicitly prohibits any public interest association from making any profits or receiving any compensation for the lawsuit it represents.[4]

While the class action device provided in the Consumer Protection Act is applicable only in consumer cases, its basic model was extended in 2003 by TCCP to be applied in all kinds of lawsuits involving common interests of members of an incorporated public interest association, and by the Securities Investors and Fortunes Trader Protection Act (SIFTP Act) to be applied in securities class action, respectively. Doctrinally, both the devices in TCCP and in SIFTP Act use public interest associations as a vehicle to drive class actions and share all of the four features described above. However, empirically, in practice the actual applications of these two devices significantly differ. To illustrate, although both devices became available in 2003, fewer than five class actions have been brought under TCCP as of 2012 but there have been more than 100 class actions brought under SIFTP during the same period. This contrast is particularly astounding in light of the fact that the TCCP class-action mechanism has general applicability in all types of claims while the SIFTP class action only applies to narrowly-defined securities-related claims.

This Chapter reports on two case studies: the first of a class action brought by a labor union on behalf of its members to seek small-claim redress under TCCP; the second of a security class action brought under SIFTP. In closing, this Chapter briefly analyzes why the two types of class actions fare so differently in practice and the challenges inherent in using public interest associations as vehicles for class actions.

[4] *See* Article 50 of Consumer Protection Act (providing that consumer protection groups shall not claim rewards from consumers for litigation); Article 49 of Consumer Protection Act.

2. A SMALL-CLAIM ACTION BY LABOR UNION: *THE PARKING-LOTS-ATTENDANT UNION V. TAIPEI GOVERNMENT*

A. Prologue

Taipei, like other major cities around the globe, provides public parking spaces on the streets. All these parking spaces are managed by the Parking-Lots Bureau of the Taipei Municipal Government (referred to as PLB) in a user-friendly manner, that is, every car is charged manually via a parking sheet issued by a parking-lot attendant (referred to as PLA) patrolling an assigned area on an hourly-basis so that vehicle owners do not have to worry about being short of coins. Obviously, such a parker-friendly system demands a substantial number of PLAs to undertake the task of patrolling the streets to issue parking sheets. As a result, the PLB hires hundreds of privately-contracted PLAs who do not belong to the public servant system and are treated as ordinary workers employed by companies.

The work of a PLA requires labor rather than expertise. Since its career outlook is not promising and this job involves working in unbearable humidity in summer as well as enduring chilly rains in winter, it is not surprising that most PLAs are not college educated. The evidently great disparity of power as well as capability between the employer—the municipal government of the capital of Taiwan—and the employees—a group of workers unequipped with high education or special skills—dictates that unionization is desirable, maybe even necessary, for the protection of those PLAs. However, due to the fact that the authoritarian regime of the Chinese Nationalist Party (KMT) government has suppressed the organization of labor unions for over 40 years since 1949, labor unions remain underdeveloped even though Taiwan has transformed into a democratic country in the twenty-first century. Nevertheless, under that then-still union-hostile environment, those PLAs formed their own union in July 1997 after a three-year effort, a rare and significant success among the workers in Taiwan. The final success of organizing the PLA Union through relentless struggle suggests the proactive nature of this Union, which distinguishes itself from most labor unions sponsored by the employer.

The fact that the PLAs are employed by the municipal government but do not belong to the public servant system, directly results in the unequal treatment between the PLAs and ordinary governmental employees. The latter enjoy superior treatment to the former in various respects. Accordingly, demanding equal treatment and better benefits became the major aim of the PLA Union. The leaders of the Union adopted various approaches in fighting for union members' interests, such as requesting local politicians to speak on their behalf, holding demonstration parades, and asking the mayoral candidates to respond to their demands during the election campaign. The PLB counteracted such efforts by attempting to penetrate the union and undermine its leadership. Their relationship is a tense rivalry.

B. The Dispute and the Underlying Battle

The dispute leading to the subsequent class action originated from the PLAs' working bonus. Starting from June 1999, the PLB agreed to pay the PLAs a monthly working bonus ranging from New Taiwan Dollars (NTD) 4,000 to 6,000,[5] according to seniority. The PLAs claimed that this working bonus constitutes part of the wage, and so their overtime wage should be calculated on the basis of including such bonus into their monthly wage. At first, the PLB disagreed. This disagreement was not resolved until the Management-Workers Meeting in December 2002 at which the management agreed to include the working bonus in the regular monthly wage as the basis of calculating the overtime pay. However, how to calculate the overtime pay for the period of June 1999 to November 2002 (42 months in total) remained disputed.

To demand that the PLB pay the difference between the overtime pay calculated by including working bonus and the overtime pay calculated by excluding working bonus, the Union, on behalf of its members, filed for labor dispute mediation against the PLB with the Labor Bureau of Taipei Municipal Government on 10 March 2006.[6] The parties settled on 15 May 2006 when the PLB agreed to pay the difference in overtime pay in question no later than 30 June 2006. However, the issue of whether the PLB should also pay the interest that would have accrued on the overtime-pay difference remained unclear and eventually resulted in the initiation of the class action.

At first glance, it seems surprisingly bizarre that after successfully recovering the disputed difference in overtime pay, the PLAs would even consider insisting that the PLB pay interest for its tardiness in paying that

---

[5] The exchange rate between US dollars and New Taiwan dollars has remained about 1:30 for the past ten years with a fluctuation within 10%.

[6] For an introduction to the labor mediation mechanism in Taiwan, *see* Huang et al., 2010.

difference. After all, even if their assertion that the difference of overtime pay is overdue stands, every member's claim for such interest, as calculated at the statutorily-prescribed annual interest rate of 5%, would be small, certainly not enough to make it economically feasible to bring an independent lawsuit. Take member C.C. Lin for example. His overtime pay for February 2001 was NTD 4,416, which was calculated by his monthly salary of NTD 32,161 without including his working bonus of NTD 4,500. If his bonus had been included, he would have received NTD 618 more. The interest on the difference of NTD 618 for a period of 63 months, from February 2001 to June 2006 (the time of actual payment), would be NTD 162. Adding interest on the difference for overtime pay in the entire period in question, his total claim in the subsequent class action was NTD 2,965, equivalent to approximately US$ 100.

The fact that the PLA Union brought lawsuits on behalf of their members for individually small amounts of money exemplifies not only the proactive nature of the Union but also its tense relationship with the employer. Examination of the conflict between the PLB and the Union during the same period helps to explain why the Union took such a hardline stance.

With the growth of the number of parking lots in Taipei city, the PLB initiated the policy of contracting with private companies to undertake the job of issuing parking sheets. For the PLB, this 'private-contractor policy' is cost-effective and financially desirable. However, for the PLAs, this policy threatens their jobs. To fight against this private-contractor policy, the PLA Union, from 2002, organized a number of collective actions, including holding parades and demonstrations, which naturally escalated the rivalry between the PLB and the PLA Union. Viewed more broadly, the dispute over the interest arising from the alleged overdue overtime pay difference is simply a product of this rivalry.

C. The Litigation

Three female members, C.L. Wei, C.I. Chu, and S.M. Huang, all in their forties, served on the executive board of the Union and played key roles in the PLAs' battle against the PLB. The three ladies took advantage of the fact that Taipei Municipal Government provided legal aid for the workers and labor unions to file claims against their employer through litigation. The maximum amount of such legal aid for hiring attorneys is NTD 100,000 per court level. Note that the most popular fee arrangement in the legal market of Taiwan is for retained lawyers to receive a fixed amount of legal fees for representation in a specific court level, no matter how the case is terminated.[7] While NTD 100,000 does not seem like much, it was sufficient to make S.T. Liu, a female attorney actively involved in labor-related cases, agree to take on this case, acting as counsel for the plaintiff, the PLA Union.

Article 44-1 of TCCP provides that an incorporated public interest association may, to the extent permitted by its purpose as prescribed in the bylaws, sue on behalf of its members who own a common interest in the subject matter of a litigation.[8] Pursuant to this provision, the PLA, on behalf of 777 members, filed the complaint in Taipei District Court against the PLB on 14 November 2006. The defendant was originally represented by C.L. Liu, an experienced attorney who had served on the bench before turning to private practice. This case was assigned to Judge C.I. Kwan, a talented woman who had sat on the civil bench for six years at the time the case was filed and was known for her specialization in civil and labor disputes.

The plaintiff's legal theory was straightforward. The working bonus was part of the PLAs' wage and therefore should be included in calculating their overtime pay. Although the defendant had paid the difference of overtime pay that occurred during the period in question (June 1999–November 2002), the payment was not made until June 2006 and therefore was overdue. Consequently, the defendant should pay all class members interest. Since the context of this action, that is, a labor union on behalf of its members suing for their aggregate claims arising from a common ground, squarely falls within the scope of Article 44-1, it was virtually uncontested that the PLA Union had standing to initiate this action. Note that while, as a matter of procedural law, TCCP does not explicitly provide that a class action cannot proceed until it is 'certified' by the court, satisfying the requirements of Article 44-1 is still a precondition for a case to be argued and decided on the merits.

The total amount of the 777 members' aggregate claims was NTD 3,251,380. The mean value of each member's claim was about NTD 4,100, ranging from the minimum of NTD 27 to the maximum of NTD 8,549. Figure 4.1 shows the distribution of the amount of all members' claims in US dollars.

The defendant raised two defenses, which in turn became the two pivotal issues in this litigation. First, the nature of the working bonus is a benefit rather than wage and, thus, a working bonus should not be included in calculating the overtime pay. While the PLB agreed to

---

7 For an introduction to legal representation in Taiwan, *see* Huang, 2008.

8 *See* Article 44-1 of TCCP.

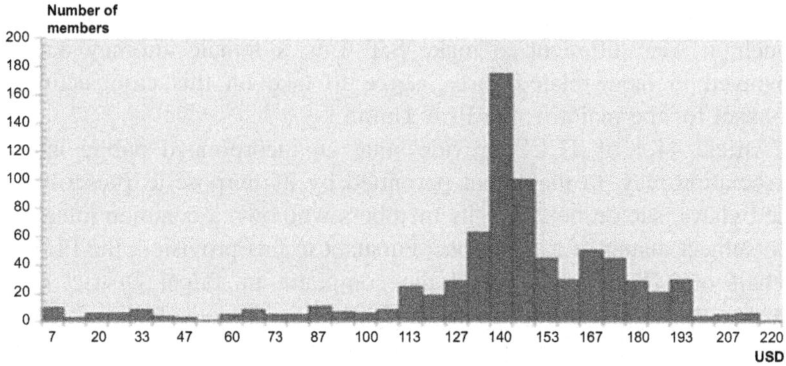

Figure 4.1 Distribution of amount of members' claims

include the working bonus in calculating the overtime pay in the settlement of 15 May 2006, that agreement was a gift from the employer rather than its legal obligation. Since the PLAs have no legal rights to ask for inclusion of a working bonus as part of their wage in calculating the overtime pay, there is no such thing as an overdue payment and thus no interest to be claimed. Second, even if the working bonus, as a matter of law, should be deemed part of the wage for the purpose of calculating the overtime pay, the statute of limitations for part of the plaintiff's interest claims had elapsed. Specifically, since the PLAs did not initiate this action to toll the applicable statute of limitations—which is five years for an interest claim—until 14 November 2006, the interest claim for the overtime pay during the period April to November 2001 was time-barred.

Judge Kwan ruled on both issues in favor of the PLA Union. She found not only that the working bonus should be deemed part of the wage but also that the PLAs' invoking labor mediation during the period of March to May 2001 had tolled the statute of limitation. On 18 April 2007, Judge Kwan issued a judgment for the plaintiff, granting the PLA Union's entire claim.[9] The proceeding in the district court took less than six months.

D. The Appeal

After losing the case in the court of first instance, the PLB terminated its relationship with C.L. Liu and retained a new lawyer, C.M. Hsu, to file

[9] *See* Taipei District Court 95 Lou-Shu-Tzi No. 206 Judgment.

an appeal with the Taiwan High Court. The PLA Union was still represented by S.T. Liu to defend its victory, again taking advantage of the legal aid for an additional legal fee of NTD 100,000 for appearing before the court of second instance. This appeal was assigned to a three-judge panel, which is specialized in hearing labor dispute cases.

Note that the court of first appeal in Taiwan adopts the standard of review *de novo*, which means that the High Court would deal with not only the legal questions but also the factual issues. On its appeal, the PLB virtually repeated its two defenses raised in the district court. While the Taiwan High Court rejected the PLB's first defense, it supported the PLB's second defense, finding that the mediation session did not toll the statute of limitations and therefore part of the plaintiff's interest claims were time-barred. Consequently, the High Court, affirming in part and reversing in part, found that the PLA Union's claim should be cut down to NTD 1,915,663, about 59 percent of its award obtained in the district court.[10] This judgment was rendered on 29 August 2007, within five months of when the first appeal was taken.

Still unsatisfied with the High Court's decision, the PLB filed its appeal to the Taiwan Supreme Court, which generally has broad discretion in deciding whether to hear an appeal on the merits.[11] On 17 April 2008, the Taiwan Supreme Court issued its ruling to procedurally dismiss the PLB's appeal without hearings. This case is consequently final and conclusive.[12] It should be noted that appealing to the Supreme Court requires that the appellant must have an interest exceeding a minimum amount of NTD 1,500,000. Since the PLA Union's interest in appealing for its loss in the High Court judgment did not exceed this minimum amount requirement, the plaintiff-Union could not have filed an appeal to the Supreme Court even if it would have liked to do so.

E. Epilogue: The Backfire After Victory

The PLA's litigation is the first, and the only, known completed class action invoking the device provided by Article 44-1 of TCCP since its amendment in 2003. By any standard, this class action is a success for the PLA Union and its members. While the PLAs did not receive the full amount of their original claim and the eventual pay-off for each member ranged from merely NTD 25 to 3,693, it is fair to say that most, if not all,

---

[10] *See* Taiwan High Court 96 Lou-San-Tzi No. 44 Judgment.

[11] For an introduction to the Taiwan Supreme Court's jurisdiction and operation, *see* Eisenberg & Huang, 2012.

[12] *See* Taiwan Supreme Court 97 Tai-San-Tzi No. 786 Ruling.

Union members would have gained nothing if they had to initiate individual lawsuits, because it would not have been economically feasible to do so. The PLA's litigation is a good illustration of why the class action is often viewed as an enabling mechanism (Hensler et al., 2000, 49–50).

On the cost side, the out-of-pocket expenses for the Union and its members incurred by this lawsuit were virtually negligible. Insofar as the attorney fee is concerned, Taiwan generally follows the American rule that each party bears its own attorney fee. The Union's attorney fee, NTD 300,000 in total, was subsidized by the legal aid system. As to the filing fee, NTD 112,949 in total, paid to the court, while Taiwan follows the English rule that the loser pays, the Union's substantial victory and only partial loss resulted in only NTD 34,040 to be borne by the Union at the end, with the rest of the NTD 78,909 to be borne by the PLB.

The Union's triumph in this lawsuit attracted an unexpected backfire from the PLB, resulting in a dear price to be paid by the Union's leaders—the three ladies Wei, Chu and Huang. After the High Court issued its judgment to uphold most of the Union's victory, the three executive directors of the Union received an ultimatum from the PLB in November 2007 to agree to the following three terms: (1) support the private-contractor policy, (2) lower the working conditions and benefits of the Union, and (3) resign from their positions on the executive board of the Union. When these demands were rejected, the PLB, in December 2007, notified Wei, Chu and Huang that their employment was terminated, citing the reason that they 'failed to show up for work without good cause' for more than six days in October 2007, which constitutes a legitimate ground for the employer to terminate employment according to article 12 of the Labor Standards Act. The three ladies claimed that this termination was an outright retaliation from the PLB. They maintained that their absence from the job on those days was used to serve their duties for the Union, which was allowed by the PLB according to a previous labor-management agreement. According to Wei, Chu and Huang, such a practice of Union directors' absence from the job for the purpose of dealing with Union affairs had lasted for a long time and did not give rise to any dispute until they turned down the before-mentioned ultimatum from the PLB.

The three Union directors filed a lawsuit against the PLB on 1 April 2008, seeking a declaratory judgment that the PLB's unilateral termination of employment was void and they were still legally employed by the PLB. Unfortunately, the court ultimately dismissed their lawsuit and, as a result, the termination of the three ladies' employment was conclusive. As of May 2011, they remained unemployed.

3. A SECURITIES CLASS ACTION BY A GOVERNMENT-FUNDED FOUNDATION: *SFIPC v. KYEC ET AL.*

A. Prologue: KYEC's IPO

King Yuan Electronics Company (KYEC), founded in 1987 and headquartered in Taiwan, is a globally leading semiconductor testing service provider with regional offices around the world, including the United States, Europe, Japan and Singapore, and net assets of US$ 750 million. The dispute giving rise to the subsequent class actions involved an abrupt huge drop of KYEC's stock price that occurred in 2001 when KYEC took steps in applying for listing its stocks on the Taiwan Stock Exchange (TWSE), which operates the national securities exchange in Taiwan, for public trading.

After obtaining approval from the TWSE and the competent authority, KYEC started its initial public offering (IPO) in March 2001 by collaborating with its underwriter, Capital Securities Corporation. The price for KYEC's stock bid auction, held on 20–23 March 2001, ranged from NTD 61 to 120 per share. The fixed price sale for KYEC's stock was set at the price of NTD 65.32 per share and was open to the public from 10 April to 30 April. On 9 May 2001, KYEC's stock was listed on the national securities exchange at the initial price of NTD 65.32 per share.

About one month before its stock was listed for public trading, on 30 March, KYEC voluntarily released a renewed financial forecast for Year 2001 and, while not statutorily required, included such renewed financial forecast report in its prospectus for the IPO. In the renewed financial forecast, KYEC slightly lowered its estimated earnings before tax from NTD 1,710 million to 1,670 million and estimated the earnings per share (EPS) to be NTD 3.83. Both KYEC's underwriter, Capital Securities, and a leading accounting firm, Diwan & Company, issued a statement to the effect that KYEC's original financial forecast remained valid.

However, what followed was an abrupt drop in KYEC's stock price. At the end of May, KYEC's stock closed at NTD 29, less than half of its original price on the first listing day. The situation deteriorated in the following months. KYEC's stock price dropped to NTD 20 on 30 June and continued to fall to NTD 14.5 on 31 July. On 27 July, KYEC announced its second renewed financial forecast where its estimated earnings had shrunk to NTD 44 million, less than 3 percent of what was estimated four months earlier, and its estimated EPS was accordingly adjusted to NTD 0.96. By the end of September, KYEC's stock was less than NTD 10 per share.

The sudden lowering of KYEC's earnings outlook by 97 percent not only led to widespread speculation on the stock market but also attracted a lot of attention from the press. All major newspapers covered this unhappy story and questioned whether KYEC deliberately concealed material information in making its first renewed financial forecast. The huge devaluation of KYEC's stock immediately after its IPO certainly hurt a considerable number of investors. Given the unusual circumstances and development, the TWSE established a taskforce to investigate whether KYEC submitted a fraudulent financial statement for the purpose of obtaining approval for listing its stock on the TWSE and whether it deliberately exaggerated its earnings outlook first and failed to promptly disclose the renewed forecast later.

On 7 September 2001, the TWSE issued a demerit to KYEC on the grounds that KYEC had failed to prudently consider a change of circumstances underlying its first renewed financial forecast in March, resulting in an overly optimistic forecast, and that it had failed to promptly renew its second financial forecast. While this demerit was not publicly announced by the national exchange, it nevertheless was reported by the press. On 3 October, the TWSE also gave Capital Securities a demerit for its involvement in the renewed financial forecast in question.

B. An Institutional Investor's Lawsuit

Although many investors were severely hurt by the abrupt decline of KYEC's stock price, only ALGA Technology Incorporation took action to sue KYEC. ALGA spent NTD 53,880,000 purchasing 812,000 shares of KYEC's stock in April 2001 and had suffered a more than 60 percent loss from KYEC's stock by the end of July. ALGA filed a civil lawsuit on 9 August 2001 against KYEC and the chairman of its board of directors, Mr. Lee, in the district court of Hsin-chu, the city where KYEC's headquarter was located, seeking damages in the amount of NTD 23,223,654. The main theory ALGA raised in support of its claim was that KYEC's first renewed financial forecast was fraudulent and induced the plaintiff as a bona fide investor to mistakenly rely upon this financial forecast in deciding to purchase KYEC's stock.

After a proceeding of more than two and half years, the Hsin-chu district court found in favor of the plaintiff ALGA on 19 March 2004 and held KYEC and its chairman, Mr. Lee, jointly responsible for an award of NTD 18,298,942, despite the fact that the prosecutor had dismissed the criminal charge filed by ALGA the same year. KYEC and Mr. Lee appealed the civil judgment to the Taiwan High Court.

While ALGA's victory in the district court was subject to change by the High Court, it was nevertheless significant enough to attract a lot of press attention, which triggered two securities class actions filed under the SIFTP Act of 2003. To explain how a private institution's civil lawsuit could be this significant when the prosecutor did not press criminal charges against the alleged securities fraud, it is necessary to briefly introduce the enforcement mechanism of securities transaction protection in Taiwan.

C. Public and Private Enforcements of Securities Laws in Taiwan

The policies of protecting investors and maintaining a fair and orderly capital market traditionally are enforced through two major mechanisms in Taiwan. The first and most important mechanism is regulatory enforcement by the Taiwan Securities Exchange Commission (SEC). The second mechanism is criminal enforcement by the prosecutors. Since the task of monitoring the order of stock markets and discovering any irregularity in securities transactions is assigned to the Taiwan SEC, in practice, most criminal prosecutions of securities fraud are triggered by the Taiwan SEC's regulatory investigations.

What is missing under this enforcement regime is civil litigation. Although private shareholder actions have always been available either in the form of a direct shareholder action or in the form of a derivate suit, they are rarely invoked and have never become an enforcement mechanism of practical importance. As a result, in case of securities fraud, even if the wrongdoers are punished, the victims remain uncompensated.

To remedy this inadequacy, the Taiwan Congress enacted the aforesaid SIFTP Act in 2003. The crux of the SIFTP Act is to establish a publicly funded organization—Securities and Fortunes Investors Protection Center (SFIPC)—to resolve disputes arising from public offering and sale of securities.

While SFIPC is chartered in the form of a private and independent foundation, its operation is under the close control and supervision of the Taiwan SEC through a board whose directors are mainly appointed by the Taiwan SEC. Moreover, SFIPC's funding comes from a statutorily required endowment from the securities industry, a design derived from the Securities Investor Protection Act of 1970 in the United States.[13]

---

[13] *See* 15 U.S.C. §78aaa.

However, SFIPC is equipped with a broader mission than its US counterpart.

Specifically, in addition to shouldering the responsibility of returning the investors' securities or cash in case of bankruptcy or financial difficulty of a brokerage firm, SFIPC also takes complaints from investors concerning offering, issuance or sale of stock or fortunes, and mediates such disputes between the investors and the issuers, the securities firms, the national exchange or other related parties. SFIPC's most significant function is that it is authorized by Article 28 of SIFTP Act to initiate a class action in its own name as long as it receives delegation from 20 or more investors who suffered damages from the same securities transaction or incident.[14]

The creation of a securities class action device as well as SFIPC is intended to assist the victims of securities fraud in seeking compensation rather than to establish a 'private attorney general' enforcement mechanism. This definition of SFIPC's function is vividly reflected by the actual practice that shows that, from its establishment in 2003 to 2011, 98 out of 102 securities class actions initiated by SFIPC piggybacked on criminal prosecutions of securities fraud, either in the form of independent civil lawsuits or in the form of ancillary civil claims to the criminal prosecutions. In essence, what SFIPC engages in is not to uncover the actionable fraudulent conducts in the securities markets, but rather to file a follow-up civil suit on behalf of a group of victims to recover their losses from securities fraud which have been discovered by the governmental authorities.

D. SFIPC's Decision to Initiate Class Action

The drama of an abrupt decline in KYEC's stock price since its first public offering naturally caught the attention of SFIPC's predecessor,[15] especially with the press' wide coverage. However, within SFIPC, there were different opinions on whether it should take action against KYEC.

Some argued that SFIPC should act for three reasons. Firstly, the unusual circumstances surrounding the incident strongly suggested that

---

[14] *See* Article 28 of SIFTP Act.

[15] It should be noted that even before the enactment of SIFTP Act and formal establishment of SFIPC in 2003, the predecessor of SFIPC had started to seek civil remedies for investors from violators of securities laws. But the litigation was initiated in the form of joinder, where the investors themselves were named as plaintiffs but authorized the in-house lawyers of the SFIPC's predecessor to act as representative counsel, rather than through the class action mechanism.

there was something very wrong with KYEC's first renewed financial forecast and KYEC should be held accountable. Secondly, it was not entirely clear at that time, as a matter of law, whether a financial forecast constituted part of the prospectus. It was also not clear whether and under what conditions misstatements in a financial forecast could constitute a cause of action for investors. A civil action would help to clarify these legal issues. Thirdly, bringing an action would promote SFIPC's public image and earn the investors' confidence.

However, others argued that since there had been no clear evidence of fraud and no criminal prosecutions filed against anyone involved in this incident, SFIPC should not rush to the courthouse. This passive attitude prevailed even after the TWSE issued a demerit to KYEC and Capital Securities in the autumn of 2001.

SFIPC did not change its attitude until the news of ALGA's victory in the district court quickly spread in the market in March 2004. Intensive inquiries from the press about whether SFIPC would continue to remain passive exerted tremendous pressure on SFIPC. The relevant regulations require that the decision to initiate a securities class action be approved by the board of directors of SFIPC. Nevertheless, since all of the board members, except for the chairman, have their own respective jobs and serving on SFIPC's board is merely one of their many duties in various capacities, the chairman's opinion, as advised by SFIPC's full-time staff, played a dominant role in the decision-making. Insofar as the initiation of a securities class action is concerned, the decision-making process is normally routine, given the fact that most class actions brought by SFIPC were piggybacking on the criminal prosecutions: after SFIPC received notice that a criminal prosecution had been filed, its staff would suggest initiation of a class action to the chairman who would in turn bring the proposal to the board meeting for approval. Rarely, if ever, has the board disapproved the chairman's proposal.

In this KYEC incident, while there still existed lingering concerns about the merits of filing a lawsuit against KYEC, a senior staff member strongly advised the then chairman to take action, which ultimately was approved by the board. After the decision was made, the case was assigned to SFIPC's in-house attorney, P.C. Huang, to act as litigation representative to bring the lawsuit.

The position of in-house counsel at SFIPC is semi-official, which reflects the fact that SFIPC itself is a publicly funded organization and its budget is under the legislature's control. As a result, in-house counsel at SFIPC is under a salary system similar to that adopted by most state-owned enterprises. While SFIPC's salary system and the career outlook for in-house counsel cannot compete with prestigious law firms, this position has the advantage of stability and a manageable workload, which attracts young talented attorneys. P.C. Huang, who specialized in the fraud-on-the-market theory in his graduate training, had had four years of experience in securities litigation when he was recruited by SFIPC to act in the KYEC matter.

E. Filings of Two Separate Class Actions

Because SFIPC's claim was grounded on the alleged falsehood and misstatement of KYEC's first renewed financial forecast and, according to Articles 20 and 32 of the Security Exchange Act in Taiwan, all parties involved in misrepresentations during public offerings and in the production of a false prospectus are jointly liable for losses suffered by bona fide purchasers,[16] SFIPC decided to go after not only KYEC but also the underwriter of KYEC's IPO, Capital Securities. While TCCP allows SFIPC to sue KYEC and Capital jointly despite the fact that their headquarters are located in the jurisdictional area of Hsin-chu district court and Taipei district court, respectively, SFIPC decided to initiate two separate lawsuits against the two corporations at their respective home courts in order to avoid unnecessary complexity.

Accordingly, SFIPC announced its decision to litigate on 3 May 2004 and started to accept investors' delegations until 21 May. 55 investors applied to SFIPC to delegate their rights to sue during the period. The total amount of these 55 investors' aggregate claims was NTD 25,351,170. The mean value of each investor's claim was about NTD 460,000, ranging from the minimum of NTD 1,160 to the maximum of NTD 5,051,500. Among those 55 members, two members were institutional investors, whose claims were NTD 3,673,300 and NTD 2,979,300, respectively.

On 1 June 2004, SFIPC filed the first class action, naming KYEC, its chairman, general manager, and financial manager as defendants, in Hsin-chu district court (hereinafter Class Action No. 1) and the second class action in Taipei district court (hereinafter Class Action No. 2) against Capital Securities and two accountants, Mr. Yang and Miss Yea, who certified KYEC's financial reports. P.C. Huang acted as SFIPC's attorney in both class actions. The four defendants in Class Action No. 1 (hereinafter KYEC et al.) were jointly represented by four attorneys, F.F. Chen, S.K. Hsian, T.H. Chen and S.W. Lo, from two well-known law firms specializing in securities laws. As to the three defendants in Class

[16] *See* Articles 20 & 32 of Securities Exchange Act.

Action No. 2 (hereinafter Capital Securities et al.), Capital Securities was represented by Z.W. Ho, a solo practitioner, as well as its own in-house counsel, I.W. Lai, and the two accountants were represented by F.F. Chen and S.K. Hsian, who also represented KYEC in Class Action No. 1.

F. The Defendants' Position and Strategy

Long before the initiation of these two class actions, all defendants and their respective legal teams had gathered to coordinate their defense in the ALGA litigation mentioned before. From KYEC's viewpoint, it did nothing wrong in its IPO. All the major decisions concerning KYEC's IPO, such as the price and timing of initial listing, were made by Capital Securities. As to the renewed financial forecast, it was made according to KYEC's performance in the preceding year without advance knowledge of the suddenly-worsening circumstances of DRAM (dynamic random access memory) industries. KYEC's top officers, who also suffered great losses from the decline of KYEC's stock price, privately blamed Capital Securities for failing to make thorough preparations and intelligent decisions in conducting its IPO. As a result, in the subsequent class actions, as a matter of litigation strategy, KYEC deliberately kept its distance from Capital Securities while coordinating closely with the two sued accountants.

The criminal charge of fraud filed by ALGA against KYEC's chairman, Mr. Lee, was taken by Mr. Lee as the worst personal insult and shame in his life. Mr. Lee thought that that criminal charge was essentially an act of extortion from an unhappy investor who tried to coerce him to compensate for its own investment loss. Given the above, KYEC decided from the very beginning that there would be no settlement negotiations.

This was exactly why KYEC did not have any inclination to settle the dispute out of court even after ALGA obtained a favorable judgment in the trial court. Instead, what KYEC did after its initial defeat was to recruit a stronger legal team for its appeal. KYEC not only hired T.H. Chen and S.W. Lo from another prestigious firm to join its legal representation but also retained three leading law professors in the field of securities laws in Taiwan to provide consultation in strengthening KYEC's arguments on appeal. KYEC was determined to fight with all its muscle. KYEC's decision to fight for ultimate victory in the ALGA case turned out to be the right strategy in the end. This decision had a decisive impact on the two following class actions.

G. The Litigation Process and Outcome

Since these two class actions were triggered by ALGA's victory in the district court, SFIPC basically followed the factual allegations and legal theory raised by ALGA and endorsed by that district court: KYEC's first renewed financial forecast was fraudulent, which induced bona fide investors to form an erroneous evaluation of KYEC's stock value and, as a result, to suffer losses. Against these allegations, KYEC argued that the falling of its stock price was caused by the unexpected abrupt decline of the DRAM price and the overall worsening circumstances of DRAM industries. The defendants explained that although KYEC's earnings were far below what was forecasted in its renewed financial report, the forecast was based upon the best available information and was made with due diligence. Requiring the defendants to compensate investors' losses under these circumstances was essentially to impose a no-fault liability on the defendants in warranting the absolute accuracy of a financial forecast, which would be blatantly unjust.

Three major issues were inherent in both class actions. The first issue was whether the financial forecast report constituted a material part of KYEC's IPO prospectus. The second issue was whether a decision to hold KYEC liable required a finding that it had acted with scienter or whether a finding of negligence was sufficient. The third issue was whether the statute of limitations for the plaintiff's claim had elapsed. It was undisputed that the applicable statute of limitations for the plaintiff's claim was two years and both class actions were filed on 1 June 2004. What was disputed was when the statute of limitations started to run. SFIPC asserted that the statute of limitations did not start to run until the investors knew the existence of their claims, that is, the rendering of ALGA's victorious judgment by the district court. The defendants argued that the investors knew or should have known the inaccuracy of the first renewed financial forecast in the fall of 2001 and that the statute of limitations, in any event, could not possibly have started to run later than by the end of May 2002.

Although the two class actions were heard by two separate courts, both proceedings were tightly linked by one common factor—the appeal taken by KYEC in the ALGA case. From the fact that the two courts propelled the cases exceptionally slowly by prolonging the period between each continental-style episodic oral-argument session,[17] one could easily tell

[17] For an introduction to the continental civil procedure's episodic oral argument sessions, as contrasted to the common law system's continuous trial, *see* Huang, 2003, pp. 66–70.

that the courts in both class actions were waiting for a final resolution in the ALGA case. The real battlefield was the ALGA appeal.

In that appeal, the strong legal team recruited by KYEC fought so hard as to force the Taiwan High Court, which normally holds only two to four sessions in most appeals, to hold more than ten sessions to hear the case. On 2 August 2005, the Taiwan High Court reversed the district court's decision and issued a judgment in favor of KYEC[18] finding, firstly, that the financial forecast should not be deemed a material part of KYEC's IPO prospectus and, secondly, that the mere fact that KYEC's earnings fell short of what was predicted did not prove that KYEC deliberately made false statements. This victory became the cornerstone of KYEC's subsequent triumphs. While ALGA immediately appealed to the Taiwan Supreme Court, KYEC had started to celebrate its success.

Although the High Court's decision in the ALGA case had set the basic tone for the whole dispute, the two district courts hearing SFIPC's separate class actions were still waiting for the Taiwan Supreme Court's final decision. According to attorney Hsian, who played a key role in KYEC's defense team, SFIPC was obviously piggybacking on ALGA's action and the litigation materials and evidence submitted by SFIPC were far less than what had been offered by ALGA's counsel. As a result, except for the issue of the statute of limitations, every factual as well as legal issue covered by the two class actions had been dealt with in the ALGA case.

What broke the silence while the Taiwan Supreme Court's decision in the ALGA's appeal was pending, was the change of the judge presiding in Class Action No. 2 after the original judge was transferred to another court. The succeeding judge decided not to wait any longer to resolve the lawsuit. Shortly after taking over the case, the new judge rendered a judgment for Capital Securities et al. on 2 May 2006, finding in favor of defendants on all before-mentioned three issues.[19] In addition to adopting the opinions of the High Court's judgment in the ALGA case, the Taipei district court in Class Action No. 2 found that, in any event, the two-year statute of limitations of those represented investors' claims had elapsed. SFIPC immediately appealed this judgment to the Taiwan High Court.

On 26 October 2006, the Supreme Court issued a judgment dismissing ALGA's appeal and finalizing KYEC's victory.[20] Thereafter, the Taiwan High Court in Class Action No. 2 quickly dismissed SFIPC's appeal on

---

[18] *See* Taiwan High Court 93 Chun-San-Tzi No. 220 Judgment.

[19] *See* Taipei District Court 93 Gin-Tzi No. 40 Judgment.

[20] *See* Taiwan Supreme Court 95 Tai-San-Tzi No. 2385 Judgment.

17 January 2007.[21] The Hsin-chu district court also found for KYEC et al. in Class Action No. 1 on 22 January 2007.[22] SFIPC decided to adhere to its routine of appealing any unfavorable judgments in both class actions. Its appeal to the district court's judgment in Class Action No. 1 was dismissed by the Taiwan High Court on 2 October 2007,[23] followed by the Supreme Court's dismissal of SFIPC's second appeal on 6 March 2008.[24] Three months later, on 19 June 2008, the Supreme Court issued another decision to dismiss SFIPC's second appeal in Class Action No. 2, concluding the whole dispute arising from the abrupt decline of KYEC's stock price immediately after its IPO in May 2001.

H. Epilogue: Peculiarities of Public-Funded Securities Class Actions

After two parallel proceedings lasting about four years, the exhaustion of all available appeals, and the incurring of substantial expenses, the two class actions initiated by SFIPC on behalf of investors ended with a total failure. Despite the ultimate defeat, the represented investors—the real plaintiffs in interest—bore virtually no costs, because SFIPC, fully funded by the government, shouldered all expenses incurred by its decision to bring lawsuits. On the other hand, the defendants in these two class actions together had spent more than NTD 2 million on legal representation alone.

From a comparative perspective, SFIPC is undoubtedly special. While the overlapping of public and private enforcement of securities laws has become a common phenomenon across countries, SFIPC seems to have no similar counterpart in other jurisdictions. Specifically, the fact that 98 out of 102 securities class actions initiated by SFIPC were filed in conjunction with criminal charges of securities fraud clearly shows that SFIPC neither performs the function of detecting nor has the effect of deterring. What it accomplishes is simply to seek civil remedies for investors injured by securities laws violations already detected by other public enforcement mechanisms through a semi-official body established by the government. While the phenomenon of private securities suits piggybacking on criminal prosecutions or regulatory actions is also

[21] *See* Taiwan High Court 95 Gin-San-Tzi No. 5 Judgment.
[22] *See* Taipei District Court 93 Chun-Shu-Tzi No. 162 Judgment.
[23] *See* Taiwan High Court 96 Gin-San-Tzi No. 5 Judgment.
[24] *See* Taiwan Supreme Court 97 Tai-San-Tzi No. 432 Judgment.

pervasive in Europe and the United States (Rubenstein 2004, 2150),[25] those private suits, either in the form of group litigation or class action, are not funded by governments. Taiwan's SFIPC represents not only a unique form of securities laws enforcement mechanism but also a new style of class action—a private means of civil remedy to be publicly funded.

From a policy perspective, the desirability of this kind of mechanism is certainly debatable. On the one hand, under Taiwan's current civil justice system, it is obvious that, without SFIPC, most individual investors cannot effectively seek remedies from the perpetrators in violation of securities laws due to the fact that their claims are too small to make individual lawsuits feasible. On the other hand, funding a specific type of private lawsuit with governmental budgets raises serious concerns of fairness and equality. Investors of any kind, including even institutional ones that have sufficient capabilities to pursue their own private claims, can take advantage of this cost-free SFIPC mechanism without facing any consequences upon defeat. Moreover, the fact that the decision makers in SFIPC are not financially responsible for whatever results from the class actions they decide to initiate also raises the question of efficiency.

The KYEC class actions provide an excellent illustration of this policy challenge. Firstly, even without the involvement of criminal prosecutions, in terms of pursuing civil remedies from potential violators of securities laws, SFIPC acts as a follower instead of a leader, piggybacking on an institutional investor's lawsuit. It is evident that without ALGA's initial victory at the district court, SFIPC would not have brought those two class actions. Secondly, although several investors, including two institutional investors, on whose behalf SFIPC filed suits have a claim sizable enough to initiate an independent lawsuit, they happily enjoyed the advantage of being a free rider. Ironically, the victors of the class actions, especially KYEC, spent considerable resources on defending the lawsuits but the losing party—the delegating investors who were the real plaintiffs in interest—incurred virtually no expenses. Thirdly, while the wise course of action for SFIPC to take was to stop any further litigation investment after the Supreme Court issued a conclusive judgment favorable to KYEC in the ALGA case, SFIPC nevertheless chose to appeal to the end in both class actions. The fact that SFIPC was not really spending

[25] Moreover, it has been shown that private suits with parallel SEC actions settle for significantly higher amounts and more quickly than other private actions without parallel SEC proceedings. *See* generally Cox, 2003.

its own money on making these appeals provides a straightforward explanation for this litigation decision.

4. CONCLUDING REMARKS

While the two cases reported in this chapter vary significantly in several aspects, they not only share the same feature of using an association as a vehicle for driving a class action but, more importantly, also reveal a pivotal concern underlying this kind of class action mechanism—whether a public interest association's incentive to represent its members can overcome the financial burden it encounters in bringing a class action. This concern underscores the contrast between the scarcity of the TCCP class action on the one hand and the copiousness of the SIFTP class action on the other hand. Where the securities class actions are sufficiently funded and driven by a semi-governmental body, the problem of how to finance litigation virtually does not exist. However, where a public interest association is prohibited from receiving any compensation for bringing a class action, the same problem becomes a powerful disincentive for most public interest associations to even contemplate initiating class actions.

The success of the PLA Union class action shall be viewed as an exception rather than a norm. Three factors contributed to the unique context of this class action. First, the subject matter of the controversy fell within the scope of the Union's ordinary operation for its members. The relevant information for preparing this class action was readily available. These facts minimized the Union's costs of organizing its members to take collective action. Second, the availability of legal aid allowed the Union to avoid the difficult question of whether it was financially justifiable to bring the lawsuit. The actual out-of-pocket expenses were almost negligible. Last, but not least, the fact that this class action was essentially one of the battles of a larger war between the employer and the PLAs provides the Union with strong incentives to act.

The same kind of unique context is rare to find for most public interest associations. Even for those associations with steady funding sources to meet the needs of their run-of-the-mill operations, the financial burden associated with initiating class action is still hard to overcome. Another illustration is the consumer class action provided in the Consumer Protection Act, from which the TCCP class action is derived. Since its availability in 1994 to 2012, there have been fewer than ten consumer class actions brought under this Act. In many instances of massive product liability incidents involving widespread damages for numerous consumers, the consumer interest associations qualified to sue on consumers' behalf simply did not have the resources to organize those victims and take their claims to court. This phenomenon has led to the criticism that the consumer class action mechanism is virtually a paper law without effect.

In order to vitalize the class action mechanism in Taiwan, some scholars have advocated that several stringent restrictions be relaxed, including broadening the categories of litigants that have standing to bring class actions, removing the absolute ban on receiving any compensation, and recognizing 'opt-out' class actions in certain types of cases. However, the fact that Taiwanese civil procedure is still deeply rooted in the German way of thinking, so far has kept those advocates from receiving enough support in the legal community to amend the rules.

Nevertheless, while the rules remain static, the practice seems to be evolving to get around the rules. Instead of relying on established public interest associations to initiate class actions, some well-known lawyers with social movement backgrounds have started to organize victims who have suffered losses from the same transaction or incident to form an association and use that association to bring a class action thereafter. This new type of class action is economically beneficial for the victims because each member is required to pay substantially less than what it would cost to bring an individual lawsuit. It is financially viable for the lawyers to take on such a case because the aggregate of a reduced individual fee multiplied by a sufficient number of clients still amounts to a handsome paycheck. Moreover, in addition to obtaining the standing to file a class action, organizing an association has another advantage: that association can also be used to advocate for the cause underlying those victims' claims, to appeal to the general public. Such out-of-court movements are believed to be helpful for class actions in court.

One prominent example of this type of class action is the suit brought in 2011 by an association organized for the purpose of representing hundreds of consumers who were victimized by the financial derivatives sold by several banks, including Lehman Brothers, as a result of the subprime mortgage crisis in 2007. This case is still pending in the district court. Where the real purpose of organizing an association is to initiate a class action, granting standing in a class action to this type of association arguably undermines the very purpose of the current class action regulations in Taiwan. However, from the perspective of making the class action mechanism workable in practice, this strategy is not entirely meritless. Whether the court in Taiwan will ultimately recognize the legality of this type of class action awaits future answer.

REFERENCES

James Cox et al., *SEC Enforcement Heuristics: An Empirical Inquiry*, (2003) 53 Duke Law Journal 737

Theodore Eisenberg & Kuo-Chang Huang, *The Effect of Rules Shifting Supreme Court Jurisdiction from Mandatory to Discretionary—An Empirical Lesson from Taiwan*, (2012) 32(1) International Review of Law & Economics 3

Deborah Hensler et al., *Class Action Dilemmas: Pursuing Public Goals for Private Gain* (RAND 2000)

Kuo-Chang Huang, *Introducing Discovery into the Civil Law: A Comprehensive Study of Discovery Through Comparative Civil Procedure* (Carolina Academic Press 2003)

Kuo-Chang Huang & Richard Thurston, *Taiwan Code of Civil Procedure* (Judicial Yuan 2006)

Kuo-Chang Huang, *How Legal Representation Affects Case Outcome: An Empirical Perspective from Taiwan*, (2008) 5(2) Journal of Empirical Legal Studies 197

Kuo-Chang Huang et al., *An Empirical Investigation of Settlement and Litigation—The Case of Taiwanese Labor Disputes*, (2010) 7(4) Journal of Empirical Legal Studies 786

William Rubenstein, *On What a "Private Attorney General" Is—And Why It Matters*, (2004) 57 Vanderbilt Law Review 2129

5. The promise and peril of media and culture: The Toyota unintended acceleration litigation and the Gulf Coast Claims Facility in the United States[1]

Byron Stier

PROLOGUE

The Toyota unintended acceleration litigation and the BP Gulf Coast Claims Fund in the United States (US) each display the difficulties and opportunities presented by media and culture for mass litigation and dispute resolution. In August 2009, far-reaching media exposure publicized claims that Toyota automobiles were accelerating unintentionally and causing serious and sometimes fatal accidents. American media attention galvanized regulatory oversight by the National Highway Traffic Safety Administration (NHTSA), as well as hearings by the US

[1] Research sources for this chapter included media reports; law review and bar journal articles; books by the claims fund administrator; executive and administrative governmental reports, press releases, public remarks, blog entries and letters; testimony and written submissions for governmental hearings; written reports by independent consulting and expert private entities; court pleadings and a verdict form; published and unpublished court opinions and management orders; and interviews, discussions and other interactions with numerous persons serving as counsel in the litigations, claims fund administrator, governmental administrators or consultants, litigation consultants, researchers and reporters. In the Toyota unintended acceleration class action discussed herein, I was a class member as a result of vehicle ownership, but declined to take any monetary compensation. I benefitted from my participation in two symposia at Stanford Law School and Mississippi College School of Law regarding the Gulf Coast oil spill involving BP and Deepwater Horizon, as well as research presentations at the Law and Society Association Annual Meeting and Southwestern Law School.

Congress, and Toyota recalled millions of automobiles in connection with floor mats and pedal mechanisms. Subsequently, the plaintiffs filed hundreds of claims against Toyota in state and federal courts in the US, alleging widespread problems with Toyota's electronic throttle control system. In 2011, a report by NHTSA found no problems with Toyota's electronic throttle system that could cause complaints of unintended acceleration. Instead, NHTSA determined that acceleration complaints likely stemmed from pedal misapplication by the driver, except for exceedingly rare instances of acceleration from pedal entrapment by a floor mat or a slow-returning accelerator pedal. A 2012 report from the National Academy of Sciences supported the conclusions of the NHTSA report. In 2013, a federal court granted final approval to a settlement of more than $1 billion between Toyota and a class of Toyota owners seeking to recoup economic losses from reduced vehicle value due to the risk of unintended acceleration. Although Toyota won several trials involving personal injuries and property damage from accidents allegedly affected by unintended acceleration, Toyota lost a 2013 trial in Oklahoma state court, and Toyota subsequently engaged in intensive settlement negotiations to resolve remaining cases.

Eight months after the 2009 accident and the media attention that led to the Toyota mass litigation, the Deepwater Horizon oilrig drilling for oil for British Petroleum (BP) exploded in the Gulf of Mexico, and before the well was permanently capped, nearly five million barrels of oil poured into the waters next to the Gulf Coast of the US. To compensate commercial fisherman and businesses and preserve residents' livelihoods and way of life, President Obama announced in his first Oval Office address a $20 billion BP claims fund to be neutrally administered. Kenneth Feinberg, a leading claims fund administrator of national repute, was subsequently appointed to oversee distribution of the fund. Feinberg then met with skeptical Gulf Coast claimants in numerous town hall meetings. Widespread media coverage not only publicized the spill and the fund, leading many claimants to opt in to the fund and settle their claims, but also led to the questioning and referral for possible prosecution of thousands of potentially fraudulent claims. Despite criticism from the Gulf Coast plaintiffs' attorneys about the fund's lack of independence from BP, the Gulf Coast Claims Facility disbursed more than $6 billion before being supplanted by a wide-reaching class settlement initially estimated at $7.8 billion.

A 51-SECOND EMERGENCY PHONE CALL BEGINS A MASS LITIGATION AGAINST TOYOTA FOR UNINTENDED ACCELERATION

In August 2009, eight months before the BP oil spill on the Gulf Coast, off-duty California Highway patrol officer Mark Saylor and three family members were driving a Lexus ES350 automobile on loan from their Lexus dealer, when the car suddenly accelerated. Officer Saylor's wife called the 911 emergency number from his car, and stated that the car had no brakes, the accelerator was stuck and the car was traveling at more than 100 miles per hour. The occupants stated they were approaching the end of the freeway, and as they approached an intersection, the driver and occupants said, 'pray, pray'. Then the call abruptly ended. In fact, their car had hit another car and fallen down an embankment, resulting in the death of everyone in their car.

What followed was a firestorm of concern and fear from Toyota drivers, attention from legislative and regulatory entities, and the development of a mass litigation in the US. Subsequent news reports across the country replayed Officer Saylor's recorded emergency call, which was also linked across the Internet.

Investigations by NHTSA and Congress of Toyota Unintended Acceleration Claims

Between the Mark Saylor accident in August 2009 and January 2010, at NHTSA's urging, Toyota undertook several recalls affecting millions of cars in the US and around the world. The recalls exchanged floor mats for cars, reconfigured gas pedals, and altered braking software so that the brakes could return an engine to idle. To decrease the possibility of a pedal being entrapped in the floor mat, which might occur when the back of the pedal was caught in the grooves in the floor mat, Toyota reduced the length of accelerator pedals and the amount of foam under the carpet in some vehicles. For other vehicles, Toyota opted to install 'smart pedals' that would eliminate engine power if the driver pressed both the brake and accelerator at the same time, particularly assisting any users unfamiliar with the need to press and hold for several seconds their push-button ignition to turn off the car while it was in motion.

In February 2010, the US Congress held hearings on unintended acceleration, which were televised on C-SPAN and available on the internet.[2] In those hearings, Toyota CEO Akio Toyoda, grandson of Toyota's founder, testified and conceded that Toyota may have grown too quickly, undermining the quality of its cars:

> Toyota has, for the past few years, been expanding its business rapidly. Quite frankly, I fear the pace at which we have grown may have been too quick. I would like to point out here that Toyota's priority has traditionally been the following: First: Safety; Second: Quality and Third: Volume. These priorities became confused and we were not able to stop, think and make improvements as much as we were able to before, and our basic stance to listen to customers' voices to make better products has weakened somewhat. We pursued growth over the speed at which we were able to develop our people and our organization, and we should sincerely be mindful of that. I regret that this has resulted in the safety issues described in the recalls we face today and I am deeply sorry for any accidents that Toyota drivers have experienced.[3]

During the hearings, uncertainty remained about the cause of unintended acceleration.

Media Coverage of Investigations into Toyota Unintended Acceleration

Studies by the Pew Research Center for Excellence in Journalism showed that Toyota recall stories were among the top five stories covered in the US for several weeks from January to March 2010, following Toyota's recalls, the congressional hearings on Toyota and a series of investigative articles in the Los Angeles Times (Vartabedian & Bensinger, 2009; Vartabedian & Bensinger, 2010), whose authors were subsequently nominated as finalists for a Pulitzer Prize for their coverage.[4] So extensive was the coverage and public discussion that the nationally popular live weekly comedy television show Saturday Night Live created

---

2 See *Response by Toyota and NHTSA to Incidents of Sudden Unintended Acceleration*: Hearing Before the Subcommittee on Oversight & Investigations of the Hearing Committee on Energy and Commerce, 111th Congress, 23 February 2010.

3 *Full Text of Akio Toyoda's Testimony*, Reuters, 24 February 2010, available at http://uk.reuters.com/article/2010/02/24/toyota-testimony-idUKTOE61N04I20100224; *Toyota Gas Pedals, Before the Hearing Committee on Oversight and Government Reform* (2010), 24 February 2010, available at http://www.c-spanvideo.org/program/Pedal.

4 *2010 Finalists*, The Pulitzer Prizes (2010), available at http://www.pulitzer.org/finalists/2010 (named '[f]or their tenacious reporting on how design flaws and weak federal oversight contributed to a potentially lethal problem with Toyota vehicles, resulting in corrective steps and a congressional inquiry').

a mock commercial referencing unintended acceleration in Toyota automobiles.[5] One ABC news report also featured a Southern Illinois University professor who claimed to have induced unintended acceleration in Toyota automobiles and who was also serving as an expert consultant in the unintended acceleration litigation, but subsequent analysis from Toyota and the Director of Stanford's Center for Automotive Research found that similar modifications could create problems with many other brands of cars as well.[6]

Of more than 9,000 complaints related to unintended acceleration for all vehicles by any manufacturer received by NHTSA between 1998 and 2010, NHTSA determined that 3,054 of the complaints pertained to Toyota automobiles, but 71 percent of those Toyota complaints were received after the first Toyota recall in October 2009, and 43 percent of the Toyota complaints occurred during and after the Toyota congressional hearings in February and March 2010. Both NHTSA and NASA determined that 'publicity surrounding NHTSA's investigations, related recalls and Congressional hearings was the major contributor to the timing and volume of complaints'.

Certain Japanese media suggested that treatment of Toyota in America was biased, stemming from opposition to a foreign automobile company, especially among American politicians who used the issue prior to the 2010 mid-term congressional elections. That view of biased treatment was seconded by a letter to Congress from the governors of four US states who claimed that 'it is unfortunate and unfair that Toyota has fallen victim to aggressive and questionable news coverage' and who noted 'the federal government's obvious conflict of interest because of its huge financial stake in some of Toyota's competitors (indeed, the federal government is a shareholder in many of Toyota's competitors)'.[7] But as

---

[5] *Saturday Night Live: Weekend Getaway (Prius Commercial)*, NBC television broadcast 13 March 2010, available at http://www.hulu.com/watch/134733. After showing a couple in a runaway Toyota automobile, the clip ended with a Ford logo and the words, 'We make hybrids too'.

[6] *See* Ahrens, 2010, also noting that Stanford's Center for Automotive Research was funded by automakers including Toyota.

[7] Letter from Steven L. Beshear, Governor of Kentucky, Mitch Daniels, Governor of Indiana, Haley Barbour, Governor of Mississippi and Bob Riley, Governor of Alabama to Hon. Henry Waxman, Chairman, House Committee on Energy and Commerce, Hon. Edolphus Towns, Chairman, House Committee on Oversight and Government Reform, Hon. Joe Barton, Ranking Member, House Committee on Energy and Commerce and Hon. Darrell Issa, Ranking Member, House Committee on Oversight and Government Reform (10 February 2010), available at http://ftpcontent.worldnow.com/wthr/PDF/toyotaletter.pdf.

the governors admitted in the letter, they all had Toyota manufacturing operations in their states, suggesting they had their own stake in the controversy as well.

From Media Story to Mass Litigation

Biased or not, all the publicity in the US also likely stoked litigation, by raising awareness of potential Toyota problems among the entrepreneurial plaintiffs' lawyers, as well as potential claimants, who may have been suing on behalf of someone who died in unclear circumstances. Hundreds of lawsuits were filed in both state and federal courts, triggering utilization of the multidistrict litigation process for coordinated pretrial management of federal cases. To assist in the efficient and timely management of mass litigation in the federal courts in the US, the Judicial Panel on Multidistrict Litigation has statutory authority to order a transfer for pretrial management of federal cases 'involving one or more common questions of fact', if the Panel determines that such coordination or consolidation will be 'for the convenience of the parties and witnesses and will promote the just and efficient conduct of such actions'.[8] Plaintiffs in several lawsuits concerning Toyota unintended acceleration moved the Judicial Panel on Multidistrict Litigation for transfer and consolidation of all related cases nationwide. After briefing and oral argument, the Panel granted the plaintiffs' motion. With the aim of reducing discovery costs and judicial resources, and avoiding inconsistent court rulings, the Panel transferred and consolidated not just lawsuits claiming economic loss, but also suits alleging personal injury. The Panel selected the Central District of California as the transferee court, in light of the district being home to the highest number of pending claims, as well as Toyota's corporate headquarters, where pertinent witnesses and documents would be located. The Panel also chose Judge James Selna as the transferee judge, highlighting his extensive private practice experience with complex litigation.

The multidistrict litigation (MDL) transferee court received more than 200 lawsuits, some of which involved claims for economic losses based on lower resale value for Toyota automobiles affected by the recall. The MDL court subsequently issued several opinions on class treatment that highlighted hurdles to class recovery. In particular, uncertainty surrounded the question of whether reduced resale value was an injury, especially for those Toyota owners who have not tried to resell their cars.

---

8 28 U.S.C. § 1407 (2012).

The MDL court held that reduced resale value was an injury for the purposes of constitutional standing to sue, but the court certified the question to the Ninth Circuit Court of Appeals. In addition, noting that several states other than California would reject recovery for diminution of value of automobiles that had not suffered unintended acceleration, Judge Selna rejected application of California law to a proposed nationwide class, leading to the likely application of less favorable law from other states, and potentially creating individual issues of choice of law. The MDL court dismissed the claims of the foreign plaintiffs claiming economic loss on the grounds that necessary foreign defendants, such as foreign manufacturers and dealerships, were not joined and could not be joined, because the court likely lacked personal jurisdiction over them.

Discovery was complicated by the need to communicate in both Japanese and English. To account for the additional time required for translation in a deposition, the MDL court permitted ten hours of deposition of non-English speaking deponents. Documents did not need to be translated into English by Toyota prior to production. The MDL court also ordered Toyota to produce documents relating to the approximately 37,000 reported incidents of unintended acceleration. In addition, the MDL court issued an order to preserve for discovery not only relevant tangible materials and vehicles involved in accidents, but also pertinent electronically stored information and email by Toyota. Additional documents were to be produced as determined by electronic database searches via keywords, based on 260 key terms agreed to by the parties.

The MDL court also undertook considerable coordination with state courts. Scheduling of corporate depositions was to be coordinated with state court actions, with cross-noticing of MDL depositions. And time was reserved at depositions for questions from the plaintiffs' counsel in the state cases. Transcripts, video recordings and exhibits from MDL depositions were also to be made available to attorneys in state actions.

Governmental and Independent Investigations Question Unintended Acceleration

Although publicity quickly disseminated news of a possible safety threat, and likely led to mass litigation, ongoing investigation suggested that widespread claims of unintended acceleration might have been unfounded. While many thought that acceleration problems could affect all cars, the problems at least in Officer Saylor's case may have been unique. Subsequent investigation determined that the loaner ES350 that Officer Saylor was driving had a mismatched SUV floor mat put in by the dealer, and that floor mat had entrapped the accelerator pedal. Indeed, the prior user of that exact loaner car had specifically complained to the dealer that the accelerator pedal had become entangled in the floor mat.

Furthermore, in February 2011, NHTSA released a full report on its investigation of unintended acceleration in Toyota vehicles. The report was undertaken at the request of the US Congress, and utilized NASA engineers to analyze Toyota electronics. The report found that the 'vast majority' of complaints involved allegations of unintended acceleration from a stop or low speed. For such incidents, NHTSA determined that no vehicle-based cause generally existed, and that:

> where the complaint included allegations that the brakes were ineffective or that the incident began with a brake application, the most likely cause of the acceleration was actually pedal misapplication (that is, the driver's unintended application of the accelerator rather than, or in addition to, the brake).

NHTSA also noted that unintended acceleration complaints disproportionately involved older drivers. In addition, NHTSA's field inspections of vehicles, which included a review of 58 alleged unintended acceleration crashes and available automobile data recorders, 'indicated that drivers were applying the accelerator and not applying the brake (or not applying it until the last second or so), except for one instance involving pedal entrapment'. That one instance involving pedal entrapment was the Mark Saylor case. NHTSA's investigation of consumer complaints of 75 fatal crashes involving 93 deaths since 2000 also pointed to the Saylor case as the only confirmed instance of unintended acceleration. NHTSA separately identified one other fatal crash in 2007, not in its complaint database, where pedal entrapment was believed to be the cause. The investigation found no electronic throttle problems that could produce acceleration,[9] and only one consumer complaint and several Toyota field reports involving a slow-returning or sticking accelerator pedal. Secretary of Transportation Ray LaHood stated:

> We enlisted the best and brightest engineers to study Toyota's electronics systems, and the verdict is in. There is no electronic-based cause for unintended high-speed acceleration in Toyotas (Press Release NHTSA, 2011; Wald, 2011).

In addition, NHTSA commissioned an additional report from the National Academy of Arts and Sciences, and in January 2012, the

---

[9] The report, however, also noted the difficulty of proving the negative proposition that Toyota's electronic throttle control did not contribute to unintended acceleration.

Academy's report concurred with NHTSA's decision to close its investigation of unintended acceleration in Toyota's vehicles.

Some claims may also not just have been unfounded, but also possibly fraudulent. In one case where questions have been raised, a man called 911 saying his car was accelerating uncontrollably on the highway, but when the operator told him to put the car in neutral, he refused to do so, later saying he was afraid the car might flip or shift into reverse. But he stopped the car when a police car rode beside him. Subsequent investigation showed the man was not consistently applying his brakes, as he had claimed (Linebaugh, 2010).

A Media-created Mass Tort?

The government studies rejecting electronic throttle problems raise the question whether a mass litigation regarding Toyota unintended acceleration may have developed in part from media attention and misinterpretation of an emotional emergency call. Indeed, one claimed injury of the Toyota litigation—lowered resale value for Toyotas generally—could be said to have been directly caused by the extensive media attention. In the late 1980s, Audi automobiles were alleged to have experienced sudden acceleration upon starting, and a report on the popular CBS television news program *60 Minutes* involving a modified Audi car also triggered widespread concern (Huber, 1989; White & Searcey, 2010). A subsequent governmental investigation, however, suggested that Audi's supposed problems of unintended acceleration appear to have stemmed from pedal misapplication by the driver, and Audi's redesign that required a driver to step on the brake pedal to start the car greatly reduced alleged problems.[10]

If unintended acceleration is generally not traceable to Toyota, but instead is the result of driver error or fraud, inquiry may be warranted into the speed and efficiency of the US civil justice system in processing the mass litigation. In 2011, Toyota won a trial in federal court in New York in which a plaintiff claimed his car accelerated and hit a tree, but where Toyota argued that the driver was the cause of the accident; the

---

[10] *See* Pollard & Sussman, 1989, stating that '[p]edal misapplications are the most probable explanation for the vast majority of sudden acceleration incidents in which no vehicle malfunction is evident' and that '[e]ven in cases where vehicle malfunctions exist which startle or otherwise distract the driver, it is often pedal misapplication which is the direct cause of high engine power'; Huber, 1989; White & Searcey, 2010.

court, however, excluded evidence involving the car's electronics.[11] In 2012 Toyota settled the Officer Saylor case involving the widely publicized accident and death of a family of four for a reported $10 million, as well as a separate Michigan personal-injury case for an undisclosed amount (Bensinger & Vartabedian, 2010). In 2013, Toyota also won another trial in Philadelphia, as well as the first bellwether trial set by a coordinating state court in California, where a 66-year-old woman crashed her car and argued the car defectively accelerated. In addition, Toyota agreed to pay two fines for $16.375 million each and another fine for $17.35 million to NHTSA, for the delay in informing NHTSA of defects involving sticky pedals and floor mat entrapment. Toyota also settled certain additional lawsuits, including a multidistrict litigation bellwether personal-injury lawsuit, a $29 million settlement of claims from 29 states and a US territory in which Toyota would also make additional safety information and assistance available to consumers, and a separate $16 million settlement of California claims brought by the Orange County district attorney (Bensinger, 2013(a); Bensinger, 2013(b)).

In autumn 2013, Toyota lost a trial in Oklahoma, and the jury found that Toyota's electronic throttle control system was defective. The jury awarded $1.5 million to each the families of two women who died in the crash, and also found that Toyota had acted with 'reckless disregard', warranting the imposition of punitive damages. Before the jury deliberated to determine the amount of punitive damages, Toyota settled the case. In December 2013, to enable intensive settlement negotiations of the remaining cases involving alleged personal injury and property damage, Judge Selna delayed the progress of federal cases in the multidistrict litigation, and set the cases for informal settlement conferences and then formal mediation for those not yet resolved (Bensinger, 2013(c)). In addition, in February 2015, Toyota was ordered to pay $11 million in a Minnesota federal court, where the plaintiffs allege that unintended acceleration caused a crash that ultimately took the lives of three persons and seriously injured two others. In March 2014, Toyota agreed to pay a fine of $1.2 billion to the US Justice Department for concealing information regarding floor mats and sticky pedals related to unintended acceleration, and Toyota also agreed to undergo ongoing independent review of its safety policies. In July 2015, Toyota attorneys

[11] Verdict, *Sitafalwalla v. Toyota Motor Sales, U.S.A., Inc.* (E.D.N.Y. 1 April 2011) (No. CV 08-3001 (ETB)), 2011 WL 1251297; Amended Verified Complaint ¶ 16, *Sitafalwalla v. Toyota Motor Sales, U.S.A., Inc.* (No. 08-CV-3001), 2010 WL 1704901; *see also* New York Times 2011; Associated Press, 2011.

informed Judge Selna that settlement agreements had been reached in 388 cases, including 146 of 171 cases in the federal multidistrict litigation.

Ongoing Corporate and Regulatory Safety Reform

In the wake of what one commentator has called the 'Great Toyota Panic' (Olson, 2010), regulatory and legislative proposals to broaden NHTSA enforcement have emerged, and Toyota has undertaken various safety initiatives. NHTSA proposed a brake-throttle override requirement that would seek to prevent crashes stemming from a trapped or stuck accelerator pedal (Press Release NHTSA, 2012(a)). In addition, NHTSA proposed a requirement for all light passenger vehicles to have event data recorders, so that automobile information such as speed and use of brakes and accelerator is preserved prior to a crash (Press Release NHTSA, 2012(b); Wald, 2011). NHTSA also planned to research design strategies to reduce pedal misapplication (NHTSA Press Release, 2011).

In 2011 Toyota again completed additional recalls to prevent pedal entrapment by floor mats and possible interference with pedals by interior panels and pads (Bensinger & Vartabedian, 2011). Toyota has also begun installing a brake override system as standard equipment in all of its cars, giving the brake precedence if both the brake and accelerator are depressed. In addition, Toyota has created a panel to hear customer complaints and swiftly relay concerns. Moreover, Toyota committed to creating a $50 million safety center in Michigan (Wald, 2011). Toyota also moved and consolidated its headquarters in the US, thereby facilitating quick communication to prevent future crises.

In December 2012, Toyota agreed to pay more than $1 billion to settle the class-action lawsuit seeking recovery for economic losses from reduced resale value of Toyota automobiles, and a federal judge subsequently granted final approval. Claims involving personal injuries are not part of the class settlement. While the class settlement created funds of $250 million for owners claiming losses from the sale or trade of their Toyota vehicles between September 2009 and December 2010, along with $250 million for owners whose cars are unable to have brake-override systems installed, much of the additional expenditures involved further safety-related initiatives by Toyota. Toyota agreed to spend between $200–400 million to provide brake override systems in cars where pedals may potentially be subject to sticking or entrapment in the floor mat, create a $400 million customer support program with free repairs on certain parts for ten years, and contribute $30 million for research on driver behavior, acceleration, and a safety education and information program for drivers. In addition, the class settlement reserves $227 million for the plaintiffs' attorneys' fees and costs. The class settlement does not, however, identify or address any Toyota electronic throttle problem, and plaintiffs' class counsel Steven Berman noted that '[w]e have not resolved the issue of is there a bug' in the electronic system (Ramsey, 2012). Toyota sales in the US have increased markedly, and in 2013 Toyota regained its prior position as global leader in automobile sales.

ONE OF THE WORLD'S LARGEST OIL COMPANIES IS INVOLVED IN ONE OF THE WORLD'S LARGEST OIL SPILLS

Eight months after the Saylor automobile accident and accompanying publicity that led to the Toyota unintended acceleration mass litigation, on 20 April 2010 the Deepwater Horizon oilrig in the Gulf of Mexico exploded, killing 11 rig workers and injuring many others. Subsequently, nearly five million barrels of oil poured into the Gulf of Mexico. After a temporary cap in July 2010, the oil well was permanently capped in September 2010. The oil spill had widespread effects on the economy of the Gulf region. Commercial fishermen, including shrimpers and crabbers, were unable to fish, resulting in cascading losses to seafood processors and restaurants. In addition, the absence of tourists in the coastal areas during the summer caused additional losses to hotels and restaurants. Soon after the oil spill, the US Coast Guard designated BP a 'responsible party' under the Oil Pollution Act of 1990, rendering BP strictly liable for losses from the oil spill.[12]

President Obama and the Creation of a Claims Fund

Media in the US devoted widespread national coverage to the spill, and media ultimately offered a live feed picture of the oil spilling into the ocean. This media attention triggered political pressure that in turn led to

---

[12] 33 U.S.C. §§ 2701–2762 (2012); Letter from the United States Coast Guard to BP Exploration and Production, Inc., 28 April 2010, available at http://www.ag.louisiana.gov/Shared/ViewDoc.aspx?Type=3&Doc=259 (Exhibit B) [hereinafter: US Coast Guard Letter to BP].

an unprecedented event: the direct, personal involvement of the President of the US in negotiating a mass tort settlement among private parties.[13]

To compensate commercial fisherman and businesses and preserve their livelihoods, President Barrack Obama announced, in his first Oval Office address which was televised and available via the Internet, the creation of a claims fund to be independently and neutrally administered. After meeting with President Obama, BP agreed to provide $20 billion for the fund, which was to be put in place by BP and overseen by the Department of Justice. BP's willingness to agree to the President's request for such a fund may have been motivated by public relations, the need for future regulatory approval for drilling by the US, or the desire to avoid protracted, expensive and uncertain litigation that might possibly lead to bankruptcy. Moreover, BP was already required to pay ongoing losses as a responsible party under the Oil Pollution Act, although the amount to be paid for economic damages was limited to $75 million in the absence of a finding of gross negligence. One motivation for the government's involvement in the creation of the claims fund, according to President Obama and Vice President Joseph Biden, was to save whole communities in the Gulf from a kind of cultural destruction, which would have occurred if parties had to wait for litigated settlements. In his Oval Office address, President Obama noted:

> [F]or generations, men and women who call this region home have made their living from the water. That living is now in jeopardy. I've talked to shrimpers and fishermen who don't know how they're going to support their families this year. I've seen empty docks and restaurants with fewer customers—even in areas where the beaches are not yet affected. I've talked to owners of shops and hotels who wonder when the tourists might start coming back. *The sadness and the anger they feel is not just about the money they've lost. It's about a wrenching anxiety that their way of life may be lost. I refuse to let that happen.* Tomorrow, I will meet with the chairman of BP and inform him that he is to set aside whatever resources are required to compensate the workers and business owners who have been harmed as a result of his company's recklessness.[14] [emphasis added by author] … .

Vice President Biden repeated this theme of cultural preservation and recovery, noting that:

---

[13] For a broad treatment of the historical role of the presidency in resolving various national and international disputes, *see* Zimmerman, 2015.

[14] The White House, Office of the Press Secretary, *Remarks by the President to the Nation on the BP Oil Spill*, 15 June 2010, available at http://www.whitehouse.gov/the-press-office/remarks-president-nation-bp-oil-spill.

> [t]here is an entire way of life in jeopardy [and that] the President … said … take care of those people now, who if they don't get help now, are going to be gone, gone, gone.[15]

A Noted Claims Administrator Gives Details About the Largest Private Claims Fund

Soon after the announcement of the $20 billion fund, BP and the White House announced that Kenneth Feinberg would direct the fund. Mr. Feinberg is perhaps the most widely known claims administrator in the US, whose prior work includes administering the September 11th Victim Compensation Fund and the Hokie Spirit Memorial Fund for victims of the Virginia Tech shooting, as well as serving as special master in the Agent Orange class settlement. Secretary of the Treasury Timothy Geithner had also chosen Feinberg to oversee executive compensation for bank executives in connection with the administration's Trouble Asset Relief Program (TARP) after the financial crisis in 2008.

Feinberg identified several challenges of the Gulf Coast Claims Facility not present in his work with prior funds. The Gulf oil spill mainly involved claims for lost wages and business income, rather than death or physical injury, and the defendant was a foreign corporation still generating considerable profits. In addition, media had focused on the ongoing spill for months, enflaming public anger. Moreover, local political officials may have sought to further their constituents' desires for maximum compensation and to express anger toward BP by criticizing the claims fund. Furthermore, the claims fund might trigger opposition from the Gulf plaintiffs' lawyers by removing claimants from traditional mass litigation involving the lawyers. Because the wrongdoer was solvent and accepted its responsibility to pay claimants, Feinberg also decided to seek his own compensation from BP, rather than undertake the task pro bono, as he had done in September 11 Victim Compensation Fund, TARP Executive Compensation Program and Hokie Spirit Memorial Fund.

The Gulf Coast Claims Facility replaced BP's prior claims process of temporary payments to claimants under the Oil Pollution Act. In that process, BP had retained Louisiana insurance adjuster Worley Catastrophe Response and created 35 claims offices across the Gulf area,

---

[15] Jesse Lee, *A New Process and a New Escrow Account for Gulf Oil Spill Claims from BP*, The White House Blog (17 June 2010, 2:35 PM), posting video of Vice President Biden's remarks, available at http://www.whitehouse.gov/blog/2010/06/17/a-new-process-and-a-new-escrow-account-gulf-oil-spill-claims-bp.

involving more than 1,300 claims adjusters. Worley authorized payments of $400 million to 80,000 claimants. Feinberg determined the pre-existing approach was too decentralized and inconsistent, with individual claims adjusters assessing evidence in person and then potentially immediately writing checks, and with claimants visiting multiple offices after being denied by one. Instead, Feinberg had persons submit their claims at local offices, or via the internet on the Gulf Coast Claims Facility website. The centralized claims facility then entered the claim into its database and reviewed the claim based upon standardized criteria determined by Feinberg's law firm, Feinberg Rozen. Pricewaterhouse-Coopers accountants reviewed business claims, because of their complexity compared to individual claims, and also reviewed other particularly difficult claims that raised new issues. When a claim was authorized for payment, Citibank issued a check, in collaboration with Gulf branches of Whitney Bank and Hancock Bank.

For the first 90 days, the Gulf Coast Claims Facility offered emergency payments without waiver of right to sue, and thereafter permitted claimants to return with additional documentation for further interim payments, also without waiver to sue. After the initial 90-day period for emergency payments, the Facility offered those already granted an emergency payment a further 'quick payment' of $5,000 to any individual or $25,000 to any business, without need for further documentation. To obtain a quick payment, however, an individual or business needed to waive further legal claims against BP. Alternatively, without waiving the right to sue, a claimant could repeatedly seek an 'interim payment' for documented costs related to the spill for the prior quarter. If claimants wished to avoid repeated submissions, and could document present and future costs in excess of the quick payment amount, claimants might seek a 'final payment' that covered all such costs, but claimants receiving final payments also had to release any claims to sue BP. With the assistance of Analysis Research Planning Corporation, the Gulf Coast Claims Facility determined that the Gulf economy would be free of spill-related problems by the end of 2013. As a result, the Facility permitted future recovery for final payments until the end of 2013, and multiplied prior documented losses to achieve the amount offered for a final payment. An exception, however, was made for oyster harvesters, in light of the longer-lasting damage to oyster beds; accordingly, final payments were based on expected future losses continuing until the end of 2015. The Facility subsequently also awarded shrimp and crab fisherman the same increased future recovery as oyster harvesters, in light of ongoing assessment of risks.

Claimants also were able to obtain their payments without an attorney, so claimants could avoid being charged an attorney's fee, as well as avoid the delays for compensation that might accompany formal litigation. This approach maximized compensation to claimants and reduced transactions costs, but claimants had to trust that the Facility's offers were fair. To assist claimants with filing, the Gulf Coast Claims Facility obtained the assistance of the Mississippi Center for Justice, which provided pro bono legal assistance and reimbursed eligible claimants for accounting expenses. The anticipated volume of claims precluded individual hearings, but each claim was to be individually assessed by claim administrators.[16]

Town Hall Meetings and Gulf Coast Claims Facility Outreach

Unlike judges and courts, where centuries of tradition contribute to a public perception of fairness, the claims facility was new, and even Feinberg, widely known in legal circles, was likely unknown in the communities of the Gulf fisherman. To address this problem, the Facility sought to build trust not only through the fund's good dealings with claimants, but also through media-enabled outreach. That work had already been significantly aided by President Obama's public announcement of the fund, as well as President Obama's assurance that the Fund would be 'administered by an independent third party' and that 'all legitimate claims [will be] paid out in a fair and timely manner'. Indeed, President Obama's endorsement of the fund might warrant considering it a quasi-public, rather than a purely private, claims fund.[17]

To further explain the Gulf Coast Claims Facility to claimants, offer claimants an opportunity to voice their concerns and participate in the process, and to curry favor with claimants, Feinberg proceeded to meet with skeptical Gulf Coast claimants in numerous town hall meetings.[18] At

---

[16] Feinberg noted that 'the right to be heard was at odds with requirements of speed and efficiency' (Feinberg, 2012).

[17] *See* Stier, 2011. Feinberg has stated that '[t]he GCCF is a unique hybrid, part public, part private ... OPA required BP to step up and process claims, but the statute never anticipated a handshake deal between BP and a US president creating an independent claims facility' (Feinberg, 2012).

[18] In the first six months of the claims facility, Feinberg visited the Gulf almost every week and attended five or six several-hour town-hall meetings in a day. Feinberg noted, '[l]ocal citizens expected—were entitled—to visit with me on their home turf, to meet the public face of the claims program. They needed an opportunity to vent, criticize, argue, demand, implore, and seek compensation for their damages'. Suggesting that such meetings would ultimately aid the Gulf

these packed meetings, however, claimants often quickly became angry while voicing their frustration and seeking payment, and that anger was amplified by the group setting.[19] Although BP was a British company, and Mr. Feinberg hailed from the northeast and had a Boston accent markedly different than that prevalent in the southern Gulf area, Gulf claimants did not openly voice regional resentment. Claimants did, however, complain that Feinberg, who worked in Washington, could not understand that business in the Gulf had been transacted by a handshake for generations, without documentation. Feinberg would not agree to payment on a claim without corroboration, and at these meetings, Feinberg generally listened to questions, provided answers and set forth the claim procedures for the Gulf Coast Claims Facility. With regard to shortcomings, Feinberg admitted a mistake in overpromising that eligible individual claims would be processed and paid in 48 hours and eligible businesses within one week. The inability to obtain a formal individual quasi-judicial hearing for each claim may also have discontented claimants.[20]

Concerns of Fraudulent Claims and a Lack of Independence for the Fund

The widespread media coverage of the spill, the fund and the town hall meetings led many claimants to opt in to the fund and settle their claims. But media coverage may have also led to the filing of frivolous claims. With regard to tax returns, certain claimants altered their submitted tax returns, turned in supposed tax returns that were never filed, sought recovery for amounts greater than listed on their tax returns, or stated

---

Coast Claims Facility, Feinberg predicted, 'many claimants would appreciate my local appearances in unfriendly environments. Even as I was battered with criticism, I would achieve some degree of credibility, even some admiration, in my choice to meet with fisherman in Louisiana, condo owners in Alabama, hoteliers in Florida, and restaurant owners in Mississippi' (Feinberg, 2012).

[19] According to Feinberg, complaints generally sought to criticize inconsistent awards, delays in processing claims, lack of transparency, absence of generosity or insensitivity to cultural differences. Feinberg observed that '[t]hose shouting the loudest received the most applause and encouragement'. Ibid.

[20] Feinberg noted that the 'inability to provide a tailored individual hearing to each and every claimant inevitably distanced the GCCF from the very people it sought to serve'. Feinberg 'wanted individual Gulf residents to believe that they were not simply cogs in a bureaucratic machine, that each claim and each claimant were important to the GCCF', but he concluded, 'I never completely solved this problem, one that will continue to bedevil any effort at mass resolution of claims'. Ibid.

their tax returns were false. Other claimants submitted fake documents pertaining to pay and ownership of boats and businesses. When claim administrators suspected fraud in a claim, they referred the claim for further investigation to Guidepost, a company specializing in corporate investigations and fraud. The Department of Justice also maintained a fraud hotline, which received anonymous tips of fraud in the fund that were subsequently investigated by Guidepost. The Facility ultimately denied more than 400,000 claims, deeming approximately more than 10,000 claims 'suspicious', and referred several thousand claims to the Justice Department for possible prosecution.

One problem with the Fund's media outreach, as well as its town hall meetings, was concern about Feinberg's independence from BP.[21] Feinberg's compensation was paid by BP and periodically renegotiated with BP. And any money left in the $20 billion fund was to be returned to BP, potentially compromising Feinberg's independence.[22] Furthermore, BP disagreed with several decisions by Feinberg, such as the creation of the emergency payment program, the eligibility for compensation of hotels and restaurants in the more distant Florida Peninsula, and the extent of the future recovery for claimants, although BP continued to state its support of Feinberg's independence.[23] Feinberg stated there was no linkage of his pay by BP to any decisions by him on payments to claimants. At the suggestion of a noted federal judge, Judge Jack B. Weinstein, Feinberg sought and obtained an opinion letter from ethics expert Professor Stephen Gillers of New York University School of Law, opining that as the administrator of the Gulf Coast Claims Facility, Feinberg was not serving as a lawyer for BP.[24] In addition, Feinberg sought and obtained an opinion letter from Michael B. Mukasey, a

[21] Feinberg stated that 'anger' at town hall meetings 'reached a crescendo within fifteen minutes, with the audience shouting, "Pay him! Why won't you listen to her! You're just working for BP!"' Ibid.

[22] Although Feinberg's compensation was not tied to the number of claims processed or the amounts being paid, he stated that a town-hall-meeting claimant complaint might allege, 'You must be getting paid by BP depending upon the money you saved'. Ibid.

[23] For example, BP argued that future recovery should be limited to less than one year, rather than the Facility's use of four years for oyster harvesters and two years for others.

[24] Letter from Stephen Gillers, Crystal Eastman Professor of Law, New York University, to Kenneth R. Feinberg, Administrator, Gulf Coast Claims Facility (28 December 2010).

former US Attorney General and federal judge.[25] After reviewing the agreed-upon monthly retainer for Feinberg's firm of $850,000, and the subsequent increase of the firm's monthly retainer to $1.25 million, Mukasey opined that the compensation was reasonable under the circumstances. Feinberg justified his compensation payments from BP in light of the extensive burdens of the work, the ability of BP as wrongdoer to pay, the inappropriateness of seeking compensation from claimants, and the unwillingness of local governments to pay.

Nevertheless, the plaintiffs' attorneys brought such concerns to the federal multidistrict litigation court in the formal BP litigation, and the court found that 'Mr. Feinberg and the GCCF cannot be considered "neutral" or "totally independent of BP"'. As a result, the court began supervising the Facility's communications with claimants, who were also potential class members in the pending litigation. It was a rare clash of formal litigation with informal claims processing, with the result that formal litigation—the multidistrict litigation process and putative class actions—emerged as dominant.

A Class Settlement Supplants the Gulf Coast Claims Facility

In March 2012, BP and the plaintiffs' lawyers in the pending BP federal multidistrict litigation announced at the eve of trial that they had reached a class action settlement for $7.8 billion via two settlement classes—one for economic losses, and one for personal injuries. Like the Gulf Coast Claims Facility, the class settlement provided eligibility criteria, payment calculation tools, and requirements for proof. Unlike the Gulf Coast Claims Facility, which covered economic losses, as well as certain physical-injury claims by workers injured by the initial explosion on the Deepwater Horizon rig, the class settlement covered claims for health problems such as respiratory illness. In addition, the class settlement covered claims relating to loss of recreational enjoyment of property as a result of the Gulf oil spill. The settlement created a Transition Process that received court approval and, as a result, the Gulf Coast Claims Facility ceased operations. A new, longstanding-Gulf-resident claims administrator, Patrick Juneau, coordinated the distribution of the class settlement. An Alabama politician welcomed the new coordinator's regional roots, stating: 'He comes from our part of the world. He didn't

---

25 Memorandum from Michael B. Mukasey, Partner, Debevoise & Plimpton, L.L.P., to Kenneth Feinberg, Partner, Feinberg Rozen (8 October 2010), available at http://www.motherjones.com/files/gulf_coast_claims_facility_feinberg_rozen_llps_compensation_october_8_201011.pdf.

have to take a plane to get here. We have someone who, for the first time, understands us' (Talbot, 2012). In December 2012, the federal district court granted final approval to the class settlement, determining it was 'fair, reasonable and adequate'.[26] In court BP subsequently challenged the breadth of claims that were granted payment by the class settlement administrator, arguing that his interpretation of the agreement impermissibly allowed recovery by those not suffering losses as a result of the oil spill, but both the federal district court and Fifth Circuit Court of Appeals rejected BP's contentions. Separately, in November 2012 BP agreed to plead guilty to felony misconduct in connection with the Deepwater Horizon oil spill and related workers' deaths, and pay approximately $4 billion in penalties to the government, including a $1.256 billion criminal fine that is the largest in US history. In September 2014, a federal court trial resulted in a finding that BP had been grossly negligent in connection with the Gulf oil spill, raising the possibility of significant additional civil penalties under the Clean Water Act. In July 2015, BP agreed to settle various remaining claims by Gulf states and localities, as well as federal claims under the Clean Water Act, for $18.7 billion.

Until the end of May 2012, the Gulf Coast Claims Facility disbursed more than $6 billion and received claim requests from more than 574,000 claimants. Of the total paid, approximately $2.4 billion was spent on emergency payments to more than 169,000 claimants in the first 90 days of the fund's operation, out of almost 450,000 who filed potential claims. Approximately 130,000 individuals and businesses waived claims to sue BP and accepted quick payments, totaling $1.3 billion. More than 35,000 individuals and businesses obtained interim payments, resulting in $495 million in payments during the first year. And more than 75,000 claimants received final payments. In contrast, the September 11th Victim Compensation Fund received only 7,500 claims in 33 months. At its height, the Gulf Coast Claims Facility employed 4,500 persons in claims processing, and was disbursing $27 million a day. An audit of the Facility overseen by the Justice Department and conducted by BDO Consulting concluded that although there were approximately 7,300 claimants who should have received an additional $64 million total in payments, and others who were overpaid, the Facility generally consistently applied its criteria and, in fact, constituted a 'significant advance' in disaster

[26] In Re: Oil Spill by the Oil Rig 'Deepwater Horizon' in the Gulf of Mexico on 20 April 2010, No. 10-2179 (E.D. La. 21 December 2012); Issacharoff & Rave, 2014, noting that '[b]y all appearances, claimants will be receiving higher payments under the class settlement than under the GCCF, and in some cases much higher payments'.

response (BDO Consulting, 2012). In addition, utilizing their statutory right to review under the Oil Pollution Act, more than 1,600 claimants obtained review of the Facility's treatment of their claims from the US Coast Guard, and the US Coast Guard uniformly upheld the Facility's treatment of their claims.

The environmental recovery of the Gulf area has made significant progress, aided by both remediation efforts by BP and the US Coast Guard, as well as natural dispersion of oil. Meanwhile, Feinberg has since been asked to assist in several other incidents involving national media and cultural concerns: the child-sexual-abuse cases relating to former Pennsylvania State University assistant football coach Jerry Sandusky, the claims fund for victims from the Aurora, Illinois movie theater mass shooting, the One Fund Boston for victims of the terrorist bombing of the 2013 Boston Marathon and General Motors' claims fund for those injured by faulty ignition switches.

CONCLUSION

Viewing mass litigation from the perspective of media and culture offers an unusual, but fruitful way to understand the dynamics and goals of mass proceedings, and could also offer insight into the important, but under-studied area of legal crisis management. Media attention in the Toyota litigation quickly disseminated information pertaining to automobile recalls, and media reports in both the Toyota unintended acceleration litigation and the BP Gulf Coast oil spill led many persons to pursue litigation, as well as informal claims resolution in the context of the Gulf Coast Claims Facility. In both settings, widespread media attention may have unfortunately also resulted in fraudulent claims, as was shown by the Gulf Coast Claims Facility's referral of various putatively fraudulent claims for governmental prosecution. In addition, the possibility of fraudulent claims requires heightened attention to individualized assessment of claimants, thereby adding further cost to processes already burdened by mass claimants. Media attention also likely stoked corporate and regulatory reform: Toyota has installed further safety mechanisms to thwart potential unintended acceleration and the government has proposed expanding its regulations pertaining to unintended acceleration, as well as its capacity to assess complicated electronic systems in automobiles; with regard to the BP Gulf Coast oil spill, the government has reviewed the efficacy of its regulatory entities for offshore drilling (National Commission, 2011).

In addition, problems of disparate culture posed challenges for effective management of both the Toyota unintended acceleration litigation and the Gulf Coast Claims Facility. The Toyota litigation confronted issues of varying language and cross-national discovery, as well as combined issues of media and culture present in allegations of cultural and political bias in media coverage. The Gulf Coast Claims Facility grappled with issues of regional informal business practices based on oral communication rather than records, and Gulf suspicion concerning the independence of the fund.

The Toyota unintended acceleration litigation and the Gulf Coast Claims Facility were also paired, factually and thematically, in another way. The federal court in the Toyota litigation appointed as settlement mediator, Mr. Patrick Juneau, who also served as the claims administrator for the BP Gulf oil spill class settlement. Mr. Juneau's presence in both cases, as well as that of leading the plaintiffs' lawyers such as Elizabeth Cabraser, offers additional evidence that a relatively small cast of legal actors, perhaps with their own culture of repeat players, appears in many mass torts in the US.

REFERENCES

Frank Ahrens, *Toyota Demo Counters Claim of Electronic Acceleration Glitch*, Washington Post, 9 March 2010

BDO Consulting, a Division of BDO USA, LLP, *Independent Evaluation of the Gulf Coast Claims Facility, Executive Summary*, 19 April 2012

Ken Bensinger, *Toyota Acts to Settle Two Big Lawsuits*, Los Angeles Times, 16 January 2013

Ken Bensinger, *Toyota to Pay $29 Million Settlement*, Los Angeles Times, 15 February 2013

Ken Bensinger, *Toyota Settles Acceleration Suit in W. Virginia: The Deal Comes a Day After the Automaker Enters Talks on a Slew of Other Such Cases*, Los Angeles Times, 14 December 2013

Ken Bensinger & Ralph Vartabedian, *Toyota Settlement May Set Bar for Sudden-acceleration Payouts*, Los Angeles Times, 24 December 2010

Ken Bensinger & Ralph Vartabedian, *Toyota to Recall 2.17 Million More Vehicles*, Los Angeles Times, 25 February 2011

Committee on Electronic Vehicle Controls and Unintended Acceleration, National Research Council of the National Academies, *The Safety Promise and Challenge of Automotive Electronics: Insights from Unintended Acceleration*, 2012

Aaron Ezroj, *Product Liability After Unintended Acceleration: How Automotive Litigation Has Evolved*, (2014) 26 Loyola Consumer Law Review 470

Kenneth Feinberg, *Who Gets What: Fair Compensation After Tragedy and Financial Upheaval* (PublicAffairs Books 2012)

Takahiro Fukada & Natsuko Fukue, *The Trouble at Toyota: Reportage Seems Source-biased*, Japan Times, 3 September 2010, available at: http://www.japantimes.co.jp/text/nn20100903f2.html

Peter Huber, *Manufacturing the Audi Scare*, Wall Street Journal, 18 December 1989

Samuel Issacharoff & Theodore Rave, *The BP Oil Spill Settlement and the Paradox of Public Litigation*, (2014) 74 Louisiana Law Review 397

Jurors Side with Toyota in Lawsuit Over Crash, New York Times, 1 April 2011

Kate Linebaugh, *Investigation Raises Questions on Prius Incident*, Wall Street Journal, 14 March 2010

National Commission on the BP Deepwater Horizon Oil Spill and Offshore Drilling, Report to the President, *Deep Water: The Gulf Oil Disaster and the Future of Offshore Drilling*, January 2011

Walter Olson, *Exorcising Toyota's Demons*, National Review, 15 March 2010

John Pollard & Donald Sussman, *An Examination of Sudden Acceleration*, January 1989 (prepared for the U.S. Department of Transportation, National Highway Traffic Safety Administration)

Press Release, National Highway Traffic Safety Administration, *U.S. DOT Proposes Updated Safety Standard to Prioritize Braking Control, Reduce Risk of High-Speed Unintended Acceleration for Nation's Cars*, 12 April 2012, available at http://www.nhtsa.gov/About+NHTSA/Press+Releases/USDOT+Proposes+Updated+Safety+Standard+to+Prioritize+Braking+Control,+Reduce+Risk+of+High-Speed+Unintended+Acceleration+for+Nation's+Cars

Press Release, National Highway Traffic Safety Administration, *U.S. DOT Proposes Broader Use of Event Data Recorders to Help Improve Vehicle Safety*, 7 December 2012, available at http://www.nhtsa.gov/About+NHTSA/Press+Releases/U.S.+DOT+Proposes+Broader+Use+of+Event+Data+Recorders+to+Help+Improve+Vehicle+Safety

Press Release, National Highway Traffic Safety Administration, *U.S. DOT Releases Results from NHTSA-NASA Study of Unintended Acceleration in Toyota Vehicles*, 8 February 2011, available at http://www.nhtsa.gov/PR/DOT-16-11

Mike Ramsey, *Toyota in $1.1 Billion Gas Pedal Settlement*, Wall Street Journal, 27 December 2012

Sheila Scheuerman, *Against Liability for Private Risk-Exposure*, (2011) 35 Harvard Journal of Law and Public Policy 681

Byron Stier, *The Gulf Coast Claims Facility as Quasi-Public Fund: Transparency and Independence in Claim Administrator Compensation*, (2011) 30 Mississippi College Law Review 255

George Talbot, *New BP Claims Boss is a Stark Contrast to Ken Feinberg*, Al.com, 8 August 2012

Toyota Wins NY Case Over Unintended Acceleration, Associated Press, 1 April 2011

U.S. Department of Transportation, National Highway Traffic Safety Administration, *Technical Assessment of Toyota Electronic Throttle Control (ETC) Systems*, February 2011

Ralph Vartabedian & Ken Bensinger, *Runaway Toyota Cases Ignored*, Los Angeles Times, 8 November 2009

Ralph Vartabedian & Ken Bensinger, *Doubt Cast on Toyota Decision to Blame Sudden Acceleration on Gas Pedal Defect*, Los Angeles Times, 30 January 2010

Matthew Wald, *Electronic Flaws Did Not Cause Toyota Problems, U.S. Says*, New York Times, 8 February 2011

Joseph B. White & Dionne Searcey, *Audi Case Set Template for Toyota's Troubles*, Wall Street Journal, 12 March 2010

Adam Zimmerman, *Presidential Settlements*, (2015) 163 University of Pennsylvania Law Review 1393

6. Collective redress in Vie d'Or: A reflection on a European cultural phenomenon[1]

Ianika Tzankova

INTRODUCTION

The collapse of financial powerhouse Lehman Brothers in September 2008 marked the start of a financial crisis the scale of which had not been experienced for almost a century. From this time onwards the bankruptcy or nationalization of a troubled financial institution would hardly be considered a rarity. The financial landscape was different in 1993 when Vie d'Or, a life insurance company established in the south of the Netherlands, went bankrupt. In the 1990s in the Netherlands, financial institutions rarely went bankrupt and the life insurance business was considered to be a safe activity. Moreover, in the Netherlands, as in other European countries, there is a strong reliance on public regulatory oversight and enforcement to prevent the collapse of financial institutions. When an exceptional event takes place, the government is expected to provide a solution or at the very least to somehow facilitate a compensation scheme for the victims.

The bankruptcy of Vie d'Or left about 11,000 Dutch consumers without life insurance policy and with damages estimated to total €80 million. It is not surprising, then, that at the time the matter attracted extensive media and political attention. In 2011, after 16 years of collective litigation, the consumers succeeded in obtaining compensation

[1] The case study was conducted in collaboration with Prof. Dr. Deborah R. Hensler, Stanford University and builds on interviews with eight individuals representing the interest of the various stakeholders in the Vie d'Or litigation. The interviews took place in March 2011. Each interview took more than an hour. Respondents were given the opportunity to review, and if necessary correct, the factual statements made in this case study. The conclusions attributed to the factual statements are those of the author. *See also* Tzankova, 2013.

of about 50 percent of their damages through a collective settlement. The latter was approved and declared binding by the Amsterdam Court of Appeal on an opt-out basis in April 2009.[2]

The case study of the Vie d'Or litigation and settlement illustrates several ways in which culture and civil society influence and shape the emergence and resolution of a mass dispute. Firstly, the study offers an insider's view on the functioning of a collective redress[3] mechanism that shares one of the most distinctive features of the European philosophy on collective redress, where standing to act is often granted to non-profit organizations rather than representative class members, such as individual plaintiffs or companies. The study helps enhance our understanding of the organizational dynamics that affect associations' behavior in collective litigation, including the existence of potential agency problems, subjects that to date have attracted little academic attention. Secondly, the study reveals how dynamics within a particular industry—in this case, the insurance industry—intersect with the political culture to shape the emergence of a mass dispute and its ultimate resolution. Thirdly, the case study illustrates the multiple roles that the Dutch State plays in the resolution of mass disputes, roles that may create yet other agency problems.

THE RISE AND FALL OF VIE D'OR: NEW KIDS ROLL DOWN THE BLOCK

Vie d'Or was founded in 1985 by Frans Maes and Gerard van Santen. Maes had a financial background and extensive investment banking experience; van Santen had relevant experience in the insurance industry. They combined their expertise to establish an insurance company built on an arguably innovative business model able to produce innovative low-priced insurance products. The products drew attention from consumers

---

2 Gerechtshof Amsterdam, 29 April 2009, NJ 2009, 448, LJN: BI2717 (Vie d'Or).

3 The use of the term 'collective redress' became popular under the watch of the two European Commissioners Neelie Kroes and Meglena Kuneva who have had the most far reaching plans to date to introduce a European collective action. The choice of the term 'collective redress' was political and intended to reflect that the plans did not intend to establish US-style class actions that are widely understood to include private regulatory enforcement as a goal. As a result of extensive lobbying by the business community, the term 'class action' has a negative connotation in Europe.

and investors alike, including international financial powerhouse Merrill Lynch. The new company's financial products became very popular among mid- and small-sized businesses, entrepreneurs and independent contractors, much to the annoyance of the established insurance industry players, who saw part of their clientele flowing away. Although relatively wealthy by Dutch cultural standards, the company's target customers were financially vulnerable because they themselves had to provide for their family's security. A low priced life insurance product was therefore very attractive to them and initially the Vie d'Or life insurance was a huge market success.

As the company expanded its subscriber base, established insurance company executives closely followed its growth and the popularity of its products. The established industry players were skeptical about the ability of a company to offer a life insurance product over the long term at such a low price. They also distrusted the company and its founders, who were not, as one respondent observed, part of the 'old boys' network'. The Netherlands is a small country with a clubby business culture. Business partners and competitors tend to know each other well. Vie d'Or was not a member of the Dutch Association of Insurers (Verbond van Verzekeraars), a powerful independent trade association with self-regulatory powers that represents the interests of private insurance companies operating in the Netherlands. The Association's members represent more than 95 percent of the Dutch insurance market expressed in terms of gross premium income and is often consulted by the government and regulators on industry-related issues and legislation.

Concerned about what it observed regarding Vie d'Or's marketing and pricing practices, the Association of Insurers advised the public insurance regulatory agency, Pensioen- en Verzekeringskamer[4] that it should initiate investigations into Vie d'Or's products, administration and funding model. Initially the warnings had no effect, but when Vie d'Or policy holders started complaining as well, the Insurance Regulator took action and in October 1993 it replaced the CEO of Vie d'Or. This measure was too little, too late. The internal investigation that the new CEO initiated immediately after his appointment revealed that nothing could be done to prevent the collapse of the company. Vie d'Or went bankrupt only a few months later. The life insurance policies of Vie d'Or were taken over by another insurance company[5] in August 1994, but only after substantial

[4] In October 2004, the Pensioen- en Verzekeringskamer merged with De Nederlandsche Bank.

[5] Twenteleven N.V., which later merged with Avéro Achmea.

reductions in the coverage of the 11,000 policy holders. The total estimated loss to the policy holders at that time was about NLG 177 million (€80 million).

Interviews with informants, along with court documents from the various civil, disciplinary and criminal proceedings and investigations that were initiated after the collapse of Vie d'Or, suggest that the bankruptcy was caused by a variety of factors. One was clearly mismanagement:[6] Vie d'Or could not handle the success of its product and effectively administer its many new policies. Furthermore, the company relied on a funding model that turned out to be inadequate. The remuneration of the intermediaries who sold the policy to the consumers was too high, and the level of company reserves was too low. The company's solvency was dependent on uncertain future profits. The products were aggressively priced and promised too much in return. In addition, it turned out that one of the company's directors had used company funds to finance other, risky, private ventures.[7] The company's balance sheets and annual financial statements did not reveal the true financial situation of Vie d'Or,[8] raising the question whether the Regulator should not have identified those omissions at an earlier stage, especially considering the early warnings of the Association of Insurers.

One of the respondents observed that normally if a small insurer such as Vie d'Or encountered financial problems, it would have been 'rescued' by one or more members of the Association of Insurers and the issues

---

[6] Mismanagement was established in the inquiry proceedings into the affairs of the company and its management before the Enterprise Chamber of the Court of Appeal in Amsterdam. Those are special Dutch proceedings often used to collect facts to be used in subsequent proceedings for damages, although the purpose of the proceedings in the case of Vie d'Or was different. Normally only shareholders of a company have standing to file a request for an inquiry before the Enterprise Chamber. In the case of Vie d'Or, an exception to this rule was made and the Public Prosecutor was permitted to file the request because it concerned a matter of public order and policy. For a discussion of discovery proceedings *see* Tzankova, Van Maanen & Rijnhart, 2014, pp. 236–237; *see also* Van Hooijdonk & Eijsvoogel, 2009.

[7] The Criminal Prosecutor started criminal investigations against the directors of the company. Although this attempt did not result in convictions, it produced some additional facts and materials in support of the civil claims of the policy holders.

[8] This finding was established in a report of independent accountancy firm KPMG, and in subsequent disciplinary proceedings against the accountant and the actuaries of Vie d'Or. Both were initiated by the Vie d'Or Foundation that was established to protect the interest of the Vie d'Or policy holders (see the following paragraphs).

would then have been sorted out within the sector. The Association of Insurers would normally try to prevent an insurer from going bankrupt, because that would damage the image of the industry and might lead to unwelcome regulatory interference. The policy holders of the troubled insurance company would thus not suffer much, if any loss. Indeed, the Vie d'Or affair eventually resulted in increased regulation of the insurance business. A respondent commented that if the insurance sector had known beforehand how Vie d'Or would fare, it might have stepped in to save the company.

A few explanations emerged from the interviews about why Vie d'Or was not rescued by the industry members. According to some, at that time the Association of Insurers did not consider Vie d'Or as a shared problem of the existing insurance companies. The new company was an outsider, and not a member of the Association of Insurers. Also, the Association of Insurers had warned the Insurance Regulator more than once about Vie d'Or's business practices and felt that it had sufficiently fulfilled its public duty, and that Vie d'Or was now an issue for the regulator, rather than the trade association. According to another respondent, by the time the problems became apparent to the outside world it was simply too late to rescue Vie d'Or. Some insiders also suggested that the fact that the policy holders were viewed as relatively wealthy might have played to their disadvantage too. Apparently it was assumed that they were able to bear the financial pain of the collapse of Vie d'Or, reflecting the relatively positive economic and financial situation in the 1990s. Some interviewees also suggested that the established industry members were not entirely unhappy with this signal to the public that there was a risk involved in trusting your money to an aggressive newcomer in the market. Finally, one respondent observed that the dilemma of regulators always is that they 'can never do good'; they are always faced with unattractive choices. On the one hand, the regulators are charged with protecting the public. On the other, they should not intervene too soon in situations where a company such as Vie d'Or claims to offer innovative business models and whose development might serve the public. For its part, the Insurance Regulator may have doubted the validity of the warnings of the Association of Insurers and wondered whether they were aimed merely at eliminating a competitor to the 'closed shop' of existing insurers. Whatever the motivations of the Association of Insurers or the Insurance Regulator to act or not to act, the result was that 11,000 of Vie d'Or's subscribers were left with substantial financial damages and without a valid life insurance policy. The matter drew the attention of politicians and, in the summer of 1994, the Insurance Regulator incorporated the Vie d'Or Foundation to protect the interests of the policy holders who suffered losses resulting from Vie d'Or's bankruptcy.

THE VIE D'OR FOUNDATION: A FAITHFUL AND UNSELFISH GUARDIAN OF COLLECTIVE INTERESTS

The Netherlands was one of the first European countries to introduce a collective action, in April 1994, coincidently only shortly after Vie d'Or went bankrupt. In line with the collective redress tradition in many European countries, only declaratory or injunctive relief is available under the collective action Act, and standing to act (Tzankova, 2012) is granted only to non-profit organizations that meet certain criteria. The latter are relatively easy to meet, and there is no separate certification stage,[9] as exists in some other jurisdictions that have adopted collective actions. Instead, the court determines whether the organization has legal standing to bring the action as part of the adjudication of the matter. The organization that brings an action may be a foundation or an association (but not a commercial entity or an individual), whose articles of association explicitly enable it to initiate legal actions for the collective protection of similarly situated individuals or companies whose rights are infringed. The organization may be a Special Purpose Vehicle incorporated for the purpose of a specific litigation or an established public or private interest association such as the Dutch Consumers' Association (Consumentenbond) or the Dutch Shareholders' Association (Vereniging van Effectenbezitters).

The Consumers' Association did not get involved in the Vie d'Or matter because it has limited resources and has to prioritize potential activities. It was clear from the outset that the Vie d'Or matter was highly complicated from a factual and legal point of view[10] and addressing the issues adequately would require substantial financial resources. The fact that the Vie d'Or policy holders were not viewed as 'average consumers' might have also played a role, according to one of the respondents.

---

[9] Article 3:305a of the Dutch Civil Code (Burgerlijk Wetboek). Before an action can be filed, the organization is required by law to attempt to obtain the desired relief by means of a negotiated out-of-court settlement (Kamerstukken II 1991/1992, 22 486, nr. 3 Memorie van Toelichting (Parliamentary Proceedings House of Representatives, Explanatory Memorandum)).

[10] The issue of State liability for the failure of regulatory oversight was at that time an open question. Also, establishing causation was problematic and the calculation of damages complicated.

In the absence of an existing organization stepping forward to bring a collective action, a Special Purpose Vehicle had to be established to collectively protect the interests of the policy holders; as a result, the Vie d'Or Foundation was incorporated by the Insurance Regulator. According to the Foundation's articles of association, a policy holder could not be a member of the Board of the Foundation, and the Board members would be appointed by the Insurance Regulator. The Insurance Regulator also funded the initial expenses of the Foundation. Despite public criticism of the role it had played in the bankruptcy of Vie d'Or—or perhaps because of this criticism—the Insurance Regulator wanted to make a statement that the matter was not only going to be dealt with vigorously, but also objectively. A more skeptical view of the decision of the Insurance Regulator to incorporate the Foundation and to appoint its Board members is that it wanted to have some influence on the investigations and follow-on actions. In any event, the Vie d'Or case is the first and only time that a Dutch regulator incorporated a Special Purpose Vehicle to collectively protect the interests of a group.

The Insurance Regulator appointed accomplished, respected and well-known individuals to sit on the Board of the Foundation. Mr. Jaap van Rijn was chairman of the Board from 1994 to 2005. He was the former chairman of the Board of Directors of ING Bank. Van Rijn accepted the appointment and viewed his tasks as a public duty. All respondents described him as a great communicator, an experienced and inspiring leader, an individual applying high moral standards and a shining example of integrity. Throughout the years, Van Rijn used his corporate connections, knowledge, experience and skills solely for the benefit of the policy holders. He was succeeded in 2005 by Jan Holsboer, also a former ING Bank director, who was suggested by Van Rijn. The remaining members of the Board were equally high profile and devoted to the cause of the consumers. Notwithstanding their dedication, the resolution of the matter took 16 years, during which time the Foundation's Board members invested substantial time and energy in the protection of the policy holders' interests on a *pro bono* basis. One respondent observed that nowadays it would probably be unrealistic to expect and find such an attitude and devotion.

But this admiring view of the Foundation only developed over time. In the beginning, the policy holders distrusted the Foundation and saw it as 'the long arm' of the Insurance Regulator. This led to the incorporation of two additional groups by disgruntled and suspicious policy holders to protect their interests. However, in the years that followed, the roles of those organizations that initially competed with the Foundation were limited to monitoring the action(s) of the Foundation through their membership on the Foundation's steering committee. As the litigation moved forward, their attitude evolved from suspicious and cautious to fully supportive of the Foundation.

One of the first decisions of the Board after its appointment in August 1994 was to instruct a lawyer for the Foundation and KPMG to investigate and collect facts about the cause of the bankruptcy, including the role of the Insurance Regulator. But the Board probably first won the trust of the policy holders with its second decision, when in 1998, after the conclusion of a few inquiries and investigations, it decided to initiate legal proceedings against the Insurance Regulator that had not only incorporated the Foundation, but also provided its initial funding. To accomplish this, the Foundation had to change its articles of association, which had initially provided for the Insurance Regulator to appoint the Board members of the Foundation and required the Foundation to report to the Insurance Regulator. Without such a change, the Insurance Regulator could have easily sabotaged the decisions of the Foundation regarding its litigation strategies and follow-on actions by simply replacing the Board members. The Insurance Regulator resisted the changes in the articles of association and, because of that, initially no notary could be found who was willing to assist the Foundation. Eventually a notary who was also a part-time academic and who probably saw this as his public duty volunteered and the change was made, which led to the Insurance Regulator filing a disciplinary complaint against that notary. Even though that complaint was granted by the respective disciplinary body, there were now no obstacles left to prevent the Foundation initiating litigation.

THE LITIGATION AND THE SETTLEMENT

In the litigation that took place between 1998 and 2006 and that moved from the District Court to the Supreme Court of the Netherlands, the Foundation faced many challenges. The picture that emerged from the interviews is that the personality of the Foundation's chairman and the devotion and determination of the Board members to protect the interests of the policy holders contributed to a large extent to the resolution of the case. The litigation was designed as a collective action for declaratory relief, combined with eleven individual test cases to determine the calculation of damages in relevant subcategories of cases. The Foundation was anticipating that a favorable decision on liability in the collective action and on causation and damages in the individual test cases would facilitate a collective settlement and overall resolution of the matter. One of the factors motivating defendants to seek a settlement is a court decision in a prior lawsuit favoring the plaintiffs.

Obviously it could be argued that the directors and officers of Vie d'Or had failed to fulfill their contractual and fiduciary duties and obligations, but their personal assets were nowhere near sufficient to compensate the policy holders since the company had not purchased Directors and Officers liability insurance. About €8 million altogether was collected in settlements with the supervisory directors and officers of Vie d'Or, the intermediaries and Merrill Lynch, which was used to initiate the fact-gathering proceedings that took place from 1994 to 1998 and the initial costs of the collective litigation action[11] against Deloitte, the accountant of Vie d'Or, its actuaries Heijnis & Koelman, the Insurance Regulator and the Dutch State. The action was initiated before the District Court in The Hague. The State was named as a defendant because the claim, if successful, would exceed the resources of the Insurance Regulator. The Foundation argued that the Insurance Regulator performed a delegated State task, making the State liable if that task was not adequately performed.

According to the Foundation, the accountant and actuaries were liable for the insureds' losses because the balance sheets of the company and its annual financial statements did not reveal the true financial situation of Vie d'Or. The Foundation claimed that the Insurance Regulator should also have identified those omissions, especially considering the several early warnings by the Association of Insurers. Although the Foundation obtained favorable court rulings before the District Court and the Court of Appeal in The Hague, in a 2006 landmark decision, the Dutch Supreme Court ruled that the Insurance Regulator enjoys a large margin of discretion in deciding whether or not to make use of its investigative and enforcement powers. In a way, the Supreme Court left the case open: it ruled—in favor of the State and the Insurance Regulator—that the Court of Appeal had applied an inadequate test to establish the civil

---

[11] Other funds that were used to fund the various fact-finding proceedings, expert opinions and the subsequent collective litigation were obtained from the legal expense insurers of the policy holders (about €1 million). With the €8 million collected by the Foundation in the various settlements, the costs related to the disciplinary proceedings, the criminal complaint, the inquiry proceedings and the administration costs of the Foundation were covered and a sufficient fund remained to initiate civil proceedings for damages. The Foundation knew that it had a long way to go, up to the Supreme Court, because the test for liability of the State and regulators was not established at that point and the matter was complicated not only from a legal, but also from a factual point of view.

liability of a regulator, but held that another court had to look into the facts again, applying the correct test. The 'new' test was less strict with regard to assessing the Regulator's liability and therefore disadvantageous to the Foundation. The Supreme Court ruling on the liability test that was used for the accountants and the actuaries was more advantageous to the Foundation, but applying it to the Vie d'Or case required further, lengthy litigation.[12] Twelve years after the bankruptcy of Vie d'Or and several millions spent on fact-gathering, expert opinions and litigating, the consumers wanted a resolution without many more years of further proceedings. During the proceedings up to this point, 600 policy holders had died. This added yet another dimension to the Vie d'Or scandal.

The Supreme Court decision led to political pressure on the national government to facilitate a final settlement of the claims, but in July 2007 the State officially refused to accede to this pressure. The Netherlands has a history of stepping in to help resolve major mass claim disputes.[13] However, when the former Minister of Finance Wouter Bos answered questions before Parliament about whether he was considering a final resolution of the matter, he answered[14] that there was no legal reason to settle, and a settlement would create a precedent to the disadvantage of the tax payer. (The State and the Insurance Regulator had previously resisted attempts to negotiate a settlement, even though the accountants and actuaries were open to such negotiations.) From the State's perspective, the question of State liability for failing regulatory oversight was a matter of principle and required a Supreme Court ruling. One of the respondents shared that it was clear from the beginning of the litigation that the State would insist on obtaining the latter.[15] The reason for this was, in part, strategic: if the Supreme Court ruling on liability for failing regulatory oversight went against the State, the State would have the ability to 'repair' this with new legislation restricting or excluding such State liability. As a result, there was little reason for the State to forgo taking the question to the Supreme Court.

---

[12] HR 13 October 2006, LJN: AW2080, C04/281HR (Deloitte & Touche e.a./Stichting Vie d'Or).

[13] Dexia and DES are examples of other major cases that were settled after political interference and under political pressure (Tzankova, 2012, 578).

[14] *See* http://www.rijksoverheid.nl/documenten-en-publicaties/kamerstukken/2008/07/28/antwoorden-op-kamervragen-over-vie-d-or.html.

[15] Since 2012, the Dutch Supreme Court can be requested to rule on questions of law prior to adjudication on a case's merits (De Jong, 2009; Ozmis & Tzankova, 2012, 27–28). Had this mechanism existed previously, at least some of the delay associated with the Vie d'Or litigation might have been eliminated.

The sequence of events in the year after the Minister's official announcement is not clear, but what emerges from interviews and media coverage is that the partial clarity provided by the Supreme Court ruling, political pressure and other external factors all contributed positively to a change in attitude of all parties involved. The State had gotten what it thought it needed: a decision formally absolving it from liability. As a result, it might have been willing to take steps 'behind closed doors' to facilitate compensation of the increasingly elderly claimants whose plight had captured the public's attention. The Association of Insurers also seems to have engaged in re-thinking its role in the process. Early in 2008, the Association of Insurers announced that although not a party in the litigation, it was willing to voluntarily contribute €6.5 million to a settlement fund. The Association's offer also responded to the political environment. Over the 14 years in which the Vie d'Or litigation unfolded, the regulatory landscape had changed and the insurance sector was facing not only stricter national and European regulation, but also negative press coverage related to insurance products, especially the so-called 'unit-linked' insurance products of the type promoted by Vie d'Or.[16] The Association might have speculated that the gesture would contribute to a more positive image of the industry. Also, if the Insurance Regulator were held liable, the costs thereof would probably be borne by the industry anyway, as the costs of the Insurance Regulator are borne by the industry. The gesture of the Association seems to have been the last push the parties needed to reach a final resolution.

In May 2008, it was officially announced that the parties had reached a final settlement agreement, creating a settlement fund of €45 million.[17] The parties contributing to this fund in addition to the Association of Insurers were the Foundation,[18] the accountant and the actuaries. Although the State and the Insurance Regulator did not formally contribute to the settlement fund, the Insurance Regulator facilitated the

---

[16] Those insurance products resemble some of the features of the product that was developed by Vie d'Or: a percentage of the insurance premium is used to invest in securities, but also to cover costs that were not made transparent to the consumer. If the market goes up the consumers will gain because they will be insured against lower premiums. However, dependent on market developments and in the most negative scenario, the costs could absorb a large part of the premium and result in a negative value of the product.

[17] *See* http://www.ed.nl/economie/3196108/Eindelijk-schikking-zaakVie-dOr.ece.

[18] With reserved funds left from the bankruptcy of Vie d'Or, which could be 'set free' only in the case of a final resolution.

settlement by retroactively volunteering to cover all costs and expenses the Foundation had incurred over the past 15 years (€8.5 million) so that the previously collected settlement funds and the new settlement fund of €45 million could be used entirely for the claims of the policy holders.[19] This resulted in compensation of about 50 percent of the policy holders' damages, not including the loss of interest, which by this time constituted a considerable amount.

A petition was filed under the 2005 Dutch Act on Collective Settlements before the Amsterdam Court of Appeal to approve the settlement and make it binding on all policy holders who chose not to opt out (Tzankova, 2012). Under the collective settlement statute, an association representing claimants such as the Foundation and potential defendants to a legal action may jointly petition the Amsterdam Court of Appeal to approve a binding settlement, on an opt-out basis. No objectors appeared and the settlement agreement was approved and declared binding by the Amsterdam Court of Appeal in May 2009. There were no opt-outs. The fund was distributed, and in 2012 the Foundation was dissolved, 16 years after the bankruptcy of Vie d'Or.

REFLECTIONS

The Vie d'Or litigation offers several useful lessons regarding collective litigation in the Netherlands and in other civil law jurisdictions that have adopted the approach of permitting associations and special purpose organizations—but not class members—to litigate on behalf of a class.

The Role and Functioning of Special Purpose Vehicles in Collective Redress

The Vie d'Or case study shows how Special Purpose Vehicles incorporated for the resolution of a specific collective matter operate in a European context, where civil society and consumers rely on the supervisory and enforcement powers of State or semi-State agencies and

---

[19] The former policy holders would receive about 50 percent of the nominal value of their claims, not including interest. Parties agreed further that defendants would settle without admitting liability, that the exact contributions of the various parties to the settlement fund would remain confidential, that they would file a petition to declare the settlement agreement binding and that the minimum participation rate of the policy holders should be 90 percent. The take-up rate was ultimately 99.8 percent.

regulators, rather than private litigation and entrepreneurial lawyers, to protect their rights.

The Vie d'Or case study suggests that if the Dutch collective action regime relies exclusively on longstanding public or private interest organizations or regulators to take the lead in the protection of the collective interests of the policy holders, those interests might go unprotected for a variety of reasons. In the first place, the inquiries and subsequent litigation in Vie d'Or required resources that longstanding organizations such as the Consumers' Association do not have. The Consumers' Association is entirely dependent on modest membership fees, and its primary tasks and objectives are to test and conduct research on consumer goods and services for the benefit of its members, not to fund protracted litigation for the benefit of a relatively small number of consumers or non-members.[20] Moreover, Vie d'Or illustrates that there could also be a conflict of interest between the relevant regulator—in this instance, the Insurance Regulator—and the disgruntled consumers that makes the regulator less appropriate as a protector of the private collective interests of consumers.

Monopolies are seldom a good idea and no less so in the case of litigation. Allowing Special Purpose Vehicles to bring collective actions can contribute to a healthy system of checks and balances with respect to longstanding public or private interest organizations. However, authorizing Special Purpose Vehicles raises a whole new set of issues, as the Vie d'Or case study illustrates. The first issue relates to the incorporation of the Special Purpose Vehicle. Who should be entitled to establish such a vehicle and is that an important issue? The second issue relates to competing Special Purpose Vehicles. Should multiple competing Special Purpose Vehicles be permitted? In Vie d'Or there were competing organizations that initially distrusted the Foundation, but eventually the three organizations managed to work well together for the benefit of the

---

[20] Apart from the insufficient resources issue that such organizations face, internal conflict of interests could also prevent long-standing organizations from playing a key role in the protection of collective consumer interests. One of our respondents observed that the experience of the Consumers' Association in the Dexia case, another massive Dutch collective action and settlement matter, resulted in a policy decision to not take a lead role in subsequent massive consumer disputes that require a collective approach. In relation to Dexia, the Consumers' Association was heavily criticized by a large group of its members for following a settlement and litigation strategy that was advantageous for a certain group of consumers, but disadvantageous for another. The position of the Consumers' Association in that matter resulted in a large group of consumers cancelling their membership fees (Ozmis & Tzankova, 2012).

consumers. However, no commercial interests were involved. The question is what happens if commercial interests are involved, which nowadays is a realistic scenario as the Shell case study illustrates.

In Vie d'Or the Insurance Regulator, who later became one of the defendants, incorporated the Foundation and initially appointed its Board members. Although the Insurance Regulator tried to influence the course of events, for example by refusing to cooperate in the change of the articles of association needed to start the litigation, in the end that did not influence the conduct or strategy of the Foundation to the disadvantage of the consumers. The Board members demonstrated integrity, devotion and dedication to the consumers despite the fact that they were not chosen by the consumers, but had been appointed by the Insurance Regulator. The performance of the *pro bono* operating Board members seems to contradict agency theories from law and economics. But as one of the respondents in our interviews observed: how realistic is it nowadays to anticipate the same conduct and level of devotion? When the Vie d'Or scandal emerged, it was 'one of a kind'. The investigations and inquiries into the bankruptcy of Vie d'Or revealed that, although many factors contributed to the collapse of the company and the finger could be pointed at many different parties, it could not be pointed at the 11,000 consumers. However, they risked being left empty-handed. That was perceived as an injustice by the Board members and also explains the noble deed of the notary who risked his reputation to assist the policy holders. The fact that the collapse of Vie d'Or and the unfortunate fate of the policy holders were considered as exceptional at that time, in combination with the fact that initially the State was not willing to offer a helping hand, motivated the Board members to assist the policy holders and protect their interests as much as they could.

Nowadays, financial disasters are not viewed as exceptional, nor are the subsequent litigation they might cause or the Special Purpose Vehicles that are being created to facilitate the latter. The emergence of Special Purpose Vehicles seems to create a new market in 'legal services'. If one studies the composition of the Board of the foundations that were a party to the collective settlements declared binding since 2005 or were involved in collective actions, in the best case scenario one would discover that those Boards, like the Board of Vie d'Or, consist of experienced, neutral and distinguished individuals. Unlike in the case of Vie d'Or however, nowadays Board members are remunerated on an hourly basis. This is not necessarily a bad thing. To the contrary, this trend demonstrates the professionalization of the collective resolution process and may enhance the quality of representation by addressing the issue of finding and appointing sufficiently qualified and experienced individuals willing to serve as Board members of ad hoc organizations. However, this also raises issues of accountability, legitimacy and conflict of interests. In the Netherlands those issues have now been acknowledged and have led to self-regulatory initiatives, such as the establishment of a so-called Claim Code.[21] The Claim Code provides guidelines for the founders of ad hoc foundations that aim to avoid conflicts of interest and enhance the transparency and accountability of those organizations (De Jong, 2010; Lemstra & Okhuijsen, 2010; Van der Velden, 2011; Tzankova, 2012, 565). However, it is not mandatory to follow the guidelines of the Claim Code. A statutory provision has been introduced that requires Special Purpose Vehicles initiating a collective action to demonstrate that the group interests at stake are sufficiently guaranteed.[22] Neither the Claim Code nor the statutory provision solves the issue of competing Special Purpose Vehicles.

To us, the question with respect to the European collective redress model that grants standing to act to non-profit organizations, rather than representative individual plaintiffs or companies, is how effective that model can be. Depending entirely on previously established associations, such as consumer organizations, would significantly reduce effectiveness. At least in the Dutch case, as demonstrated by the Vie d'Or litigation, there also needs to be a provision for a special purpose organization such as the Special Purpose Foundation that led the action on behalf of Vie d'Or's policy holders. However, if Special Purpose Vehicles are part of the system of collective redress, issues such as conflict of interests, accountability and competing organizations need to be addressed. To date, in the Netherlands at least, the latter issue has not been sufficiently addressed (Ozmis & Tzankova, 2012).

Another question that remains unanswered is how legitimate the association-based European collective redress philosophy truly is. In the end individuals following an organizational or personal career agenda with no stake in the matter at hand make decisions that have a major impact on the lives of others, without necessarily being 'chosen' by the latter. Although different from the US private attorneys general model, the fact that it has a different label does not make agency problems disappear, nor does it eliminate questions about legitimacy and adequacy of representation. Those are the kind of questions that any legal system of collective

---

[21] Claimcode, Commissie Claimcode (2011), available at http://www.consumentenbond.nl/morello-bestanden/pdf-algemeen-2011/compljuniclaimcodecomm2011.pdf.

[22] Kamerstukken II 2011/2012, 33 126, nr. 2 (Parliamentary Proceedings House of Representatives).

redress needs to address, whether it builds on an association or a private attorney general model. Much has been written about the agency problems (Tzankova, 2012, 553–556) in a system of collective redress that builds on the private attorney general model, but we know very little about the agency problems that arise in a system built on an association model of collective redress. In light of such a lack of knowledge, the European endorsement of the role of associations and foundations or 'designated entities' as outlined in the European Recommendation on Collective Redress in class actions is remarkable, at the very least.

The Influence of Business and Political Culture on the Emergence and Resolution of a Mass Dispute

The Vie d'Or case study reveals how dynamics within a particular industry and political culture can play a significant role in the emergence of a mass dispute and in its ultimate resolution. As noted before, the Netherlands has a clubby business culture, the kind of business culture that could have prevented the collapse of Vie d'Or, as one of the respondents observed, if the life insurance community had realized that the bankruptcy of the company was not only an issue for the Insurance Regulator, but damaging for the whole life insurance industry. Ultimately, the case resulted in stricter regulation of the life insurance business, a result that the insurance community would have preferred to avoid. Whether its motivation was damage control, shame and guilt, a public relations trick or something else, the decision of the Association of Insurers to voluntarily contribute to a settlement fund created momentum for the settlement and generated the positive vibes needed for a final resolution. The Association of Insurers should get credit for the constructive role it played in that process. Ironically, in Vie d'Or the insurance industry would have preferred, retrospectively speaking, an early rather than a late collective settlement but that was not a realistic option because of the position and the legal strategy of the State and the Insurance Regulator.

The initial position of the State in relation to the resolution of the Vie d'Or matter is in contrast with the choices the State made subsequently in the aftermath of the global financial crisis. On a macro level Vie d'Or shows that the State's policy with regard to the protection of consumers against financial disasters is inconsistent. As one legal commentator observed in relation to the Supreme Court rulings in Vie d'Or:[23]

[23] CC van Dam, in his annotation on the Vie d'Or rulings of 13 October 2006, NJ 2008, 527–529 [translation by the author].

> In times of a financial crisis, banks are being nationalized and tax payers' money spent with not much hesitation to establish protective warranty schemes and to maintain the trust in the financial markets. In practice this means that money paid by individuals and companies who have nothing to do with the crisis or malpractices is being used to make up for the consequences of irresponsibly acting entrepreneurs, failing regulatory oversight or failing regulation.

It is ironic that, in the end, the same State that could be held responsible for failing regulatory oversight or regulation can easily create political pressure on parties to settle litigation that resulted from a failure of regulation, and introduce legislation that practically exonerates its liability in such situations. In doing so it plays a dual role. The Netherlands has a history of political interference with the resolution of mass disputes.[24] This is commonly accepted, even sometimes demanded by the public, and could be viewed as a feature of the Dutch mass claims dispute resolution culture. A question remains whether such State interference should be seen as part of the cultural identity and evaluated as something positive. We identify at least two issues for concern. The first one is that such a reliance on State interference is problematic when the State itself is involved as a co-defendant: the State would have, and has the power to present the final bill of a failure to regulate to third parties, as the Vie d'Or case illustrates. The second concern is that there are apparently no other sufficiently effective means in the Netherlands to achieve a fair resolution in case of a mass dispute, so the intervention of the State and the organization of a political lobby for ad hoc solutions are required. Initially this approach might work in a compact and relatively small or clubby society such as the Netherlands, where social actors know each other and problems are solved in a less antagonistic environment. Whether that would be the case for the long term in a globalized world, remains to be seen.

REFERENCES

Marieke van Hooijdonk & Peter Eijsvoogel, *Litigation in the Netherlands, Civil Procedure, Arbitration and Administrative Litigation* (Kluwer Law International 2009)

Bas de Jong, *Prejudiciële vragen aan de Hoge Raad bij massavorderingen*, Ondernemingsrecht 2009, 106

---

[24] For example, the Dexia and the DES case were also settled under political pressure.

Bas de Jong, *Een Claimcode voor stichtingen die collectieve acties initiëren?*, Ondernemingsrecht 2010, 46

Jurjen Lemstra & Rob Okhuijsen, *Consultatiedocument Zelfregulering claim-stichtingen*, Tijdschrift voor Financieel Recht 2010, 6

Denise Ozmis & Ianika Tzankova, *De evaluatie van de WCAM: de kernthema's uitgelicht*, Tijdschrift voor Civiele Rechtspleging 2012, 2

Ianika Tzankova, *Funding of Mass Disputes: Lessons from the Netherlands*, (2012) 8 Journal of Law, Economics & Policy 549

Ianika Tzankova, *Resolving Mass Claim Disputes in Europe: Lessons from the Netherlands*, IADC International Committee Newsletter, February 2013, Second Edition

Ianika Tzankova, Martijn van Maanen & Martijn Rijnhart, *A Dutch View on Discovery: Short and Sweet*, Defense Counsel Journal, July 2014, Vol. 81, no. 3

Brechje van der Velden, *Juridische afwikkeling van massaschade nu (bijna) perfect*, Tijdschrift voor de Ondernemingrechtpraktijk 2011, 6

PART III

Economics

7. Economic enablers

Camille Cameron, Jasminka Kalajdzic and Alon Klement

INTRODUCTION

Perhaps the most significant feature of any collective litigation regime is its economic viability: who pays, what does it cost, and does the aggregative mechanism adopted by the legislator provide the necessary incentives for pivotal actors to pursue litigation. Statutes tell us very little about the economics of class actions or the identity of the actors who economically enable class actions to exist. The case studies in this Part help fill that void.

This chapter provides a comprehensive framework within which the economics of class actions can be better appreciated. First, we review the case studies. Then, we consider them within an analytical discussion of alternative class action enablers and the institutional and economic conditions for their operation. As the case studies show, the selection of enablers will differ across jurisdictions. Finally, we examine the case studies from a broader legal and doctrinal perspective of the dominant enablers in each of the case study jurisdictions.

OVERVIEW OF THE CASE STUDIES

The case studies explored in this part illustrate the various mechanisms for funding class actions, and the impacts of these funding mechanisms on the initiation, conduct and resolution of class action litigation. As featured in these case studies, the identity of the enabling agent is a product of institutional and contextual factors. These factors go beyond the mere legislative framework that is apparent when reading each jurisdiction's class action law. The cases studies thus facilitate our understanding of the choices made in these jurisdictions among alternative class action enablers.

Chapter 8 discusses the *Royal Dutch/Shell Transport* litigation in the United States (US) and the Netherlands. In January 2004, Royal Dutch Shell disclosed that it had overstated its reserves in oil and gas by approximately 20 percent. The disclosure resulted in an immediate drop in the prices of shares on both the New York and London stock exchanges and subsequently further losses for investors worldwide. Multiple class actions were commenced in a US federal court by shareholders, resulting in large institutional investors and their allied law firms jockeying to be appointed lead plaintiff, in accordance with the US Private Securities Litigation Reform Act. By mid-June 2004, the securities class actions were consolidated and a lead plaintiff, the Pennsylvania Teachers' pension fund, was appointed to represent a putative worldwide class including investors on exchanges outside the US.

Foreign institutional investors were not pleased with this appointment. Among the largest of these investors were two Dutch pension funds, which retained a self-described American 'entrepreneurial' law firm in Delaware to represent their interests in the US court proceedings. A motion brought by the defendants challenging the jurisdiction of the US court over investors who purchased shares outside the US created uncertainty for the Dutch pension funds, whose ability to bring suits in their own country would soon become time-barred. This uncertainty, coupled with Royal Dutch Shell's position that the claims of foreign investors should not be resolved in a US Court, resulted in a unique dynamic. Both the defendants and the foreign institutional investors sought a forum outside of the US to resolve their claims—and they found it in Amsterdam under the umbrella of the Dutch Collective Mass Claims Settlement Act (WCAM). The settlement was negotiated by Royal Dutch Shell and the pension funds' American lawyers.

The Amsterdam Court of Appeals approved a binding opt-out settlement of all foreign investors' securities fraud claims totaling \$358 million, and payments of lawyers' fees to the Dutch funds' American lawyers of roughly \$50 million. The settlement was conditional on the US judge dismissing the non-US investors' claims. Carving out the foreign investors meant the size of the US class—and hence the settlement value and the American class counsel's fees—would be significantly reduced. Not surprisingly, class counsel objected to the elimination of the foreign class members from the American class action. Their objection was unsuccessful, and they ultimately reached a settlement on behalf of a much smaller class of US investors in the fall of 2008. As part of the deal, the American class action lawyers received fees for their contribution to the Dutch settlement on a scale commensurate with US rather than Dutch practice.

The next two case studies, described in Chapter 9, arose in Australia approximately ten years ago. The first, *Multiplex*, involved allegations that the company failed to disclose information about its construction projects, including a multi-million dollar stadium project in Wembley Park, in northwest London (UK). The case was initiated by Australian lawyers who, after having watched a television documentary recounting the delays and costs associated with Wembley Stadium, determined that there was a viable action on behalf of Multiplex investors who had suffered losses as a result of the company's non-disclosure. Finding a suitable and willing representative plaintiff, however, proved difficult. While institutional investors had about 95 percent of the claims against Multiplex, none were prepared to step forward. Chapter 9 explores the possible rationales for such reticence.

Though committed to prosecuting the action, the lawyers' firm was not willing to assume all of the financial risks of the litigation. In Australia, unlike Canada, Israel and the US, lawyers are not permitted to charge contingency fees, and the cost-shifting rule prevails; as a result, to pursue complex litigation, funding must be secured from another entity. In Australia, that entity is a commercial litigation funder, which invests in litigation in pursuit of profit. The lawyers in *Multiplex* ultimately found a Canadian commercial funder willing to step in. The presence of the funder led to significant satellite litigation that has shaped the class action landscape in Australia.

Multiplex settled before trial, as most Australian class actions do. However, the second Australian case study, *Aristocrat*, broke that mold. The case went to trial in 2007 and was settled after a four-week trial, before a judgment was issued. Commenced in late 2003, shareholders in *Aristocrat* alleged that they had suffered losses due to the defendant Aristocrat's misrepresentations about sales and projected profitability. The action arose when a commercial litigation funder became aware of problems at Aristocrat, conducted its own investigation, and brought its findings to a class action law firm. The funder was also instrumental in identifying a lead plaintiff and eventually signed funding agreements with approximately 600 individual shareholder plaintiffs. A further 2,300 claimants were unfunded and only came forward to participate in the settlement after it was announced.

Securities fraud and misrepresentations were also at the center of a long-running class action in Israel, which is the case study featured in Chapter 10. In 1995, an investor named Moshe Shemesh filed suit alleging fraud against the majority shareholders of Reichart Industries, several of its officers, directors, accountants and others. A class action was certified in 1996, and soon after, the plaintiff's lawyers negotiated settlements with all but two of the defendants—the company's accountant, who was one of the primary culprits in the fraud, and Dan Reichart, one of the majority shareholders against whom there was very little evidence of wrongdoing. Importantly, distribution of the settlement proceeds reached with the other defendants could not be effected until the case against Reichart and the accountant was either settled or concluded by way of final judgment.

The claims against the two remaining defendants went to trial in 2002, and the court found in favor of the plaintiffs. Dan Reichart appealed on both liability and damages grounds. The plaintiff cross-appealed on the calculation of damages and quantum of lawyer's fees. Shemesh's lead attorney, however, faced a dilemma: should he pursue the appeal and thereby delay distribution of settlement funds to the class, or abandon the claim against Reichart, who consistently refused to settle? The lawyer proceeded with the appeal, and only after three visits to the Supreme Court and strong pressure from the bench did the parties eventually settle the case, some 15 years after it had begun. The prolonged litigation and delayed settlement garnered little benefit for the class. Because class counsel chose to protract the litigation, the class and counsel both received the benefits of the litigation far later than would otherwise be the case.

The final chapter in this part of the book examines two Canadian cases. The first, *Atlas*, focuses on familiar allegations of securities misrepresentations and shareholder losses. The second, *Hislop*, concerns a claim of discrimination on the basis of sexual orientation against the federal government. Both cases illustrate the ways in which the entrepreneurial litigation model affects the initiation, conduct and resolution of class proceedings.

Atlas was initiated in February 2004 as a result of alleged misstatements in its 2001 and 2002 public offerings. Two of the three representative plaintiffs were recruited by the two plaintiffs' firms prosecuting the action. Indemnities against the risk of adverse costs were obtained from Ontario's Class Proceedings Fund because the plaintiffs were not willing to pursue the litigation without such insurance. Several interlocutory motions were argued in the case before it settled in 2008—a few months before the certification motion was to be heard. Although the judge approved the settlement, she agreed with objecting class members that the fee requested by the plaintiffs' firms was not reasonable. Her order discounting the fee was then appealed by class counsel to the Ontario Court of Appeal, which agreed with the lower court judge.

Hislop was a national class action on behalf of approximately 1,000 class members whose same-sex partners paid into the Canada Pension

Plan (CPP) and died between 1985 and 1998. The plaintiff, George Hislop, volunteered to represent the class when he heard that an LGBTQ advocacy group wanted to sue the federal government over discriminatory provisions in the CPP. Hislop did so despite the fact that he would be exposed to adverse costs if the class lost, and he would be precluded from settling his own personal claim if the government offered to do so.

Hislop was the first national class action to go to trial in Canada. The trial took place in 2003 and was a complete victory for the class. In Canada, as in the US, the trial judge awards fees to class counsel when the class prevails. At the time *Hislop* was decided, the Canadian practice was to award a base fee plus a multiple of that base, if the judge believed it was merited. The trial judge in *Hislop* awarded plaintiff's counsel their base fee plus a multiplier of 4.8, the highest multiplier awarded up to that time. Defendants were also ordered to pay adverse costs of almost $2 million. The federal government appealed the trial judge's rulings, and was partially successful at the Court of Appeal and then again at the Supreme Court of Canada. While the case was winding its way through the courts, the government refused to pay any of the CPP benefits that were indisputably owed to the class members, creating a dilemma of both an ethical and economic nature for the plaintiff's lawyers; should they offer to settle the appeals and obtain lower fees so that class members would immediately receive the benefits owed to them by the government, or should they hold on to maintain the potential for higher damages for the class, and greater fees for themselves, at the cost of delaying compensation for class members?

Another dilemma arose regarding the plaintiff's lawyers' fees. Just prior to the fee approval hearing, counsel for the government alerted the plaintiff's attorneys that section 65 of the CPP provided that pension benefits could not be assigned or charged for another purpose. While section 65 was enacted to protect pensioners from ordinary creditors, government lawyers in *Hislop* argued that it also applied to pensioners' lawyers, who sought to deduct their judicially-approved contingency fee from class members' pension arrears or from future payments. Because of the government's challenge, plaintiff's counsel was forced to pursue their clients (the class members) individually to collect their proportionate share of the contingency fee awarded by the judge. The precedent set by the fee issue made future litigation over government entitlements unappealing for class action lawyers, who rely on the certainty and efficiency of payment once a contingency fee is approved.

The case studies provide a rich and nuanced demonstration of the different avenues class actions may take, as initial facilitators later interact with other enablers in an effort to maintain control of the litigation. Plaintiffs, attorneys and funders, both local and foreign, may be involved in prosecuting a class action, and their interaction may be collaborative at times, and competitive at others.

ECONOMIC ENABLERS

As the case studies demonstrate, class actions may be initiated and controlled by various actors—class members (local and foreign), entrepreneurial attorneys, and funders (public and private). We next explore the distinctive characteristics of each of these actors, which allow them to initiate and control class action litigation.

Representative Plaintiffs

Many class actions involve a large number of claims of relatively modest value. If pursued individually, each claim would have a negative expected value, because the cost of litigation would far outweigh the monetary value of the claim. The rational decision in such circumstances is not to litigate. Aggregating claims via a class action or other collective procedure changes the calculus for the group, as the costs and risks of litigation are spread over the group members. However, each class member has a minimal stake in the aggregate litigation, and therefore none has a sufficient incentive to pursue it. This incentive problem is further exacerbated by collective action issues. Even when class members have a sufficient stake in the class action—for example, because their claims have greater value—they would rather take a *free ride* on the efforts and investments of other class members, thus gaining the same benefit without incurring the cost and risk involved in such litigation. In addition to these economic realities, class members are often ignorant of their cause of action, and even if they suspect that they have a valuable claim, they lack the liquidity to pursue it in court.

Yet, initiating the class action may require information which is held by class members only. Even if they do not fathom its legal implications, class members may nevertheless have some information indicating that their interests may have been adversely affected by an act or omission of a potential defendant. Class members may hold the best, and often only, information about their injuries from tortious acts. Initiating a class action in such cases requires class members to come forward and demonstrate their injury. The named plaintiff would then serve the same purpose as the plaintiff in an individual lawsuit. He or she is the representative, or typical, example for courts to grapple with when adjudicating a class action.

The class representative may also help the court in monitoring the class attorney and guaranteeing that he or she fulfills his or her duties to the class. This function requires, though, that the class representative will not only have similar incentives to those of the represented class, but will also have sufficient motivation to effectively monitor the attorney. Unfortunately, these two requirements often conflict. When each class member has small stakes in the litigation, any one of them would have similar interests to those of all the others, yet none may have sufficient resources and incentives to monitor the class attorney.

Depending on their views about which of these functions is most significant, legal regimes have taken alternative approaches to achieve meaningful representation of the class by its representative.

One such approach is to look for class members whose stakes are sufficiently high to justify their investment in initiating the class action and monitoring it. This is the approach mandated by the US Private Securities Litigation Reform Act, which creates a rebuttable presumption that the shareholder with the largest financial stake in the litigation serve as class representative. This Act governed the appointment of the class representative ('lead plaintiff') in the Royal Dutch Shell litigation. In the absence of such legislation in Australia, it has been difficult to convince institutional investors to assume the role of lead plaintiff. In *Multiplex*, institutional investors had most of the claims against the defendant, but none were willing to be the lead plaintiff. Among the possible explanations offered by our interviewees for this reticence were that the business community is small and there is a preference 'to settle things at the club', that institutional investors want to avoid discovery and the adverse costs risk, and that they were not yet familiar with the role of commercial funders in litigation and, in particular, the funders' assumption of the risk of an adverse costs order.

Another approach is to forgo the requirement that the class representative should be a member of the plaintiff class, and instead to require that representation be provided by non-profit organizations, consumer/investor associations or special purpose foundations who represent similar interests outside the class action context. This approach has been favored by civil law jurisdictions that have adopted class action procedures and was the approach that led to the appointment of a special purpose foundation to represent non-US investors in the Royal Dutch Shell settlement proceedings in Amsterdam.

Finally, some commentators have proposed forgoing class representation altogether, preferring scrutiny of the class attorney's adequacy of representation and focusing attention on certification requirements that pertain to the substantive and procedural attributes of the case and the qualifications of the class attorney.

Entrepreneurial Lawyers

More than 80 years ago, Judge Jerome Frank of the US 2nd Circuit coined the term 'Private Attorney General' to describe the statutory authorization of a non-official person to pursue public proceedings to vindicate the public's interest.[1] Since then, the term has often been used to describe the role of private attorneys who initiate and litigate class actions. Indeed, the class action attorney is pursuing public goals, most notably law enforcement and deterrence, by using private litigation. Yet, the class attorney is a mix of public and private, not only in the type of litigation he or she pursues but also in his or her motivation for pursuing it. A distinctive feature of the class action procedure is its potential for enlisting the attorney's private economic incentives, to the benefit of the represented class and the public at large. Hence, the class attorney is not only described as a 'Private Attorney General', but also as a 'Bounty Hunter' and an 'Entrepreneur'.

Aggregation is essential for rendering class members' claims *marketable* for lawyers. The expected return on the lawyer's investment of time and money must exceed his or her opportunity costs. Since complex litigation might entail high fixed costs, aggregation of claims is necessary to provide economies of scale. At the same time, lawyers are potentially good litigation funders. Although they may be required to make substantial monetary investments in payouts for investigatory work, complex pretrial procedures, and expert reports and testimony, their main investment is often their time and effort. This relaxes their liquidity constraints, compared to other litigation enablers. They have the necessary expertise and experience to evaluate the risk and value of a lawsuit, and they can diversify their investments among different class actions. Thus, the combination of scale economics, with a bounty or contingent fee mechanism, renders attorneys prominent and effective candidates for pursuing public goals, through the class action, for private gain.

---

1 *Associated Industries of New York State, Inc. v. Ickes*, 134 F. 2d. 694, 704 (2d Cir. 1943).

Indeed, some of the cases studied in this part demonstrate the prominent role played by attorneys in initiating class actions and litigating them. They feature the complexities that may arise due to interrelations between the class and the attorney (*Hislop*), among attorneys competing for control of the class (*Royal Dutch Shell/Transport*) or sharing carriage of the action (*Atlas*), and between attorneys and private funders (*Multiplex*). Whether attorneys fully control the class action or not, their enabling function in each of the case studies cannot be overstated.

This framework, however, is subject to two significant critiques. One, the *external* critique, is based on the doctrinal, constitutional and often cultural aversion in various legal systems to lawyer-initiated litigation. The other, the *internal* critique, is based on the economic theory of *agency*, which recognizes the adverse implications created by the divergence between the class attorney's private interests and the interest of the class and the public at large. In fact, both critiques are driven by the absence of a significant plaintiff-client who may initiate the lawsuit and monitor its progress.

The external critique is demonstrated by the doctrines of barratry, maintenance and champerty. These doctrines prohibit the lawyer from initiating a lawsuit or financing it for his or her client. The practice of entrepreneurial lawyering in class actions stands in stark conflict with these doctrines. It therefore comes as no surprise that many legal systems do not allow lawyer-initiated class actions, and even when allowing them, proscribe the use of contingency fees for class attorneys, or prohibit lawyers from fronting litigation expenses for the class. Objections in such legal systems to attorney-driven litigation seem to be rooted in a strong resistance to the common perception of hyper-litigious Americans. Although empirical data do not support this perception, it has taken root in many parts of the world, where the 'US-style' class action is considered to be emblematic of the dangers of incentivizing lawyers to litigate. As a formal matter, American lawyers cannot initiate class actions themselves, but they may search for candidate class representatives for potential class litigation. As explained further below, in American class actions, judges award attorney fees when the class prevails, which by law may reflect the risk the class counsel took on to represent the class.

The internal critique maintains that attorneys do not fully realize the interests of class members—their clients—because these client interests are misaligned with the attorneys' own private interests. This divergence is created by the nature of entrepreneurial attorney litigation, in which the attorney bears the *full* costs and risks of litigation, yet enjoys only *part* of the stakes. It is often suggested that this divergence results in the class attorney's inclination to invest too little in litigating the case, and to settle for too little and too early, when these decisions are evaluated from the represented class' perspective (Hensler et al., 2000, 79). However, as the Israeli case study of *Shemesh* demonstrates, agency does not always play out the way economic models predict. In a case that was completely controlled by the lead attorney, that attorney decided to pursue litigation for an additional ten years after most defendants had settled. This suggests that he understood his duties toward the represented class as requiring him to litigate the case vigorously and decline settlement offers he deemed inappropriate.

Whereas agency problems are thought to be mitigated in individual litigation by client monitoring and by attorney bonding through market reputation, these mechanisms are often absent in attorney-initiated class actions (Macey & Miller, 1991, 19–22) where the client, whether it be the class as a whole or the class representative individually, does not select the attorney and rarely has a sufficient stake to justify monitoring her performance. It is this lack of a significant stake in the litigation that perhaps explains why the representatives in *Atlas* would have agreed to increase their attorneys' contingency fee retroactively, on the eve of the settlement approval hearing.[2]

Thus, although attorneys enjoy inherent advantages in funding and litigating class actions, many legal systems are reluctant to entrust the public cause to their private hands. Legal regimes diverge in the incentives they allow class attorneys, mainly whether they allow for their fees to be contingent upon litigation success, and in the selection and monitoring mechanisms they employ to control against attorneys' agency problems.

Commercial Funders

A striking feature of class action litigation in recent years has been the increasing presence of commercial litigation funders as class action

---

[2] In Canada, representative plaintiffs sign retainer agreements with class counsel at the outset of the litigation, setting out the proposed contingency fee (as a percentage of the class' recovery, a base fee and multiplier, or some combination of both). This agreement is taken into consideration by the judge who ultimately sets the fee when and if the case is successfully concluded. In *Atlas*, the representative plaintiffs originally signed fee agreements in 2004 providing for a 25 percent contingency fee; four years later, they agreed to a 30 percent fee or a base fee times a multiplier of 4, whichever was greater.

enablers. Companies that are in the business of assuming the substantial financial risks of a class action in exchange for a share of any damages awarded are now a permanent feature of the class action landscape in Australia, Canada and increasingly Europe, although less so in the US and Israel.[3] Two Australian authors have reported the view of an experienced litigation lawyer that 'the capacity for plaintiffs to bring an equality of arms to large scale litigation through [commercial litigation funding is] one of the most significant changes in the litigation landscape' in more than 30 years (Watson & Donelly, 2014, 27).

Whether and to what extent there are commercially funded class actions in any jurisdiction will depend on that jurisdiction's costs and fees rules and practices. Costs shifting and the related risk of an adverse costs order, prohibitions on lawyers' contingency fees, the lack of any 'after the event' insurance, and the unavailability of legal aid or any public fund to support class action litigation are all factors that create a gap in class action financing. In Australia, for example, all of these factors are present, which is why entrepreneurial commercial funders now occupy a central place in class action litigation. Their role has also been facilitated by positive court decisions that have endorsed commercial funding of class actions[4] and by entrepreneurial lawyers who have been willing to change their litigation business models. In the US, in contrast, the American fee rule (each side bears its own costs), legal acceptance of contingency fee agreements in individual litigation and judicial fee awards that recognize risk in class actions mean that there has been far less demand for third-party funding of litigation. Large plaintiff law firms with healthy credit lines dominate the class action landscape.

This is not to suggest that the entry of commercial litigation funders into class action litigation has been smooth. In Australia, the country that has led the way in private commercial funding of class actions, the role of commercial funders has been hotly contested, from:

> challenges on the basis of maintenance, champerty and abuse of process, to the permissibility of 'closed classes' ... , to the question whether various existing financial regulations apply to litigation funding arrangements (Cameron & Kalajdzic, 2014, 5).

---

[3] *See* Cameron & Kalajdzic, 2014, and Kalajdzic, Cashman & Longmoore, 2013, for an analysis of the role of commercial litigation funders in class actions in these three jurisdictions.

[4] *Campbell's Cash and Carry Pty Ltd v. Fostif Pty Ltd* [2006] HCA 41 ('*Fostif, HC*'); *Fostif Pty Ltd v. Campbell's Cash and Carry Pty Ltd* (2005) NSWCA 83; *Multiplex Funds Management Limited Pty Ltd v. P. Dawson Nominees Pty Ltd* [2007] FCAFC 2000.

In the US, common law strictures against maintenance and champerty have been abandoned by some states but not all, and yet third-party funding of class actions is still uncommon.

While some of the central questions about commercial funding of class actions are similar across jurisdictions, the answers vary just as the legal cultures and the legal architectures and institutions of those jurisdictions vary. Australia and Canada have, for example, both grappled with the question of the degree of control that commercial funders should be allowed to have in the litigation they are funding, but their answers differ. In *Fostif*, the High Court of Australia endorsed a relatively broad degree of funder control.[5] In contrast:

> [l]ong-standing principles related to the independence of counsel have informed Canadian courts' opposition to [commercial funding] contracts that would provide the funder with control over the litigation (Kalajdzic, Cashman & Longmoore, 2013, 145).

Another challenge common to all jurisdictions in which commercial funders are operating is how best to regulate the commercial funding industry. A dominant theme in many discussions about regulation is concern about consumer protection.[6] In Australia, the courts were of necessity the first regulators, because the industry was new and existing financial and securities regulations had not been drafted with commercial litigation funding arrangements in mind. This judicial regulatory role is evident in *Multiplex*; much of the interlocutory litigation in that case arose because of the presence of a commercial funder. The courts were called on to determine whether the funding arrangement was a 'managed investment scheme' under corporate legislation and whether requiring class members to sign an agreement with the funder was inconsistent with the opt-out nature of Australia's class action regime. What has evolved in Australia is a combination of regulatory sites—judicial, legislative and self-regulation by funders. All of the regulation in Canada,

---

[5] *Fostif, HC*, n. 23.

[6] In the Australian class action context, defendants have been the prime agents of court challenges to the participation of litigation funders. While consumer protection has been one of the arguments advanced, it is safe to assume that the capacity of commercial funding to shift the traditional balance of power in litigation is also a key reason for most of the challenges that have been advanced by defendants.

however, is still occurring by way of judicial scrutiny.[7] In the US, regulation of third-party funding is still under debate.

The 'access to justice' value of commercial litigation funding is another frequently debated topic.[8] The risks assumed by commercial funders, especially in cost-shifting jurisdictions, require them to do a robust risk analysis. They are interested in cases with a high prospect of success and significant money damages. This excludes much public interest litigation. Among those cases that funders are willing to take on, however, there will be individual and institutional claimants who have suffered financial loss as the result of the defendant's misconduct. The availability of commercial funding enables their meritorious claims to be litigated. It may be limited access, but it is access.

Public Funders

In addition to commercial firms, the state may also facilitate class action funding by creating public funding entities, such as in two provinces of Canada, as well as in Israel.[9] In many respects, commercial and public funding models are similar: both seek to invest in class actions that have a high probability of success, for a return on investment based on the monies recouped in the action. They both provide indemnities against adverse cost awards, and both purport to increase access to justice for representative plaintiffs and their lawyers, in situations where counsel are not willing to serve on a purely contingent basis with respect to both time and disbursements.

There are, however, important differences. While commercial financiers invest with a view to making a profit that can be distributed to their investors, public funders seek to make a return that can then be used to finance other cases. In selecting cases to fund, profit maximization is not the only consideration for public funders; rather, they are statutorily required to consider the public interest when assessing applications for

---

[7] *See* Kalajdzic, Cashman & Longmoore, 2013, 141–145, for a discussion of the regulation of commercial litigation funding in Australia, Canada and the United States.

[8] For a fuller discussion of this issue, *see* Watson & Donelly, 2014; Cameron & Kalajdzic, 2014; Kalajdzic, Cashman & Longmore, 2013.

[9] *Quebec*: le Fonds d'aide aux recours collectifs, available at http://www.farc.justice.gouv.qc.ca/. *Ontario*: Class Proceedings Fund, available at http://www.lawfoundation.on.ca/class-proceedings-fund/. *Israel*: The Class Action Fund, available at http://index.justice.gov.il/Units/YeutzVehakika/TovanotYitzugiyot/Pages/TovanotYitzugiyot.aspx

funding. While both public and private funders seek to be kept informed of developments in the funded action, public funders have no input in the cases; conversely, where judicially permitted, commercial funders may seek some control of the litigation strategy. Commercial funding firms have the flexibility that contractual relationships provide, so that they can, for instance, limit their exposure to adverse costs[10] or provide for a cap or sliding scale on their percentage return. Public funders, on the other hand, are constrained by their enabling statutes and regulations; in the case of Ontario's fund, for example, exposure to costs is limitless, and the ten percent levy on successful actions is fixed.[11]

Although budgets can be constrained in both commercial and public funding models, commercial funders' budgets may be more influenced by investors' confidence in the perceived viability of the action, while public funders have the more rigid limitations of government budgets. This is more true in Israel than it is in Canada, where the self-funded model provides opportunities for growth that do not depend on the largesse of government. Both the Quebec and Ontario funds are self-perpetuating in that they impose a levy on successful cases. The Quebec government also guarantees the liquidity of that province's fund.[12] Ontario's fund was created in 1993, at the same time that class proceedings legislation was enacted, with seed money of $500,000. Since then, it has grown exponentially, with no additional government funding, to a balance of over $19 million at the end of 2014.

Although there is no similar public funding for class actions in the US, where the publicly-funded Legal Service Corporation was prohibited from funding class actions by a 1999 statute, the leading US corporate law firms assist the prosecution of public interest class actions by providing legal services *pro bono*. Private lawyers frequently work on such cases in tandem with lawyers from non-governmental organizations that receive financial support from law firms and individual lawyers. In effect, *pro bono* legal services operate as a quasi-public source of funding. While not subject to public regulation, *pro bono* lawyering is subject to private law firm decision-making, which is responsive both to the firms' financial circumstances and to concerns about the effects of specific legal engagements on their market reputation. Corporate law

---

[10] *See* for example *Baynes v. Kinross* 2013 ONSC 4974, where the commercial litigation funder limited its exposure to costs to $1 million in respect of the certification motion and $5 million thereafter up to the conclusion of the common issues trial.

[11] Class Proceedings, O Reg 771/92, s. 8(4)(c).

[12] Act respecting Class Actions, s. 44.1.

firms are unlikely to provide *pro bono* support for litigation against corporate defendants, and plaintiff firms may be unable to assume further financial risks given the nature of their practices.

INSTITUTIONAL VARIABLES THAT AFFECT THE SELECTION OF THE ENABLING AGENT

Representative plaintiffs, entrepreneurial lawyers, and private and public funders are all potential class action enablers. Each may initiate the class action and then control (to varying degrees) its litigation. Comparisons among different legal regimes show that the dominant class enabler in each is different. Before examining who the dominant enabler is in four jurisdictions where the cases presented in this Part arose, we briefly review two economic institutional factors that may influence who the enabler may be in each specific legal regime—attorney contingency fees and cost-shifting rules.

Attorney Contingency Fees

Monetary class actions create a common fund, whose benefits extend to the whole class.[13] The common fund is created either by a court decision when the class prevails, or by a settlement. The class attorney's fee may then be paid out of this common fund, thus allocating the proceeds from the lawsuit between the class and the attorney. Since the class is dispersed and most class members do not actively approve the lawsuit, and often are not even aware of it, the attorney may not collect a fee higher than the common fund. Hence, the attorney's fee must be contingent on winning the class action, or on settlement. A non-contingent fee, which is paid independent of the suit's outcome, is not feasible in opt-out class actions.

The attorney's contingent fee may be set as a percentage of the common fund, in which case it is *output* based, and inherently contingent upon winning the case or settling it. Alternatively, the attorney's fee may be based on the hours spent by the attorney, in which case it is *input* based. In the US, when this latter fee structure is used, it is called a *lodestar* fee.[14]

---

[13] We discuss below the absence in Australia of a 'common fund' approach as that term is understood in Canada, the Unites States and Israel.

[14] Klement & Neeman, 2004, 109; Conte, 2014, § 2:3, 2:6; Hirsch & Sheehey, 2005, 72–75.

Two implications follow. The first is immediate: any legal regime that bans contingent attorney fees, whatever form such a fee may take, is effectively ruling out the possibility of attorneys as class enablers.[15] To facilitate class actions, such a regime must therefore allow for public or private class action funding that pays the attorney's non-contingent fee.

The second implication is more nuanced. Allowing the attorney fee to be contingent is not sufficient to induce lawyers to initiate and litigate class actions. To do so, the fee must be larger than the lawyer's reservation (or alternative) fee for her time investment, assuming such investment is reasonable given the merits of the case. Since the fee is contingent upon winning the case or settling it, there is always some risk (and sometimes a significant risk) that the defendant will prevail and the attorney will earn no fee. The contingent fee must therefore compensate the lawyer for this risk. To demonstrate this point, suppose that the attorney's reservation fee is 100, and the risk of not earning any fee in the class action is 0.5. The attorney must be paid 200 in case of settlement or winning. Only then would his expected (mean) fee be 100 (0.5x200). If the attorney is paid a lower fee, then he would be better off not litigating the class action. Hence, to facilitate entrepreneurial lawyering in class actions, the fee paid must be higher than the actual value of the attorney's time input. This is often the case when the fee is set as a percentage of the common fund. When the fee is hourly based, a multiplier or risk premium must therefore be applied.

More generally, the contingent fee must compensate the attorney for her costs of investigating the class action and litigating it, and for the risk of losing it. Any regulation of the attorney's compensation would limit the types of class actions filed, and the quality of attorneys filing it. The lower the maximum fee, the more difficult it would be for attorneys to pursue complex cases, and the less inclined would the best attorneys—who have the highest reservation fee—be to file and litigate class actions.

Cost-shifting

The cost barrier to litigation in some parts of the world, including jurisdictions discussed in this Part of the book, has two components: the cost of one's own legal services, and the potential cost of paying the opposing parties' fees if one is unsuccessful in the litigation. Cost-shifting has a long history outside the US and serves two fundamental

---

[15] A limited exception is the early role of Australian class action lawyers, which we discuss below.

purposes: deter wasteful steps in litigation and unmeritorious lawsuits, and at least partially compensate the successful party for costs incurred.

Not surprisingly, the impact of the compensation and deterrence functions of cost-shifting is amplified in mass litigation. As the cost of prosecuting or defending large, complex claims mounts, so, too, do the disincentives in initiating them or risking judgment at trial. Where the representative plaintiff and not the class is liable for adverse costs (as is the case in many of the case study jurisdictions), the individual plaintiff's exposure to the risk of paying a successful defendant's costs creates a significant barrier to justice. After all, such costs, which may run into the hundreds of thousands of dollars, will inevitably dwarf any award the individual plaintiff might hope to recover.[16] No rational person would expose himself or herself to such risk. As one Ontario judge put it, the 'grim reality is that no person in their right mind would accept the role of representative plaintiff if he or she were at risk of losing everything they own'.[17]

To overcome this barrier to justice and ensure the availability of representative plaintiffs, systemic responses have evolved. One is the practice among some Canadian plaintiff lawyers to indemnify their clients against adverse costs. The willingness of lawyers to 'self-insure' depends upon their confidence in the case, business arrangements at their firm and the general state of the economy. However, in some jurisdictions (for example, Israel) such indemnification is considered illegal. A second reaction to risks posed by cost-shifting is the creation of funding mechanisms, either of a public or a commercial nature, from which plaintiffs obtain an indemnification against costs. Although commercial litigation funders operate even in jurisdictions where parties are not subject to cost-shifting, the type and cost of funding arrangements can vary substantially as a result of the risk of adverse costs. Finally, a third response to this problem is to increase the incentive payment to class representatives, to afford them sufficient compensation for their risks, in case they win or settle the litigation. This is the response taken by the Israeli law. In contrast, in Canada and the US, incentive payments to class representatives are limited out of fear that more generous payments would create a conflict between the representative and other class members.

---

[16] In Ontario, the average costs award to a successful defendant falls in the range of $300,000: *Dugal v. Manulife Financial Corp.*, 2013 ONSC 6354 at para. 5.

[17] *Dugal v. Manulife Financial Corporation*, 2011 ONSC 1785 at para. 28.

There is considerable debate about the utility of maintaining the cost-shifting rule in class action litigation. The need for litigation deterrence in mass litigation can sometimes be overstated, particularly in jurisdictions where plaintiffs' lawyers operate on a contingency fee or other speculative basis. After all, even without the possibility of paying the successful party's legal costs, the risk of prosecuting lengthy litigation without any fee recovery can be sufficient to dissuade lawyers from taking on unmeritorious cases. Nevertheless, the specter of frivolous class actions, launched simply to blackmail defendants, has persuaded some governments to retain cost-shifting rules for class actions.[18]

The compensation function of adverse costs awards may be more important in class actions than in other litigation, despite the fact that it is usually the attorney, not the successful litigant, who is being compensated. The historic role of compensation or indemnification of a successful party is largely inapplicable in class actions, where the plaintiff has not paid or been billed by her lawyer. The lawyer, however, has incurred disbursements and committed significant resources to representing the class. It is the lawyer, therefore, who seeks compensation from the unsuccessful defendant; the class members' access to justice is indirectly facilitated by way of a costs order to the lawyer.[19] In addition to making the lawyer funding the plaintiff's lawsuit whole, costs awards paid as a result of interlocutory steps in the proceeding can become an important source of ongoing funding for the law firm, paying experts and other disbursements throughout the case.

Allowing contingency fees in class actions all but guarantees that entrepreneurial lawyers will be the primary enablers of class actions. Yet, the existence of cost-shifting rules complicates this dynamic. If representative plaintiffs bear the risk of cost-shifting, they must also be compensated for this risk, which increases the overall burden on the class; alternatively, if lawyers bear these costs then they must either become even more risk-tolerant, obtain a higher fee proportionate to the risk assumed, or obtain third party indemnities. Failure to secure any of these solutions would expose representative plaintiffs to the unacceptable

---

[18] There are references to this line of thinking in the debates leading up to Ontario's enactment of its class proceeding statute: Hansards, 12 June 1990 at 1739 (C. Harnick).

[19] The 'fiction' of the plaintiff paying or receiving costs was exposed by Justice Paul Perell in a lengthy decision on costs: *McCracken v. Canadian National Railway Company*, 2010 ONSC 6026, reversed on other grounds 2012 ONCA 445.

risk of bankruptcy if the lawsuit proves unsuccessful, without a countervailing benefit, and might therefore spell the demise of the class action regime as a whole. At a minimum, cost-shifting complicates the search for a suitable representative plaintiff; in *Atlas*, the action was delayed as a result of the difficulties faced by counsel in locating a suitable investor who was willing to be named as a representative, and only then after an indemnity was obtained for him, at his insistence, from Ontario's Class Proceedings Fund. In *Multiplex*, efforts to identify a suitable institutional investor as a lead plaintiff failed, although those investors had about 95 percent of the claims against Multiplex. One of the reasons for their reticence was the fear of an adverse costs order. In contrast, in the US, in the absence of cost-shifting, pension funds (and their lawyers) competed avidly to be appointed lead plaintiff in the *Royal Dutch Shell/Transport* class action.

MAPPING THE FRAMEWORK

United States

The modern American class action was adopted in 1966. One result of the 1966 Rule was to facilitate class actions for money damages (Hensler et al., 2000). All but one state in the US have adopted class action rules modeled on the federal rule.

Private civil litigation in the US is facilitated by the 'American fee rule' and by the availability of contingency fees. Unlike in most other jurisdictions, in most US litigation each side must bear its own costs, win or lose. With few exceptions, the same fee rules prevail in class actions.

The prevalence of contingency fee representation has contributed to the development of a vibrant risk-tolerant plaintiff bar. Successful plaintiff law firms maintain an inventory of cases such that fees from successfully concluded cases provide up-front funding for new cases. The most successful firms have substantial lines of credit from commercial banks to smooth out cash flow. Class counsel are not permitted to enter into contingency fee agreements with class representatives, but the contingency fee business model works equally well for class actions, in which judges award fees for successful representation. Whether applying the percentage of fund approach or the lodestar approach (see below), the result is that plaintiff counsel are rewarded in proportion to the amount they secure for the class, and all class members contribute proportionately to paying the attorneys' fees.

Representative Plaintiffs: As a result of the American fee rule neither the representative plaintiff nor other class member bears any risk of adverse costs. As a result of equitable fund doctrine, if the class prevails, the representative's share of attorney fees and expenses will be the same as any other similarly situated class member. Perhaps as a result, a class member's financial wherewithal has little consequence for being approved by the judge as a class representative. In certifying a class, the judge must find that a proposed representative is typical of other class members and will provide adequate representation. But adequacy of representation has long been interpreted as applying to class counsel's ability to effectively represent the interests of the class, including having resources to prosecute the action.

Because they bear no adverse cost risk nor disproportionate responsibility for class counsel fees, class members have little or no financial disincentive for serving as class representative—but also little incentive for monitoring the class attorney. Monitoring might be incentivized if class representatives received special payment for their services (Nagareda, 2006), but because of fear that incentive payments might create conflicts of interest between the class representative and other class members, they are strictly limited in class actions generally (Eisenberg & Miller, 2006) and forbidden altogether in securities class actions.

Somewhat anomalously, under the Private Securities Litigation Reform Act, the financial stakes in the litigation of candidates for class representative is the primary basis for their being selected as lead plaintiffs by the trial judge. The rationale is that the class member with the greatest financial interest in the litigation will have the greatest incentive to monitor the class attorney. In effect, the lead plaintiff provision substitutes for paying meaningful incentive payments to the class representative.

Class Attorneys: The growth of the plaintiff bar that contingency fee representation enabled has led in turn to the development of plaintiff firms that specialize in mass and class action litigation. The Multi-District Litigation (MDL) procedure that consolidates claims arising out of a common set of facts and law and assigns them to a single judge created the possibility that a judge would find herself dealing with dozens or more attorneys all representing plaintiffs in the same litigation at the same point in time. To rationalize this process, MDL judges began appointing lead plaintiff counsel and Plaintiff Steering Committees (PSCs) to guide the litigation. To assure quality and efficiency of representation, judges tended to appoint the same national and regional law firms to serve on these committees. These positions are widely sought after as they offer an opportunity to shape the litigation, including negotiating group-wide settlements. Often lead counsel and PSC members receive special fees on top of whatever contingency fees they may have negotiated with their clients. As judges became comfortable with the idea of appointing lead counsel in mass non-class actions it seemed reasonable for them to also appoint class counsel. Now the judge's responsibility to appoint class counsel is enshrined in the class action rule. Lawyers compete vigorously for class counsel appointment, because whatever firm is appointed will, if successful, receive the fee award. A large class action will require at least several million dollars to prosecute and complex cases may cost more. The class counsel firm must lay out all these funds without any promise that they will be compensated in the end.

Third-Party Funders: As commercial funding has entered the US market, it has largely avoided class action litigation (Hensler, 2014). This may be in part a strategy calculated to disarm corporations (the usual class action defendants) that offer potentially attractive targets for funding commercial litigation. It may also reflect uncertainty on the part of these relatively new market actors about how to assess class action litigation risk in the US. The recent line of US Supreme Court decisions making it more difficult to obtain class certification may also diminish third-party funders' appetite for investing in class actions. Notwithstanding this general pattern, there are examples of complex high-value class actions, chiefly in the antitrust domain, that have attracted outside investment. And some law firms have provided funding to lead counsel firms in mass and class actions in return for a share of eventual fee awards (Goral, 2016).

There is no public institutional funding for class actions in the US, but leading corporate law firms have contributed substantial time pro bono to prosecuting public interest litigation and also have contributed to non-governmental organizations that often lead such litigation.

Canada

Class actions in Canada have existed in Quebec since 1979 and in English-speaking Canada since 1993. All but one province and territory now have a class action statute. All statutes require the court appointment of a representative plaintiff in whose name the lawsuit is filed by counsel. All jurisdictions allow lawyers to act on a contingency fee basis, with the ultimate fee to be approved by a judge. Roughly half of the statutes maintain the cost-shifting rule in class action litigation, with the representative plaintiff (not the class) liable for such costs.[20] The other provinces specifically provide that the usual two-way cost rule is suspended in class actions.[21] In terms of opting in and out, all statutes operate on an opt-out basis, at least for their own residents, with some also permitting out-of-province residents to be included in the class on the same basis.

Given these institutional variables, three types of enablers facilitate class action litigation in Canada: representative plaintiffs, class attorneys and public funders.

Representative Plaintiffs: Representative plaintiffs are the least influential economic enablers in Canadian class actions. Individual plaintiffs do not fund class actions, they are not responsible for paying their own lawyers' fees, and they are almost always indemnified against the risk of adverse costs. There is some empirical and anecdotal evidence that most class actions are initiated by class counsel, not class members.[22] The two Canadian case studies discussed in this book were both initiated by the lawyers, not the representative plaintiffs.

Despite their lack of economic influence, representative plaintiffs are a necessary feature of the Canadian class action regime. Indeed, in both *Atlas* and *Hislop*, much effort was expended to identify and persuade suitable individuals to represent the class. The representatives did so without the guarantee of any benefit over and above what they would receive as passive class members. But for their willingness to stand as representatives, the class actions could not have been commenced. Still, for the reasons explored above, there is a serious debate about the extent to which representative plaintiffs actually exercise any influence over the litigation or effectively monitor the conduct of the class attorneys. Some judges have expressed the view that representative plaintiffs are usually

---

[20] Ontario, Alberta, New Brunswick and Nova Scotia apply their normal 'loser pays' rules with respect to costs in class actions. *See* Winkler et al., 2014, 368.

[21] British Columbia, Manitoba, Newfoundland, Saskatchewan and the Federal Court have modified no-way costs rules for class actions. Winkler et al., 2014, 366.

[22] A 2009 survey of 13 leading class action firms in Canada revealed that less than 25 percent of the reported 332 cases were initiated by clients. Kalajdzic, 2009, 20.

figureheads.[23] The courts' endorsement of client recruitment, counsel indemnification of the client, and judicial insistence that the client in a class action is not just the representative plaintiff but the class itself, all serve to mitigate whatever authority the individual representative theoretically possesses by virtue of the statutory requirement.

Class Attorneys: The availability of contingency fees, sometimes at multiples of the lawyers' usual hourly rates, has created a decidedly entrepreneurial class action bar. Fees in the millions of dollars are routinely awarded.[24] While some lawyers choose to pursue a particular class action for ideological reasons, most decide to initiate a suit because of the likelihood of success coupled with the potential size of the damage award.[25] The bigger the damage award or settlement, the bigger the contingent fee. The economic incentive created by contingency fees is what drives class actions in Canada. Just what constitutes an adequate incentive, however, is the subject of some debate. In *Atlas*, the case management judge and then the Ontario Court of Appeal agreed that a $6.3 million fee in a $40 million settlement (or 2.6 times the lawyers' usual hourly rates) was an adequate incentive.[26] The plaintiffs' lawyers in the case, however, who had requested approval of a $12 million fee, thought otherwise.

Public and Private Funders: As described above, public funding entities exist in Ontario and in Quebec. These funds provide an indemnity against adverse costs to those plaintiffs whose applications are approved. In exchange, in Ontario the Fund receives 10 percent of the class' recovery, net of the lawyers' fees. In *Atlas*, this amounted to a levy of approximately $3 million. In Quebec, the rate of return varies. Commercial litigation funders have provided indemnities to representative plaintiffs in a small number of cases in Ontario for slightly less than a 10 percent return (Kalajdzic, Cashman & Longmoore, 2013). Still, the predominant source of insurance against adverse costs remains the plaintiff's law firm. With far more to gain than any individual class member, and far more to lose (both in terms of no fee, and liability for costs to the successful defendant), entrepreneurial lawyers are unquestionably the most important economic enabler of class actions in Canada.

---

[23] One judge interviewed for one Ontario study stated that there 'are cases where it's a joke, frankly, to think the client is doing anything. The client was recruited and just accepts instructions'. Kalajdzic, 2011, 17.

[24] For an empirical analysis of fees, *see* Alarie & Flynn, 2014.

[25] Kalajdzic, 2009, 22.

[26] Kalajdzic, The engine that drives, infra Chapter 11 at ff. 41 and accompanying text.

Australia

In the almost 25 years since the modern class action was introduced in Australia, entrepreneurial lawyers and commercial litigation funders have been the economic enablers of class actions. To these two class action enablers we can add a third, uniquely Australian, enabler: the 'closed class'. In the context of a commercially funded class action, the closed class mechanism limits membership in the class to those who have signed an agreement with the funder. In exchange for taking on the considerable risk of a class action, funders want the benefits that the closed class provides: elimination of the 'free rider' problem and greater certainty as to the number of claimants and the likely return for the funder should the action be successful. This private contract approach to funding arrangements is necessary because, unlike Canada, Israel and the US, there is not yet a 'common fund' option in Australia such that class counsel can count on a judge to award them fees and expenses if the class prevails, which will be allocated as a share of the total amount defendants pay to resolve the litigation. There are signs of a shift, but until that shift occurs commercial funders will continue to use closed classes in this way to manage their risk.[27]

Entrepreneurial Lawyers: Unlike their counterparts in other jurisdictions, who were encouraged to be entrepreneurial because of the availability of contingency fee arrangements, early class action lawyers in Australia were forced to be entrepreneurial because of the unavailability of contingency fee arrangements or any other funding vehicle to nurture a nascent class action regime. Prior to the entry of commercial funders into the market, a few Australian law firms were willing to take on the very significant financial risk of large class actions. They did this on a 'no win, no fee' basis, without the advantages provided by contingency fee arrangements or a 'litigation war chest', and in circumstances in which costs-shifting and the liability of lead plaintiffs for costs made it very difficult to find willing lead plaintiffs (Murphy & Cameron, 2006, 432–434). Notwithstanding these initial obstacles, they demonstrated that class action litigation, effectively managed, could be lucrative. This encouraged commercial funders, who had traditionally limited their activity to insolvency cases, to develop new business models to fund class actions. Those funders might eventually have entered the market in

---

[27] A request to make a 'common fund' order was rejected by the court in *Blairgowrie Trading Ltd v. Allco Finance Group Ltd* [2015] FCA 811. For a consideration of the arguments in favor of a common fund approach in Australia, *see* Hoffman-Ekstein, 2013.

any event, but the initial willingness of some plaintiff lawyers to 'fund' complex class actions probably expedited that entry.

Commercial Litigation Funders: Encouraged by the successes of some pioneering entrepreneurial lawyers and bolstered by favourable court judgments,[28] commercial funders stepped in to fill the huge funding void in Australian class actions. They are now a dominant presence in the Australian class action landscape and the main class action enabler. They thrive because, unlike Australian lawyers, they are able to fund litigation in exchange for a percentage of the damages award or settlement sum.

One of the early criticisms of the Australian funding market was that there were too few players and, therefore, too little competition. While there is still room for growth, the number of funders has increased and now includes both Australian and overseas funders. There are at least 11 active funders in the Australian class action market—six from Australia, two from the UK, and one each from The Netherlands, Singapore and the US (King & Wood Mallesons, 2014). This globalization trend works both ways; several Australian funders are active in overseas markets.

While legislative scrutiny has increased in recent years, funders are still operating in what can accurately be described as a 'light touch' regulatory regime. Courts were the first 'regulators' and dealt with a number of early challenges to the very existence and legitimacy of litigation funding arrangements. There has been a gradual shift in the site of regulation away from the courts to the legislature. In July 2013, legislative amendments came into effect that exempt litigation funders from the need to hold an Australian Financial Securities License but require them to have in place suitable practices to manage conflicts of interest.[29]

Perhaps the biggest question about the future development of commercial funding of Australian class actions is whether Australian courts will endorse the common fund approach. If they do, there will be a significant change in Australia's class action landscape. This is discussed below.

The 'Closed Class': 'Closed' or limited classes are those defined to limit the class to fewer than the total number of people who have suffered the alleged loss. While closed classes were used in the early days of Australian class actions, they remained uncontroversial until the *Multiplex* decision. The *Multiplex* class was limited to people who had signed a funding agreement with ILF, the Canadian commercial funder. Having

---

28 *Fostif, HC* and *Multiplex*, n 23.

29 *Corporations Amendment Regulation 2012 (No 6) (Cth)* and Australian Securities and Investment Commission Guide 248 (ASIC Guide).

entered the class action market, funders demanded as the price for staying there the increased certainty provided by a class limited to those who had signed a funding agreement. This particular use of the closed class was challenged by the defendants in both of our case studies, *Multiplex* and *Aristocrat*, and finally resolved in *Multiplex*.

One of the bases on which the defendants in *Multiplex* challenged the funding agreement was that any clause limiting the class to those who had signed an agreement with the funder was contrary to the opt-out nature of Australia's class action regime. When that regime was introduced for proceedings in the Federal Court of Australia,[30] it was intended to be an opt-out regime. In preferring the opt-out approach, legislators had accepted the recommendations of the Australian Law Reform Commission (ALRC) in its *Grouped Proceedings* report.[31] The authors of that report recommended an opt-out regime for access to justice reasons.[32] The Attorney-General agreed, stating that the opt-out approach was 'preferable on grounds of both equity and efficiency'.[33]

The opt-out nature of the Federal Court of Australia class action regime was generally accepted in the first 10 to 15 years of its operation. During that period, however, classes were defined in various ways that limited those who would benefit from and be bound by any judgment to fewer than the total number of potential claimants.[34] These practices continued without adverse judicial comment or defendant objection and, often, with explicit judicial approval and encouragement.

This is the class actions landscape in which commercial litigation funders began to assume a dominant presence. Funders take on the cost and risk associated with complex class action litigation in a cost shifting jurisdiction and take a percentage of the damages recovered, in the 20–45 percent range. In exchange, they require as a condition of class membership that members sign a funding agreement with them.[35] Their attempt

---

[30] Federal Court of Australia Act 1976 (Cth) Pt IV ('Federal Court Act').

[31] LRC Report No 46, 1988, para 101. They did not, however, accept LRC advice about the need for lawyer contingency fees and a public fund of the kind operating in Ontario.

[32] LRC Report No 46, 1988, paras 104–108 and 126–127.

[33] Commonwealth, Parliamentary Debates, House of Representatives, 14 November 1991, 3174 (Michael Duffy, Attorney General).

[34] For a detailed study of these cases, *see* Morabito, 2007.

[35] In the absence in Australia of a common fund approach, funders will continue to demand closed classes as the price of assuming the financial risk. However, commercially funded open classes will be possible if courts accept, as they are being asked to do, that they have the discretion to approve a common

to define a class in this way was challenged by the respondents in *Multiplex*.[36]

The Federal Court first instance and appeal judges disagreed with the arguments advanced by Multiplex and confirmed the appropriateness of the funder criterion as a prerequisite to class membership. In doing so the court relied less on overarching principles about the intent of the legislation and more on a close reading of the relevant provisions. They concluded that the words 'as representing some or all of them' in section 33C, which is the provision that sets out the threshold requirements for a class action, contemplated a class composed of fewer than all of the possible group members.[37] Such 'closed classes' are now commonplace in commercially funded class actions in Australia and, as a result of *Multiplex*, no longer contested.

Interviews we conducted confirmed that there are some Australian class actions that would not have been brought but for the availability of commercial funding (and see Watson & Donelly, 2014). They also confirmed that the closed class has enabled Australian class actions; by providing certainty for funders, it encourages them to stay in or to enter the market.

A looming question for commercial funding in Australia is whether Australian courts will endorse a common fund approach. If they do, funders will be able to obtain court approval at the commencement of a proceeding to recover their funding premium from all group members, not only from those who have signed a funding agreement. Advocates of this approach argue that it is permitted by the broad power given to the court by Section 33ZF(1) of the Federal Court Act to 'make any order the Court thinks appropriate or necessary to ensure that justice is done'. If the common fund approach is endorsed, funder reliance on closed classes will diminish and funders will be inclined to bring more 'open' class actions. The need for the extensive and time consuming book-building that funders now do to identify class members and to get signed contracts will also diminish, which in turn may make it possible for claims to be filed more expeditiously and with less expense for funders. Such a shift

---

fund application at the beginning of a class action that allows the funder to receive a percentage of any settlement or award of damages.

[36] *P. Dawson Nominees Pty Ltd v. Multiplex Limited* [2007] FCA 1061 (Finkelstein J) and *Multiplex Funds Management Limited Pty Ltd v. P. Dawson Nominees Pty Ltd* [2007] FCAFC 2000.

[37] The relevant section states that where the threshold requirements are met by a group of persons, 'a proceeding may be commenced by one or more of those persons as representing some or all of them'.

to a common fund approach would further solidify the role of commercial funders as Australia's primary class action enabler.

Israel

Israel has had class actions for more than 20 years. The Israeli legislature has incorporated class action procedures into substantive laws in various sectors such as consumer protection, banking, insurance, securities, equal pay for equal work and equal rights for people with disabilities. Although not identical, these procedures were modeled on Rule 23 of the American Federal Rules of Civil Procedure, yet each was limited to a specific cause of action that was defined by the relevant statute. For example, the case studied in this part, *Shemesh v. Reichart* was initiated in 1995, based on a class action procedure enacted into the Israeli Securities Law.

In 2006, the Knesset (the Israeli legislature) enacted a new Class Action Law (hereinafter the CAL or the Law) which superseded all previous specific statutory arrangements. The new law maintained the substance-specific framework of the preceding statutes. Nevertheless, those causes of action were prescribed in a much broader manner, rendering certification easier, especially in consumer protection (including banking and insurance), in labor and anti-discrimination, and in restitution lawsuits filed against unlawful payments collected by state and public authorities. In addition, the new law prescribed various procedures for managing class actions which were not specified in detail by any prior legislation. These included certification of settlement and withdrawal from the class action, possible alternatives to individual remedies, attorney and representative plaintiff remuneration, and processing of multiple class action filings over similar issues and questions of law and fact.

In the ten years since its enactment, the CAL has generated a significant amount of litigation, from 26 class actions filed in 2006, to 820 filings in 2012.[38] Courts have been addressing numerous questions of interpretation of the new law, and have experimented with novel issues they had not previously encountered. Much has been written on those issues, focusing on the legal and normative implications of the act and proposing how it should be applied.

---

[38] All empirical data mentioned in this subsection are based on Klement et al., 2014, available (in Hebrew) at http://elyon1.court.gov.il/heb/Research%20Division/doc/25122014.pdf; Klement &Weinshall Margel, 2016.

The CAL provides specific arrangements that facilitate class actions through three types of enablers: representative plaintiffs, class attorneys and public funders.

Representative Plaintiffs: The law prescribes three categories of representative plaintiffs: (1) individual class members; (2) non-profit organizations; and (3) specifically designated public regulators. Nevertheless, in the first six years since its enactment, nearly all of the representative plaintiffs—99.3 percent—were individual class members. Very few class actions were filed by non-profit organizations and none were filed by public regulators.

When the class representative is a class member, he or she is required to show that his or her cause of action is one of the causes specified in the law. If loss is a necessary element of this cause of action, then the class representative must show that he or she suffered some loss. He or she also has to convince the court that he or she will represent class members adequately and in good faith.

However, even if the representative plaintiff does not satisfy one or more of these requirements, the court may nevertheless certify the class action and substitute the representative. The court will do so if it finds that other certification requirements are satisfied, namely that:

(1) there are common issues of fact or law pertaining to the class;
(2) there is a reasonable likelihood that these issues will be decided in favor of the class; and
(3) litigating the case as a class action will be efficient and fair.

This undermines the significance of certification requirements that pertain to the class representative. Indeed, in all motions to certify that were denied between 2006 and 2012, the court never based its decision to deny on requirements that pertain to the representative plaintiff only. This is one indication that the role of plaintiffs as enablers is often not significant.

Representative plaintiffs may be ordered to reimburse defendants for their litigation costs if class certification is denied or if the case is eventually lost. However, as in other civil cases, Israeli courts have wide discretion whether to award costs, and if they do, in what amount. The costs awarded in class actions therefore cover only part of the actual litigation costs borne by defendants (the median is NIS15,000 and average is NIS40,000). On the other hand, representative plaintiffs are rewarded if they win the class action or if it is settled. Incentive awards for representative plaintiffs in Israel are substantial, amounting to between one-fifth to one-third of the fee awarded to the class attorney.

Class Attorneys: The CAL delineates the duties of the class attorney toward the class, before and after certification. Like the representative plaintiff, the class attorney may be substituted by the court if other certification requirements are satisfied, but courts have almost never used this power. Class attorneys are paid a contingent fee, which is often set as a percentage of the common fund created in judgment or in settlement. The law lists a number of considerations the court must take into account when setting the attorney fee, including the benefit to the class, the risk and difficulty in litigating the class action, its public significance, the way the class action was conducted and the difference between the remedies sought and those actually awarded. In practice, class attorneys are awarded between 15 percent and 30 percent of the total remedy, depending on its amount.

It is commonly agreed among judges, practitioners and scholars that most class actions are attorney driven. Since the representative plaintiff's remedy is usually very low (median equal to NIS250), they are seldom the initiators of class actions. The facilitative goal of class attorneys has also been recognized by the Supreme Court, although the justices were divided on the question whether class action attorneys may initiate class actions by identifying causes of action and then approaching potential representative plaintiffs.[39] Moreover, courts expect class attorneys to take responsibility for the important litigation and settlement decisions, and some have even expressed their preference for attorneys over class representatives when the two disagree.

Public Funding: The CAL has established a designated public fund, whose purpose is to help representative plaintiffs in funding class certification motions and class actions, which it deems socially and publicly important. However, since the fund's budget is small (NIS1 million annually), its capability to facilitate class actions is limited, at best.

The designated fund cannot provide funding for securities class actions. Those class actions may be funded only by the Israeli Securities Authority (ISA), which has also designated a small share of its budget for this purpose. Although its designated funds are not substantial, the ISA has succeeded in increasing the number of securities class action filings since the enactment of the CAL. This facilitative effect can be attributed to the probative value of ISA's decision to fund a class action. Such a decision may indicate to the court that the ISA believes that the case is sufficiently strong and that it has significant social value.

[39] CA 8037/06 *Barzilay v. Prinir* (decided 4 September 2014).

To conclude, Israel has experienced an increasing number of class action filings in the past ten years. This trend is mainly attributed to the intense involvement of entrepreneurial attorneys in this field. Although the Israeli class action law recognizes alternative facilitators—class representatives and public funders—their significance as class action enablers does not seem to have been significant.

CONCLUSION

Class actions rely on entrepreneurial incentives for private actors to pursue public goals. Such incentives are created by institutional economic mechanisms, which result in different enablers dominating aggregate litigation. This Part presents case studies from diverse regimes and demonstrates the operation of class representatives, attorneys and funders within each of those regimes.

Two questions remain open for further research. The first is the question of agency. Since private and public incentives do not overlap, agency problems arise. Private enablers pursuing private economic goals might misuse the class action procedure for their own benefit, at the expense of represented class members. Which of the class action enablers is more prone to such problems, whose problems can be more effectively addressed, and how competition, monitoring and collaboration among different enablers affect their performance are all questions that should be examined more closely.

The second question is that of control. With the multiplicity of class action enablers comes a competition among them for control of the process. This creates potential conflicts which courts must address. For example, in exchange for assuming the considerable financial risk of complex litigation, funders want some control over how that litigation is conducted and managed. However, funder control of litigation can quickly run up against longstanding views about independence of counsel. This issue of funder control has arisen in both Canada and Australia, with markedly different results. How the debate about control will unfold in each jurisdiction is a matter of great importance, for practitioners, judges and scholars.

REFERENCES

Benjamin Alarie & Peter Flynn, *Accumulating Wisdom: An Updated Empirical Examination of Class Counsel's Fees in Ontario Class Actions*, (2014) 9(2) Canadian Class Action Review 355

Camille Cameron & Jasminka Kalajdzic, *Commercial Litigation Funding: Ethical, Regulatory and Comparative Perspectives*, (2014) 55(1) Canadian Business Law Journal 1

Alba Conte, *Attorney Fee Awards, 3d* (Trial Practice Series 2014)

Theodore Eisenberg & Geoffrey Miller, *Incentive Awards to Class Action Plaintiffs: An Empirical Study*, (2006) 53 UCLA Law Review 1303

Radoslaw Goral, *The Color of Money: A Story of One Complex Case and Its Many Financiers*, (2016) 12 NYU Journal of Law & Business.

Deborah Hensler et al., *Class Action Dilemmas: Pursuing Public Goals for Private Gain*, (RAND Corporation 2000)

Deborah Hensler, *Third-Party Financing of Class Action Litigation in the United States: Will The Sky Fall?* (2014) 63 DePaul Law Review 499

Alan Hirsch & Diane Sheehey, *Awarding Attorneys' Fees and Managing Fee Litigation* (Federal Judicial Center, second edition 2005)

Jarrah Hoffman-Ekstein, *Funding Open Classes Through Common Fund Applications*, (2013) 87 Australian Law Journal 331

Jasminka Kalajdzic, *Access to Justice for the Masses? A Critical Analysis of Class Actions in Ontario* (Masters' Thesis 2009), available at https://tspace.library.utoronto.ca/bitstream/1807/18780/6/Kalajdzic_Jasminka_200911_LLM_Thesis.pdf

Jasminka Kalajdzic, *Self-Interest, Public Interest and the Interests of the Absent Client: Legal Ethics and Class Action Praxis*, (2011) 49 Osgoode Hall Law Journal 1

Jasminka Kalajdzic, Peter Cashman & Alana Longmoore, *Justice for Profit: A Comparative Analysis of Australian, Canadian and U.S. Third Party Funding*, (2013) 61 American Journal of Comparative Law 93

King & Wood Mallesons, *The Review, Class Actions in Australia 2013–2014*, available at http://www.kwm.com/~/media/SjBerwin/Files/Knowledge/Downloads/au/2014/07/01/kwm-the-review-class-actions-in-australia-201407.ashx?la=en

Alon Klement & Zvika Neeman, *Incentive Structures for Class Action Lawyers*, (2004) 20 The Journal of Law, Economics, and Organization 102

Alon Klement et al., *Class Actions in Israel—An Empirical Perspective*, 2014, available (in Hebrew) at http://elyon1.court.gov.il/heb/Research%20Division/doc/25122014.pdf

Alon Klement & Keren Weinshall Margel, *Cost-Benefit Analysis of Class Actions – An Israeli Perspective*, (2016) 172 Journal of Institutional and Theoretical Economics, 75

Law Reform Commission, *Grouped Proceedings in the Federal Court*, Report No 46, 1988, available at http://www.austlii.edu.au/au/other/lawreform/ALRC/1988/46.html

Jonathan Macey & Geoffrey Miller, *The Plaintiffs' Attorney's Role in Class Action and Derivative Litigation: Economic Analysis and Recommendations for Reform*, (1991) 58 The University of Chicago Law Review 1

Vince Morabito, *Class Actions Instituted only for the Benefit of the Clients of the Class Representative's Solicitors*, (2007) 29(5) Sydney Law Review 5

Bernard Murphy & Camille Cameron, *Access to Justice and the Evolution of Class Actions in Australia*, (2006) 30 Melbourne University Law Review 399

Richard Nagareda, *Restitution, Rent Extraction and Class Representatives: Implications of Incentive Awards*, (2006) 53 UCLA Law Review 1483

Andrew Watson & Michael Donelly, *Financing Access to Justice: Third-Party Litigation Funding and Class Actions in Australia*, (2014) 55 Canadian Business Law Journal 17

Warren Winkler et al., *The Law of Class Actions in Canada* (Canada Law Book 2014)

8. A class action 'mash-up': *In Re Royal Dutch/Shell Transport Securities Litigation*[1]

Deborah R. Hensler

INTRODUCTION

The global expansion of class actions and other group litigation devices over the last decade provides rich fodder for comparative law scholars interested in legal transplants. The conventional analysis of legal transplants is that they are rarely successful. Unless a transplanted doctrine or procedure meshes well with other aspects of legal regimes and legal culture it is difficult for it to take root. Over the last two decades, collective litigation procedures have spread outside the United States (US). But, consistent with the comparativists' analysis, except where additional changes have occurred in substantive law, procedural rules and professional codes, the formal adoption of a class action procedure outside the US has failed to produce much class-based litigation. The three most significant formal obstacles to the use of class action procedures in jurisdictions that have adopted them are:

(1) a bar against monetary damages in many jurisdictions' class action statutes;
(2) an almost universal prohibition against lawyers charging contingency fees in any civil litigation; and
(3) fee-shifting rules.

[1] This is the formal title of the case. When referring to the corporation itself, we use 'Royal Dutch Shell', as does the corporation. This case study is based on published and unpublished court documents (available electronically through the US federal court PACER system) and information obtained in confidential interviews with in-house and outside defense counsel and plaintiff counsel in the US and the Netherlands, and with representatives of NGOs. The case study was conducted in collaboration with Prof. Ianika Tzankova.

As discussed in Chapter 1 of this book, these rules limit incentives for attorneys to represent parties in class actions while imposing substantial risks on both class counsel and class representatives.

However, formal rules provide an incomplete picture of the operations of legal regimes. 'Law in action', shaped by interested parties, lawyers and judges, may produce legal behavior that is not anticipated by formalist analysis. One vehicle for such unanticipated outcomes can be termed a legal 'mash-up'. Like internet users who create new media content by combining bits and pieces of songs and video,[2] lawyers from different jurisdictions, with judges' approval, are informally combining the legal rules of multiple jurisdictions in ways that serve their own and their clients' interests. These informal combinations of rules are both incentivized and enabled by the availability of class action and other collective litigation procedures. *In re Royal Dutch/Shell Transport*, a securities class action lawsuit pursued in parallel in a US federal court[3] and the Amsterdam (Netherlands) Court of Appeal, is an example of such a mash-up. By combining US legal fee rules with Dutch class action rules, US lawyers were able to earn fees arguably unavailable to Dutch lawyers in Dutch courts and a multi-national corporate defendant was able to craft a global settlement in the Netherlands that was beyond its reach in US courts.

BACKGROUND OF THE LITIGATION

As is true of many securities class actions, the Royal Dutch Shell litigation began with the announcement of untoward news that immediately depressed the corporation's share price. On 9 January 2004 Royal Dutch Shell disclosed that it had 'overbooked' its proven oil and gas reserves by 20 percent. Investors use information about energy companies' reserves, which are drawn down gradually over time, as a basis for estimating future revenues. Analysts estimated that Royal Dutch Shell's disclosure that it had overstated its reserves translated to

---

[2] According to Wikipedia, the term 'mashup' describes a variety of user-created combinations of digital media that produce 'derivative works' that often have new functionality. *See* http://en.wikipedia.org/wiki/Mashup.

[3] *In re Royal Dutch/Shell Transp. Sec. Litig.*, 380 F. Supp. 2d 509 (D.N.J. 2005).

$67.5 billion less in expected future revenue from its oil reserves alone (Cummins, Warren & Schroeder, 2004).[4]

Calculating the volume of petroleum and natural gas reserves is a complicated and somewhat uncertain business. Accounting for reserves is subject to US Securities and Exchange Commission (SEC) guidelines. Although Royal Dutch Shell claimed its reserve accounting practices complied with SEC rules, some analysts regarded its accounting approach as 'aggressive' and the 20 percent reserves reduction attracted immediate negative attention. Royal Dutch Shell is a wholly owned subsidiary of Netherlands-based Royal Dutch Petroleum and United Kingdom-based Shell Transport & Trading. Royal Dutch's shares trade on multiple exchanges in Europe and on the New York Stock Exchange (NYSE). On the day of the disclosure that Royal Dutch Shell had overstated its reserves, Royal Dutch Petroleum ADRs[5] traded on the NYSE dropped 7.9 percent and Shell's shares traded on the London exchange dropped 6.7 percent.

Over the next few months, Royal Dutch Shell issued three further restatements of its oil and natural gas reserves. The total reduction in reported reserves was equivalent to a reduction in reported earnings of $402 million for 2001 to 2003, or 1.2 percent of total income. As a result of the company's reserves restatements, government regulators launched investigations in the US, UK and the Netherlands and heads rolled at Royal Dutch Shell. Shell also launched its own internal investigation. In early March, the board of Royal Dutch Shell's parent companies fired its Chairman, Sir Philip Watt, and his top deputy. Share prices on the New York Stock Exchange rose modestly on the news.

A few days after the announcement of the Chairman's firing, the Wall Street Journal reported that Sir Philip and his deputies had been warned two years earlier that Royal Dutch Shell's reporting appeared to be non-compliant with SEC guidelines, and that the company might need to restate its reserves. The Journal wrote that Shell's internal investigators had reported to Shell's board that they had "found a 'trail of communications' showing Sir Philip appeared to have known about longstanding internal questions over the validity of the reserves bookings" (Cummins, 2004). In response to the reserves restatements the three major rating

---

[4] Information on the disclosure of Royal Dutch Shell's reserve booking practices and the reactions to the disclosures is drawn primarily from Wall Street Journal articles appearing in January–June 2004. Cummins was the lead reporter on the story.

[5] American Depository Receipts, traded on US exchanges, represent shares in foreign-owned companies.

agencies downgraded Shell's credit rating. The story of energy industry leaders' restatements of their reserves, highlighting Royal Dutch Shell's trespasses and travails, received front section attention in the business media for months.

THE LITIGATION BEGINS

As Royal Dutch Shell and its parent companies scrambled to correct its accounting and allocate responsibility for past errors and government investigations slowly geared up, class action lawyers and institutional investors in the US and Europe quickly responded to Royal Dutch Shell's disclosures by filing suit in the US. On 23 January 2004, just two weeks after the company issued its first reserve restatement, Milberg, Weiss—at that time the nation's leading securities class action plaintiff firm—filed a shareholder class action lawsuit in the US federal court in the district of New Jersey. A few days later, on 29 January 2004, a second similar lawsuit was filed in the same court, followed over the next few months by a dozen more suits. Shareholder plaintiffs sued Royal Dutch and Shell Transport, the Dutch and English parent companies of the Royal Dutch Shell Group, Sir Philip and his deputy, Royal Dutch Shell's accountants, KPMG and Price Waterhouse Coopers, and assorted others.

Competing class actions brought by different law firms representing different parties, each of which is seeking to be appointed as class representative, are a common characteristic of class action litigation in the US. Courts have long responded to the challenge of managing multi-party, multi-claim litigation by appointing lead plaintiff counsel to coordinate the litigation. Such appointments are eagerly sought by plaintiff attorneys who then not only control the course of the litigation but also stand to receive substantial fees if the class prevails. The promise of substantial fees incentivizes lawyers to seek out parties to serve as class representatives, reversing what is assumed to be the normal course of litigation in which parties who wish to sue seek counsel to represent them. In an effort to inject more party control into securities class action litigation, in 1995 the US Congress passed the Private Securities Litigation Reform Act, which authorizes federal judges presiding over securities class actions to appoint the 'most adequate plaintiff' as class representative and creates a presumption that the class member with the largest financial stake in the action, usually an institutional investor, will satisfy the 'most adequate' requirement. Typically, the law firm that represents the lead plaintiff is appointed as lead counsel.

In *Royal Dutch/Shell Transport* multiple state pension funds and their law firm allies jockeyed for the lead position. Seven groups of funds that had filed complaints offered themselves as lead plaintiffs and proposed the lawyers representing them as lead counsel. One team comprised Pennsylvania public employee pension funds and KBC-AM, a Belgium-based publicly traded asset management fund that had purchased Royal Dutch Shell shares on a foreign exchange. The Pennsylvania funds had not routinely appeared as lead plaintiffs in securities class actions but became involved at the suggestion of the law firm that they proposed as lead counsel. The presence of KBC-AM signaled the intent of the team's lawyers to file a 'global' class action, representing all investors worldwide who claimed financial loss due to Royal Dutch Shell's allegedly fraudulent reporting of its reserves in the period prior to the restatements. The Pennsylvania team proposed New York-based plaintiff class action firm Bernstein, Liebhard & Lifshitz as lead counsel.

In early May 2004, trial Judge John Bissell appointed the Pennsylvania Employees Retirement System and the Pennsylvania Teachers' Retirement System as lead plaintiffs (excluding KBC-AM) and Bernstein, Liebhard & Lifshitz as lead counsel. Named partner Stanley Bernstein would lead the team. The lead attorneys for Royal Dutch Shell were Ralph Ferrara and Anne Ashton, then partners at Debevoise & Plimpton, a leading New York-based corporate law firm.

On 30 June 2004, Judge Bissell issued a consolidation order that not only formally combined all previously filed securities class action complaints arising out of the Royal Dutch Shell reserves restatements but mandated that any subsequent complaints arising out of the same matter would be treated as part of this single litigation, which became known as *In re Royal Dutch/Shell Transport*. Henceforth, Stanley Bernstein would drive the securities class action litigation on behalf of shareholders. But the potential for competition among the many plaintiff lawyers representing institutional clients in the litigation was scarcely resolved. Over time, Bernstein's approach to dealing with the defendant would open up an opportunity for Royal Dutch Shell's lawyers to resolve the litigation in quite a different manner than the lead plaintiff counsel had initially anticipated.

THE JURISDICTIONAL DISPUTE

From the inception of the litigation, the parties and their counsel understood that deciding whether the court had jurisdiction over foreign investors who had purchased their shares in Royal Dutch Shell on foreign exchanges was the key to its resolution. In 2010, the US Supreme Court resolved this issue of prescriptive jurisdiction, holding that the reach of the *Securities Exchange Act of 1934, §10(B)* and the SEC Rule 10b-5 that implements it is limited to transactions on US exchanges.[6] But in 2004, when *In re Royal Dutch/Shell Transport* began, whether the district court would hold that US securities regulations reached beyond the US to foreign investors and foreign transactions was less certain. The 1934 statute that provided the basis for the *Royal Dutch/Shell Transport* securities fraud claims was silent on its reach beyond the US. For more than 70 years, federal judges answered that question themselves. Over time, appellate courts converged on an approach that looked to whether the underlying conduct took place within or had significant effects on investment or investors in the US. But the strictness of the test varied across circuits. Importantly, the Third Circuit, whose jurisprudence the New Jersey court was required to follow, had adopted one of the more relaxed standards, providing class counsel with hope that Judge Bissell would rule that their case could move forward as a 'global' class action on behalf of all investors worldwide.

Although the issue of jurisdiction could be expected to arise in any securities fraud class action involving foreign investors or foreign exchange transactions, the issue was particularly significant in *Royal Dutch/Shell Transport* because the value of foreign investments that allegedly declined as a result of the reserves restatements far outweighed the value of domestic investments. When appointing the Pennsylvania funds as lead plaintiffs, Judge Bissell had formally recognized the disproportionate foreign investors' stake in the litigation but nonetheless rejected KBC-AM, the Belgian entity with the largest stake, as lead plaintiff because of the possibility that foreign claims would ultimately be dismissed on jurisdictional grounds.

Other foreign investors besides those that KBC-AM represented also had a stake in the outcome of the jurisdictional dispute. Among the largest of these were ABP and PGGM, two leading Dutch pension funds. Between them, in 2012, these funds reported managing (directly or through their asset management funds) about €440 billion. A substantial share of the assets managed by the two Dutch funds was invested in US-based companies, either through purchase of ADRs on

---

[6] *See Morrison v. Nat'l Austl. Bank Ltd.*, 130 S. Ct. 2869 (U.S. 2010). *Morrison* was a so-called 'f-cubed' case involving foreign investors who had purchased shares on a foreign exchange suing a foreign defendant. The putative class in *Royal Dutch/Shell Transport* included US and foreign investors who had purchased ADRs on the New York Stock Exchange.

US exchanges or purchase of shares on foreign exchanges. (ADRs, or American Depository Receipts, represent shares in foreign companies that can be traded on US exchanges.) Senior fund managers saw US securities class actions as important for protecting the value of the funds invested with them and for promoting sound corporate governance of the companies in which they invest. ABP had some experience serving as co-lead plaintiff in US securities class actions but was more likely to monitor US litigation from a distance and had been criticized for not taking a more proactive stance in pursuing compensation for losses due to security fraud. ABP's pension scheme was administered by APG Asset Management.

For representation in US class actions, APG generally looked to Grant & Eisenhofer, a Delaware-based securities class action firm, with whom it had negotiated a standing contingency fee agreement. Grant & Eisenhofer was founded in 1997 by two self-described 'entrepreneurial lawyers' who saw new opportunities for representing institutional investors after the passage of the Private Securities Litigation Reform Act. By 2004, Grant & Eisenhofer was representing various European investment management funds in several different US securities class actions. Concerned about the uncertainty surrounding US courts' jurisdiction over foreign investors' claims, APG attempted to bring together Dutch pension funds to consider coordinated non-class litigation against Royal Dutch Petroleum in the Netherlands under Dutch securities law. At the same time, under the broad description of the putative class in *Royal Dutch Shell*, the Dutch funds along with other European investors were class members, represented by Bernstein, Liebhard & Lifshitz.

It was Royal Dutch Shell of course that had the largest stake in the outcome of the jurisdictional dispute. Shell's General Counsel, Beat Hess, was the key defense strategic decision-maker. Hess had taken up the reins in Shell's London office shortly before the reserves issue erupted into public view. He understood immediately the regulatory, litigation and public relations ramifications of the issue. Prior to joining Shell, Hess had been the General Counsel at ABB, a Zurich-based multinational industrial power products and technology company. Having spent ten months prior to joining Shell negotiating with the leaders of the US plaintiff asbestos bar to resolve long-running asbestos worker injury litigation against ABB-owned Combustion Engineering, Hess had a keen understanding of US plaintiff lawyers' entrepreneurial mindset and litigation skills. As General Counsel, Hess rejected the notion that Royal Dutch Shell had violated the SEC guidelines for reserve reporting, but understood that the reports that had surfaced in the US of e-mails showing that Royal Dutch Shell's Chairman and other senior managers had been warned in the early 2000s that reserves were being overbooked had the potential to weaken the company's defensive position.

The disclosure of 'bad documents' is often the key to promoting settlement in US litigation. Even when corporate defendants and their legal representatives think their legal position is quite strong, the possibility of a jury responding negatively to the appearance of a corporate cover-up and the attendant possibility of punitive damages create a climate of willingness to consider reasonable settlement demands by plaintiffs. At an early stage of the litigation, Hess might have been willing to consider a reasonable settlement demand from US investors who had purchased shares on the New York exchange; he also might have been inclined to settle the claims of foreign investors, for whom there was the possibility—however small—of litigating individually in Dutch courts. He was adamant however that he would never agree to settle the claims of foreign investors in a US court.

After the consolidation of the various class action complaints and the appointment of lead plaintiffs and lead counsel, *Royal Dutch/Shell Transport* moved forward in the usual fashion for US securities class actions. The parties engaged in preliminary skirmishes over discovery and other pretrial issues; the plaintiffs filed amended complaints. On 30 June 2005, a year and a half after the litigation commenced, Royal Dutch Shell filed a motion to dismiss for lack of subject matter jurisdiction, which Judge Bissell shortly denied. The lead plaintiff for the class had overcome the first hurdle in achieving an outcome for the class but a long path lay ahead: the class had not yet been formally certified and issues of law and fact remained to be decided.

In late autumn 2005, *In re Royal Dutch/Shell Transport* moved into a new phase. Judge Bissell had retired and Judge Joel Pisano was assigned to the case in his place. On 4 January 2006, the judge issued a joint scheduling order, setting aside the first three weeks in November 2006 for 'hearings and a potential mini-trial of all issues related to plaintiffs' motion for class certification'.

By early 2006, the Dutch pension funds had become increasingly concerned about the possibility that the US court would dismiss the claims of foreign investors. The clock was ticking on their ability to bring suit in the Netherlands and if they waited too long they might be left without any legal recourse to claim compensation for their losses. If a settlement was reached before the judge ruled on the jurisdictional issue, its terms might discount the value of foreign claims, as had been their experience in other mass settlements including US and foreign investors. Class counsel Bernstein's hard-edged style was not encouraging Royal Dutch Shell to negotiate a settlement and the parties reportedly were more than a billion dollars apart in their assessment of the value of the claims. In January 2006, to protect their interests and perhaps to open up an independent avenue for settlement, ABP and Deka Investment GmbH, a Frankfurt-based investment management company, filed individual lawsuits in the federal court in New Jersey against Royal Dutch Shell. In a letter to the court, Grant & Eisenhofer indicated that it was the intention of the 'Dutch funds' to opt out of the class, should one be certified. At the request of Royal Dutch Shell, the individual foreign investor complaints were consolidated with the class action for pretrial management, and Grant & Eisenhofer was given permission to access discovery materials, and to engage in settlement discussions on behalf of its Dutch clients.

In April 2006, Judge Pisano held a lengthy hearing on the procedure and schedule for resolving the evidentiary issues relating to class certification, including the jurisdictional issue, and decided on a new tri-partite approach. First up would be a bench trial (earlier referred to as a 'mini-trial') in May 2007 to decide whether the foreign investors met the Third Circuit's substantive jurisdictional test. Thereafter, the court would consider summary judgment motions. Finally, the court would hear and decide the plaintiffs' motion for class certification.

The new schedule, with clear milestones for court disposition of the central issues in the litigation, created a framework for formal court-based settlement negotiations, which began at Judge Pisano's request in July 2006 with retired district court Judge Nicholas Politan serving as mediator. The official court mediation ultimately proved unsuccessful. However, outside the court, other negotiations were beginning to take place between Royal Dutch Shell and the representatives of the foreign investors.

THE DUTCH SOLUTION

From the beginning of the litigation, Royal Dutch Shell's position was that the claims of foreign investors, whose purchases accounted for more than half of total alleged damages, should not be resolved in a US court. Although Judge Pisano was not scheduled to decide this issue until 2007 Royal Dutch Shell's lawyers knew that the judge was concerned about the possibility that the foreign investors would have no remedy for their alleged losses if he dismissed their claims. Whether foreign plaintiffs have a remedy outside the US is a factor US courts consider when deciding motions to dismiss claims that are 'legally within their jurisdiction' on *forum non conveniens* grounds. The threshold issue in *Royal*

Dutch/Shell Transport, however, was whether the court had jurisdiction over foreign investors' claims, the answer to which depended on the application of Third Circuit jurisprudence interpreting the Securities Exchange Act, not on criteria for dismissing claims on *forum non conveniens* grounds. Nonetheless, given the somewhat relaxed jurisdictional standard in the Third Circuit, Royal Dutch Shell had reason to worry that Judge Pisano might reject its arguments for dismissing the foreign claims. An appellate battle over the issue, perhaps up to the US Supreme Court, would be lengthy and expensive even if it were ultimately successful. And as is often the case in high stakes litigation, Royal Dutch Shell was interested in getting the reserves overbooking story and ensuing litigation out of the headlines. For practical reasons then, there might have been a price at which Royal Dutch Shell would have been willing to resolve the foreign claims in the US despite its principled opposition to doing so. But class counsel Bernstein's aggressive negotiation style did not encourage Royal Dutch Shell's European General Counsel to bargain with him.

However, there was a forum outside the US in which Royal Dutch Shell might be able to resolve the foreign claims and do so on a mass basis—indeed, in Royal Dutch Petroleum's home country. The vehicle for the settlement had been created by the Dutch legislature in 2005, after *In re Royal Dutch/Shell Transport* was already underway: Wet Collectieve Afwikkeling Massaschade (WCAM), the Dutch Collective Mass Claims Settlement Act.[7] Under WCAM, parties that wish to resolve a dispute involving money damages (whether or not they have engaged previously in formal litigation against each other) may jointly petition the Amsterdam Court of Appeal to approve a binding opt-out collective (class) settlement. Building on the European civil law tradition in which associations have standing to bring diffuse 'social' claims, WCAM specifies that civil society associations or special purpose foundations—rather than one or a few class members, as in the US—should serve as representatives of the claimants' collective interest. To assure that the claimants' interests are properly protected, the Amsterdam Court of Appeal must approve the representatives. After filing their petition with the court, the parties must provide notice of the proposed settlement to everyone whose claims would be resolved under the settlement's terms. After the notice period has run, the court holds a public hearing on the settlement, at which putative class members may come forward to support or object to its terms. If the court approves the settlement, a

[7] Stb. 2005, pp. 340, 380.

second notice is provided to class members so that they will have an opportunity to opt out. Those who choose to opt out may pursue individual litigation; those who do not opt out are bound to the terms of the settlement and may collect damages according to its terms. As *In re Royal Dutch/Shell Transport* was wending its way through US courts, WCAM was in the process of being implemented in two domestic mass settlements in the Netherlands.

Royal Dutch Shell did not need Bernstein or the lead plaintiffs for the putative global class filed in the New Jersey federal court to petition the Amsterdam Court of Appeal for approval of a settlement of foreign investors' claims; it simply needed a representative of the foreign investors that would be acceptable to the Dutch court. Among the candidates was ABP, which had filed its individual lawsuit against Royal Dutch Shell and communicated its intention *not* to be part of a US class action early in 2006. Just when the idea of using WCAM to resolve the foreign investors' claims in *Royal Dutch/ Shell Transport* was first floated and by whom is not clear. However, our research interviews suggest that the idea originated either with Royal Dutch Shell or its American outside counsel,[8] and that it had been informally shared with Judge Pisano by the time the judge issued his plan for hearing and ruling on the jurisdictional issue and the motion for class certification. Whoever first proposed it, by late 2006, as pre-trial activity ground on in the US district court in New Jersey, Royal Dutch Shell's lawyers were negotiating a settlement with ABP and Grant & Eisenhofer that could be taken to the Amsterdam Court of Appeal for approval.

The idea of resolving what was arguably a Dutch problem in a Dutch forum was attractive to ABP, as was the possibility that this approach would prove less expensive for them than continuing to litigate in the US. However, in order for Royal Dutch Shell to support the plan, the settlement would have to include *all* non-US investors' claims, not just ABP's or the other Dutch funds' claims. To test support for the idea of using WCAM to resolve all non-US claims, ABP began consulting with other European funds within and outside the Netherlands.

As Grant & Eisenhofer and Royal Dutch Shell's lawyers were hammering out the details of the settlement, Grant & Eisenhofer hired a Dutch law firm to establish a foundation that would join in petitioning

---

[8] *But see* CV-04-374, Dist. N.J. Royal Dutch/Shell Transport Defendants' Memorandum of Law in Support of Motion to Sever and Dismiss Non-U.S. Purchasers' Claims, 18 April 2007 at 11, stating that various European funds and investors approached Shell.

the Amsterdam Court of Appeal to approve the settlement.[9] Worried that the Amsterdam Court of Appeal might balk at approving the petition if a newly created foundation were the sole representative of claimants' interests, the negotiating parties initiated discussions of the proposed settlement with Vereniging van Effectenbezitters (VEB), a long-established Dutch association that is the public face of smaller investors in the Netherlands.

The parameters of the WCAM settlement had already been set by the time VEB was brought into the process. From VEB's perspective, the compensation Royal Dutch Shell was offering to non-US investors was found money: were it not for the WCAM option, if the US court ultimately dismissed these investors' claims on jurisdictional grounds, they would likely be left with no option to collect on their losses. However, VEB recognized that its co-signing the petition had value to the institutional investors, their US lawyers and Royal Dutch Shell. As a result of its efforts, a provision was added to the settlement offering equal shares of a $12.5 million fund to every VEB member that submitted a claim form.[10] VEB ultimately gained positive publicity in the Netherlands for having come forward to represent non-institutional investors' interests in the Amsterdam Court of Appeal.

DENOUEMENT

On 11 April 2007, Royal Dutch Shell, Stichting Shell Reserves Compensation Foundation, VEB, ABP and PGGM filed a petition in the Amsterdam Court of Appeal seeking approval of a binding opt-out settlement of all foreign investors' securities fraud claims arising out of the reserves overbooking of the early 2000s.[11] The proposed settlement offered $340.1 million to the foreign funds, plus $12.5 million to individual foreign investors, $6.25 million to VEB and other shareholder organizations to assist in outreach to individual investors, and payments of lawyers' fees that Royal Dutch Shell estimated to constitute 12.5 percent

---

[9] The Foundation formally filed its Deed of Formation in April 2007.

[10] The $12.5 million capped fund was intended to compensate each of an estimated 125,000 claimants $100. Instead, about 500,000 individual investors filed claims forms and each netted $25.

[11] The Foundation filed its Deed of Incorporation one day before the petition was filed with the Amsterdam Court, on 10 April 2007, available at http://shellsettlement.com/docs/Exhibit%202%20Articles%20of%20association%20of%20the%20Foundation.pdf.

of the total settlement value or roughly $50 million.[12] The settlement was conditioned on Judge Pisano dismissing the non-US investors' claims and, in the event of a settlement of US investors' claims on more favorable terms than offered to foreign investors, committed Royal Dutch Shell to adjust the foreign investors' settlement's terms to match.

One week later, Royal Dutch Shell filed a motion in the US court to sever and dismiss the claims of non-US investors, informing the court that it had signed a settlement contract with the Foundation, VEB and two Dutch pension funds. Although Judge Pisano had not yet ruled on the question of whether the court had jurisdiction over the foreign investors' claims, Shell's lawyers argued that he had 'discretion' to dismiss these claims on *forum non conveniens* and international comity grounds. Bernstein Liebhard & Lifshitz quickly responded with a motion on behalf of lead plaintiffs to enjoin the defendants from pursuing their Dutch settlement strategy.

The stakes could not have been higher for Stanley Bernstein. If Judge Pisano, in recognition of the availability of a Dutch remedy, were to dismiss the foreign investors' claims, Bernstein, Liebhard & Lifshitz would be left as lead counsel for a much smaller class, with a much smaller sum of alleged damages.[13] Moreover, without the foreign investors' claims, lead plaintiffs would have less leverage to negotiate an attractive settlement for the US investors' claims, lowering the total settlement value even further. In US class actions, lead counsel invest their firm's funds and their lawyers' time in preparing class action lawsuits for trial or settlement and are only paid if and when the class action is resolved, often some years later.[14] The judge assigned to the case awards fees and reimbursement for reasonable expenses to class counsel, who are not permitted to enter into a separate contingency fee

---

[12] CV-04-374, Dist. N.J. Royal Dutch/Shell Transport Defendants' Memorandum of Law in Support of Motion to Sever and Dismiss Non-U.S. Purchasers' Claims, 18 April 2007 at 15. Royal Dutch Shell's memorandum mentions only the 12.5 percent figure; it does not include the absolute value of lawyers' fees.

[13] How much smaller was a matter of contention as the amount of losses attributable to the reserve overbooking disclosures, much less their allocation between US and foreign investors, still had not been decided. Royal Dutch Shell claimed that only 10.7 percent of the shares at issue in the litigation were traded in the US and that less than 3 percent of shares traded in Europe were traded by US investors.

[14] By the time the proposed WCAM settlement was disclosed, Bernstein, Liebhard & Lifshitz claimed to have taken more than 50 depositions in the US and Europe, said it had received more than two million pages of documentary evidence and had engaged in multiple mediation sessions.

contract with the representative plaintiff lest this creates a conflict of interest between the representative and other class members. Although the formal rules for deciding the appropriate fee differ among the federal circuits, in practice the amount awarded is proportional to the total settlement value, with the actual fee percent, relative to settlement value, declining with the size of the settlement (Eisenberg & Miller, 2010). In large, complex class actions such as *In re Royal Dutch/Shell Transport*, direct expenses, not including lawyer time, normally amount to hundreds of thousands of dollars, and firms may invest millions of dollars in lawyer time, with the expectation that they will recoup these expenses plus a handsome profit if they prevail.

At the time that Bernstein, Liebhard & Lifshitz filed the complaint on behalf of the Pennsylvania funds, Bernstein was taking a gamble that a 'global' class of Royal Dutch Shell investors would be certified. A year and a half later, when Judge Bissell rejected Royal Dutch Shell's motion to dismiss the putative class claims, it appeared as if Bernstein had made the right call. Now he faced the possibility that even if lead plaintiffs prevailed on their substantive claims and Judge Pisano certified the class, his firm would earn only a modest fraction of the fees they had anticipated.

In their motion for an injunction, lead counsel asserted that it was unaware of the negotiations between Royal Dutch Shell and the Dutch pension funds over a settlement of their claims in the Amsterdam Court of Appeal until the parties filed their petition on 11 April.[15] They argued that the co-petitioners' action was 'a clear affront to this Court's jurisdiction and to US Policy regarding the conduct of securities class actions',[16] and asked Judge Pisano to enjoin Royal Dutch Shell and the Dutch funds from pursuing their settlement petition in the Amsterdam

---

[15] Our research interviews are consistent with this assertion. Despite interacting with Grant & Eisenhofer during pretrial discovery activities, Bernstein, Liebhard & Lifshitz appears to have had no inkling that the other firm was negotiating a 'Dutch solution' to *In re Royal Dutch/Shell Transport*.

[16] CV-04-374, Dist. N.J. Lead Plaintiff's Memorandum in Support of Motion for An Order Enjoining Royal Dutch/Shell Transport Defendants and Opt-Out Plaintiffs From Seeking Approval of Settlement Contract, 30 April 2007 at 2. Lead counsel noted that the two foreign investors' individual complaints had been consolidated with the class action proceeding subject to a condition that the individual plaintiffs would communicate with the defendant 'solely on their own behalf and not on behalf of the putative class'. Although lead counsel's motion was grounded on jurisdictional issues, it also raised questions about the fairness of the settlement to US investors.

Court of Appeal until he had decided the US jurisdictional question and ruled on class certification.

With the defendants' motion to sever and dismiss the foreign investors' claims and the class action lead plaintiff's motion to enjoin defendants' from pursuing their proposed settlement before him, Judge Pisano announced that he would conduct hearings first on the defendant's motion and lead plaintiff's counter-motion and then revert to the schedule for deciding jurisdiction, summary judgment motions and class certification that he had previously laid out.

With decisive hearings and decisions looming, Royal Dutch Shell and the US class action lead plaintiff, as well as representatives of the newly created Dutch foundation and VEB (which had no formal standing in the US litigation) met singly and together with Judge Politan in an attempt to work out a plan for resolving the multiple issues now before the court. The parties agreed in these sessions to ask Judge Pisano to appoint Judge Politan—who had earlier attempted to mediate the conflict—as a Special Master to review the evidentiary record and make findings and recommendations on the jurisdictional issue.

In September 2007, Special Master Politan delivered his report to Judge Pisano advising him that the court did not have jurisdiction over the foreign investors' claims. Royal Dutch Shell moved for dismissal of all foreign investors' claims and the lead plaintiff promptly objected. On 15 November, Judge Pisano ruled that the lead plaintiff had not satisfied the factual requirements under Third Circuit jurisprudence for the court to assert jurisdiction over the foreign investors' claims and dismissed the foreign investors' claims from the case. In his opinion, Judge Pisano noted:

> … this holding does not leave the Non-US Purchasers without an alternative recourse to address their alleged injuries. Significantly, the Non-US Purchasers can seek recovery through the Settlement Agreement entered into before the Amsterdam Court of Appeal or through procedures available within their respective jurisdictions.[17]

Henceforth, *In re Royal Dutch/Shell Transport* would proceed as a class action solely on behalf of US investors who had purchased their shares on the NYSE.

After the parties petitioned the Amsterdam Court of Appeal for approval of their agreement to settle the non-US investors' claims, the

[17] *See In re Royal Dutch/Shell Transp. Sec. Litig.*, 522 F. Supp. 2d 712, 723, 724 (D.N.J. 2007).

case moved smoothly albeit slowly through the process prescribed by the Dutch legislature. In this first instance of using WCAM trans-nationally, the Court proceeded carefully, paying particular attention to insuring that all those who would be bound by the proposed settlement had an opportunity to be heard and opt out if they chose. After a preliminary hearing in July 2007, the Amsterdam Court of Appeal issued a case management order that called for an extensive worldwide notice process that ultimately reached 96 countries outside the European Union. In addition to public notices in mass media, a leading bailiff[18] firm issued 350 personal writs of summons (notices of the pending action) and sent 240,000 letters to potential class members. The costs of the notice process were borne by Royal Dutch Shell and were not included in the total settlement amount. To ensure that few if any objectors would appear at the settlement hearing, during the lengthy notice period Grant & Eisenhofer lined up support for the proposed settlement from institutional investors and their lawyers within and outside the EU. Ultimately about 150 institutional investors as well as individual shareholder associations from throughout Europe joined in supporting the settlement.

Meanwhile, back in the US, negotiations on settling the US investors' claims moved into a new phase. By early 2008, the lead plaintiff and Royal Dutch Shell had agreed on a settlement, and in June 2008, as the Netherlands petitioners were informing foreign investors of their proposed settlement, the US lead plaintiffs filed a motion for class certification and preliminary approval of their settlement with Royal Dutch Shell.[19] Under the terms of the US settlement, Royal Dutch Shell would pay US purchasers of shares on US exchanges $79.9 million (described as equivalent on a per share basis to the value to the $341.1 million Royal Dutch Shell had agreed to pay foreign investors under the WCAM settlement). On top of this amount, Royal Dutch Shell would pay $6.658 million to US purchasers, which under the 'most favored nation' clause of the WCAM settlement would add $28.342 million to what foreign investors would receive. To match the $12.5 million that VEB had negotiated to be divided equally by all individual investors who filed claims under the WCAM settlement, US class members would receive another $2.95 million. Adding all these sums together, Royal Dutch Shell was agreeing to pay $471.5 million to settle all claims worldwide, with

---

18 In the Netherlands a bailiff is an officer of the court authorized to conduct certain judicial procedures, such as issuing summons. In civil cases, bailiffs are paid by the parties.

19 CV-04-374, Dist. N.J. Notice of Lead Plaintiff's Motion for Preliminary Approval of Settlement Agreement and Class Certification, 17 June 2008.

US investors to receive just under one-fifth of the total and foreign investors to receive the remainder. Royal Dutch Shell would also pay the costs of administering both settlements, plus attorney fees.[20]

On 26 September 2008, Judge Pisano certified a settlement class of US investors and declared the terms of the settlement 'fair, reasonable and adequate'. Two months later, the Amsterdam Court of Appeal held a hearing on the proposed settlement of foreign investors' claims. On 29 May 2009, the Amsterdam Court of Appeal formally approved a binding opt-out settlement of the non-US investors' claims against Royal Dutch Shell,[21] according to the terms that they had negotiated with Grant & Eisenhofer in the US three years earlier. The Court ruled that it had jurisdiction over all foreign claims not resolved in the US litigation under the terms of the WCAM statute and the Brussels I regulation on jurisdiction and enforcement of judgments. The Dutch settlement resolved the claims of more than 50 institutional investors in the Netherlands, UK, Germany, Sweden, Luxembourg, France, Denmark and Norway, and an estimated 500,000 shareholders. The litigation that began five years earlier had concluded.

PAYING THE LAWYERS

From 2003 to 2009, the average percentage fee award on US class action settlements over $175.5 million was about 12 percent (Eisenberg & Miller, 2010). This implies that had Bernstein, Liebhard & Lifshitz obtained a global settlement of claims equal to the amount Royal Dutch Shell ultimately agreed to pay investors on both sides of the Atlantic, the firm might have had a chance of obtaining a fee award approximating $56 million, or about 12 percent of $471 million. For their efforts on behalf of US investors the firm requested that the court award $30 million in fees—or about 33 percent of the approximately $89 million Shell had agreed to pay to settle US claims. At the time, the average

---

[20] CV-04-374, Dist. N.J. Stipulation of Settlement, 17 June 2008 at 3–4. An additional provision committed to pay $10.5 million more to US investors if, during the claims administration process, they were determined to have purchased shares on non-US exchanges accounting for more than 10 percent of all non-US claims by value. *Id.* at p. 4.

[21] ShellSettlement.com, 'Case History', available at http://shellsettlement.com/index.php?page=history. The Amsterdam Court's decision included a summary of the proceedings in the US and the terms of the US settlement.

percentage fee award for settlements in this range was considerably less: 19 percent (Eisenberg & Miller, 2010). However, Bernstein, Liebhard & Lifshitz argued that the 'potential benefit' of the settlement, including the fees and expenses that Royal Dutch Shell had agreed to pay was 'well over $180 million'. They argued that a fee rate of 16 percent calculated against this suggested base was 'well within the range that is customarily sought' and proper given the 'excellent result' they had achieved for the class.[22] On 26 September 2008, Judge Pisano approved the settlement and fee request as submitted.

The $30 million in fees that Bernstein, Liebhard & Lifshitz received for *In Re Royal Dutch/Shell Transport* was in addition to a $27 million fee that the firm had earlier negotiated with Royal Dutch Shell for their contribution to the resolution of the foreign investors' claims, an agreement that was disclosed to and formally approved by Judge Pisano.[23] Judge Pisano formally approved the $27 million fee although it is not clear as a formal legal matter that he needed to do so, given that he had dismissed the claims with which the fee was associated. The evidence suggests that this was part of Bernstein's price for withdrawing opposition to the settlement, a price that Royal Dutch Shell was willing to pay. Altogether, US lead counsel received $57 million, just about the average fee ratio when calculated in relation to the total $471 million that Royal Dutch Shell agreed to pay to settle all claims, even though the US firm had only secured $89 million of the total amount for their clients.

But what about Grant & Eisenhofer? The question of their fees never came before Judge Pisano, as they were not lead counsel in the US class action and normally, US courts do not inquire into fee arrangements between individual civil litigants, such as the Dutch pension funds, and their legal representatives. Nor did Grant & Eisenhofer's fees ever come officially before the Amsterdam Court of Appeal, for in the Netherlands, as in the US, fees in individual civil litigation are regarded as a matter between the law firm and its clients, and there is no provision in WCAM for the court to award or even review lawyer fees in collective settlements. Nor is there any requirement in WCAM to include information on lawyers' fees in the notice of a pending settlement, as is usual in US class actions. Grant & Eisenhofer had a contingency fee agreement with the Dutch pension funds to represent them in individual litigation in the US.

---

[22] CV-04-374, Dist. N.J., Lead Plaintiff's Memorandum in Support of an Award of Attorney's Fees and Reimbursement of Expenses, 19 September 2008 at 3–4.

[23] *See In re Royal Dutch/Shell Transp. Secs. Litig.*, 2008 U.S. Dist. LEXIS 32040, 14 (D.N.J. Apr. 17, 2008).

Contingency fee contracts are unlawful in the Netherlands (as in most other jurisdictions), but Grant & Eisenhofer's representation of its clients had taken place primarily in the US. In the settlement negotiations, Royal Dutch Shell agreed to pay Grant & Eisenhofer approximately $50 million. Our research did not provide information about how this fee was calculated but it appears to be in line with the firm's usual contingency fee agreements for representing individual institutional investors.

The lawyers that Grant & Eisenhofer hired to represent the Dutch Foundation in the Amsterdam Court of Appeal were paid by Grant & Eisenhofer on a normal—for Dutch litigation—hours and expenses basis. The Dutch firm's fees were covered by the fees that Grant & Eisenhofer earned in the US. Our research interviews suggest that Grant & Eisenhofer also may have shared a portion of the fees they negotiated with Royal Dutch Shell with other US law firms, perhaps to smooth the way for approval of the Dutch settlement. VEB's outside lawyers were also paid in the normal Dutch fashion, but the association's legal expenses were covered by the $6.25 million awarded to them in the WCAM settlement.

The $50 million Grant & Eisenhofer is said to have received from Royal Dutch Shell is equivalent to about a 13 percent fee award for the approximately $382 million settlement fund they negotiated for foreign investors—about what they would have won in a US court.

Together, Bernstein, Liebhard & Lifshitz and Grant & Eisenhofer earned about $107 million in fees, a fee percent of about 23 percent in relation to the total settlement fund of $471 million, about twice the average fee percent either firm might have obtained in a US court for a settlement that large. Although they were competitors in *In re Royal Dutch/Shell Transport*, the two firms have since served as co-lead counsel in other securities class actions.

REFERENCES

Chip Cummins, Susan Warren & Michael Schroeder, *Shell Cuts Reserve Estimate 20% as SEC Scrutinizes Oil Industry*, Wall Street Journal, 12 January 2004, p. A1

Chip Cummins, *Former Chairman at Shell Was Told of Reserve Issues—Memos as Early as 2002 Show Energy Giant's Tally Might Overstate Holdings*, Wall Street Journal, 8 March 2004, p. A1

Theodore Eisenberg & Geoffrey Miller, *Attorneys' Fees and Expenses in Class Action Settlements: 1993–2008*, (2010) 7 Journal of Empirical Legal Studies 248.

9. Litigation as 'core business': Analyzing the access to justice and regulatory dimensions of commercially funded class actions in Australia[1]

Camille Cameron

INTRODUCTION

Class actions have come a long way in Australia in a relatively short period of time. Since Part IVA of the Federal Court of Australia Act 1976 (Cth) (the FCAA) was introduced in 1992, group litigation has shifted from the old-fashioned representative action to a modern, 'North American style' class action regime. Statutory class action procedures were also adopted in Victoria in 2000 and in New South Wales in 2005. While the empirical evidence available clearly shows that there has not been the explosion of cases that some have predicted (Morabito, 2010), Australia now has what may fairly but not unreservedly be called a robust class action regime. Most class action litigation in Australia has taken place in the Federal Court, and that jurisdiction will be the focus in this chapter.

A unique feature of Australia's class action culture is the dominant role of commercial litigation funding. From about 2001, funded class actions have gradually become commonplace. This can be attributed to a variety of factors, including entrepreneurial class lawyers and funders, judicial decisions affirming the legitimacy of litigation funding and the positive contributions it makes to access to justice, and a costs jurisdiction with a cost shifting rule that prohibits lawyers (but not litigation funders) from charging contingency fees. It is safe to say that among the jurisdictions

[1] This chapter uses information obtained from 14 interviews with key actors (lawyers, clients, judges, funders), judicial decisions and media reports.

examined in this book, Australia has been a leader in the development of commercial litigation funding for class actions.

In this chapter, case studies of two securities class actions are used, the *Multiplex* and *Aristocrat* cases,[2] to analyze the development of class action litigation in Australia, the claims for and against their contributions to facilitating access to justice, and the central place that commercial litigation funders now occupy in Australia's class action landscape. Any consideration of modern class actions in Australia must take into account the growth and impact of commercial litigation funding. Not only were commercial litigation funding issues prominent in both *Multiplex* and *Aristocrat*, but as these cases were winding their way to a resolution, commercial litigation funding was emerging more broadly as a significant issue in Australia's litigation landscape. That emergence was characterized by questions about its advantages and disadvantages and how best to regulate it, and those questions are still being asked. These two cases, and especially *Multiplex*, played a dominant role in this evolution. This makes them an excellent lens through which to scrutinize the growth, roles, impact and probable future of commercial litigation funding of class actions in Australia.

Both *Multiplex* and *Aristocrat* were settled with favorable results for class members, and both were possible only because of the availability of commercial funding. These facts justify high marks on any 'access to justice' report card. This research has also revealed, however, the possible negative impact of commercial litigation funding on access to justice. One of these is the tendency of plaintiff lawyers who would previously have taken on risks as 'private funders' of high stakes cases to be less willing to do so. These and other positive and negative 'access to justice' dimensions of commercial litigation funding will be analyzed through the *Multiplex* and *Aristocrat* lenses.

The chapter also analyzes the relationship between a jurisdiction's legal financing structures and commercial litigation funder models, philosophies and approaches. While there are various reasons for the increasing presence of commercial litigation funding in securities class actions in Australia, the main catalysts are the risk of an adverse costs order against an unsuccessful litigant and the prohibition against lawyers charging contingency fees. The chapter analyzes the practical and ethical issues raised for class counsel in cases funded by commercial litigation funders, and how these might vary across lawyers and funders. The case

---

2 *Multiplex Funds Management Ltd v. P. Dawson Nominees Pty. Ltd* (2007) 164 FCR 275; *Dorojay Pty. Ltd v. Aristocrat Leisure Ltd* [2005] FCA 1483.

studies offer a good opportunity for this analysis—both were commercially funded, the *Multiplex* funder was Canadian and the *Aristocrat* funder was Australian, and each of these funders operates according to markedly different business models.

Finally, the chapter considers trends in commercial litigation funding, including how the industry is being, and should be, regulated. It is a relatively new industry, and the extant laws and regulations that might be looked to for guidance were not drafted with commercial litigation funding in mind. As the *Multiplex* case study demonstrates, courts are being asked to fill perceived (by some) regulatory gaps. This analysis will include a consideration of some emerging 'best practice' discourse about how to regulate the activities of commercial litigation funders.

OVERVIEW OF THE CASES: *MULTIPLEX* AND *ARISTOCRAT*

Multiplex

The defendant in the *Multiplex* class action was Brookfield Multiplex Limited, an Australian construction company with a substantial international presence. The claims against it alleged that Multiplex had failed to disclose information about delays and costs increases on several projects, including the Wembley Stadium project, and the effect these would have on its profit statements. The class members were investors who were alleged to have suffered a loss as a result of these non-disclosures. The case settled prior to trial and without any admission of liability, but only after substantial satellite litigation. Much of that litigation related to the role of commercial litigation funding and the relationship between the funder and the plaintiff lawyers.

The origins of the *Multiplex* class action can be found in several places, including an Australian Broadcasting Corporation television documentary, *The Road to Wembley*, that explored delays and costs associated with the Wembley Stadium project. Lawyers from the law firm that would subsequently become the class lawyers, Maurice Blackburn, watched the documentary and decided that further inquiry was warranted. They undertook a substantial investigation, including interviewing witnesses in England and reviewing other ongoing litigation between Multiplex and one of its subcontractors. They concluded that the facts would support a class action with good prospects of success.

This is an example of the kind of lawyering that is required to make Australia's class action regime work, and it is a far cry from the traditional roles of lawyers. It is sometimes called entrepreneurial lawyering, a term that has negative and positive connotations depending on who is using it. Some have criticized entrepreneurial lawyers and litigation funders for stirring up litigation that would otherwise not have been brought. Others have observed that 'solicitation is not improper per se', and that it may be a good thing if it identifies clients who would not otherwise have sought redress or even have known they were entitled to it.[3] One of the benefits of litigation funding, looked at from the perspective of class lawyers and potential class members, is that some funders take on much of this entrepreneurial investigative and 'book building' activity that would otherwise have to be done by the lawyers.

Having concluded that there was a good prospect of success, the lawyers then had to find a way to pay for what would be a very expensive piece of litigation. Maurice Blackburn are one of the most experienced class action law firms in Australia. In fact, they were one of only two plaintiff law firms with the experience to run a case like *Multiplex*. They had been the lawyers for the class in the *GIO* securities class action, the first successful securities class action in Australia. That case settled for about AUD$110 million. Maurice Blackburn financed the *GIO* class action themselves, that is, without a commercial litigation funder. Their *GIO* experience made them acutely aware of the financial risks associated with such litigation, in a jurisdiction with a cost shifting rule and where lawyers are not permitted to charge contingency fees, against a determined defendant with deep pockets. They went looking for assistance to fund the *Multiplex* class action and they found a funder, International Litigation Funding Partners Pte Ltd (ILF) willing to step in. ILF is a Singapore-based company in which a Canadian law firm has a substantial interest. ILF works closely with Maurice Blackburn and is actively involved in litigation funding in Australia. Since its formation in 2006, ILF has been involved in several landmark class actions, including the *Multiplex* case and shareholder claims against National Australia Bank (NAB) which were settled for AUD$110 million and AUD$115 million respectively. If Maurice Blackburn had been unable to find a commercial funder, there would likely have been no *Multiplex* class action.

Another prerequisite was to find a suitable lead plaintiff. The aim was to find one who would be representative of the class and who had a strong case. Several were considered, and the one finally chosen was a sophisticated private investor of substantial means who had an alleged

---

[3] Finkelstein J in *Kirby v. Centro Properties Ltd* [2008] FCA 1505, [5].

loss of approximate $40,000. He responded to advertisements about the class action and contacted the plaintiff firm.

If we contrast these facts with the selection of the lead plaintiff in *GIO*, we get a sense of the substantial change in class action practice in a relatively short period of time. (The *GIO* class action was commenced in August 1999 and settled in August 2003. The *Multiplex* class action was commenced in December 2006.) The search by plaintiff lawyers in *GIO* for a suitable lead plaintiff was more difficult, in part because there was no funder involved who would take on the risk of adverse costs otherwise carried in an Australian class action by the lead plaintiff (but not class members). It is much easier to be a lead plaintiff in Australia in a funded case, and much better to be a class member, but *not* the lead plaintiff, in one that is not funded.

Here the role of institutional investors in Australian class actions requires comment. Institutional investors had about 95 percent of the claims against Multiplex, yet none were willing to be lead plaintiffs. There were explicit refusals from some of these investors to take the lead; they were willing class members but unwilling lead plaintiffs. This is bad for the class because it has a negative effect on settlement. The presence of large institutional investors as lead plaintiffs and in settlement negotiations sends a message to defendants that can expedite the settlement and increase the settlement amount.

People who were interviewed offered various explanations for the unwillingness of institutional investors to assume the lead plaintiff role. One suggestion was that this attitude reflected the nature of the business market in Australia, where 'things are settled at the club'. In such a culture many (but not all) business people hesitate to sue one another. Another explanation offered was the fear of discovery. If an institutional investor is a lead plaintiff, they expose themselves to full discovery of the particulars of their claims and their losses. Many would prefer to avoid the risk of having any of their internal investment secrets and strategies revealed, either to protect their perceived commercial advantages or because disclosure might reveal that there is nothing about their investment strategies that is different from the strategies of many other institutional investors. It might also be the case that these investors have not yet adjusted to a class action regime in which astute litigation funders manage cases and risks, including the risk of adverse costs. Whatever the reasons for their reticence, the consensus among those interviewed was that institutional investors are unlikely to change their approach and will continue to hide behind other lead plaintiffs. In *Multiplex*, the result was that an individual came forward to serve as lead plaintiff.

The *Multiplex* class action settled before trial, as most Australian class actions do, and without an admission of liability by Multiplex. The alleged wrongdoing that led to the class action happened in the period between August 2004 and May 2005. Action was commenced in December 2006, and the settlement occurred about four years later. The beneficiaries were approximately 120 individual and institutional investors. Of the settlement amount of AUD$110 million, about AUD$10million went to the class lawyers for their costs. Of the remaining sum of approximately AUD$100 million, the funder received its commission of 35 percent and the balance was distributed to the class members. During the four-year life of this class action, there were approximately 46 interlocutory hearings, four Full Federal Court appeals and two Special Leave applications to the High Court of Australia (one of which was pending when the case settled).

Regulation of Commercial Litigation Funding: The *Multiplex* Satellite Litigation

The *Multiplex* case became a battleground over the role, and the regulation, of commercial litigation funders in Australian class actions. The defendant challenged the arrangement between the funder, ILF, and the class lawyers on the basis that the aggregate of the arrangements between them constituted a managed investment scheme as defined by the Corporations Act and was therefore required to be, but had not been, registered under that legislation. Multiplex asked for an injunction restraining ILF from providing any further funding for the class action and preventing the class lawyers from taking any further steps in the action. Justice Raymond Finkelstein, the judge who gave the first ruling in response to the defendant's request for an injunction, opined that 'what lies behind this allegation is Multiplex's desire to stop the action in its tracks'.[4] This is not an overstatement. My research confirmed that both of the securities class actions being studied here would not have been brought but for the availability of commercial litigation funding. If the funding source was cut off, then it is unlikely that the class action could have continued.

Here the role of Justice Finkelstein should be noted. During his tenure as a Federal Court judge (he joined the court in 1997 and retired in 2011), Justice Finkelstein presided over and made major decisions in

---

4 *Brookfield Multiplex Ltd v. International Litigation Funding Partners Pte Ltd (No. 3)* [2009] FCA 450 (6 May 2009), [2].

many of Australia's landmark class action cases. In his role as a judge he brought a keen intellect, years of experience as a barrister and a strong managerial style to these cases. He has had a very significant impact on the development of Australian class action jurisprudence.

The request by Multiplex for an injunction took this litigation down a path that the class lawyers and funders could not reasonably have predicted. The attempt to use the managed investment scheme provisions of the Corporations Act to catch an arrangement between a commercial litigation funder and class lawyers was akin, in the view of some, to trying to put a square peg into a round hole. The first instance judge (Finkelstein) agreed, but on appeal, two of the three judges hearing the matter disagreed. In their view the funding arrangement was a managed investment scheme as defined in the legislation. The decision that the litigation funding arrangement constituted a managed investment scheme had ramifications well beyond the *Multiplex* class action, as it was broad enough to catch all other pending class actions with similar funding arrangements.

One result of this appellate decision was a shift in the locus of the regulatory debate from the courts to the securities regulator and to the Commonwealth of Australia Minister responsible for corporate law. First, the securities regulator, the Australian Securities and Investment Commission (ASIC) stepped in to issue temporary exemptions under the legislation for the *Multiplex* class action and for all other funded class actions. In doing so, ASIC took into account the consequences of the appellate decision for the *Multiplex* class action and the members of that class, and for all other funded class actions as well. ASIC also considered the broader regulatory issues, including the case for and against regulating class actions and the additional obligations that would be created if funded class actions were treated as managed investment schemes. It concluded that without immediate intervention on its part, by way of temporary exemptions for all affected cases, existing class actions would immediately suffer delay, disruption and further expense.

But the ASIC exemptions were temporary, and the very considerable uncertainty created by the Appellate Court decision still had to be addressed. The *Multiplex* predicament was resolved by the intervention of the Commonwealth of Australia Minister responsible for corporate law. After consultations with stakeholders, including the parties in the *Multiplex* class action, he decided that regulations would be introduced to make the ASIC temporary relief permanent. The effect of these regulations was to confirm that the type of funding arrangement in *Multiplex* was not a managed investment scheme and was therefore exempt from those provisions of the Corporations Act.

Starting from the view that class actions enhance access to justice for consumers, the Minister noted that one effect of the Appellate Court's decision had been to halt the commencement of new class actions. Another concern was the impact the decision would have on existing class actions, once the ASIC temporary relief provisions expired. Consistent with the 'square peg, round hole' metaphor that some observers (and the Minister) had used to describe the effects of the Appellate Court's decision, the Minister noted that the managed investment scheme provisions of the Corporations Act had been adopted before litigation funding for securities class actions even existed, and simply had not been prepared with funded class actions in mind.

Broader regulatory theory principles also informed the Minister's decision. Imposing new compliance measures, and the related costs, had to be balanced with the benefits and protections created by the new measures. The substantial measures already in place to protect Australian consumers made the compliance costs that would be created if the Appellate Court's decision were allowed to stand disproportionate to any added benefits that might accrue. Those existing protections include provisions in the federal class action statute shielding class members from an adverse costs order and requiring court approval of settlements. When new regulations are adopted, there should be solid evidence that they are needed, but in this case there had been no complaints from consumer groups that consumers were suffering losses or otherwise encountering problems in the conduct of class actions. For the Minister, this was further persuasive evidence that it would be ill-advised to create the added compliance costs at stake.

There was another stream of satellite litigation in *Multiplex* that arose because of the presence in that proceeding of a litigation funder. The class definition in *Multiplex* limited class membership to those investors who had, at the commencement of the proceeding, entered into a litigation funding agreement with ILF. Multiplex applied to discontinue the proceeding, arguing among other things that this requirement created an impermissible opt-in arrangement, because the federal statute provided for opt-out class actions only. Multiplex failed at first instance and on appeal.[5] The judges on appeal expressed the view that using a funder criterion to limit class membership was not entirely consistent with the access to justice and efficiency principles on which the class proceedings legislation was based. They also noted, however, that the statute expressly

[5] For the decision on appeal see *Multiplex Funds Management Ltd v. P Dawson Nominees Pty Ltd* [2007] FCAFC 200 (21 December 2007).

contemplated such limitations with the words in section 33C that an action could be brought by a representative party 'as representing some or all' of those who have suffered the alleged loss.

This decision, and the use of these limited or 'closed' classes more broadly, has been criticized as inimical to the 'access to justice' goals of the Australian class action regime. Similar issues arose in *Aristocrat*, but in that case the main issue was a class limited by a 'solicitor criterion' rather than the *Multiplex* funder criterion. The 'access to justice' issues raised by these closed classes are explored below in the discussion of the *Aristocrat* case.

The *Multiplex* settlement received a considerable amount of media attention because of the substantial discrepancy between the recovery of the shareholders in the commercially funded class action and the recovery of those who participated in a separate settlement between ASIC and Multiplex. Two days after the *Multiplex* class action began, ASIC and Multiplex announced that they had reached a settlement following an ASIC investigation into the conduct of Multiplex. The subject of that ASIC investigation was the conduct of Multiplex regarding its continuous disclosure obligations. While Multiplex admitted no liability for its conduct, it acknowledged the compliance concerns ASIC had raised. It also gave an undertaking to undergo an independent review of its disclosure policies and procedures and to implement the recommendations that would emanate from that review.

The amount of the ASIC settlement was AUD$32 million; it extended only to shareholders who had purchased shares in a three-week period, rather than the nine-month period at issue in the funded class action. It was a condition of the ASIC settlement that any security holder who participated was barred from participating in the *Multiplex* class action. Only two of the *Multiplex* class action members chose to participate in the ASIC settlement, and only $20 million of the $32 million was taken up. Lawyers for the *Multiplex* class estimated their recovery for class members to be about 20 times greater than what their clients would have received if they had accepted the offer made by Multiplex in the ASIC proceeding (The New Lawyer, 2010).

It is hard to be too critical of ASIC, either for the discrepancy between the 'public' and 'private' settlements or for the other, arguably lenient terms in its settlement with Multiplex. Regulators are generally overworked and under-resourced. Just as it is difficult for an individual citizen to match resources with deep-pocketed multinational corporations, so do regulators face similar challenges. They may be repeat players, but they also have an explicit public interest duty, one component of which requires them to spread their limited resources across many cases.

The *Multiplex* class action settlement also received attention because of some public claims by Multiplex that the matter would have settled faster but for the conduct of the class lawyers. Multiplex claimed, in particular, that the class lawyers had failed to provide accurate data to Multiplex regarding the share trades of class members. The class lawyers countered by agreeing with Multiplex that the matter could have been settled earlier, but they attributed the failure to do so to Multiplex's litigation by attrition strategy, including its application for the proceeding to be discontinued because of the use of the funder criterion to create a closed class.

Settling any commercial dispute when the stakes are high is a challenge, and that challenge is compounded in an Australian securities class action. They are conducted in an adversarial system and, as the *Multiplex* class action demonstrates, they can become an interlocutory battleground. The tendency of Australian class actions to become bogged down in interlocutory proceedings, and the attendant expense, has attracted criticism from judges, practitioners, academics and litigation funders. Class actions promote access to justice and the vindication of shareholder rights, but sometimes at a huge cost. That cost is contributed to by interlocutory warfare and is one of the reasons why an increasing percentage of Australian class actions are commercially funded. Without funding they are beyond the financial reach of citizens and class lawyers.

Finally, while settlements have obvious advantages, they do little to clarify the key legal issues at the heart of securities class actions in Australia—the nature of continuous disclosure obligations, the nature and extent of the reliance required, and the calculation of damages and loss. Notwithstanding the fact that the majority of class actions in Australia are securities class actions, these questions have not yet been resolved. This will eventually be a job for the High Court of Australia.

Aristocrat

The *Aristocrat* class action was commenced in November 2003 by Dorojay Pty Ltd against Aristocrat Leisure Ltd. Aristocrat was in the business of making and selling gaming machines. Shareholders alleged that they suffered losses due to the defendant's misrepresentations and non-disclosures about its sale of poker machines in South America and its expected profitability in 2002 and part of 2003. Their complaint was that they had purchased shares at an inflated price and that when the true state of Aristocrat's business was revealed, the value of their shares plummeted.

Most Australian class actions settle before trial, but *Aristocrat* broke that mold. The claim went through a full (four-week) trial in October 2007, and settled *after* trial and while judgment was reserved. Had it not settled, some highly contested issues in Australian securities class actions around continuous disclosure obligations, causation and calculation of loss would finally have been the subject of judicial comment.

The total settlement amount was AUD$144 million. The class lawyers received about $8.5 million of this amount, while the funder, Insolvency Litigation Fund Pty Ltd, a wholly owned subsidiary of IMF (Australia) Ltd (which later changed its name to IMF Bentham Limited and is referred to below as IMF), received $37 million. This left about $100 million for distribution among shareholders. Some will criticize the diversion of such a substantial amount of money from those whose rights were affected—the shareholders—to a litigation funder. But looked at through an 'access to justice' lens, this is in significant respects a good outcome. Even with the substantial IMF fee, the shareholders were much better off than they would have been had they not participated in the class action. Without significant changes in the architecture of litigation costs and funding in Australia, including increased funding options for class actions, this need for commercial litigation funding will continue. It is highly unlikely that significant structural change will occur.[6] What might reduce the amount recovered by funders, however, resulting in more of the settlement proceeds being available for the class, is increased competition in the litigation funding market. See further comment on this issue in this chapter, Looking ahead—Whither the litigation funding industry in Australia?

While in *GIO* the plaintiff lawyers looked for but could not find a willing funder, and in *Multiplex* they looked for and found a funder, in *Aristocrat* the funder, IMF, brought the case to the lawyers. IMF had become aware of litigation between Aristocrat and its former chief executive for, among other things, non-disclosure and misuse of company funds. IMF investigated and brought its findings to the eventual class lawyers, Maurice Blackburn, who had also represented the *Multiplex* class. The lawyers conducted further investigations, which included attending the trial between Aristocrat and its former chief executive and

[6] But recent recommendations from the Productivity Commission to do away with the ban on lawyer contingency fees might be a harbinger—see below, in this chapter, Looking ahead—Whither the litigation funding industry in Australia? for a discussion of the Productivity Commission report.

obtaining and reviewing the court documents from that case. They concluded that it was a case with a good prospect of success.

IMF was also instrumental in identifying the lead plaintiff in this case. The person it recommended to the class lawyers (Jack Graham, carrying on business as Dorojay) became the lead plaintiff. We can contrast this with *GIO*, in which there was no litigation funder and the plaintiff lawyers made at least 70 requests before they found a willing lead plaintiff (Murphy & Cameron, 2006, 432–434). One of the advantages of litigation funding is that the funders take on much of the considerable leg work, such as identifying the class and a suitable lead plaintiff, which would otherwise be done by the class lawyers.

During the four years between the commencement of the *Aristocrat* class action and the trial, there was considerable interlocutory litigation. Much of that litigation concerned the attempts of the class lawyers (and, indirectly, the funder) to restrict the size of the class, thus creating what is referred to as a 'closed class'. These efforts ran up against a judicial view that Australia has an opt-out class action regime, that this means all persons similarly affected are in the class unless they take some positive action to opt out, and that any attempt to create a closed class by requiring a positive step to opt in is contrary to the spirit and the intent of the legislation. The 'opt-in' requirement in this case was limiting the class to those shareholders who had suffered the loss alleged *and* who had signed a retainer agreement with Maurice Blackburn, the class lawyers (the 'solicitor criterion'). It was also a provision of that retainer agreement that all class members would sign a funding agreement with IMF.

In the opinion of Justice Stone, the presiding judge, this solicitor criterion subverted the opt-out process.[7] She had no complaint about the solicitors having made a separate funding agreement between the client and the funder a condition of their retainer. That was a matter between the lawyers, the clients and the funders. Her concern was that the solicitors went further by making the retainer agreements a condition of class membership. She ordered either that the solicitor criterion be dropped, and the class opened up, or that the action be discontinued as a class action. The solicitor criterion was removed and the proceeding continued, albeit with a much larger number of class members.

One striking feature of this decision is that there were already numerous examples of Australian class actions in which the claim was brought on behalf of only some of those affected by the alleged wrongful

---

7 *Dorojay Pty Ltd v. Aristocrat Leisure Ltd* (2005) 147 FCR 394, 431.

conduct, among them the *GIO* case.[8] In many of these cases judges had not been concerned that some part of the definition of the class had the effect of closing the class or requiring some positive 'opt-in' step in order for people to be included. A review of these cases indicates that there are various reasons for 'closing' a class, including predictability, certainty and cost. A smaller group of identifiable individuals is much easier to manage than a larger group, many of whom are known to be 'out there somewhere' but not yet identified and their precise number not known.

Devices to limit and better define classes also help to manage and spread the risk and the cost of a proceeding, and to discourage 'free riders'. For example, a class defined by reference to people who have signed a funding agreement with the litigation funder (as in *Multiplex*) ensures that all those who get the benefit of the action will also contribute to its cost. This is based on the assumption prevailing in Australia that a funder can only be paid for its litigation services if it has entered into a contract with the class member from whom payment is requested.[9]

Regardless of what we may think are the advantages and disadvantages of closed classes, it is clear that section 33C contemplates such limitations, stating as it does that a class action may be commenced by one or more of the class 'as representing some or all' of the entire group.[10] Finally, it is noteworthy that the 'solicitor criterion' issue was taken up by Justice Stone in *Aristocrat* on her own, not in response to a complaint by the respondent. This makes intuitive sense, because some of the benefits of the ease of management and certainty referred to above accrue to class action respondents as well as applicants.

Quite apart from the fact that closed classes in various forms had previously occurred and were consistent with the language of the legislation, there are other reasons to question some of the reasoning on

---

[8] For a review of these cases, see Morabito, 2007. For his specific reference to the limiting device used in *GIO*, see p. 19.

[9] Some have argued that a judge has the discretion to order at the commencement of proceedings that all class members must share the costs of funding even in the absence of a contractual arrangement. In the one case thus far in which this 'common fund' argument has been made, however, the court refused to make such an order. See *Blairgowrie Trading Ltd v. Allco Finance Group Ltd* [2015] FCA 811. It is beyond the scope of this chapter to canvass these issues here. Readers are referred to Kalajdzic, Cashman & Longmoore, 2013, for some analysis of this issue in the Australian context: *see* especially pp. 108–109.

[10] This is how the Federal Court first instance and appeal judges interpreted the legislation and determined the issue in *Multiplex*.

which this *Aristocrat* decision was based. The judge relied on the report of the Australian Law Reform Commission (ALRC) that led to the FCAA class action legislation to support her view that closed classes were inconsistent with the opt-out philosophy of the Australian class action legislation. But there are some substantial recommendations of the ALRC that did not find their way into the FCAA legislation, namely, methods to fund class actions and thus to make them viable tools to achieve the 'access to justice' aims of the legislation. These exclusions, especially of a class action fund of the kind that exists in the Canadian provinces of Ontario and Quebec, combined with the preservation of the costs shifting rule and the prohibition on contingency fees, go a long way in explaining why limited classes have become the norm in commercially funded class actions.

FUNDER PHILOSOPHIES AND APPROACHES CONTRASTED

IMF, the *Aristocrat* funder, has been the leader (along with some entrepreneurial class action lawyers) in making commercial litigation funding the dominant force that it is in Australian class actions. It brings a new business model to the conduct of litigation, one that is unapologetically entrepreneurial. In fact, as a listed company with responsibilities to shareholders, it must be entrepreneurial. As explained above, it was IMF that conducted the initial investigations of the lawsuit between Aristocrat and its former CEO and brought the results of its investigations to Maurice Blackburn, the lawyers who subsequently became the class lawyers. IMF also played the central role in locating a suitable lead plaintiff.

These origins of the *Aristocrat* class action and the relative roles of the funder and the class lawyers represent a very substantial departure from the way in which traditional litigation is conducted. Just as the Australian class action relies on entrepreneurial lawyers for its viability, so too does it rely on entrepreneurial litigation funders. This is highlighted if we recall how the unfunded *GIO* securities class action was commenced and conducted. The plaintiff lawyers, Maurice Blackburn, had to find a lead plaintiff. They made many requests before they finally found one willing to assume that responsibility. They also had to explain to that lead plaintiff the costs consequences should the claim fail, because there was no litigation funder to assume the adverse costs risk. They took on all of the responsibility for advertising the class action and identifying class members.

In a funded securities class action, many of these responsibilities shift from the class lawyers to the funders. A sometimes overlooked consequence of commercial funding is that a funder like IMF is often also better able to get institutional investors on board. Funders like IMF work hard to build relationships with large institutional investors and can bring them into a class action more quickly and efficiently than plaintiff lawyers can on their own.

When the *Multiplex* and *Aristocrat* cases were being litigated and settled, there were about half a dozen funders in Australia, and IMF was the leader by a wide margin. IMF has been a change agent. It has participated actively in discussions about civil justice reform, especially but not exclusively in matters directly related to commercial litigation funding. IMF made a decision early on in its existence to list publicly, thus making itself subject to the same reporting and accountability requirements as any public Australian company. Its choice of this model was prescient. IMF had sufficient insight into the nature of the business on which it was embarking to know that substantial legal and regulatory challenges would arise. By taking the self-regulating step of public listing, IMF armed itself for some of these battles. One of these was overcoming the long-held view that funding litigation in this manner amounted to one or more of the following: officious meddling, champerty, maintenance or abuse of process.

The High Court of Australia was called on to address these issues in 2006 in *Campbell's Cash and Carry v. Fostif.*[11] *Fostif* was a representative proceeding brought on behalf of tobacco retailers to recover allegedly invalid licence fees from wholesalers. The representative claims were financed by Firmstones, a commercial litigation funder who sought out the claimants, agreed with those who joined the action that Firmstones would get 33⅓ percent of any award and would pay any adverse costs order should the claim be unsuccessful, and asked in exchange for some control over key litigation management decisions. The funding arrangement was challenged by the wholesalers on the basis of maintenance, champerty and abuse of process. The High Court rejected the wholesalers' arguments, thus giving a green light to the legality of commercial litigation funding in Australia and endorsing the legitimacy of a degree of funder control of litigation.[12]

---

[11] *Campbell's Cash and Carry Pty Ltd v. Fostif Pty Ltd* [2006] HCA 41 ('Fostif, HC'); *Fostif Pty Ltd v. Campbell's Cash and Carry Pty Ltd* (2005) NSWCA 83.

[12] As President Mason pointed out at para. [100] in the Court of Appeal: 'many people seek profit from assisting the processes of litigation. That a person

Fostif has had a major influence on the growth of commercial litigation funding in Australia. One of the results of that case is that funders have been given a considerable amount of control in the management of cases. IMF likes the amount of control that *Fostif* permitted, and it takes full advantage of that control. IMF's view is that it is taking the risk and should therefore also have substantial control. From a plaintiff lawyer's perspective, this can be problematic. As a practical matter, it results in a new and important role for that lawyer—managing the funder and ensuring that the amount of control the funder wants to take does not compromise the lawyer/client relationship.

The *Multiplex* and *Aristocrat* case studies offer some interesting contrasts with regard to the allocation of control over the litigation between the funder and the plaintiff lawyer. ILF, the Singapore-based Canadian funder that funded *Multiplex*, takes the view that a funder ensures that expert lawyers are in place and then lets them take charge of the case. If we imagine a control spectrum, IMF is close to the opposite end. It is entrepreneurial in a way ILF is not (although ILF did nonetheless collect about AUD$35 million in the *Multiplex* settlement).

I asked Australian class lawyers about the class lawyer/funder relationship, and specifically about funder control. They agreed that the impact of funder control on the relationships between the class lawyer and the class, and on the overall management of the case, is a matter for concern. They differed, however, as to degree. One view was that it is a serious matter, serious enough that if there were any way to run these cases without commercial litigation funders, that would be the clear choice. Another view was that funder control presents challenges, but none that robust class lawyers cannot handle.

COMMERCIAL LITIGATION FUNDING AND ACCESS TO JUSTICE?

What do these two case studies tell us about the relationship between commercially funded class actions and access to justice? They indicate—emphatically—that the availability of the kind of commercial litigation funding provided by IMF and ILF in these cases enhances access to justice. To some this may seem self-evident, because any additional funding option must expand the number of people and cases that can be

---

who hazards funds in litigation wishes to control the litigation is hardly surprising.' (see *Fostif*, n. 14, para. 41).

litigated. Litigation is expensive. Class actions, through aggregation of large numbers of claims, make it possible to litigate claims that would not be brought but for the class action. But class actions are very expensive, and very robustly defended. In Australia there are few law firms able to provide the private funding and to take the associated financial risks associated with securities class actions.

The intuitive view that commercial litigation funding enhances access to justice is supported by my inquiries into the *Multiplex* and *Aristocrat* cases. Respondents said that the claims would not have been brought if commercial funding had not been available. The *GIO* case was litigated before commercial litigation funding for securities class actions had become commonplace in Australia. The *GIO* class lawyers were financing that class action, and carried the very substantial risks inherent in any complex litigation and in a jurisdiction with a costs shifting rule. Securities class actions in Australia have not become less expensive since *GIO*. There had to be a successful securities class action like *GIO* to encourage funders to take on subsequent cases like *Multiplex* and *Aristocrat*. But the cost and risks associated with class actions in Australia make it unlikely that any law firm will want, or be able, to fund a securities class action. There may never be another *GIO*.

These case studies also show us, however, that while commercial litigation funding enhances access to justice in significant ways, there may be an unintended negative impact. My inquiries revealed that the availability of commercial litigation funding might make lawyers less willing to take on cases on a conditional fee basis (no win, no fee). This seems a logical outcome if we put ourselves in the position of a plaintiff lawyer who is responsible, over several years, for carrying the financial risk of a hard fought class action. That person must periodically explain to her law firm partnership why the case is taking so long, why it is so expensive and how an adverse interim ruling in the case might make the law firm's risk position worse than it already is. If in this climate the availability of commercial litigation funding improves, due to favorable court decisions and some natural growth in the commercial litigation funding market or to the emergence of one strong player in the market, experienced class action lawyers might gradually become accustomed to running large cases without the risks and associated stresses that self-funding can bring. In these circumstances it is not surprising that there might be a tendency to forego the cases that would require self-funding in preference for those that are attractive to commercial litigation funders.

To the extent that these unintended negative consequences for access to justice do occur, they are not limited to large cases. If it becomes possible for lawyers to take on more of these large cases because of the availability of commercial funding, this may leave them with less time and inclination to take on smaller cases that are not attractive to commercial funders. During the period in which I was conducting this research, IMF's practice was rarely to take cases worth less than AUD$5 million. It may be that cases that lawyers might once have been willing to take on fall through the cracks. This is somewhat speculative, but supported by the comments of one experienced interviewee who had seen this happen in a few situations.

The small number of commercial funders in Australia and the inability of Australian lawyers to charge contingency fees both potentially exacerbate these 'access to justice' problems.[13] One of the reasons why IMF has been so successful in the Australian market is that it identified and filled a gap in Australia's market for legal services. Lawyers can charge conditional fees but are prohibited from charging contingency fees. If lawyers' business models are shifting, intentionally or otherwise, to represent plaintiffs in more cases that are commercially funded and fewer that are not, the prohibition on contingency fees means there is no other incentive for them to fill the gaps their shifting business models might create.

This may help to explain why IMF added a pro bono public portfolio to its business and is giving some time and money to public interest cases. IMF acknowledges that its business model, with its high monetary threshold and rigorous risk analysis, can only advance access to justice for a limited category of cases. In 2011, IMF estimated that it funded fewer than 5 percent of the approximately 350 cases it looked at each year. But in that small group of cases at least, access to justice is promoted. Our two case studies attest to this. The *Multiplex* and *Aristocrat* class members received reasonably good recoveries. Courts exist to resolve disputes and to vindicate rights, and in both cases the rights of a large number of Australian shareholders were vindicated. This is highlighted when we compare the settlement in *Multiplex* with a parallel ASIC settlement. The subsequent recovery of the shareholders in the private class action (as a percentage of their individual losses) was much better that the recoveries in the ASIC settlement. Not only did those in the private class action have *access* to justice, in the sense that the class action vehicle and the commercial litigation funding meant that

[13] Since we have conducted our research for this book, the number of Australian and overseas funders active in the Australian market has grown: see below.

their claims could be brought, they also had access to *justice*, in the sense that they had a good outcome.

REGULATION OF COMMERCIAL LITIGATION FUNDERS

Courts have had a central role in addressing questions about the regulation of the commercial litigation funding industry in Australia. It was tempting to think that after the High Court of Australia decision in *Campbell's Cash and Carry v. Fostif* in 2006, litigation about the legitimacy of commercial litigation funding arrangements might cease. That case gave the green light to commercial litigation funding and eliminated concerns that had been raised about 'trafficking in litigation'. It also endorsed the need for funders to assume a degree of control in the cases they fund. But as the *Multiplex* case shows, this was only the beginning. Following the ruling in *Fostif* on the general principles of maintenance, champerty and abuse of process, the focus of litigation about funding arrangements then shifted to the 'nuts and bolts' of those arrangements. The discourse shifted from common law first principles to definitions in legislation governing corporations and financial services. There were many calls for (and against) regulation, and courts continued to be called on by defendants to fill a perceived regulation void.

This is a reflection of several factors. First, commercial litigation funding for securities class actions was still a relatively new industry when the *Multiplex* litigation began, one that the drafters of the corporate laws had not contemplated being called on by some to define that industry's proper roles and boundaries. Second, securities class actions are themselves a relatively new phenomenon in Australia, one made possible by the availability of commercial litigation funding. This is not a welcome development among many potential defendants, and it is not surprising that they would use the courts to try to proscribe the potential reach of these arrangements. Just as the satellite litigation in class actions was intense as class actions became more common and the class action legislation was being tested and interpreted, so it was with the advent of commercially funded securities class actions.

As a result of the *Multiplex* litigation concerning commercial litigation funders and their funding arrangements, the locus of regulation shifted from the courts to the legislature. The intervention of the relevant Commonwealth Government ministry, mentioned above, resulted in a set of regulations that took effect on 12 July 2013. Those regulations clarify the status of commercial litigation funding arrangements under Australia's corporate law and rectify the uncertainty created by the *Multiplex* litigation. Just as it was tempting, after *Fostif*, to predict that the legitimacy and status of funding arrangements had been settled, so is it tempting, again, to make this prediction post-*Multiplex* and its progeny, the Corporations Amendment Regulation 2012 (No. 6).[14] One contrary indication, however, was the *Chameleon Mining*[15] case, decided by the High Court of Australia in October 2012. In that case, which was not a class action, Chameleon purported to rescind its funding agreement with funder ILP on the basis that the funding agreement was a 'financial product', and that under the Corporations Act ILP should have been, but was not, licensed to deal in such a product.[16] The Commonwealth of Australia then immediately intervened again to amend the regulations it had prepared to address the issues created by the *Multiplex* managed investment scheme litigation. As things now stand, class action funding arrangements are neither managed investment schemes nor financial services.

It may be that *Chameleon Mining* represents the tail end of resorting to Australian courts to declare the rights and responsibilities arising from litigation funding arrangements. But there is room for a cautionary note. When the Commonwealth of Australia released the above-mentioned regulations for comment, two of Australia's funders criticized them as inadequate. IMF and Litigation Lending Services stated that the proposed regulations, which would exempt funders from the managed investment scheme and financial services license regimes but would require them to have in place appropriate conflict of interest protocols, did not go far enough to protect consumers.[17] IMF, the only Australian funder to hold a financial services license, estimated its audit and compliance costs related to that license to be in the range of AUD$50,000, in addition to the

---

[14] Corporations Amendment Regulation 2012 (No. 6) Amendment Regulation 2012 (No. 1).

[15] *International Litigation Partners Pte Ltd v. Chameleon Mining NL (Receivers and Managers Appointed)* 2012 HCA 45.

[16] Of all the Australian cases in which the funding arrangements have been challenged, this was the only one in which the challenge was made by the plaintiff. The funding agreement obliged Chameleon to pay an 'early termination fee' should there be a 'change in control' of Chameleon. That change occurred, obliging Chameleon to pay the fee. In response, Chameleon purported to rescind the funding agreement. The High Court described this at [11] as a 'counter-attack'.

[17] 'Litigation funders say licenses needed', The Australian Financial Review, 19 May 2011, p. 22.

$2,500 license fee. In the view of then IMF's managing director, this cost is minimal. He suggested that the compliance costs argument is one 'put up by funders who wanted to avoid scrutiny or by offshore funders "who don't want to pay Australian tax"'.[18]

One person I interviewed took a different view. In that person's opinion, the call for all funders to be licensed could be used by those already established in the market to restrict entry and competition. Recalling the discussion above about the need to grow Australia's litigation funding market, this is a legitimate concern. It is one to which the Minister adverted when choosing his 'light touch' regulatory strategy. While litigation funding has become a dominant feature in Australia's class actions landscape, the industry is still developing. In such a market, new players can increase competition, which in turn gives consumers more choice. One risk of creating heavy compliance burdens is that they become a barrier to entry. The Minister was aware of this risk and the detrimental effect such an outcome would have on Australian consumers when he rejected the *Multiplex* Appellate Court's characterization of funded litigation arrangements as managed investment schemes. He acknowledged the positive contribution of litigation funding to improving access to justice for consumers, the risk of impeding access to justice with heavy compliance burdens, and the need for increased regulation to be based on evidence, not speculation.

One area in which it was thought some immediate consumer protection might be called for, however, was potential conflicts of interest. The example offered by the Minister was when class action lawyers or funders were assessing settlements. He left it to class action funders and lawyers to ensure that they have adequate conflict management provisions in place including, for example, procedures to refer disagreements about settlements to an independent party for resolution.

LOOKING AHEAD—WHITHER THE LITIGATION FUNDING INDUSTRY IN AUSTRALIA?

A preliminary question is whether it is accurate, yet, to refer to the business of litigation funding in Australia as an industry. The litigation funding landscape in Australia has until recently been dominated by one or two funders. One consequence of this is that there is little competition or concomitant downward pressure on fees. But just as IMF is looking to

[18] The Australian Financial Review, 19 August 2011.

expand its business beyond Australia's borders, so are overseas funders like ILF increasingly willing to invest in Australian class actions. In a 2010 speech, Chris Bowen, the Minister responsible for corporate law and related matters stated that, as of 4 November 2009, 21 funded class actions were in progress, involving about 35,000 class action members and claims totaling approximately AUD$2.6 billion. He also observed that a further 16 funded class actions were proposed, with claims totaling an estimated $810,000 million. By the end of 2014 there were at least 11 active funders in the Australian class action market—six from Australia, two from the UK and one each from the United States, Singapore and the Netherlands. As the number of funders operating in the Australian class action market has increased, funder interest in cases other than securities class actions has also emerged.[19] The market is maturing.

In December 2014, the Productivity Commission released its report on Access to Justice.[20] One of its recommendations was that the ban on lawyer contingency fees in Australia should be lifted for most types of cases.[21] Among the reasons they offered in support of this recommendation were increased access to legal advice for consumers, an assurance of proportionality between legal fees and the value of taking legal action, the need to create incentives for innovative billing practices, and some competition for funders. It is hard to say whether this recommendation will be taken up. If it is, it will be a game changer for class actions and the commercial litigation funding industry in Australia.

REFERENCES

Jasminka Kalajdzic, Peter Cashman and Alana Longmoore, *Justice for Profit: A Comparative Analysis of Australian, Canadian and U.S. Third Party Litigation Funding*, (2013) 61 American Journal of Comparative Law 93

Vince Morabito, *Class Actions Instituted only for the Benefit of the Clients of the Class Representative's Solicitors*, (2007) 29(5) Sydney Law Review 5

Vince Morabito, *An Empirical Study of Australia's Class Action Regimes*, Report 2, September 2010

---

[19] Examples include cases arising from the spread of equine influenza (*Clasul Pty Ltd v. Commonwealth of Australia*, NSD368 of 2013) and the spread of an abalone virus (*Regent Holding Pty Ltd v. State of Victoria and Southern Mariculture Pty Ltd* (SCI 2010 6132).

[20] Productivity Commission, *Access to Justice Arrangements*, No. 72, 2014, available at www.pc.gov.au/projects/inquiry/access-justice.

[21] Recommendation 18.1. See especially pp. 625–626.

Bernard Murphy & Camille Cameron, *Access to Justice and the Evolution of Class Actions in Australia*, (2006) 30 Melbourne University Law Review 399
Multiplex settles $110m class action, The New Lawyer, 21 July 2010, available at http://www.lawyersweekly.com.au/the-new-lawyer/law-firms/13585-multiplex-settles-110m-class-action

10. The class attorney—an agent without a principal: The Israeli case of *Shemesh v. Reichart**

Alon Klement

Justice, like rain, is a blessing only if it comes at the right time[1]

PROLOGUE

Economic literature has taught us the importance of agency problems in class actions. Class litigation involves significant investments of time, effort and financial resources, in addition to the intrinsic risk of loss without reimbursement. While class action attorneys bear the entirety of costs and risk, they enjoy only part of the returns. This discrepancy leads the attorney's interests to diverge from those of the class. Under the simple agency model, such divergence predictably results in suboptimal investments of time and effort by the attorney, and in excess motivation to settle too early and for too little.

Nevertheless, examination of the prolonged Israeli class litigation case of *Shemesh v. Reichart* generates a more complex picture of the class attorney's agency. The case was filed as a securities fraud class action in 1995. By 2002, most defendants had settled for an aggregate amount of 10 million New Israeli Shekels (NIS).[2] As of that date, only two defendants still declined to settle: one was insolvent and the other bore

---

* This case study is based on my review of all court records in the District Court, archival records in various attorney offices and interviews with key participants in the proceedings: judges, attorneys and parties. This research was supported by the Israel Science Foundation (grant No. 709/12).

[1] CA 520/71 *Goldberg v. Belga*, 26 PD 456, 462.

[2] Since 1995 the exchange rate between the NIS and the US dollar has obviously fluctuated. However, an exchange rate of NIS 4 per $1 can be used as a rough approximation.

only indirect liability for the fraud charged in the case. Nevertheless, the class attorney persisted in litigating the case against them. In doing so he performed very skillfully, argued some of Israel's most significant precedents in securities litigation, invested significant time and effort, and consistently refused to settle the case for offers he deemed inadequate. This additional litigation, in which the class prevailed both on trial and on appeal, produced an extra NIS 3 million for the class.[3] However, it delayed the distribution of the initial settlement funds by another ten years.

Acting as an agent without a principal, the class attorney adopted a tough and relentless litigation strategy, contrary to the predictions of the simple agency model. This chapter examines the class attorney's strategy, in view of other factors that contributed to the prolonged litigation: court delay, uncompromising defendants and complications of securities class action substantive and procedural law. Viewed against these other factors, the question whether the class attorney's strategy was in the best interest of his invisible principals—the class—is a question that remains unresolved.

CLASS ACTIONS IN ISRAEL

Unlike most jurisdictions outside the United States (US), Israel has had modern US-style class actions for more than 20 years. Class action procedure in Israel has always adhered to the three basic features of the modern class action as adopted in common law jurisdictions:

(1) representation by a representative class member;
(2) contingent fee compensation for the representative attorney; and
(3) an opt-out provision, according to which all class members are bound by the outcome of the class action unless they request to be excluded from it.

The Israeli legislature has incorporated class action procedures into substantive laws in various areas such as consumer protection, banking, insurance, securities, equal pay for equal work and equal rights for

---

3 By 2012, when the total funds were distributed to the class, the present value of the initial settlements was NIS 13.25 million. Of the additional NIS 3.4 million earned, the class attorney received NIS 1 million.

disabled persons.[4] These procedures were modeled on Rule 23 of the US Federal Rules of Civil Procedure (FRCP), and were similar, albeit not identical, to their US counterpart. Thus, in contrast to Rule 23, each Israeli class action procedure was limited to a specific cause of action specified by the statute, tying different procedures to different substantive categories.

The first of these substance-specific class action procedures to be enacted was Chapter 9A of the Securities Law.[5] Chapter 9A allowed any holder of a security to file a motion to certify an opt-out class action, in the name of all security holders who held the same cause of action. To certify a class action, the representative plaintiff had to show that he satisfied the following requirements:

(1) that the lawsuit was filed in good faith and that there is reasonable likelihood that substantial common questions of law or fact would be decided in favor of the class;
(2) that the size of the class justifies litigating the lawsuit as a class action;
(3) that the class action is the most fair and efficient method to resolve the dispute at hand and
(4) that there is a sufficient basis to conclude that the plaintiff would adequately protect the interests of the class.

At the time *Shemesh v. Reichart* was filed, in 1995, only a few securities class actions had been litigated. Therefore, the parties, as well as the Courts, were presented with unprecedented issues concerning the law's interpretation and the mechanics of class action procedure.

In 2006, the Knesset (the Israeli legislature) enacted a new Class Action Law (CAL) which superseded all previous specific statutory arrangements.[6] The new law automatically applied to all pending class actions, including *Shemesh v. Reichart*. The new procedure was very similar to its predecessors, preserving historical requirements for certification and upholding the substance-specific framework of preceding statutory arrangements that designated which causes of action could possibly be brought as a class action.[7]

---

[4] For a complete list of these statutory class action procedures, *see* Klement, 2007.

[5] It was later superseded by sections 207–218 of the Corporation Law (1999).

[6] Sefer Hachukim 2054, p. 264 (12.3.2006).

[7] Class Action Law (2006), sections 3 and 8.

Even after the enactment of the CAL, class actions in Israel rarely proceed to trial and judgment. *Shemesh v. Reichart* remains one of the few class actions that proceeded to trial and was decided on its merits. It was appealed before the Supreme Court three times during its various stages, producing significant precedents on securities class action law and practice.

LITIGATION BACKGROUND

Faibel Reichart was born in Warsaw, Poland in 1900. In 1924, he immigrated to Israel (then Palestine) and in 1951 he opened a small factory for concrete products, that later developed into a prospering business with factories in two locations. Faibel had two sons: Ezra, the eldest, who—the facts indicate—was his father's favorite, and Dan. When Faibel died in 1968, he left Ezra all his shares in the family business, except half the ownership of the smaller factory, which was given to Dan.

In 1983, Ezra hired Menashe Cohen as the firm's controller. Ezra and Menashe managed the business successfully, and it became the Israeli market leader in underground concrete products. By the end of 1992, the two had realized that in order to further expand the business, they had to relocate the factory. To fund this relocation, as well as necessary investments in additional machinery, the two decided to take the company public.

In February 1993, preparing for the public offering, the business was reorganized under a new firm named Reichart Industries Inc. (hereinafter 'the firm'), which acquired both factories' assets. Dan, who owned half of the smaller factory, received 10 percent of the consolidated firm's issued stock in return for his shares. The rest of the shares were issued to Ezra, his wife and their three children. These shareholders, including Dan, signed a voting arrangement under which they were required to vote in tandem with Ezra on any subject brought before the firm's general shareholder meeting. Ezra and two of his children were appointed members of the firm's board of directors, Ezra was appointed as the firm's CEO, and Menashe as its CFO. Dan was appointed director of quality control, research and development, but held no role in the daily management of the firm, its financial business or its accounting. He maintained his old job as the smaller plant's manager.

Thereafter, on August 1993, the firm offered 12.5 percent of its outstanding shares to the public. In this public offering the firm raised about NIS 28.5 million, which reflected a market capitalization of about NIS 165 million.

On 3 April 1995, the firm issued an immediate press release reporting that Ezra and Menashe were detained and investigated by the Israeli Tax Authorities, on suspicions of fraud and tax evasion. On 28 April the firm reported that, due to accounting irregularities, it was suspected that the firm's financial statements did not accurately reflect its financial condition, and that restated financial statements would likely indicate impairments to the firm's value. By 30 April, the Tel Aviv Stock Exchange (TASE) suspended trading of the firm's shares. From 20 March to 30 April the firm's stock price dropped by about 71 percent. On 5 June 1995, the firm reported that it had terminated Menashe's employment due to his suspected responsibility for the accounting irregularities. On 9 July 1995, the firm filed for bankruptcy.

CLASS ACTION LITIGATION BEGINS

Moshe Shemesh, a carpet dealer, purchased options and shares of the firm on the TASE for a total of NIS 60,000 in February 1994. He had never sold the securities and therefore lost the entirety of their value upon dissolution of the firm. As it happened, Shemesh had a friend whose son, Shay Adler, had just finished his LLM degree at New York University Law School, specializing in securities litigation and regulation. The young lawyer advised Shemesh to file a class action suit in Israel.

On 16 July 1995, Adler, along with two other attorneys, filed a motion to certify a class action in the name of Moshe Shemesh, on behalf of all shareholders from the public who had held the firm's securities (stocks and options) on 3 April 1995 (the date upon which it was first reported that Ezra and Menashe had been detained and investigated). The class action was filed against Ezra, his wife and three children, his brother Dan, two independent directors, the leading underwriter for the initial public offering (Israel Discount Capital Management and Investment Inc.), the firm's accountants before the IPO (Rassuli) and after the IPO (Harpaz), and Menashe. The suit claimed that the firm misrepresented its financial status in its prospectus and in consecutive quarterly reports, thereby artificially inflating its stock price. The suit also claimed that the defendants were responsible, directly or indirectly, for the misrepresentations, and that by such misrepresentations they had violated various sections of the Israeli Securities Law. The estimated minimum total loss by class members was about NIS 13 million.

The class action was filed only one week after the firm filed for bankruptcy. At the time, the class attorneys were still uncertain about what exactly had led to the firm's dissolution. The complaint and motion to certify the class action were based solely on the firm's reports to the stock exchange and on the documents that were publicly filed in support of the firm's motion for bankruptcy, including an affidavit by Ezra. The affidavit reported suspicions of fraud, forgery and inaccurate financial reports. As it turned out, the firm's total liabilities were greater than its total assets.

Under Israeli securities law, the defendants' liability is joint and several, rendering possible differences in proportional liability irrelevant from the plaintiff class' perspective. Still, the plaintiff lawyers understood that some of the defendants had no direct responsibility for the fraudulent disclosures. One such defendant was Dan Reichart, against whom liability allegations rested entirely on the voting agreement with his brother Ezra. According to the plaintiff attorney's interpretation of the law, this voting agreement was enough to establish that Dan was legally considered a controlling shareholder, despite the fact that direct involvement in the fraudulent scheme was never claimed against him.

The defendants' main strategy was to challenge Shemesh's adequacy as a class representative. Their lawyers cross-examined him for two days, demonstrating that he had little understanding of the securities market, had not read the prospectus or any of the firm's reports, had actually bought the shares based on casual advice from a source he failed to recall, and knew nothing more than what was reported or mentioned in the bankruptcy motion. Furthermore, the lawyers showed that Shemesh was utterly oblivious to the grounds on which liability allegations were based against each of the defendants, and that he had insufficient resources to finance litigation.[8] In addition, each of the defendants argued that the complaint failed to state a claim upon which relief could be granted, and that it was sued only for its deep pocket.

On 15 October 1996, the Tel Aviv District Court certified the class action against all of the defendants. Relying on the firm's bankruptcy documents and immediate releases, the Court concluded that there was a reasonable likelihood that substantial common questions of law or fact would be decided in favor of the class.

Regarding adequacy of representation, the defendants' strategy backfired against them. The judge expressed her sympathy for Shemesh, as

[8] The Israeli Securities Authority (ISA) agreed to provide limited financial support, but it could not cover all future expenses of litigating the class action.

she wrote that she found it difficult to 'see him humiliated' by the defendant attorneys during cross-examination. In her view, Shemesh represented the unsophisticated investor, who naively invested his savings in the stock market. She held that his lack of financial expertise should not disqualify him as a class representative.

However, the judge questioned the adequacy of legal representation provided by the three class attorneys. She was concerned that the attorneys' rush to file the class action, only a week after the firm filed for bankruptcy, did not allow them sufficient time to conduct a proper investigation of the pertinent facts. Additionally, the judge was critical of the lawyers' decision not to sue the company. The judge also expressed dissatisfaction with the way that the lawyers had drafted Shemesh's affidavit, which was replete with legal conclusions that Shemesh could not explain upon cross-examination.

Therefore, the judge conditioned certification of the class action on three requirements:

(1) that the plaintiff would file a motion before the Bankruptcy Court to allow it to join the corporation as a defendant;
(2) that the plaintiff would provide the Court with a comprehensive plan for financing litigation of the class action; and
(3) that the plaintiff attorneys would be joined by an additional 'lawyer who is experienced in economic litigation'.[9]

This last requirement proved to be most significant for the way the class action developed thereafter. Adler, the young attorney who initiated the class action, approached Rami Ben-Nathan, a prominent Israeli lawyer who had mentored Adler during his internship, and asked him to join in representation of the class. Ben-Nathan, who by that time had already handled several successful class litigations, decided to join as lead attorney and soon took control of the case.

CLASS ACTION SETTLEMENTS: 1997–2002

The defendants appealed class certification before the Supreme Court. In addition, one of the defendants—the underwriting bank—brought a motion to dismiss Shemesh's claim, alleging that he had failed to pay the required court fees. This motion was denied by the District Court, and the bank appealed to the Supreme Court, claiming that the court fee Shemesh

9 CC (T.A.) 1134/95 *Shemesh v. Reichart* (Nevo, 15.10.96), p. 21.

paid was calculated based on the value of his individual claim and not on the total value sought for the class. The defendants were aware that Shemesh would be incapable of paying the 2.5 percent court fee calculated as a percentage of the class claim's face value, and hoped that the Supreme Court would reverse the District Court's Decision, effectively blocking the class action proceedings.

During the time that this appeal was pending before the Supreme Court, the underwriting bank sustained a stonewalling strategy and declined to engage in settlement negotiations. As for the other defendants, Ben-Nathan's team approached each of them in an attempt to reach an inclusive settlement. However, the plaintiff team soon realized that an all-inclusive 'global' settlement was not achievable. Therefore, the plaintiff team shifted to what they called a 'divide and conquer' strategy, trying to negotiate a separate and independent settlement with each defendant. This strategy proved successful. On 23 December 1999, the Supreme Court dismissed the underwriting bank's appeal over the court fee. This decision set the ground for the defendants to settle. Within a few months, most of the defendants agreed to settle for amounts that were, to a great extent, covered by their insurance.

The first to settle, on 27 December 1999, were the company's liquidator (also the trustee for Ezra's individual bankruptcy) and Harpaz, the accountant that reviewed the periodical reports subsequent to the public offering. Together, they settled for an aggregate NIS 5 million.

Next to settle, on 13 April 2000, was the underwriting bank, for NIS 2.5 million. Both the loss on appeal in the court fee matter and the fact that the liquidator had already settled persuaded the bank, and more so, its insurers, that settlement was in their best interest. These first two settlements essentially paved the way for the remaining defendants to settle.

According to section 54d of the Securities Law, class action settlements were contingent upon court approval. Unlike the new 2006 Class Action Law, this section did not include any further provisions that define exact procedures for the Court to follow in certifying the settlement.[10] Nor were there any precedents to guide the Court in the settlement approval procedure. This lack of systematized procedure culminated with the District Court's failure to notify the class—directly or publicly—that a settlement had been reached. Thus, the only objectors to the settlements were the other (non-settling) defendants, who were concerned about potential adverse effects on them, particularly since the settlements

---

[10] For the current procedure, *see* Class Action Law, sections 16, 18–19.

guaranteed that the liquidator and the accountant would participate and assist the plaintiff attorneys in the class action proceedings. On 17 May 2000, in a short three-page decision, the Court rejected the objections and approved both settlements, finding them fair and reasonable.

Between June and August 2000, each of the directors, including Ezra's wife and children, settled separately. Together, these settlements totaled approximately NIS 550,000. The Court granted certification, based on its prior certification of the first two settlements.

Three defendants remained: Rassuli, the accountant who had reviewed the firm's prospectus before the IPO, Menashe Cohen and Dan Reichart. Rassuli's insurer declined to provide the necessary funds for settlement, contending that the accounting firm's liability was not covered by the insurance policy.

On 12 July 2001, the Supreme Court dismissed the remaining defendants' appeal over class certification. In its decision, the Supreme Court affirmed the District Court's decision to certify the class action and endorsed its reasoning. Although the District Court had formally declined to stay the proceedings while the appeal was pending before the Supreme Court, hearings of witness testimony did not begin until the Supreme Court's decision. On 17 December 2001, the case moved to trial. According to Ben-Nathan, a day before Rassuli was scheduled for cross-examination he finally decided to settle. On 3 March 2002, Rassuli settled the case against him for NIS 2 million.

Thus, by the beginning of 2002, Ben-Nathan had already managed to accrue about NIS 10 million in settlements. Only two defendants remained adamant in their refusal to settle: Menashe Cohen and Dan Reichart.

At the time, Menashe's financial condition had deteriorated and he faced personal bankruptcy. Therefore, it came as no surprise that he did not settle the class action against him. Dan, on the other hand, maintained that he should not have been named a defendant in the first place since he had no responsibility, direct or indirect, for the firm's collapse: he did not serve on the firm's board, was not involved in its management, had no control over its daily business and accounting, and was utterly unaware of the alleged misstatements, fraud and accounting irregularities. Furthermore, due to the firm's bankruptcy, Dan had lost the total value of his shares. As described earlier, Dan had received these shares in return for transferring the 50 percent share he held in the smaller factory to the firm. Thus, in his own mind, Dan should have been a member of the plaintiff class and not one of the defendants.

In fact, Ben-Nathan's team recognized that, compared with all the other defendants' alleged liability, Dan's responsibility was rather feeble and that he could not have benefitted from any of the alleged misconduct. In this sense, he differed from all the other defendants, including Ezra's wife and children, who like him were not involved in the firm's management but stood to benefit from the firm's alleged misconduct. The poor nature of Dan's relationship with his brother Ezra before the firm's collapse could not be reconciled with allegations that he was responsible for the firm's actions. Therefore, when Ben-Nathan's team approached Dan, they made him a low settlement offer of about NIS 100,000. Dan, concerned that a settlement would constitute acknowledgment of his responsibility for the firm's collapse, declined the offer. Convinced of his ability to prove his innocence in court, he was unwilling to make such admissions.

CLASS ACTION LITIGATION: 2002

While the pursuit of quick and easy settlements and avoidance of prolonged and complicated litigation are characteristic features of Israeli class actions, the case of *Shemesh v. Reichart* played out differently. Ben-Nathan, lead attorney for the class, resumed litigating the class action before the District Court even while conducting settlement negotiations with the defendants. Ben-Nathan moved the Court to order discovery of documents held by the firm's liquidator and by tax authorities. He was also granted access to records of interrogations of firm employees—including Menashe and Ezra—conducted by the liquidator and by tax authorities. Based on the discovered documents and on cross-examination of Ezra, Dan, Menashe and some other firm employees, Ben-Nathan managed to expose a fraudulent scheme contrived by Menashe and Ezra.

On 27 November 2002, the Court decided the class action for the plaintiff class and against the remaining two defendants. The Court found that Ezra and Menashe were indeed responsible for the firm's collapse, as they depleted assets and squandered business opportunities for their own private gain. Their fraudulent scheme included production and issuance of fake invoices to customers and suppliers, profit inflation in periodical reports and financial statements, unreported salary payments, and surreptitious money and benefit payments to Menashe, Ezra and their relatives.

The Court found Menashe liable for violating his duties of care and loyalty to the firm and held him responsible for the aforementioned fraudulent conducts, which he performed by abusing his power as the firm's CFO. The Court concluded that these violations precipitated the firm's collapse.

As for Dan, the Court held that 'there is no dispute that Dan was not involved in the fraudulent acts conducted in the firm, nor did he supervise its accounting'.[11] Nevertheless, the Court found him liable for those fraudulent acts. His voting agreement with Ezra made him (together with Ezra, his wife and children) a controlling shareholder. As such, he owed a duty of care to the firm, which he violated by failing to supervise management and prevent the fraudulent acts, as well as by neglecting to inform other shareholders about suspicions he held with respect to the way the firm's business was being handled.

Regarding compensation, the Court encountered difficulties in accurately quantifying the defendants' liability. Since at least part of the firm's share price decline was attributable to market factors independent of the fraudulent activity, the Court found that an exact calculation would not be possible. Therefore, the Court determined the class compensation by way of estimate, setting Menashe's liability at NIS 3 million and Dan's liability at NIS 400,000. The Court awarded Ben-Nathan 13 percent of the total sum accrued in settlement and litigation in fees, and Shemesh an additional fixed amount of NIS 300,000 as an incentive payment.

Dan and Menashe appealed this decision on issues pertaining both to liability and calculation of damages. Shemesh appealed the decision on damages, attorney fees and representative plaintiff awards, all of which he claimed were set too low. Menashe, who had begun bankruptcy proceedings a month before the District Court delivered its class action judgment, lacked the financial resources to post the necessary bond for appeal, and his trustee was unwilling to make the payment. Therefore, his appeal was dismissed and Dan remained the sole defendant on appeal.

This marked a decisive moment for Ben-Nathan. He had to decide whether to pursue Shemesh's appeal against Dan Reichart alone, or to agree to drop the appeal against him and conclude the class proceedings.

Since the District Court had determined the remaining defendants' liability by estimate, without directly addressing the question of how the plaintiff losses should be calculated, its decision left no guidance on how to allocate the total fund accrued in judgment and settlement among class members. In a supplementary decision, the Court ordered that those sums should be prorated among class members according to the number of shares held on 3 April 1995 (the date of the first report on Ezra and

[11] CC (T.A.) 1134/95 *Shemesh v. Reichart* (Nevo, 27.11.02), p. 25.

Menashe's arrest).[12] However, the Court stayed the final distribution until the Supreme Court's decision on appeals over the class action judgment.

Importantly, all of the prior settlement agreements provided that distribution of the settlement funds would be contingent on final judgment rendered in the class action, and on completion of execution and collection procedures against all defendants. This was how the settling defendants secured themselves against subrogation claims by the remaining defendants. Thus, Ben-Nathan could not distribute the funds from the settling defendants unless he also settled with Dan and Menashe, obtained a final judgment against them, or decided to drop the appeal against Dan and concede his lack of liability. Ben-Nathan decided to move along with the appeal. Ultimately, this delayed distribution of the settlement funds by ten years.

CLASS ACTION APPEALS: 2002–2012

The Supreme Court only decided the appeal in 2007. On the question of liability, the Supreme Court approved the District Court's conclusion that Dan was a controlling shareholder. It also confirmed the District Court's conclusion that Dan failed to follow up on information and signs that the firm might be violating the Securities Law and therefore found him liable for the losses incurred by the class.

Nevertheless, the Supreme Court ruled that joint and several liability should not apply in Dan's case, and instead held that damages should be allocated proportionally between defendants, consistent with each defendant's relative degree of liability, which was to be decided by the District Court.[13]

On the question of loss quantification, the Supreme Court opted for an out-of-pocket measure, according to which the suffered loss is equal to the difference between the shares' 'true value', as established by the Court on the date the prospectus was issued, and the actual price at which those shares were sold. The Supreme Court returned the case to the District Court for calculation of those losses as well as the proportional liability shares.

However, by the time the case was returned to the District Court, the original judge had retired, and so a new judge was assigned to preside over the calculation of damages. The Court proceeded in the determination of Dan and Menashe's relative liability and issued judgment in

12 The decision was delivered on 9 March 2003.

13 CA343/03 *Reichart v. Successors of the late Moshe Shemesh*, 62 PD 437.

January 2010. Nonetheless, this decision too was bilaterally appealed by both Dan and Ben-Nathan, acting on behalf of Moshe Shemesh's heirs (by then Moshe had passed away).

In 2011, on the 'third round' before the Supreme Court, the judges expressed dissatisfaction with the parties' failure to settle. The justices advised Dan that in view of the litigation risk he was facing, he would be better off settling the case. They strongly encouraged him to rethink his stubborn insistence on litigating the appeal.

And so finally, for the first time in 15 years, Dan was willing to settle. He had given up. Yet, the price he had to pay for his insistence on litigating the case that far was high. He agreed to settle with the class for NIS 1.5 million,[14] and on 29 March 2011, the Supreme Court approved the settlement. Five days before, Ben-Nathan had also settled with the trustee who had been appointed for Menashe Cohen, who by that time had also passed away. That settlement was for an additional NIS 2.5 million.

At last, the case was over and the money could be distributed among class members (or in several cases, their heirs). Still, one last issue was yet to be decided by the Supreme Court—that of Ben-Nathan's attorney fee.

CLASS ATTORNEY FEE

Section 54H of the Securities Law provided that:

> The court will award the class attorney fee, irrespective of any prior agreement between the attorney and a plaintiff. The class attorney will not receive any payment in addition to the fee set by the court.

The new 2006 Class Action Law upholds the same principle, although the specific arrangement is more detailed and includes a list of considerations that the court must take into account when awarding the attorney fee.[15]

In 2001, following class certification and most settlement agreements, Ben-Nathan had moved the District Court to award interim fees for himself as well as for the class representative. He had requested 25 percent of the available settlement funds as an attorney fee and 10

[14] Dan accumulated an additional NIS 1.5 million in legal costs throughout this litigation.

[15] *See* section 23 of the 2006 Class Action Law.

percent of those funds as a class representative award. Ben-Nathan reported that his office had spent 1,733 billable hours on the case, and claimed that together with the three other attorneys who filed the class action and including the time spent on negotiating the settlements, a total of 3,350 billable hours had been invested in litigation.

The possibility of awarding interim fees was not specifically stated in the Securities Law.[16] Nevertheless, on 25 December 2001, the District Court awarded Ben-Nathan 10 percent of the available settlement funds. The Court reasoned that 'litigating the case required both skill and significant effort, continuing for a significant number of years', and that the billable hour report submitted by the attorneys exhibited sustained daily activity on the case. As for Shemesh, the class representative, the Court awarded him NIS 100,000 as an advance payment for his actual loss from investing in the firm's shares and options.

Eventually, in the class action judgment delivered on 27 November 2002, the District Court awarded Ben-Nathan a fee amounting to 13 percent of the total amounts collected in settlement and litigation. The Court reasoned that:

> the class attorneys invested much effort and skill in handling both settlement negotiations and litigation. One should take into consideration the case's complicated nature, the prolonged litigation, and the amount of material that was required to uncover the truth.

The Court also awarded Shemesh an additional NIS 300,000 incentive fee.

On 18 March 2003, Ben-Nathan moved the Court to allow him to collect his fee, as well as the class representative award, from the sums already collected. The Court accepted the motion, albeit stipulating that the actual distribution of funds would be contingent on the Supreme Court's final decision in the appeals of its class action judgment.

When the total damages were decided by the District Court on remand from the Supreme Court, on 27 January 2010, it was a different judge than the one who had given the class action judgment seven years earlier. This judge was very critical of what she perceived to be Ben-Nathan's insistence on litigating the case instead of settling it. She wrote:

> The class representative and his attorneys undoubtedly invested thousands of hours in litigating this case. However, since the actual damages awarded after litigation are lower than the total settlement amounts, it is evident that there

---

[16] *See* now section 23(c), which specifically allows for such interim fee.

> was no justification for continuing litigating the case after the initial settlements. Thus, the additional effort in litigating the case after reaching those settlements did not bring any additional benefit to the class … it even harmed them, in that during those years the settlement funds were not distributed and additional costs were spent on attorney fees and expert evidence.[17]

Therefore, she decided that the class attorney fee should remain 13 percent of the total damages decided, and fixed it at NIS 1.3 million. Remarkably, this implied a lower fee, in present value, than had been awarded seven years earlier.[18]

Ben-Nathan appealed the decision on attorney fees together with the appeal on the class judgment. As explained before, the parties settled the damages portion of the litigation, leaving the Supreme Court to render a final judgment on the issue of attorney fees alone. On 23 May 2012, the Supreme Court delivered the final judgment in this prolonged litigation. In its decision, which is now the leading precedent on attorney compensation in class actions, the Court held that the percentage fee should be preferred over the alternative lodestar fee mandated by some US Circuit courts.[19] It further held that the percentage should be higher for a litigated case than for a case that was settled early on, that the percentage should be inversely correlated with the total fund obtained in settlement or judgment, and that it should be calculated from sums actually recovered and distributed to the class.

Accordingly, the Court awarded Ben-Nathan a total fee of NIS 3.25 million. Thus, Ben-Nathan collected only an additional NIS 1 million over and above the present value of what he had already been awarded by the District Court in 2002.

In its prior decision, which approved the settlement with Dan Reichart, the Supreme Court stated that:

> We can only praise the excellent work done by attorney Ben-Nathan and his team in resolving this class action, in succeeding to reach settlements where he could, and in declining to settle on terms he could not agree to; as well as on his last settlement offer which was accepted. It is unfortunate that the trial

---

[17] CC(T.A.) 1134/95 *Successors of the late Moshe Shemesh v. Reichart* (Nevo, 27.1.10), pp. 35–36.

[18] It should be noted that although the District Court held that the class damages should be adjusted for inflation and accrue interest according to the law from 3 April 1995, it did not do the same for the class attorney fee.

[19] For a discussion of these two alternative fee methods in the US, *see* Eisenberg & Miller, 2004, 29–31, and Eisenberg & Miller, 2010.

court blamed Ben-Nathan for proceeding with unnecessary litigation, even though these proceedings added millions to the common class fund.[20]

In its final decision, the Supreme Court added: 'There is no doubt that the class action was well litigated by the class attorney and the class representative.'[21]

DISTRIBUTION TO THE CLASS

Even after this long litigation, one issue still remained unresolved: the exact loss suffered by class members owing to the defendants' fraudulent scheme was still unknown. In its class action judgment, the District Court refrained from deciding on this matter and chose to attribute liability to the two remaining defendants—Dan and Menashe—based on estimation. On appeal, the Supreme Court decided that the proper method for calculating damages was the out-of-pocket method, yet it refrained from applying this method to the case at hand, and remanded it to the District Court. The District Court, on remand, applied a different method—the 'constant dollar back-casting' method. However, its decision was later vacated, when the Supreme Court approved the settlement between the remaining parties. Thus, no conclusive determination of the total class total damages was reached by either Court.

At first glance, the measure of damages may seem irrelevant to the case of *Shemesh v. Reichart*, since the total amounts of indemnification were determined through settlement.[22] This, however, is far from true. The choice of method for calculation of damages in securities fraud class actions has direct implications for the definition of the class, as well as for the computation of each class member's share in the total fund.[23]

On 9 March 2003, the District Court held that irrespective of the suitable method of calculation, the accrued settlement fund should be allocated among class members according to their holdings on 3 April

---

20 CA 2046/10 *The Estate of late Moshe Shemesh v. Reichart* (Nevo, 29.3.11), p. 5.

21 CA 2046/10 *The Estate of late Moshe Shemesh v. Reichart* (Nevo, 23.5.12), p. 9.

22 It must be emphasized, though, that to decide whether the settlement is fair and reasonable the court must compare it to the expected outcome in litigation, which clearly necessitates reference to the proper method for calculating damages.

23 Explanation of this statement goes beyond the scope of this chapter. *See* Hannes & Klement, 2013 and Ferrell & Saha, 2012.

1995 (the date of the first report of Ezra and Menashe's arrest). This formula was, in the Court's view, the simplest and least expensive to implement.

By the end of 2002, the total value of settlements was NIS 10 million. This amount was placed in a trust, and accrued about 33 percent in interest until 2012. After paying the attorney fees and representative plaintiff awards in 2002, along with other costs incurred in the litigation, the remaining fund was about NIS 10 million, in 2012 values.

Following the final settlement in the Supreme Court, an additional NIS 3 million was added to the common fund, of which NIS 1 million was added to the class attorney fees. Thus the net amount that remained for distribution among class members totaled about NIS 12 million. This fund was distributed among 810 class members in 2012.[24]

Had the case been concluded in 2002, after everyone except Menashe Cohen and Dan Reichart had settled, the net sum available for distribution (after deducting Ben-Nathan's attorney fee as set by the District Court's class action judgment, and Shemesh's incentive award) would have totaled about NIS 8 million. If this fund was kept in the same trust account in which the settlement funds were actually invested, it would have accrued an additional 33 percent, so that the future value for 2012 would have equaled around NIS 10.5 million. This back-of-the-envelope calculation demonstrates that the class gained, at most, NIS 1.5 million in 2012 values, from ten years of litigation.

EPILOGUE

This case leaves quite a few questions unresolved. Why was litigation prolonged for ten years after the District Court's judgment? Why was distribution of the NIS 10 million in settlement funds delayed during those ten years? Would the class not have been better off receiving only those settlement funds, ten years earlier? And in particular: what was Ben-Nathan's responsibility for this delay, and were his decisions regarding settlement and litigation after 2002, which increased the total fund to be distributed but delayed its distribution by ten years, optimal from the class perspective?

Litigation was prolonged, first and foremost, owing to long delays in both Courts, and especially in the Supreme Court. Most significantly, it took the Supreme Court five years to decide the appeal of the class action

---

[24] 5/12 of the total claims were held by five institutional investors. The rest were held by private investors.

judgment. Even then, instead of rendering a final judgment on the remaining defendants' liability, the Supreme Court remanded the case to the District Court, to a new judge who enjoyed no advantage over the Supreme Court since she had not heard the evidence or rendered the initial class action judgment.

Litigation was also prolonged because Dan Reichart insisted on litigating the case and not settling it. After each major court decision, Ben-Nathan made Dan a settlement offer (which obviously increased from stage to stage), and yet he always declined.

Finally, Ben-Nathan could have stopped pursuing litigation subsequent to the class action judgment, even though this would entail giving up compensation from Dan Reichart, and possibly also from the main culprit, Menashe Cohen. Yet, Ben-Nathan never considered this a conceivable option.

Regardless of the prolonged litigation, why were the initial settlement funds not distributed to the class (possibly appropriating certain sums to cover future expenses, including additional attorney fees)? The simple and straightforward answer is that this was a decision made by the District Court in January 2003. Yet, given the malleability of procedural and substantive decisions throughout the case's litigation, this answer is unsatisfactory.

One factor that stood in the way of distributing those funds was a provision that was included in all settlement agreements, which provided that no funds would be distributed until final and conclusive judgment. This provision was meant to protect the settling defendants from the risk of subrogation claims by remaining defendants. Another barrier to distribution was the absence of a definitive method for calculating class members' damages, and consequently for distributing the funds among them. Yet, it seems reasonable to assume that both barriers would not have been insurmountable, if Ben-Nathan had wished to overcome them.

Ben-Nathan's litigation and settlement decisions were, then, a *sine-qua-non* for the prolonged litigation and the delayed settlement. Of course, one should not forget that nobody could have anticipated that the litigation would last ten years. At each point it would have been perfectly reasonable to suppose that one of the Courts was about to deliver its judgment soon, and that this judgment would bring litigation to a close. Still, Ben-Nathan's choices were pivotal throughout the entire course of litigation, and therefore his responsibility for its outcomes, good or bad, cannot be set aside.

There is no doubt that Ben-Nathan conducted this litigation brilliantly, and that he invested maximum skill and effort in every action he took—litigation, settlement negotiation, identification and location of class members, and distribution of settlement funds. His determination and uncompromising litigation strategy have probably also been a significant motivator for the defendants to settle.

Moreover, unlike most lawyers who file class actions in Israel and belong to relatively small law offices, Ben-Nathan had a well-established law firm (in Israeli terms), which grew from seven attorneys in 1996, when he was appointed class attorney, to more than 60 attorneys in 2012, representing some of Israel's largest corporations. Unlike most Israeli class action lawyers, Ben-Nathan's office kept a detailed record of the billable hours spent on the case. Altogether, he reported 7,736 billable hours, of which about 3,701 hours were spent before the class action judgment. Since the total attorney fee he was eventually awarded in 2012 was NIS 3,242,280, his average hourly fee was about NIS 400, probably less than his reservation fee (the average fee he charges regular clients).[25] Moreover, the hourly fee he received for litigating the case after the class action judgment in 2002 was actually even lower, since the additional fee he received for the 4,000 hours spent was only NIS 1 million, which amounts to no more than NIS 250 per hour. Thus, in retrospect, the additional litigation after 2002 was not worth its reservation value for Ben-Nathan, even without accounting for the inherent risk of loss. Furthermore, given the Israeli courts' unwillingness to award large attorney fees in class actions,[26] there was no reasonable basis for Ben-Nathan to expect a fee much higher than the one he eventually received. Therefore, although Ben-Nathan did take care to have his attorney fee paid by 2002, before distribution of the funds to the class, his litigation and settlement strategy cannot be explained on a purely economic, private profit maximization basis.

So, why did Ben-Nathan insist on litigating this case all the way? As he told me, he felt all along that being a class attorney, and having no client or principal, he owed a duty to the public. He refused to pursue the easy way out through settlement and insisted on bringing the defendants to justice.[27]

---

[25] Ben-Nathan actually had to share this fee with the three attorneys who had filed the class action, whose percentage of the fee I cannot disclose.

[26] There are no exact statistics on attorney fee awards in Israeli class actions. However, the fee awarded in this case was among the 20 largest fees ever awarded in class actions.

[27] In retrospect, this proceeding was the only one that imposed liability on the defendants, since the criminal proceedings that were initiated against Ezra, Menashe and the accountants were rescinded by the State.

Would the principal—the class—approve of this strategy? It should be emphasized that this strategy must be examined from the forward-looking perspective of the class at the time the attorney was making the relevant decisions, and not in retrospect. One can only speculate what the answer would be.

REFERENCES

Theodore Eisenberg & Geoffrey Miller, *Attorney Fees in Class Action Settlements: An Empirical Study*, (2004) 1 Journal of Empirical Legal Studies 27

Theodore Eisenberg & Geoffrey Miller, *Attorneys' Fees and Expenses in Class Action Settlements: 1993–2008*, (2010) 7 Journal of Empirical Legal Studies 248

Allen Ferrell & Atanu Saha, *Forward-Casting 10b-5 Damages: A Comparison to Other Methods*, (2012) 37 Journal of Corporation Law 365

Sharon Hannes & Alon Klement, *Loss Causation in Securities Class Actions*, (2013) 35 Iyuney Mishpat, The Tel-Aviv University Law Journal 639 (in Hebrew)

Alon Klement, *Guidelines for the Interpretation of the New Class Action Law—2006*, (2007) 49 Hapraklit 131 (in Hebrew)

11. The engine that drives: Fees, costs and the Canadian class action

Jasminka Kalajdzic

INTRODUCTION

There are certain fundamental truths about civil justice for victims of mass harm in Canada. Litigation is the predominant mechanism for obtaining redress. Litigation is prohibitively expensive. Those who are harmed cannot afford to pay for legal representation. Lawyers cannot afford to work on a no win, no fee basis unless there is the possibility of recovering their fees at a premium to compensate for their time and expertise. For these reasons, class proceedings statutes in all Canadian provinces provide for contingency fees and multipliers,[1] and thus create financial incentives for lawyers to pursue litigation that otherwise would not be economical for individual litigants to advance. 'This is the entrepreneurial aspect of class proceedings legislation that enhances "access to justice".'[2] While not an end in itself, the creation of a profit-centered litigation bar is the accepted means to achieve the 'access to justice' objectives of class proceedings in Canada.

Entrepreneurial plaintiffs' lawyers, therefore, are the engine that drives class action litigation. This simple truth gives rise to complex consequences. Tensions arise between the economic incentives inherent in class actions and a legal culture still firmly rooted in traditional professional norms. For instance, although it is inevitable that lawyers for the

[1] The multiplier method is a calculation that includes the base fee, or 'lodestar' as it is called in the United States of America (the number of hours docketed by all lawyers on the file multiplied by their usual hourly rates), increased by some multiple ranging from just over one to seven.

[2] *Fantl v. Transamerica Life Canada*, 2009 ONCA 377 at para. 67 (per Chief Justice Winkler). *See* also *McCracken v. Canadian National Railway Company*, 2010 ONSC 6026 in which Justice Perell stated that the 'Legislature has purposely designed a system for class actions that anticipates that entrepreneurial lawyers will be the vehicle for access to justice' (at para. 11).

class have a far greater financial stake in the litigation than any one class member, many judges remain ambivalent about—if not altogether uncomfortable with—the large fee awards sought by counsel at the conclusion of a case. Some judges are also skeptical that genuine plaintiffs drive the litigation, especially where representatives are recruited by class action firms.

The risk of adverse costs raises the stakes for entrepreneurial lawyers, and thereby creates further barriers to litigation. Representative plaintiffs reasonably expect to be indemnified against such costs, but class action firms, the traditional providers of such insurance, are increasingly unwilling or unable to bear the risk of paying a successful defendant's costs. Public litigation funders, and more recently commercial litigation funders, thus have an important role to play in the class action regime.

In this chapter, I explore the nature and consequences of entrepreneurial class action litigation in Canada. I define what is meant by entrepreneurial litigation in Canada and discuss in detail three consequences of this litigation model:

(1) lawyers actively seek out potential lawsuits;
(2) lawyers recruit representative plaintiffs; and
(3) representative plaintiffs are 'absent clients'.

I then discuss two specific features of Canada's civil procedure—fee approval process and the two-way (or 'loser pays') costs regime—in terms of their peculiar impact on the class action regime. But first, two concluded class actions will serve as case studies to situate the analysis in the actual conduct of litigation on the ground.

CASE STUDIES

Summary of Canadian Legal Context

Canada's collective action regime borrows significantly from the United States class action. A lawsuit is commenced by one or more persons who propose to act as representatives of the class. The plaintiffs must satisfy certain legislative requirements, including commonality and preferability, in order for the action to be certified by the court as a class proceeding. Assuming there is no settlement or a successful motion by the defendant to dismiss the suit, a certified class action proceeds to a trial of the common issues and then, if necessary, individual trials or damages assessments. A certified action cannot be settled or discontinued without court approval. Similarly, plaintiffs' lawyers' fees must be approved by the court as fair and reasonable. If the case is not successful, the plaintiffs' lawyers do not receive a fee.

Two cases studies, one a constitutional challenge to pensions legislation on the basis that it discriminated on the basis of sexual orientation, the other a securities class action alleging misrepresentation in the prospectus, help illustrate the ways in which the entrepreneurial litigation model affects the initiation, conduct and resolution of class proceedings. Brief summaries of each case study follow.[3]

Hislop v. Canada (Attorney General)

Hislop was a national class action on behalf of approximately 1,000 class members whose same-sex partners paid into the Canada Pension Plan (CPP) and died between 1985 and 1998. In 2000, omnibus legislation called the Modernization of Benefits and Obligations Act (MBOA)[4] was passed following successful litigation by gay and lesbian groups, in particular the Supreme Court of Canada's ruling in *M. v. H.*[5] The MBOA amended sections of the Canada Pension Plan and 67 other statutes that discriminated against same-sex couples.

In the case of the CPP, survivor benefits were extended to same-sex couples, but in a way that denied eligibility to same-sex survivors whose spouses died before 1 January 1998. Benefits were not retroactive to April 1985, when the equality provision of the Charter[6] came into effect, or the date of the spouse's death (whichever was later), but rather were limited by a second provision in the legislation to July 2000. Conversely,

---

[3] Information about the two cases was obtained from publicly available sources (for example reported judicial decisions and court documents linked to law firm websites), interviews with plaintiffs' and defense counsel, and case documents obtained from counsel. All interviews were conducted on a not-for-attribution basis, in accordance with research ethics board clearance.

[4] S.C. 2000, c. 12 (MBOA). The statute came into force on 31 July 2000.

[5] [1999] 2 S.C.R. 3. In this case, the Court struck down the heterosexual definition of 'spouse' in the Family Law Act as contrary to the equality rights guarantee of the Canadian Charter of Rights and Freedoms, thus triggering sweeping changes to all legislation which defined spouses in a discriminatory manner.

[6] The Canadian Charter of Rights and Freedoms, section 15 states: 'Every individual is equal before and under the law and has the right to the equal protection and equal benefit of the law without discrimination and, in particular, without discrimination based on race, national or ethnic origin, color, religion, sex, age or mental or physical disability.'

opposite sex survivors were eligible for one year of retroactive pension payments (from the date an application was received).

With a mandate to pursue public interest litigation, the Canadian AIDS Society decided that a class action was the optimal method for addressing the discriminatory impact of the revised CPP provisions, because the government would not be able to preclude a determination of the constitutionality of the provisions by settling the action with the representative plaintiff individually. George Hislop, a longtime gay activist in Toronto, agreed to assume the role of representative plaintiff. Importantly, he did so despite the risk of adverse costs, and despite being advised that he could likely succeed in settling an individual claim, but would be prohibited from doing so as a representative plaintiff.

In the fall of 2003, *Hislop* became the first national class action to go to trial in Canada. Following a 15-day trial in Toronto, Justice Ellen Macdonald found that the impugned provisions of the MBOA contravened the equality guarantee of the Charter and were therefore struck.[7] She granted a constitutional exemption to the operation of a general one-year legislative cap on arrears, thus permitting eligible class members to obtain pension arrears as far back as April 1985, when the Charter came into effect. She declared that the class members were entitled to retroactive pension payments up to one month following the date of death of their partner, and interest on arrears. She also awarded costs to the plaintiffs, payable by the defendants, of approximately $1.3 million, the highest adverse costs order in a class action at that time.

The Canadian government appealed, and in 2004, the Ontario Court of Appeal reversed Justice Macdonald in part.[8] The Court upheld Justice Macdonald's decision to strike down as unconstitutional the sections of the statute that restricted eligibility to same-sex survivors whose partners died after 1 January 1998, but set aside the trial's judge's grant of an exemption to the general legislative cap that limits retroactive benefits to a year prior to the date a claimant applies for benefits. As a result, unless a class member had applied for benefits before sexual orientation was recognized as protected by the Charter (a highly unlikely event), class members were entitled to, at most, eight years of arrears, as opposed to the 20 years or more permitted by the trial judge.

Class counsel had incurred fees in excess of $5.3 million by the time the appeals had concluded. The trial judge awarded them their base fee plus a multiplier of 4.8, the highest multiplier awarded up to that time.

---

7 *Hislop v. A.G.* (2003), 234 DLR (4th) 465 (Ont SCJ).

8 (2004), 73 OR (3d) 641.

Defendants had been ordered to pay slightly less than $2 million as a result of adverse costs awards; the remainder of the plaintiffs' lawyers' fees would, in the normal course, be paid out of the class members' trial awards.[9] These awards, however, comprised not just cash (representing pension arrears and pre-judgment interest) but also future pension payments. Just prior to the fee approval hearing, counsel for the government alerted the plaintiffs' attorneys that section 65 of the CPP provided that pension benefits could not be assigned or charged for another purpose. While section 65 was enacted to protect pensioners from ordinary creditors, government lawyers in *Hislop* argued that in principle it also applied to pensioners' lawyers, who sought to deduct their contingency fee from class members' pension arrears or from future payments.

In a second round of litigation, the parties made legal arguments about the applicability of section 65 of the CPP to the case. In the interim, the government would not advance any pension payments to the class members on the basis of provisions in the statute which precluded partial payments if entitlement issues remained outstanding. In 2008, Justice Macdonald ruled in favor of the government's interpretation of section 65, while acknowledging that the operation of provisions such as section 65 would render it difficult for class counsel to collect contingency fees in this and any other class action involving government entitlements.[10]

After losing on the section 65 CPP issue, class counsel negotiated a revised retainer agreement with the representative plaintiffs that permitted class counsel to contract with each individual class member to pay half of their pension arrears to counsel in satisfaction of outstanding fees. The revised retainer agreement was approved by Justice Macdonald. Class counsel subsequently contacted each class member and offered three options:

(1) pay class counsel a pro rata share of the outstanding legal fees, calculated as 50 percent of the class member's pension arrears;
(2) contract to pay this amount once the class member receives payment of benefits; or

---

[9] Class Proceedings statutes provide that approved counsel fees are a first charge on any settlement funds or judgment awards. See for example Ontario's Class Proceedings Act, 1992, S.O. 1992, c.6, s. 32(3).

[10] *Hislop v. Attorney General*, 2008 CanLII 8248 (Ont. S.C.J.), affirmed (2009), 95 O.R. (3d) 81 (C.A.), leave to appeal denied 2009 CanLII 59424 (S.C.C.).

(3) do nothing while Justice Macdonald's decision regarding section 65 was under appeal.

Those class members who selected options 1 or 2 would be eligible to start receiving their pension benefits, because class counsel would confirm to the defendants that no entitlement issues remained and the prohibition against partial payments in the CPP statute, therefore, did not apply. Class members who selected option 3 continued to wait for payment.

In late 2009, once the section 65 appeals were exhausted, those class members who did not voluntarily agree to contribute to lawyers' fees, or who had contracted to pay but were in default, were the subject of enforcement proceedings instituted by the plaintiffs' firm. Class counsel ultimately collected approximately $6 million from cost awards, pre-judgment interest payments and payments by the class. This amount represents payment of class counsel's base fee and a multiplier of less than 1.5, about one-third of the multiplier awarded by the judge.

Lawrence v. Atlas Cold Storage Holdings Inc

In 2001 and 2002, Atlas, which operated North America's second largest temperature-controlled distribution network of storage and logistics services, made five public offerings of units on the Toronto Stock Exchange. In the spring of 2003, an anonymous letter was sent to the Ontario Securities Commission (OSC) and copied to Atlas' Audit Committee claiming that there were serious irregularities in Atlas' financial reporting. The Audit Committee hired forensic accountants to conduct an internal review of the company's accounting policies and practices. In late August 2003, Atlas announced that the independent investigation had revealed a number of accounting errors, and that Atlas' net earnings were overstated. As a result of the announcement, the trading price of units fell. Three months later, the OSC issued a cease trade order against management and insiders. On 30 January 2004, the company announced that it was filing amended financial statements for fiscal 2001 and 2002; altogether, earnings were approximately $43 million less than originally stated. According to experts subsequently retained by the parties in the class proceeding, overstated earnings artificially inflated the unit price anywhere from $1.80 to $6.80 per unit.

Following Atlas' public announcement in August 2003, a lawyer at a Windsor, Ontario law firm 'flagged' Atlas as a potential litigation target and started researching the company, including obtaining and identifying key documents available on public databases and in the press. The firm eventually located a potential plaintiff, Anne Eagles, by way of a stockbroker with whom a firm lawyer was acquainted. Separately, Paul Lawrence, a chartered accountant and Atlas unit-holder, contacted a Toronto law firm to inquire about the possibility of suing Atlas for recovery of his losses. The two law firms had worked together on other class actions; a casual conversation between lawyers at the firms revealed that both were interested in pursuing an action against Atlas. Counsel decided to work together, and soon approached a third law firm, with expertise in securities law, to join the counsel team.

A proposed class action was launched in February 2004 against Atlas, its directors and officers, the auditor and the underwriter of the public offering. The plaintiffs sought monetary damages in the amount by which the unit price had been inflated as a result of the alleged misstatements in the prospectus.

In the early stages of the lawsuit, plaintiffs' counsel determined that neither Eagles nor Lawrence had purchased their units in the primary market during the periods of distribution under the prospectuses. Where and when the plaintiffs (and other class members) had purchased their units was critical to the action because under the Securities Act, investors are deemed to have relied on misrepresentations contained in a prospectus or offering memorandum during the period of distribution, a provision that had only been interpreted to apply to purchases in the primary market.[11] Conversely, as a matter of tort law, secondary market purchasers need to prove individual reliance on a misrepresentation, a rule that is usually fatal to class certification. To insure against the risk of a non-certifiable class action, lawyers for the plaintiffs actively sought an Atlas unit-holder who made the purchase during the period of distribution in the primary market. They published an advertisement in a national newspaper. Charles Simon, a retired lawyer, responded to the ad and agreed to act as a representative plaintiff if given an indemnity against any potential adverse costs awards.

Class counsel applied to Ontario's Class Proceedings Fund, which had been established under the Law Society Amendment Act in 1993, when Ontario passed its class proceedings statute. The Fund provides financial support to class action plaintiffs for disbursements. More importantly, the Fund indemnifies the representative plaintiff against all costs orders. In return, the representative plaintiff agrees to a 10 percent levy on the settlement or judgment in the action (after counsel fees have been deducted). In June 2004, the Class Proceedings Committee, made up of

[11] Securities Act, R.S.O. 1990, c.S.5, s. 130.

five lawyers appointed by the Attorney General and Law Foundation of Ontario, approved class counsel's application for funding in *Atlas*. Thus, Charles Simon and the other representative plaintiffs were insulated from adverse costs orders, and their own lawyers were not obligated to provide such an indemnity as has become the norm in class action litigation in Ontario.[12]

In addition to a number of interlocutory motions of lesser significance, the defendants brought a motion to strike out the statement of claim in 2006. The defendants were partially successful in striking out some of the causes of action as against some defendants, but the bulk of the action remained intact. The judge, however, expressed some misgivings about the strength of the plaintiffs' claim that class members who made the purchase during the period of distribution were deemed to have relied upon the misrepresentations under securities legislation, even if they did not purchase their units from the underwriter. Her reasons for this decision were interpreted by many of the lawyers in the litigation as sending a subtle signal that they should consider discussing settlement. Notwithstanding this view, settlement discussions did not begin for another 15 months, on the eve of the certification motion.

A settlement agreement was executed in June 2008, over four years after the initiation of the lawsuit. The parties agreed to a $40 million settlement fund, on a 'claims made' basis, with no reversion to the defendants.[13] Approximately 10,000 individual notices were delivered electronically to brokers for dissemination to their clients and mailed to class members. There were no objections to the settlement registered.

---

[12] *McCracken v. Canadian National Railway Company*, 2010 ONSC 6026 at para. 7, reversed on other grounds 2012 ONCA 445 (CanLII) ('it is well known that if the plaintiff is unsuccessful in obtaining certification or if the class is ultimately unsuccessful, the plaintiff will be insulated from costs liability by having obtained funding from the Class Proceedings Fund of the Law Foundation of Ontario or by having obtained an indemnity agreement from class counsel').

[13] 'Claims made' settlement structures require class members to apply for their portion of the settlement fund. The claims administrator (either the plaintiffs' law firm or a third party) determines eligibility and processes the claims. 'Reversion' refers to the practice of returning to the defendant any monies not claimed by class members or paid to counsel as fees. Canadian courts generally do not favor reversion clauses on the basis that the full deterrence value of a class action is not realized if defendants are permitted to recoup any part of the settlement fund. In *Atlas*, any money left in the settlement fund once all claims had been paid were to be distributed cy pres; this proved unnecessary as the entire fund was distributed to class members.

The certification and approval hearing for the proposed settlement was heard in August 2008. At this hearing, counsel for the class also sought approval of their fee. Justice Lax certified the action,[14] and approved the $40 million settlement as fair and reasonable in light of the complexities of the legal issues, the rapidly depleting insurance limits, and the possibility that additional encumbrances were registered against Atlas' assets when the company was taken private in 2006.[15]

The question of counsel fee, however, was more fraught. Justice Lax heard from three class members who objected to the $12 million fee sought by counsel. The three law firms that had prosecuted the action had accumulated base fees of CAD 3.25 million and were seeking a 3.7 multiplier, or what amounted to a total fee that was 30 percent of the gross settlement amount. The objectors argued that the fees were disproportionate to the settlement achieved, in an action that settled well before trial. Justice Lax found these objections to be valid. Although she accepted that the litigation was risky and that counsel had obtained as good a result as could be achieved under the circumstances, she did not find the base fee to be reasonable. She reduced the fee by 25 percent and set the multiplier at 2.6, thereby slashing the contracted for contingency fee to approximately $6.3 million.

Class counsel unsuccessfully appealed the fee order and were ordered to pay the objectors $10,000 in costs.[16] In the course of rendering its decision, the Court of Appeal affirmed that while judges must consider the fee agreement signed by representative plaintiffs, they are not bound to accept it. The courts are the ultimate arbiters of what is fair and reasonable for lawyers to charge class members.

ENTREPRENEURIAL LITIGATION

The main component of the engine that drives Canadian class actions is the contingency fee. This is due to what Gillian Hadfield calls the 'brute economics of modern litigation': 'if there isn't a lot of money to change hands, there's no way to pay the lawyers who are by and large necessary

---

[14] In Canada, consent certifications still require the approval of a judge, though the test for certification in such instances is less stringent: *Bellaire v. Daya*, [2007] O.J. No. 4819 (S.C.J.) at para. 16.

[15] *Lawrence v. Atlas Cold Storage Holdings Inc.*, 2009 CanLII 55128 (ON SC).

[16] *Sutts, Strosberg LLP v. Atlas Cold Storage Holdings Inc*, 2009 ONCA 690 (CanLII).

for the costly process of adjudicating complex legal claims.' (Hadfield, 2005). By permitting class counsel to collect either a percentage of the class' recovery in the action, or a multiple of the usual hourly rates charged,[17] class action lawyers are incentivized to pursue the cases with the highest possibility of success coupled with potentially large monetary damages.

The ramifications of this financial model are well-known. Firstly, the profit motive encourages lawyers to actively seek out viable class actions. Law firms spend considerable resources researching potential class actions, on their own initiative, sometimes as a result of media coverage of an event (as occurred in the *Atlas* case). This departure from the traditional paradigm of the lawyer who waits for an aggrieved party to seek out legal representation is not surprising in the mass harm context. For one, the information asymmetry that exists in many (though not all) situations of mass harm between the wrongdoer and the wronged renders it unlikely that members of the class will have the wherewithal to seek legal advice. Even where the naming and blaming of the harm has occurred, the amounts at issue for an individual can be too low to warrant the effort of making a claim.[18] Moreover, some events causing mass harm —for example, the production of harmful consumer products, or anti-competitive behavior—result in geographically diffuse classes, whose members have little ability to identify and communicate with each other. Class counsel's active search for potential class actions can thus be viewed as bridging the informational divide that would otherwise make mass harm litigation unfeasible.

A second ramification of the entrepreneurial model is the active recruitment of representative plaintiffs. Both *Hislop* and *Atlas* involved the search for suitable plaintiffs to initiate the claims; in the case of *Hislop*, the lawyers' search for activists in the lesbian and gay community led them to George Hislop. In the case of *Atlas*, lawyers' contacts in the financial services sector were tapped to find one plaintiff, and an advertisement published in a national newspaper resulted in another plaintiff being added subsequently. Again, such recruitment activity is a marked departure from the usual barrister's practice. Although the solicitation of plaintiffs has a long history in test case litigation in the civil rights movement, that it is done in class actions for purely monetary

---

[17] Although most statutes refer only to a contingency fee on the basis of a percentage of recovery, the courts have regularly approved contingencies calculated on the lodestar, or multiplier, method.

[18] I am here referring to the well-known dispute resolution theory described in the seminal article by Felstiner, Abel & Sarat, 1981.

gain is unpalatable for some judges. Their discomfort with the practice is most evident in the jurisprudence regarding the test for the 'appropriate' representative plaintiff.

The test for certification in Canadian class action statutes requires, among other things, that there be a representative plaintiff who:

(1) would fairly and adequately represent the interests of the class;
(2) has produced a plan for the proceeding that sets out a workable method of advancing the proceeding on behalf of the class and of notifying class members of the proceeding; and
(3) does not have, on the common issues for the class, an interest in conflict with the interests of other class members.[19]

Some courts have viewed the fact that the proposed representative was recruited by the plaintiff law firm to become involved in the litigation as evidence of a representative who is not adequately motivated to protect the interests of the rest of the class.[20] Other courts have adopted the pragmatic view that recruitment is inevitable.[21]

The current judicial approach to the question of recruitment is one of cautious acceptance. In this regard, in a case denying certification of a proceeding against a sunscreen manufacturer, Justice Strathy of the Ontario Superior Court of Justice (as he then was[22]) stated:

> I agree that recruitment of the class representative is not fatal. After all, not many people wake up in the morning and decide that they want to start a class action. They may well need the encouragement of experienced counsel to take up the cudgels and put their name to a worthy cause. Recruitment was obviously not fatal in *Fantl v. Transamerica Life Canada*; however, the recruitment of the plaintiff is a factor to be considered in determining whether the plaintiff has the necessary interest, independence and incentive to fulfill his or her duties to the class. It is also a factor to be considered in assessing

19 Ontario CPA, supra note 9, s. 5(1)(e).

20 See for example *Singer v. Schering-Plough Canada Inc.*, 2010 ONSC 42 (CanLII).

21 *Fantl v. Transamerica Life Canada*, 2008 CanLII 17304 (ON SC). In this case, Mr. Fantl was recruited but still found to be a 'genuine' plaintiff, with the right to change lawyers and provide instructions as would an ordinary litigant. For a critical discussion of Fantl and the notion of the genuine plaintiff in class proceedings, see Kalajdzic, 2011.

22 In June 2014, Justice Strathy was promoted to Chief Justice of Ontario's Court of Appeal.

> whether there is indeed an underlying class with an actual grievance, as opposed to an issue identified by the industry of counsel.[23]

Justice Strathy's passage reveals the pervasive tension between the profit-centered model of lawyering endemic to class actions and a judicial culture still firmly rooted in traditional professional norms. Notwithstanding the deterrence objectives of class actions, judges remain devoted to the corrective justice goal of this form of litigation, and with it, an adherence to the classic lawyer-client paradigm. According to Ontario's former Chief Justice Warren Winkler, the 'representative plaintiff in a class action lawsuit is a genuine plaintiff, who chooses, retains and instructs counsel and to whom counsel report.'[24] Canadian jurisprudence continues to subscribe to the view that the representative plaintiff is a 'genuine client' of class counsel, to whom all of the usual duties are owed.[25] This normative view proves problematic in the class action context, where the client is largely an absent one.

A third consequence of the entrepreneurial model is that the client, especially when recruited to participate in an action devised by counsel's own ingenuity, has little incentive to monitor his or her lawyers or the conduct of the case. The nature of mass harm is such that class members typically have small monetary losses. Class counsel's financial stake in the lawsuit is always exponentially bigger than that of any one class member, including that of the representative plaintiff. The representative plaintiff and the rest of the class do not finance the litigation, and are usually not exposed to the risk of adverse costs. In light of the plaintiffs' firm's investment in the litigation, it is inevitable that control of the litigation, including key strategic decisions around settlement and trial, will reside not with the 'client' but with the lawyer.

There are other reasons for this absent client phenomenon. In many actions, it is not possible for the lawyers to know the identities of the class members; indeed, their names may not be ascertainable until a settlement claims process is concluded. In any event, class counsel's professional obligation is to promote the best interests of the class, not those of any individual class member. For these reasons, class action clients are figuratively, if not physically, absent from the litigation relative to their traditional non-representative counterparts.

---

[23] Supra note 20, at para. 221 (per Strathy J., as he then was).

[24] *Fantl v. Transamerica Life Canada*, 2009 ONCA 377 (CanLII) ('Fantl, OCA') at para. 44.

[25] Kalajdzic, 2011, at 13–24.

Both *Hislop* and *Atlas* illustrate the usual entrepreneurial features of class actions in Canada described in this Part. *Atlas* was the product of an Ontario law firm's research of a potential class action following the public announcement of the company's pending restatement of financial earnings. *Hislop* was conceived by a public interest organization as part of a larger litigation strategy to promote equality rights for same sex couples. Both cases, therefore, were initiated by lawyers who then found clients, and not the usual scenario of clients seeking legal advice. In neither case was client recruitment viewed as objectionable by the presiding judge; indeed, in *Hislop* the identification of a suitable representative advanced 'access to justice' for many same-sex widows and widowers who would have faced psychological and emotional barriers in coming forward publicly.

Arguably, the case studies also reveal elements of the absent client phenomenon in action. The defense lawyers interviewed for this study viewed the representative plaintiffs as 'typical' of class action plaintiffs—not visible, not vocal, not involved.[26] The plaintiffs were not present at the negotiating table, the norm in settlement discussions. Class counsel in *Atlas*, however, described the plaintiffs, particularly Lawrence and Simon, as sophisticated, interested and personally bothered by the conduct of the company. Simon insisted on obtaining independent legal advice before signing the retainer agreements, not surprising given that he was a retired lawyer. George Hislop, a gay rights activist himself, was more personally invested in his litigation than most representative plaintiffs, but was not extensively involved in the litigation strategy. Sadly, he passed away before the final appeals in the action were decided.

FEES

Lawyers' contingency fees played a significant role in each of the case studies. Although triggered by different causes and agents, the fee issue in *Hislop* and *Atlas* represented to both sets of lawyers important tests of the entrepreneurial model of class action litigation. All provincial class action statutes require that a judge approve the contingency fee sought by counsel, but provide little guidance as to the criteria for assessing the appropriateness of a fee.[27] Ontario's statute, for example, directs judges

---

[26] Interviews of five defense lawyers representing six defendants in *Atlas*, and two defense lawyers in *Hislop*, were conducted in the spring of 2011 and 2012, respectively, on a not-for-attribution basis.

[27] Ontario CPA, supra note 9, sections 32, 33.

to approve a contingency fee multiplier that 'results in fair and reasonable compensation to the solicitor for the risk incurred in undertaking and continuing the proceeding under an agreement for payment only in the event of success'.[28]

Since most class actions that are certified settle,[29] the fee approval takes place in the context of the fairness hearing at which the overall settlement is approved. For ethical reasons, judges have made it clear that approval of the fee cannot be a condition of approval of the settlement as a whole.[30] There is no rule against negotiating the fee and settlement simultaneously.

The proper approach to assessing a proposed contingency fee is well settled in the jurisprudence. The court will consider:

(1) the percentage of the fees sought from the gross recovery;
(2) whether the resulting multiplier is appropriately placed within the acceptable range, usually between 1 at the low end and 3 to 4 at the high end;
(3) how the fees sought relate to the fees that would be payable under the retainer agreement entered into with the representative plaintiffs; and
(4) whether the compensation sought is viewed by the court as 'sufficient to provide a real economic incentive to solicitors in the future to take on this sort of case and to do it well'.[31]

Specifically, judges look to the following factors in determining the reasonableness of the fee:

(1) the time expended;
(2) the factual and legal complexities of the matters to be dealt with;
(3) the degree of responsibility assumed by the lawyer;
(4) the monetary value of the matters in issue;
(5) the importance of the matter to the client;
(6) the degree of skill and competence demonstrated by the lawyer;
(7) the results achieved;

---

[28] Ibid., section 33(7).

[29] In only the last few years, the trend increasingly has been to go to trial. Settled actions still outnumber tried cases by a large margin.

[30] *Stewart v. General Motors of Canada Ltd.*, [2008] O.J. No. 4426 at para. 22.

[31] *Gagne v. Silcorp Ltd.* (1998), 41 O.R. (3d) 417 (C.A.) at paras. 25–26.

(8) the ability of the client to pay; and
(9) the expectations of the client as to the amount of the fees.[32]

Since the Ontario Court of Appeal first laid out the proper approach to assessing fees 15 years ago, two developments are worth noting. Firstly, the 'acceptable' range is no longer capped at a multiplier of 4; in a recent decision a trial-level judge approved a 25 percent contingency fee, which represented more than a 7x multiplier.[33] Secondly, a few judges have broached the issue of what constitutes enough of an economic incentive in entrepreneurial litigation. One judge concluded that a 2.25 multiplier was not so low as to create an economic disincentive to pursue class action litigation[34] and another—Justice Lax in *Atlas*—accepted a multiplier of 2.6 as adequate enough. A third judge has opined that predictability in fees is paramount to ensure the viability of class action litigation and has accordingly endorsed a rule that a one-third contingency fee is presumptively valid.[35]

As is typical in negotiated settlements, the defendants in *Atlas* agreed to a so-called 'clear sailing provision', pursuant to which they took no position regarding the appropriateness of class counsel's proposed fee at the fairness hearing. As a result of the effective notice campaign, however, three objectors came forward to dispute the $12 million fee (or 30 percent of the amount recovered for the class) sought by plaintiffs' counsel. The objectors argued that the fees were disproportionate to the settlement achieved, in that the case settled before discovery and trial. Justice Lax held that 'these [were] all valid objections'. She agreed that 'it is important to encourage experienced counsel to take on meritorious cases that are tough and this is particularly so in shareholder class actions, which are really in their infancy in Canada', and that the lawyers in this case were 'deserving of being fairly compensated at a level significantly above an amount that might be considered a reasonable base fee given the risks involved'.[36] However, Justice Lax viewed the requested fee of $12 million, representing 30 percent of the gross recovery and a much greater percentage of the net recovery, as excessive

---

[32] *Lawrence v. Atlas*, supra note 15 at para. 51.

[33] *Helm v. Toronto Hydro-Electric System Limited*, 2012 ONSC 2602 (CanLII) at paras. 20–27. Class counsel's docketed time or base fee was $203,669.50, and their 25 percent share of the $5.8 million settlement amounted to $1,458,970.50.

[34] *Martin v. Barrett*, [2008] O.J. No. 2105 (S.C.J.) at para. 55.

[35] *Cannon v. Funds for Canada Foundation*, 2013 ONSC 7686.

[36] *Lawrence v. Atlas*, supra note 15 at para. 54.

in relation to the recovery for the class. She concluded that a 2.6 multiplier was 'more than adequate incentive to prosecute actions of this kind'.[37]

Beyond the issue of economic incentives, Justice Lax was also mindful of the concept of proportionality that has become the touchstone of much civil justice reform in Canada and elsewhere. While she accepted that the *Atlas* litigation was risky and that success was achieved in the circumstances, she concluded that their $3.25 million of docketed time was excessive given the work performed.[38] Quoting a judge in an earlier proceeding, Justice Lax observed that:

> the approach of plaintiffs' counsel to the provision of their services in this and other class proceedings has departed quite radically from that traditionally adopted by solicitors representing clients in other litigation. The discipline imposed by the normal constraints in acting for a client who will be personally liable for the fees has been abandoned. The issues in this case were of some complexity but no more so than those that arise in cases in which the plaintiffs represented no one but themselves, and in which the expenditure of over 8,000 hours of preparation would not be considered acceptable.[39]

Justice Lax's reaction to the number of hours docketed in the file—what one plaintiff's lawyer described as 'sticker shock'—reflects a view shared by others that class actions are over-lawyered. It is not just large corporate defendants who expend enormous sums on complex litigation; several judges have observed that 'because of the contingent fee arrangements that drive class proceedings, overlawyering and an over-generous expenditure of time are endemic in class proceedings'.[40] Justice Lax gave effect to this view in her decision on fees. On the basis of proportionality and the assumption that there was inevitable duplication of effort between the three plaintiffs' firms, she reduced the base fee by 25 percent before applying the multiplier of 2.6 for a total contingency fee of $6.3 million, approximately one-half of the sum contemplated by the contingency fee agreement entered into by the representative plaintiffs.

---

[37] Ibid. at para. 72.

[38] Ibid. at para. 54.

[39] Ibid. at para. 68 (quoting Justice Maurice Cullity in *Martin v. Barrett*, supra note 34).

[40] 2038724 *Ontario Limited v. Quizno's Canada Restaurant Corporation*, 2010 ONSC 5390 (CanLII) at para. 25, *per* Justice Perell; *Sutherland v. Hudson's Bay Company*, [2006] O.J. No. 2009 (S.C.J.) at para 20, *per* Justice Cullity; *Boulanger v. Johnson & Johnson*, [2007] O.J. No. 2043 (S.C.J.) at para. 10, *per* Justice E.M Macdonald; *Cannon v. Funds for Canada Foundation*, 2013 ONSC 7686 at para. 5, *per* Justice Belobaba.

Class counsel—not the representative plaintiffs—appealed Justice Lax's decision. The objectors appeared at the Court of Appeal and argued that only the representative plaintiffs, not the lawyers in their personal capacity, had standing to appeal Justice Lax's order. The Court of Appeal rejected this argument, as well as the objectors' position that class counsel were in a position of conflict of interest with the class by seeking to increase their fee (and thereby reducing the sums available for distribution to the class).[41] The Court went on to endorse Justice Lax's approach to fees, her assessment of the risks involved in the litigation, and her observation that 'a fee in this range would be more than adequate incentive to solicitors to take on and prosecute an action of this nature'.[42]

Lawyers involved thought otherwise. Two of the three class counsel interviewed believed that the resulting multiplier of 2.6 was insufficient, while the third lawyer stated that the fee still made the class action economically viable. All three rejected Justice Lax's conclusion that there was inevitable duplication of effort given the different roles taken on by each plaintiff firm, and that they could have done less work or settled sooner. They also pointed out that defense's costs were higher than their own; at one hearing, for example, the dozens of defense lawyers present were cumulatively charging over $30,000 per hour—a figure accepted by one of the defense lawyers interviewed.

Their lack of success in defending their fee caused all of the plaintiffs' lawyers to reconsider the optimal business model for class actions. One specified that it made his firm more cautious about what kinds of cases to take on. Another lawyer explained that the fee result made co-counsel arrangements, particularly on very large files, less attractive. Smaller cases would be more profitable in the long run, because a judge is less likely to be shocked by a $2 million fee request than a $12 million proposal, even if it represents a multiplier of 5.

For the lawyers in *Hislop*, the court's ruling precluding a deduction on account of a contingency fee also triggered a re-thinking of the entrepreneurial litigation model. Class counsel viewed the court's interpretation of section 65 of the CPP as deterring any lawyers from challenging statutes with similar limits on solicitors' liens, and therefore insulating the government from future constitutional class actions.

The lawyers in both *Hislop* and *Atlas* emphasized that lawyers require the certainty of being paid in the event of success for the class action regime to function. One suggested that the court ought to approve a

---

41 *Sutts Strosberg v. Atlas*, supra note 16.

42 Ibid. at para. 32.

contingency fee agreement at the outset of litigation, not at the end, to create that zone of certainty.[43] Although contingency fees are by their nature an acceptance of risk of non-payment, the lawyer did not agree that the risk of a judge arbitrarily reducing a base fee or ignoring the contingency fee agreement was a necessary or appropriate risk for counsel to bear. Another lawyer argued that the contingency fee agreement ought to be construed like any other contract—*prima facie* enforceable as against the representative plaintiff and by extension the class. Quite apart from the latter proposal being contrary to the provisions of class action statutes, it also fails to account for the absent client phenomenon discussed earlier. Even with the benefit of independent legal advice, would a lone representative plaintiff have the necessary leverage to bargain effectively for reasonably priced legal services? Consider, for example, that the representatives in *Atlas* originally signed fee agreements providing for a 25 percent contingency fee; these agreements were replaced on the eve of settlement negotiations, in March 2008 (made effective as of February 2004), with a 30 percent contingency fee or a multiplier of 4, whichever was higher.

Interestingly, neither set of plaintiffs' lawyers expressed any discomfort with the conflict that arose between them and some of their clients regarding the issue of fees. In *Atlas*, three members of the class (admittedly a very small percentage of the class) actively opposed counsel's position on fees. In *Hislop*, class counsel was forced to take collection proceedings against class members who reneged on their commitment to pay a pro rata share of legal fees, or who refused to pay fees from the outset.

The government lawyers in *Hislop* pointed to this apparent conflict of interest as evidence that a class proceeding was not the preferable procedure to resolve the dispute. They argued both that the fee issue resulted in satellite litigation that unduly lengthened the proceedings and delayed payment of pension benefits to class members, and put class counsel in the unseemly position of choosing between their financial self-interest and the interests of their clients.[44] Nevertheless, the representative nature of the class action defeated what class counsel perceived

---

[43] It is worth noting that one province in Canada permits approval of fee agreements at the outset of litigation: Class Proceedings Act, SA 2003, c C-16.5, s. 39(1)(a).

[44] Plaintiffs' counsel correctly pointed out that it was the Government that delayed payment of benefits in reliance on the 'partial payment' restriction in the CPP.

to be a government strategy of piecemeal settlements in order to avoid a systemic remedy.

In addition to the risks of non-payment in the event of defeat on the merits of a case, of a radical reduction in the requested fee and of additional expenses incurred to collect an approved fee, class counsel must include in their risk calculus the potential of an adverse costs order payable to the defendants. This risk is absent in the US class action model, given that American courts do not operate, for the most part, on a loser-pays system. The impact of the risk of adverse costs is the second critical component of the entrepreneurial model of Canadian class actions.

COSTS

The usual rules of civil procedure apply to class actions, and in four provinces, this includes the provisions on costs.[45] Courts retain a broad discretion with respect to whether to order the unsuccessful party to pay the successful party's legal costs, and how much. For this purpose, courts may consider whether the class proceeding was a test case, raised a novel point of law or involved a matter of public interest.[46] In the first decade or more of Ontario's class action regime, courts were usually quite cautious about ordering unsuccessful plaintiffs to pay costs, for fear that large cost awards would undermine the 'access to justice' objectives of class proceedings.[47] In recent years, however, very large costs orders have been made against representative plaintiffs who were unsuccessful

---

[45] New Brunswick, Nova Scotia and Alberta adopted Ontario's two-way costs rule for class actions. British Columbia's class action statute specifies that costs may not be ordered against a party to a class proceeding, unless a party engages in vexatious behavior: Class Proceedings Act, RSBC 1996, c 50, s. 37. Manitoba, Saskatchewan and Newfoundland have a similar provision, as do the Federal Rules which govern class actions within the Federal Court's jurisdiction. In Quebec, costs may be ordered against the representative plaintiff but are subject to a tariff, which significantly minimizes the impact of costs on the plaintiff.

[46] CPA, supra note 9, s. 31.

[47] *Garland v. Consumers' Gas Co.*, 1995 CanLII 7179 (ON SC), affirmed 1996 CanLII 1022 (ON CA). ['The case law reflects the court's inclination to refrain from awarding costs against unsuccessful plaintiffs in class proceedings where some or all of the criteria in s. 31(1) are present' (at para. 53).]

at the certification stage[48] and at trial.[49] Courts have repeatedly stated that 'in class actions, the ordinary rule is that costs will follow the event'.[50]

Representative plaintiffs, therefore, are exposed to the risk of being ordered to pay the defendants' costs in the event certification is denied, or judgment is rendered in favor of the defendants at trial. Given the sheer scope of such liability, the 'grim reality is that no person in their right mind would accept the role of representative plaintiff if he or she were at risk of losing everything they own'.[51]

In light of this grim reality, three options are available to ensure the viability of the class action regime:

(1) either the two-ways cost system is suspended vis-à-vis class actions; or
(2) we dispense with the requirement of a representative plaintiff altogether; or
(3) we devise a system of insurance by which the plaintiff is protected against having to satisfy any adverse costs order personally.

The first option is not likely to be taken up soon by those provinces within Canada with two-way costs rules, despite the precedent set by British Columbia and others. The view in Ontario and elsewhere remains that the principles which entitle a defendant to its costs in the event it is

---

48 By way of example, the plaintiff in *McCracken v. Canadian National Railway Company*, 2012 ONSC 6838 was ordered to pay the defendants $475,000 for the certification motion. Note that before winning on appeal, the defendants originally lost the certification motion, and had been ordered to pay the plaintiffs over $1 million in costs: *McCracken v. Canadian National Railway Company*, 2010 ONSC 6026.

49 See for example *Smith v. Inco*, 2012 ONSC 5094, in which the trial judge awarded the successful defendants costs in the sum of $1.7 million. The defendants had sought more than twice that amount; they unsuccessfully appealed the costs order as too low: 2013 ONCA 724, leave to appeal denied 2014 CanLII 29446 (SCC).

50 *Pearson v. Inco Ltd.*, 2006 CanLII 7666 (ON CA), (2006), 79 O.R. (3d) 427 (C.A.) at para. 13. Courts continue to consider whether the class action was a form of test case or involved a matter of public interest in exercising discretion regarding costs.

51 *Dugal v. Manulife Financial Corporation*, 2011 ONSC 1785 at para. 28.

successful apply equally to a class proceeding.[52] It is also assumed that costs perform a useful deterrent function against the initiation of unreasonable claims, and can be an effective case management tool to encourage efficient and economical litigation.[53] In any event, there is no empirical evidence to date which supports the view that no-costs regimes encourage frivolous claims, nor is there evidence that the two-way costs rule has pre-empted the initiation of meritorious claims.

The second option is even less likely. Although some have questioned the need for class representatives in other countries (Grave & Adams, 2005, 131–132), no serious discussion about removing the representative plaintiff requirement from class action statutes has taken place in Canada. Indeed, given the extent to which judges are wedded to the traditional client-lawyer paradigm discussed above, there is no reasonable possibility that class actions could be prosecuted in the name of a class without even a nominal representative plaintiff.

The third option, then, has naturally developed as a market response to the economic disincentives created by two-way costs regimes. Indemnities were historically provided by class counsel firms. In Ontario and Quebec, public funds established to assist class members with the expenses of class action litigation also indemnify representative plaintiffs for costs that may be awarded against them.[54] Public funders, however, indemnify only a minority of class representatives in Ontario.[55] Class counsel are increasingly unwilling or unable to provide indemnities; the ever-increasing magnitude of adverse costs orders, among other reasons, makes the giving of such indemnities unpalatable for many law firms (Kalajdzic, Cashman & Longmoore, 2013). Commercial litigation

[52] Note, however, that the question of two-way costs is being considered by the Law Commission of Ontario in its current Class Action Project, available at http://www.lco-cdo.org/en/class-actions-project-scope.

[53] Alberta Law Reform Institute, Class Actions Final Report No. 85 (December 2000) at 152, available at http://www.law.ualberta.ca/alri/docs/fr085.pdf.

[54] In Ontario *see* Class Proceedings Fund, available at http://www.lawfoundation.on.ca/class-proceedings-fund/; in Quebec *see* Le Fonds d'aide aux recours collectifs, available at http://www.justice.gouv.qc.ca/francais/ministere/organisation/organism.htm#recours.

[55] Lawyers representing class representatives must apply to Ontario's Class Proceedings Fund, which in 2012 agreed to fund seven cases and rejected two: http://www.lawfoundation.on.ca/wp-content/uploads/LFO-2013-Annual-Report-English-final-E-Web-4.pdf.

funders have recently emerged in Canada to fill the void, providing modest funding and indemnification against costs.[56]

The entry of commercial litigation funders creates further distance between the traditional client-lawyer paradigm and the entrepreneurial class action model. For it is quite clear that funders share none of the ethical and fiduciary duties that counsel owe to the class; their only duty apart from their contractual obligation to indemnify the plaintiff is to their own partners or shareholders to make a profit from the litigation. Ethical questions arise and have only begun to be addressed in what is currently an unregulated industry in Canada (Kalajdzic, Cashman & Longmoore, 2013). To date, the courts alone have exercised their supervisory jurisdiction to curb potentially unethical behavior. For example, Canadian courts have parted company with their Australian counterparts by insisting that control of the litigation must remain with the representative plaintiffs, not the commercial funders.[57]

Given the nature of the entrepreneurial model of litigation described in this chapter, and the onerous financial risks facing class counsel, commercial litigation funding may ultimately advance the 'access to justice' goals of class actions. It is still in the early stages for such activity in Canada, but there is little doubt that the securitization of litigation that commercial funding represents only further entrenches the entrepreneurial nature of class action activity.

CONCLUSION

Judges continue to wrestle with the new paradigm of the private attorney general who pursues litigation for profit. It is clear, however, that the

---

[56] *Dugal v. Manulife Financial Corporation*, 2011 ONSC 1785 (CanLII); *Fehr v. Sun Life Assurance Company of Canada*, 2012 ONSC 2715; *The Trustees of the Labourers' Pension Fund of Central and Eastern Canada v. Sino-Forest Corporation*, 2012 ONSC 2937. In these cases, only $50,000 was advanced by the funder to the plaintiffs' firm; indemnities were provided in return for a commission of 5 percent if the case settled before the pre-trial conference (with a cap of $5 million) and 7 percent if the case was concluded thereafter (with a $10 million cap).

[57] Dugal, supra note 56. *See* also *Fontaine v. Canada (Attorney General)* 2012 BCSC 1671, where the judge found certain loans by a funder to claimants in the Individual Assessment Process of the Indian Residential School settlement to be improper. The judge also removed the law firm acting for the claimants from the record, on the basis that they had engaged in misconduct in arranging the loans with the funder.

profit motive is what the drafters of Canada's class action statutes envisioned would sustain the class action regime. As one Ontario judge recently noted:

> The Legislature has decided that 'access to justice' can be promoted by means of entrepreneurial lawyers taking on the risks of group litigation in exchange for a share in the claimant's recovery.[58]

This model of litigation is driven largely by the availability of contingency fees that provide successful counsel with multiples of their usual hourly rates. As a result, and as the case studies show, the unpredictability of fee approval or the inability to collect approved fees significantly impacts lawyers' decisions about the kinds of cases worth pursuing in the future. It should not be surprising, therefore, that 'worth' in this regard is measured only in monetary terms.

The entrepreneurial model is made more complicated in parts of Canada where there is the risk of adverse costs. If lawyers are no longer in a position to accept this additional risk on behalf of the representative plaintiffs, third-party funding mechanisms must fill the void. To what extent these parties affect the calculus of case selection and settlement is an open question. While class actions are an integral part of the civil justice architecture of Canada, who gets access to this institution is for its economic enablers to decide.

REFERENCES

William Felstiner, Richard Abel & Austin Sarat, *The Emergence and Transformation of Disputes: Naming, Blaming, Claiming*, (1981) 15 Law and Society Review 631

Damian Grave & Ken Adams, *Class Actions in Australia* (Lawbook Co. 2005)

Gillian Hadfield, *The September 11th Victim Compensation Fund: 'An Unprecedented Experiment in American Democracy'*, (2005) University of Southern California Law School Legal Studies Working Paper Series, Working Paper 3, available at: http://law.bepress.com/usclwps-lss/art3

Jasminka Kalajdzic, *Self-Interest, Public Interest and the Interests of the Absent Client: Legal Ethics and Class Action Praxis*, (2011) 49 Osgoode Hall Law Journal 1

---

[58] Fehr v. Sun Life Assurance Company of Canada, 2012 ONSC 2715 at para. 51.

Jasminka Kalajdzic, Peter Cashman & Alana Longmoore, *Justice for Profit: A Comparative Analysis of Australian, Canadian and U.S. Third Party Litigation Funding*, (2013) 61 American Journal of Comparative Law 93

PART IV

Politics

12. The public dimension of private collective litigation: A comparative analysis

Deborah R. Hensler and Elizabeth Thornburg

INTRODUCTION

Lawyers love to put things in conceptual boxes: over here are private law, private legal actors, private litigation and compensation, over there are public law, public actors and public policy making and regulatory enforcement. Such boxes can be helpful in bringing clarity and consistency to legal analysis. They can also be misleading when they purport to draw distinct lines that are in reality quite blurry. Such is the case with the popular public/private dichotomy used in distinguishing 'private' litigation from 'public' regulation.

Allegations of mass harms present a number of process options. All of these apply both informal social norms and formal legal rules about what should be regarded as harm, who should be held accountable for what, by whom, who should be compensated, by whom, and what recompense should be made if it is owed to victims. But how public and private actors and methods of processing disputes combine to achieve accountability and compensation is often a very messy business—a fact frequently overlooked in conventional legal analysis. Collective litigation has both public and private dimensions; it is too much a shape-shifter to fit neatly in a categorical box.

This Part of the book, rather than re-drawing the edges of the private and public categories, shows the many ways in which they can be folded and re-assembled. This chapter draws on case studies from Germany, Belgium, England, the United States (US), and Chile[1] to examine the interactions of public and private actors and the intersection of public and

[1] As indicated in footnotes many of the cases described in previous sections of the book exhibit the same patterns.

private processes both in responding to and resolving mass claims. Although our research focused on private civil litigation, we found that public officials and institutions played important roles in the dispute resolution process: as defendants, plaintiffs, prosecutors, legislators, regulators, mediators and gate-keepers—and of course as judges and other court personnel. Depending on what they did and when they did it, public actors constrained or facilitated private litigation, reduced or increased the efficiency of dispute resolution, and limited or expanded the remedies available to private litigants. Focusing on the behavior of individuals and institutions—rather than the formal rules—it became clear that the public/private dichotomy that is the topic of political and academic debate on regulatory enforcement is neither very informative nor particularly helpful in understanding the evolution and resolution of collective claims. Rather than being independent processes, we found that private and public enforcement were often intimately connected, sometimes to the point where it was difficult to discern where one process ended and the other began.

This chapter begins by briefly summarizing the case studies included in this part of the book. It then examines the different roles played by government officials and institutions in both litigation and regulation, highlighting the mixed identities and functions of public actors. Next, the chapter turns to process: the interrelationships among criminal proceedings, regulatory processes, and both public and private civil litigation, demonstrating that attempts to label types of processes as public or private are inadequate when describing the complex reality of mass claims and collective litigation. The chapter then considers whether the outcomes of public regulation and private litigation are substantially different, and whether either is more effective in achieving accountability or compensation. The chapter concludes with a summary of the argument.

OVERVIEW OF THE CASE STUDIES

The case studies highlighted here provide examples of the wide variety of ways in which public and private actors and institutions address mass claims. Chapter 13 analyzes the German experience in the Deutsche Telekom litigation. The case study focuses on the third public offering of shares in formerly state-owned Deutsche Telekom AG in 2000, part of the government's privatization of the federal mail and telecommunications service. The combination of the internet bubble and an unprecedented marketing scheme aimed at ordinary German citizens had caused this tranche of shares to sell for a very high price. Unfortunately, over-valuation of real estate plus the disastrous acquisition of a US mobile phone company and the general burst of the internet bubble caused share prices to plummet only eight months after the offering, decimating the retirement savings of many small investors.

Ultimately, thousands of those citizens sued based on errors in the prospectus. Their suits were funded by legal expenses insurance, which is widely available in Germany. In order to process the 15,000 individual claims expeditiously, the German government passed the 'Capital Market Investors' Model Proceedings Act' (Kapitalanleger-Musterverfahrensgesetz, abbreviated as KapMuG). Under this Act individual claims arising from an alleged investment fraud are entered into a registry and a single case is selected from the registry for litigation and trial. The verdict on liability binds all of the claims in the registry: if the defendant(s) prevail, the claimants cannot pursue compensation; if the defendant(s) are deemed to be liable, the claimants can pursue compensation in individual litigation. The Deutsche Telekom litigation is still ongoing in Germany, although the US dimension of the case was resolved years ago in a US class action. The outcome of the parallel criminal investigation in Germany was inconclusive, although Deutsche Telekom voluntarily agreed to make a contribution of €5 million to charity.

Chapter 14 provides insight into Belgium's civil compensation process in which individual plaintiffs can piggyback on a criminal prosecution, actually becoming parties to the case—an option provided in some other European jurisdictions as well. The Belgian case study describes the litigation arising out of the financial collapse of Lernout & Hauspie Speech Products (L&H), a speech recognition technology company headquartered in the Belgian town of Ypres. Although L&H's text-to-speech technology led to rapid expansion and high stock prices in 1995, the company collapsed when it was revealed that a combination of accounting tricks and fictitious clients had artificially inflated its revenue. L&H entered the Belgian bankruptcy process in 2001 and that liquidation is still pending.

While the bankruptcy proceedings were ongoing, the Public Prosecutor and the examining magistrate in Ypres launched a criminal investigation into L&H. During this investigation, many deceived shareholders lodged complaints against L&H and its managers. Belgian law did not permit them to bring a private class action to prosecute their claims, but large numbers of investors participated in the criminal proceeding.[2] Unfortunately for the civil claimants, while the court found some individual executives guilty, it acquitted the several solvent entities that could have actually paid a judgment, finding that their fraudulent intent had not been proved beyond a reasonable doubt.

The third case study, described in Chapter 15, arose out of a single-incident mass disaster: a huge explosion at an oil storage facility in Buncefield, north of London, which occurred in 2005. The blast injured 40 people, damaged hundreds of adjacent business facilities and required the evacuation of a couple of thousand nearby residences. The estimated losses approached £1 billion. Several different government entities handled the legislative, regulatory and compensatory issues raised by the disaster through three separate processes. Regulatory, criminal and civil proceedings operated in parallel and were completed in five years, with the most contentious issues being the allocation of blame among the defendants rather than whether the victims were owed compensation. The amounts of compensation paid to victims were negotiated in a consensual process.

Chapter 16 is a case study of the US litigation arising out of the use of the gasoline additive Methyl Tertiary Butyl Ether (MTBE). It was once thought to be a cheap, safe and environmentally friendly route to cleaner air. Unfortunately, it turned out to be an extraordinarily efficient polluter of water. When it predictably ends up in drinking water through spills and pipeline leaks, its foul taste and odor make the water functionally undrinkable; it may also pose health risks to those who inhale or consume it. Legislation and regulation, both influenced by political forces, limited the ability of the US federal Environmental Protection Agency (EPA) to step in to limit MTBE use, although the agency did convene a task force that recommended expanded enforcement tools and health studies. At the state level in the US, agencies investigated the extent and effects of MTBE in the water supply, issued reports and adopted legislation capping the allowable level of MTBE in drinking water. They did not, however, have the ability to provide remedies to those with MTBE in their water supply.

Resorting to the courts, a large number of individual plaintiffs sued for damages and remediation plans. This litigation was funded by private plaintiff's attorneys, who hoped that the risk involved in their investment

---

[2] In 2014 Belgium adopted an opt-in class action for consumer claims. Shareholders' claims such as those in the L&H case are not eligible for class treatment.

of time and money would ultimately yield a profit. While the first generation of cases failed when the judge refused to approve class treatment (because individual damage claims were too small to justify the cost of the claimants proceeding individually), a second generation involving larger value claims succeeded.

Finally, Chapter 17 examines the interaction of government and private attorneys in consumer class actions in Chile. The Chilean story centers on SERNAC, the public administrative agency in charge of protecting Chilean consumers. Under Chilean law, SERNAC must be notified of any class action filed in the country and it can become a party in any stage of any class action case. In addition, the agency, if not a party, has to be notified of any attempt by the parties to withdraw a class complaint and is given the choice to continue cases for the absent members of the class, even if a court-appointed private class counsel has settled the case.

In the first case described, a private attorney discovered that VTR, a cable television company, was illegally assessing fees on consumers. He spent significant time and effort developing the claim, first individually and then collectively, but the cable company reached an informal agreement with SERNAC in a way that provided some compensation to potential class members but avoided fines, and cut the lawyer out of any ability to collect attorney's fees.

The second Chilean case involved mass claims against a leading Chilean department store, La Polar, for improperly manipulating customer accounts. SERNAC first attempted to resolve these claims with a collective mediation process and, when that failed, filed a class action on behalf of the store's account holders. When the company's Board of Directors revealed a massive accounting fraud affecting shareholders, political turmoil ensued, and SERNAC's consumer class action attracted thousands of individual claimants and associations. However, rather than aggressively prosecuting the class action, SERNAC hung back, perhaps concerned about the impact of a huge settlement on La Polar, whose new chair was trying to rescue it. An entrepreneurial private lawyer moved in to fill the gap and when he demonstrated that he had both the wherewithal and claimant support to pursue the litigation, the court named him as counsel for the class. After dueling settlement negotiations, SERNAC pulled the rug out from under the private attorney by negotiating a settlement that built on the private attorney's efforts but was somewhat more attractive to the consumers.

THE MANY ROLES OF PUBLIC ACTORS

The case studies described in this Part (and elsewhere in this book) show that when mass harms occur, public officials and institutions play a variety of roles in addressing their causes and consequences. Public sector entities might investigate the causes of incidents, review the actions of public or private actors, institute administrative or regulatory actions, including litigation, and oversee some forms of redress.

The assignment of these tasks to specific agencies, officials and levels of government varies across jurisdictions, and sometimes over time within jurisdictions. In addition, governments acting as claimants may sue for damages and those acting as defendants may be sued. Legislatures may revise or adopt new laws to address failures to protect public health and safety or to ensure financial stability, acting on their own initiative, in response to specially appointed investigatory commissions or task forces, or in response to private litigation (or fear thereof).

Sometimes criminal prosecutors take the lead in investigating events leading up to mass harm, sometimes they follow the lead of regulatory agencies, which may or may not decide to pursue a civil enforcement action themselves. For example, public prosecutors initiated proceedings in the German Deutsche Telekom case and the Belgian L&H case; in the US, the Securities and Exchange Commission (SEC) initiated an investigation of L&H after the US subsidiary filed for Chapter 11 bankruptcy protection. UK public authorities investigated and prosecuted those responsible for the Buncefield explosion.[3] Chilean criminal prosecutors indicted most of La Polar executives after SERNAC filed the class action lawsuit. Government institutions also played a prospective regulatory role

---

[3] The same is true in other cases we studied, for example, the Brazilian tobacco litigation in which the Office of Public Prosecutor filed the first collective suit against tobacco companies for deceiving consumers (Chapter 3) and the BP *Deepwater Horizon* disaster in which the US Justice Department launched a criminal investigation that ultimately resulted in a multi-billion dollar fine against British Petroleum (Chapter 5). In other instances, as in the Taiwanese securities fraud case, a government prosecutor declined to open a criminal investigation although a public regulatory agency brought an enforcement action (Chapter 4). The Australian Securities and Investment Commission brought a civil enforcement action when investors alleged that Brookfield Multiplex, a leading Australian construction company, had failed to disclose information about delays and costs increases on several projects (Chapter 9). The US National Highway Traffic Safety Administration investigated claims that Toyota cars suddenly and uncontrollably accelerated, leading to economic losses and personal injuries (Chapter 5).

in the cases we studied, reviewing and sometimes amending existing regulations or proposing new regulations to prevent similar incidents from occurring in the future.

When multiple government institutions were engaged, they sometimes acted at cross purposes, defying conventional descriptions of rational public policy making. Reflecting political contests among opposing stakeholders, the US Congress adopted legislation allowing MTBE as a gas additive, the federal EPA recommended stricter regulation of its use, and some state legislatures used their powers to regulate drinking water quality to set limits and even adopt outright bans on its use. In contrast, in the UK, public bodies worked in concert to respond to the Buncefield explosion. The government appointed a special panel to consider whether the authority itself bore partial responsibility for not properly managing the site and whether the event revealed a need for regulatory amendments. At the same time, the authority pursued its mandate to investigate what had gone wrong on the ground, and if appropriate, impose criminal sanctions.

Multiple courts were engaged in resolving the litigation we studied. The Commercial Court in Ypres declared L&H bankrupt after its business unraveled. Early in the criminal investigation, the case was transferred from the examining magistrate in that court to a more experienced examining magistrate in the Court of Appeal in Ghent. After the Public Prosecutor indicted a private lawyer who was involved with L&H but had also served as a substitute judge in the Ypres Commercial Court, the case was formally re-assigned to the Ghent appellate court to avoid any conflict of interest. The effect of the re-assignment was to eliminate the second consideration of law and facts that is normally available to parties whose cases are first decided in the lower court. The case ultimately went up to the Court of Cassation (the Belgian Supreme Court) on appeal, but the Court rejected the appeal.

By design, the original version of the German model case proceeding (KapMuG) assigned decisions in the 'model case' to the state appellate court, while the claims that would ultimately be governed by decisions in the model case remain in the court of first instance. As a result, the German Deutsche Telekom case made multiple trips up and down the ladder from the state court of first instance to the state appellate court. The state court's decision in the model case was ultimately appealed to the highest German federal civil court, which reversed part of the state court's decision and sent the case back downwards. Movement of disputes among courts—normal in most jurisdictions—increases the number of opportunities for the individual characteristics of decision makers—with diverse experience, expertise and political and ideological orientations—to influence decisional processes and outcomes. In the lengthy processes that are characteristic of mass litigation, this movement can lead to surprising twists and turns in the development of cases and unanticipated outcomes.

Governments were not just regulators or adjudicators in the cases we studied; they were also plaintiffs and defendants, sometimes playing both roles in the same litigation. Because the Commercial Court in Ypres had declared L&H bankrupt before the criminal trial began, the L&H litigation involved the government in two distinct ways. The bankrupt company appeared as a criminal defendant and as such was represented by a public curator appointed by the Commercial Court. The government also supplied five public liquidators, also appointed by the Commercial Court, to bring civil claims on behalf of L&H creditors. In the MTBE litigation, both state and local governments appeared as plaintiffs with damage claims. A handful of local authorities were among the damage claimants in the litigation phase of the Buncefield dispute. In cases described elsewhere in this book, the government itself was the accused wrongdoer, and hence the defendant in litigation.[4]

Individuals also sometimes switched between public and private roles in the course of litigation or activities leading up to it. In the Chilean VTR class action, the corporate defendant had a lawyer on its legal team who had previously been employed by SERNAC, the public consumer protection agency. The case study suggests that his recruitment was calculated to put the private corporate defendant in a strong position when contesting consumer class actions, which would likely involve negotiating with the public agency as well as private class counsel. The research on the VTR class action suggests that this was a successful strategy.

Some of the lawsuits we studied involved entities that had both public and private dimensions themselves or played roles straddling the border between public and private litigation. Deutsche Telekom, the defendant in the German securities litigation, was created by the German government's decision to privatize the holdings of what had been a single public entity, Bundespost, which provided postal, financial and telecommunications services. The third issue of shares in the new telecommunications company (Deutsche Telekom) netted about €15 billion for the German government. After the newly privatized company negotiated a class action

---

[4] For example, the Canadian government was the defendant in the *Hislop* case (Chapter 11), in which same-sex couples sued for survivor benefits. The Taipei municipal government was sued in its capacity as employer for failure to properly pay its parking lot attendants (Chapter 4).

settlement with US investors in the US, it turned around and sued the German government (as its former majority shareholder) in a German proceeding to recover its lawyer fees for the US litigation—and won.

In many civil law jurisdictions, public officials have exclusive standing to bring class actions in some or all circumstances.[5] Their use of that power to represent private interests has mixed results. Consider Chile: SERNAC has the power to demand more compensation for class members by threatening prosecution or other enforcement actions. But by taking charge of a class action and negotiating its settlement, the agency essentially ousts the private lawyers that invested in developing it and deprives them of the fees they would have received had they settled it themselves, diminishing the likelihood that the private bar will step in to fill gaps in public action in future cases.

The funding of litigation reveals another curious private/public entanglement. When government bodies act as rule-makers or enforcers, taxpayers bear the cost of those processes. And of course the government pays to maintain the public court system in which both public and private claims are brought, and sometimes may also provide other dispute resolution services, as in SERNAC's collective mediation process. What is less widely recognized is that government may at times subsidize private parties' litigation costs wholly or in part, and conversely that private parties may provide the basis for public prosecution.

In principle, criminal prosecutions that allow formal piggybacking of civil claims may decrease the litigation expenses of private claimants who can rely on government officials to conduct factual investigations and frame winning complaints. But in the Belgian L&H litigation the reverse seems to have occurred, as it appears that the public prosecutor relied on an investigative report prepared by one of the associations that represented the civil claimants. Similarly, in the Chilean litigation against La Polar, SERNAC took advantage of the negotiations undertaken by the private class action lawyers and even borrowed the latter's strategies. On the other hand, during the trial phase of the L&H criminal proceeding, court personnel set up a system to help pro se civil claimants, offering them draft forms to complete and advising the claimants on which documents to submit. Having a public agency take the lead in pursuing defendants does not always help the private claimant; if the public

[5] Assigning responsibility for bringing class actions on behalf of private individuals and entities is not unique to Chile; in Brazil and Denmark, public officials have exclusive authority to bring class actions for damages and in many European and Asian jurisdictions only certain government-approved associations have standing to bring class actions (Hensler, 2009).

prosecutor does not have the skill or funding to adequately pursue the case, it may end up losing on the merits, thereby eliminating the claimants' ability to pursue their claims.

THE MIXED NATURE OF PROCESS

With public entities playing so many different roles in responses to mass injuries, it is not surprising that ostensibly separate public and private processes co-mingle, with each influencing the other, sometimes proceeding in parallel and sometimes sequentially, either by design or practice. Sometimes public and private actors compete with each other to control the ultimate resolution and preserve their separate domains, but in other instances the processes are symbiotic.

The fact that public decision-making shapes private litigation is not in itself surprising: statutes (and sometimes constitutions) determine what types of claims are justiciable and procedural rules determine how those claims may be prosecuted (and often whether they can, as a practical matter, be prosecuted at all). But our research shows that mass injuries and the claims that inevitably follow evoke special public responses that shape the course of private litigation and its resolution. This occurs prospectively when legislators adopt new laws to enable or bar certain types of future claims, and reactively, when legislators or jurists devise special substantive or procedural rules to deal with extant claims. Often procedures adopted to address the perceived exceptional needs of a specific mass litigation become the standard response to other mass claim situations.

Nowhere is the co-mingling of public and private more evident than in the Belgian criminal process that provides the primary vehicle for civil claimants to prosecute their claims in a 'piggyback' action. As described in the case study of the L&H litigation, in Belgium, when serious crimes appear to have been committed an examining magistrate investigates the facts and turns the case over to the Public Prosecutor who will decide whether and whom to indict. Victims are formally parties to the criminal proceedings that may ensue. The criminal case is prosecuted by the state, while the civil claimants are represented (or not) by private lawyers. In the L&H litigation, where there were approximately 15,000 claimants, some claimants proceeded on their own, some hired their own lawyers and some chose to be represented by non-governmental associations, which in turn hired private lawyers to represent them. The judge in the Belgian scheme is first charged when deciding the criminal case, and then only if he finds the defendants guilty when deciding the civil claims.

This aspect of Belgian litigation reflects a key feature of civil law regimes, in which criminal judgments establish material or undeniable truths that can subsequently be used in civil proceedings. This has the potential to expedite the resolution of civil claims although whether it is successful in doing so, on average, is uncertain.

The intersection of public and private processes is also vividly demonstrated by the German Deutsche Telekom case. Here, the government as lawmaker created the legal claim of prospectus liability and the federal court facilitated investors' claims by ruling that their legal expenses policies covered such claims. Nor was that the only public dimension of the German litigation saga: when the private German lawyers sought documents that had been obtained in the parallel US shareholders' litigation for use in the German civil proceeding, the German government stepped in to object on the grounds of 'national sovereignty' and succeeded in blocking document sharing.[6]

The MTBE case study illustrates a different and even more complicated intersection of public and private processes, involving all three branches and multiple levels of government in the US. This case also shows how private actors affect public processes, when representatives of interest groups, corporate lobbyists and the like promote or obstruct legislation and rule-making, and encourage or subvert regulatory enforcement. Some of the earliest regulatory investigation of MTBE was conducted by administrative agencies at the state level. During the 1990s, US chemical manufacturers and oil refiners lobbied vigorously for federal legislation and environmental regulations that permitted the use of MTBE. The industry's decisive political victories at the national level were the backdrop for the public and private civil litigation over MTBE ground and water contamination that ensued. Private plaintiffs seeking compensation for pollution filed state common law claims—nuisance, negligence, fraud and trespass—in state courts. MTBE manufacturers and distributers fought back by removing cases to federal court and arguing that the federal Clean Air Act preempted state law. Defendants also sought to have the federal judge stay the litigation on the grounds that the technical issues surrounding MTBE contamination should properly be decided by the competent administrative agency, rather than a court. Notwithstanding these efforts, some individual lawsuits remained in state courts, and local opposition to MTBE prodded state legislators to adopt

---

[6] Trans-border sharing of documents for litigation is governed in the US by 28 USC 1782 and internationally by the Hague Convention on the Taking of Evidence Abroad in Civil or Commercial Matters, 1970, available at http://www.hcch.net/upload/conventions/txt20en.pdf.

restrictions on its use, helped along by local agricultural industry lobbyists seeking to expand the market for bio-fuels.

Yet another example of the intersection of public and private processes is illustrated by the Chilean La Polar case. When individual consumers claimed that the company had improperly added interest charges and non-payment penalties to their bills, SERNAC attempted to mediate with La Polar on a collective basis. Ultimately that informal mediation failed, and when SERNAC moved slowly to prosecute a public class action on behalf of La Polar's customers, it created an opening for an entrepreneurial attorney who was ultimately appointed by the court as class counsel. While SERNAC held back, La Polar decided to pursue a settlement with the private class counsel, who in turn asked higher level public officials to press SERNAC to support the settlement he and La Pola had agreed to. Seeking to regain the political high ground, SERNAC instead negotiated a separate settlement with somewhat more attractive provisions for consumers, which meant that the private class counsel was deprived not just of a victory but also of his fees.

In contrast to the messiness of the Chilean La Polar case, the response to the UK Buncefield explosion seems to have followed a neater course, even though it also engaged different public entities, as well as private lawyers and claimants and three separate processes. Although each process had a different goal—to assess whether the regulatory regime for oil storage facilities needed to be amended, to determine whether the private companies responsible for the facility should be prosecuted for criminal violations, and to resolve civil damage claims—their dynamics were to some extent intertwined. For example, the oil companies that were popularly viewed as responsible moved quickly to offer compensation to householders, at least in part to be perceived by the regulatory authorities as 'doing the right thing'. The special investigatory board that was established to conduct an inquiry into the causes of the accident produced multiple reports that were an important source of evidence for the civil damage claims. The agencies charged with regulatory enforcement (the Competent Authority) also produced reports; however, disclosure of some of this information was barred until the criminal prosecution had run its course. The criminal prosecution itself was complicated by decisions in the parallel civil litigation, which outpaced the criminal proceedings.

ACCOUNTABILITY, COMPENSATION AND BEHAVIOR CHANGE

Remedial Options

In many jurisdictions, authority for determining responsibility for harmful events is lodged in public agencies that investigate the circumstances of the injury, and when warranted impose civil sanctions and conduct or assist in the criminal prosecution of wrongdoers. Civil and criminal penalties, including prison terms, are the means of holding wrongdoers accountable. Legislatures and regulatory agencies have a responsibility for behavior change, by issuing new or amended statutes and regulations. In theory, in these jurisdictions, the role of private civil litigation is limited to compensating victims: 'redress'. Therefore, the measure of damages in private litigation is what is required to make the victim whole, not what might be required to deter future wrongful behavior. Whether and to what extent civil and criminal fines—alone or in addition to compensatory payments—create meaningful incentives for behavior change are empirical questions.

In contrast, common law jurisdictions such as Australia, Canada and the US have long recognized the potential deterrent value of requiring law-breakers to compensate their victims. In the US, the availability of punitive damages and treble damages in certain circumstances reflects the belief that civil litigation may have a deterrent value. Private class actions have long been justified in the US, in part, by their contribution to the enforcement of legal norms and regulations (Coffee, 1986; Crane, 2010; Davis & Lande, 2008 & 2011; Miller, 2013; Rosenberg, 2002). In Canada, behavior change is recognized in law as a goal of class actions.[7] During debate in Australia's parliament about adopting class actions, the then Minister of Justice and Consumer Affairs asserted that the ability of shareholders to bring class actions 'will be a great aid to the more formal regulators, such as the Australian Securities Commission'.[8]

As a practical matter, it seems likely that any legal regime that requires those who have engaged in negligent or intentional wrongful acts to pay the actual costs of others' injuries or damage (and sometimes more than that) will have deterrent effects whether or not deterrence is recognized formally as a goal of private litigation. This notion is the foundation of

---

[7] *Hollick v. Toronto* [2001] 205 D.L.R. 4th 19, 28–29 (Can. S.C.C.).

[8] Australia Commonwealth Parliamentary Debates, 13 November 1996 (Welsh & Morabito, 2014: 43).

modern economic analysis of law (Calabresi, 1970; Shavell, 1987; Miller, 2013). Law and economics theorists argue that the inability to externalize the costs of harm changes a potential defendant's cost/benefit calculation when deciding whether to undertake a course of action. The costs of litigation may be direct or may be mediated by liability insurance (Abraham, 2002; Baker & Parrish, 2005). The empirical evidence that liability law effectively deters is mixed (Eisenberg & Engel, 2014) and some commentators question its theoretical underpinnings (Hodges, 2015). However, litigation's deterrent consequences are often denounced by corporate representatives who argue that the expected costs of litigation negatively affect investment in research and development and professional service and marketing decisions, and there is a sizeable analytical literature on these asserted effects (Baker, 2005; Huber & Litan, 1991; Komesar, 1994, Chapter 6). Arguably, in mass litigation, the deterrent potential of compensatory damages is larger than usual since the cost of paying modest claims adds up when the number of claims is in the thousands or hundreds of thousands. Aggregating claims amplifies this effect by requiring defendants to compensate small value claims that absent aggregation would not be prosecuted at all. Mass litigation also attracts extraordinary media attention that may result in reputational losses for those targeted as defendants, which may in turn lead to a loss of market share. A loss of market share, in turn, combined with perceived liability exposure may result in a loss of share value for publicly traded companies. Moreover, if private litigation spurs more aggressive regulatory investigation or legislative action, it may amplify public enforcement, as discussed above.

The case studies in this Part show that public and private enforcement activities do yield different immediate outcomes: in these cases, regulatory agencies and criminal prosecution determined responsibility and imposed fines and sometimes prison terms, neither of which directly benefitted victims; civil litigation sometimes (but not always) produced compensation for victims, but because settlement was usually preferred to trial, the question of who was responsible for injuries was often left unresolved. The fines imposed by civil enforcers or criminal prosecutors were exceedingly modest, compared to estimates of the total cost of mass harms or (in the case of corporate responsibility) of company value. The compensation obtained by civil complaints varied across jurisdictions and cases but in several instances was substantial.

Redress

Of the six cases described in this Part (two in Chile and one each in the other jurisdictions), four produced compensation for victims. The outcomes of the two Chilean cases were starkly different: in the VTR case, under threat of a class action, the cable TV company offered modest cash compensation or discounts on future services that amounted in total to far less than the $400 million the company arguably might have faced if local courts had tried all of the individual claims of improper charges and applied the maximum available fines. In the La Polar case, the final settlement negotiated by SERNAC reduced the contractual debt of hundreds of thousands of the company's customers while granting credits to tens of thousands of customers. Because the cases settled there was no formal court decision on their legal or factual merit.

In the US MTBE case, private plaintiffs with relatively modest individual claims for compensation were unsuccessful because they were denied the right to proceed collectively. Subsequently, public and private entities with larger claims (which justified the predicted cost of litigation) obtained a $422 million aggregate settlement from thirteen large oil companies, and a commitment to pay a substantial percent of future well decontamination costs. Because of the settlement, those cases never resulted in a decision on the merits. ExxonMobil, however, adopted a strategy of refusing to settle most cases, and some of these cases resulted in merits litigation, with mixed results. New York City won a $104 million verdict and New Hampshire won $236 million against ExxonMobil. On the other hand, while ExxonMobil was ordered to pay a total of $1.65 billion to more than 500 families and businesses in Baltimore County, Maryland for harm alleged from a 25,000-gallon fuel leak there, Maryland's Court of Appeals in 2013 threw out most of the awards, including $1 billion in punitive damages, finding no fraud and no physical harm.

In the UK Buncefield case, defendants voluntarily came forward to compensate victims for their property damage and negotiated consensual settlements in court but did not formally admit responsibility. The researchers were unable to calculate the total sum of compensation paid but estimated it to be several hundreds of millions of pounds. By comparison, the estimated total value of claims was £894 million (Creutzfeld & Hodges, Chapter 15, Table 2). As a result of the civil litigation, the court determined the comparative legal responsibility of the defendants for this liability exposure.

The Deutsche Telekom and the L&H cases are still ongoing, so it is unclear whether the German or Belgian plaintiffs will ever obtain redress for their losses. The Belgian court held the individual officers of L&H criminally liable and imposed fines and prison terms, but ruled that the 'deep-pocket' corporate defendants (L&H's bank, Dexia, and its statutory auditor, KPMG) were not criminally liable. In essence, the court held that Dexia and KPMG were victims themselves of the fraud perpetrated by L&H's principals.[9] The German federal high civil court cleared the giant telecom corporation of liability on most of the counts against it, but sent the case back to the lower court for a determination on a single civil charge that may be enough to provide compensation for the plaintiffs.

In sum, taken together, the litigations described in this Part most often produced limited redress and rarely determined—as a formal matter—who was accountable for the mass injuries that led to the litigation. Where plaintiffs did obtain redress—as in the VTR, La Polar, MTBE and Buncefield cases—it was at least in part a consequence of public outcry and political pressure.

Regulatory Enforcement

While the private litigation process failed some claimants entirely and only compensated others because of the social and political dynamics that the injuries gave rise to, the public investigatory and regulatory enforcement process often did not seem to measure up to its primary goal—holding liable parties responsible for the consequences of their actions—either. In some instances, regulatory agencies were hamstrung by a lack of resources, expertise or a full complement of regulatory enforcement powers. In other instances, the competent regulators may have hesitated to act against powerful economic actors. In at least one instance, in the US, the public regulatory process was deliberately undermined by successful corporate lobbying of both the legislature and the responsible regulatory agency.

Across jurisdictions, alleged legal violations often only came to light or were treated seriously by competent regulatory authorities when mass injuries attracted attention from media or elected officials. It was the American Wall Street Journal not the US Securities Exchange Commission or the Belgian public prosecutor who first brought the L&H fraud to light. The public prosecutor indicted multiple parties, including individuals and corporations, but in the end only the individuals were held legally responsible for the fraud.

---

[9] Dexia and KPMG did not fare as well in the US, where they paid $60 million and $115 million respectively to US investors to settle securities class actions.

In Germany, the public prosecutor in Bonn opened an investigation of the Deutsche Telekom stock issue and while it ended without a formal indictment, the German public prosecutor indicated in a press release that he believed that Deutsch Telekom had engaged in fraudulent accounting. Press releases, however, have no legal force. And the Frankfurt court subsequently held that a decision by the prosecutor—even if such had been reached—would not be binding on the civil court.

Chilean consumers of La Polar won compensation for their losses and relief from disputed contractual obligations as a result of action by the consumer protection agency. But the agency's vigorous activity on behalf of the consumers only came after a private entrepreneurial lawyer negotiated a settlement with La Polar that threatened to call SERNAC's status as the country's preeminent consumer protector into question. Moreover, the unraveling of La Polar that enabled SERNAC's class action settlement on behalf of consumers was not a result of its own investigations, but rather followed the corporate board's disclosure of its shaky financial situation, which led in short order to a collapse of its stock value and a cascade of legislative and regulatory investigations, egged on by mass media.

In the US, vigorous lobbying by the oil industry precluded public efforts by Congress and the EPA to rein in use of MTBE long after its deleterious effects on groundwater were recognized. Private lobbying stymied congressional efforts to give the EPA authority to enforce limits on MTBE and to authorize those injured by MTBE to bring claims in federal court. When public and private water agencies pressed civil claims, the US Senate came within two votes of allowing legislative action that would effectively have granted oil company defendants protection against pending and prospective litigation. At the national level, rather than Congress or regulatory agencies taking the lead on protecting well owners and consumers against MTBE groundwater contamination, it was the private litigation that ultimately encouraged amendments to the law and rules, and often the primary concern of the legislators was to protect oil companies against liability exposure rather than to protect water users.

In contrast to all of these, the UK case study illustrates a vigorous investigatory and regulatory enforcement process, combining a specially appointed public board to determine what caused the oil storage facility to explode, and an investigation and enforcement program by the competent authority. The latter imposed a total of £6.7 million in fines plus £4.08 million in costs on five companies found responsible for various offenses. The total sum of fines plus costs (approximately £11 million) is less than 10 percent of the estimated total £269 million cost impact of the explosion (net of compensation payments). The rationale for the total amount of fines is unclear: amounts of fines in these circumstances are calculated according to complex formulas that depend in part on precedents.

CONCLUSION

The chapters in this Part demonstrate that a public/private dichotomy is of little use in analyzing legal responses to mass harms. Their relationship is more like a complex origami figure than two adjacent boxes. Actors, processes and outcomes overlap and intersect on a number of levels.

First, rather than proceeding independently, the processes that are called into play when mass harms occur interact in significant ways. Public processes often rely on private fact-gathering (including factual investigation by private media). The viability of private processes often depends on the outcomes of public regulatory investigations and criminal prosecutions. And some processes simultaneously involve public and private features.

Second, the actors in these mass action dramas play multi-faceted roles. Public entities may act as government regulators, but they may also appear in private litigation as private plaintiffs seeking compensation for their own harms. Public agencies may play a kind of *parens patriae* role, representing the interests of a class of private claimants. Individual people also switch roles, working for a government agency at one point and a private party at another. Politicians, functioning as government actors, are influenced by private parties lobbying for specific legislative or administrative rules.

Third, the outcomes of actions that are conventionally labeled as public and private overlap and interact. Redress, viewed as a private remedy, can act like regulation when it incentivizes compliance with legal norms. Public regulatory or criminal findings can provide a legal basis for redress, or unearth information that makes private litigation feasible. And information developed as part of private litigation can aid criminal prosecution or lead to future regulation.

None of this should be surprising. When harm is done on a large scale, it affects individuals and institutions in so many ways, on so many levels, that trying to assess the extent and causes of the damage calls upon multiple resources of both private and public actors. Efforts to make victims whole and to avoid future harms add further complexity to the search for solutions. Different countries have worked out the details in different ways that are compatible with their own legal institution and legal culture, but across all systems the law in action has disregarded technical labels in an effort to find ways to unravel the harms and move forward. While formal legal and technical analysis may support assigning different tasks to public and private actors, when mass harms occur, it's all hands on deck.

REFERENCES

Kenneth Abraham, The Insurance Effects of Regulation by Litigation, in Kip Viscusi (ed.), *Regulation Through Litigation* (AEI-Brookings Joint Center for Regulatory Studies 2002)

Tom Baker, *The Medical Malpractice Myth* (University of Chicago Press 2005)

Tom Baker & Thomas Farrish, Liability Insurance and the Regulation of Firearms, in Timothy Lytton, *Suing the Gun Industry: A Battle at the Crossroads of Gun Control & Mass Torts* (University of Michigan Press 2005)

Guido Calabresi, *The Costs of Accidents: A Legal and Economic Analysis* (Yale University Press 1970)

John Coffee, *Understanding the Plaintiff's Attorney: The Implications of Economic Theory for Private Enforcement of Law Through Class and Derivative Actions*, (1986) 86 Columbia Law Review 669

David Crane, *Optimizing Private Antitrust Enforcement*, (2010) 6 Vanderbilt Law Review 675

Theodore Eisenberg & Christoph Engel, *Assuring Civil Damages Adequately Deter: A Public Good Experiment*, (2014) 11 Journal of Empirical Legal Studies 301

Christopher Hodges, *Law and Corporate Behaviour: Integrating Theories of Regulation and Enforcement* (Hart Publishing 2015)

Peter Huber & Robert Litan, *The Liability Maze: The Impact of Liability Law on Safety and Innovation* (Brookings Institution Press 1991)

Neil Komesar, *Imperfect Alternatives: Choosing Institutions in Law, Economics and Public Policy* (University of Chicago Press 1994)

Robert Lande & Joshua Davis, *Benefits from Private Antitrust Enforcement: An Analysis of Forty Cases*, (2008) 42 University of San Francisco Law Review 879

Robert Lande & Joshua Davis, *Comparative Deterrence from Private Enforcement and Criminal Enforcement of U.S. Anti-trust Laws*, (2011) Brigham Young University Law Review 315

Geoffrey Miller, Group Litigation in the Enforcement of Tort Law, in Jennifer Arlen (ed.), *Research Handbook of Economic Analysis of Torts* (Edward Elgar 2013)

David Rosenberg, The Regulatory Advantage of Class Actions, in Kip Viscusi (ed.), *Regulation Through Litigation* (AEI-Brookings Joint Center for Regulatory Studies 2002)

Steven Shavell, *Economic Analysis of Accident Law* (Harvard University Press 1987)
Michelle Welsh & Vince Morabito, *Public v. Private Enforcement of Securities Laws: An Australian Empirical Study*, (2014) 14 Journal of Comparative Legal Studies 39

13. Litigation without end? The *Deutsche Telekom* case and the German approach to private enforcement of securities law[1]

Axel Halfmeier

INTRODUCTION: THE *DEUTSCHE TELEKOM* CASE AND ITS IMPLICATIONS

When 15,000 plaintiffs sued Deutsche Telekom AG in 2001 and 2002 after a sharp decline in the company's share price, this prospectus liability case became the biggest mass litigation in Germany. It also sparked new legislation: the Kapitalanleger-Musterverfahrensgesetz (KapMuG), the Capital Markets Model Case Act, which is the first collective litigation instrument in German civil procedure. It was developed by the German legislator as a mechanism to deal with the thousands of individual Telekom lawsuits. Due to this origin, the KapMuG focused on the treatment of individual cases instead of creating a more efficient 'summarized' aggregate procedure. The result was a decade-long litigation that is still going on as we go to press. With regard to its original goals of more efficient case handling and better access to justice, the KapMuG may have taken the wrong path.

Beyond its legal relevance, the Telekom case must also be seen in a broader social and political context. It highlights the lack of confidence in the stock market within German society. Traditionally, German citizens did not participate much in the stock market but preferred low-yield investments such as bank savings accounts or life insurance. This started to change during the internet bubble in the late 1990s, but after

[1] This chapter is based on published court decisions in the Telekom case, media coverage and interviews with participants. Some of these interviews were done in connection with an earlier study: Halfmeier, Rott & Feess, 2010.

Telekom's share issue produced extreme losses for many small investors, the scepticism toward the stock market returned, possibly supported by a feeling that the legal system was either unable or unwilling to adequately protect small investors' interests. On the other hand, the Telekom case may also have contributed to a change in perception of the social relevance of litigation, and it has accelerated the creation of a sophisticated plaintiff bar in Germany.

The aim of this case study is to explore these implications by describing the legal and economic context of the Telekom litigation, the development of the case, the creation of the KapMuG and possible legacies for the future.

LEGAL CONTEXT

At the beginning of the Telekom case in 2001, German procedural law had no collective litigation instrument that could be compared to a US class action. In some areas such as environmental law, consumer protection and unfair commercial terms, there are 'associations' suits' in the sense that certain institutions have standing to sue for an injunction. Although these rights are frequently used against corporate misconduct, their economic impact is limited as they do not provide for damage claims. Any damage claim must be brought individually as an ordinary civil action.

The threshold to file such individual damage actions is quite high, particularly in view of the risk of adverse costs under the 'loser pays' principle that governs German procedural law. For example, a shareholder who claims to have lost savings of €5,000 due to securities fraud faces a cost risk of more than €2,000 for court and lawyers' fees in the court of first instance alone, not counting any expert witnesses' costs. It is therefore often not rational to sue for compensation, even if one suspects fraud on the other side. This situation is aggravated by the procedural rule that there is no discovery in German civil procedure, so the plaintiff must have gathered the necessary evidence before starting the legal action. As securities fraud cases often implicate complex issues within the accounting department and management of the defendant company, it is rare that a potential plaintiff can gather sufficient evidence by himself.

Under these circumstances, it is not surprising that prospectus liability cases were only rarely brought by smaller investors before the advent of the Deutsche Telekom IPO.

ECONOMIC CONTEXT

The case described here relates to the third public offering of shares in the formerly state-owned Deutsche Telekom AG in 2000. This offering was part of the large-scale privatization project of state-owned companies carried out by the German government since the 1990s. The federal mail service was split up into several stock companies which were then privatized. The shares of Deutsche Telekom AG were deemed to be particularly interesting, as they were issued in the period of the first internet bubble of the late 1990s, in which investors' demand for telecommunication companies was high.

The German government seized this opportunity to gain comparatively high prices: the first tranche in 1996 was sold for €14.57 per share, the second tranche in 1999 for €39.50 per share, and the third tranche in May and June 2000—subject of the massive litigation that followed—for a price of €63.50 per share. Even this price was considered a bargain by many investors at the time, as Telekom shares had peaked at €103.50 at the Frankfurt stock exchange earlier in 2000. The demand for Telekom shares was huge, and many small investors were disappointed when their bankers told them that they had not been able to secure any Telekom shares for them.

It was not only the internet bubble that had fuelled this demand, but also a massive marketing strategy formerly unknown in Germany with regard to the sale of securities. Ordinary German citizens traditionally had not held a lot of company shares or other securities for savings purposes; this was considered to be the domain of the super-rich. Most citizens could rely on a system of state-organized healthcare, social security and retirement payments that guaranteed sufficient funds for old age. If people invested extra money for retirement purposes, they usually did so in a risk-averse fashion with life insurance policies or low-yield savings accounts.

The Telekom stock issue set out to change this culture and thus complemented the general social change in the late twentieth century towards the individualization of risks, driven by demographic factors and global competition. The Telekom shares were advertised in newspapers and on TV. The term 'Volksaktie' (people's share, similar to the famous Volkswagen) was used in connection with the Telekom shares. In a TV commercial, the famous German actor Manfred Krug—who usually played trustworthy, down-to-earth, common-people characters—advised everybody to buy Telekom shares.

For the new shareholders, disappointment came quickly. In July 2000, Deutsche Telekom announced a costly takeover of VoiceStream, a US mobile phone company, and in February 2001 Telekom said that it had to write down its real estate portfolio by €2 billion. Together with the burst of the internet bubble, this led to a decline of the share price to about €10 in late 2001. The stock price remained at that level for a long time and has only recently picked up towards a level of about €16 in 2015. Many investors had bought relatively small amounts of Telekom stock, usually in the region of €5,000 to €10,000, leaving them with a loss of about 80 percent of their savings. Manfred Krug later apologized publicly 'to every fellow citizen who has bought shares recommended by me and who was disappointed' and said that starring in the Telekom commercial was the 'biggest mistake' of his professional career.[2]

THE FLOODING OF THE FRANKFURT COURT

The public disappointment with the Telekom shares led to the first legal actions. There was not much of a tradition of securities litigation in Germany before 2000, in view of the comparatively high court and attorneys' fees, a prohibition on contingency fees[3] and a strict 'loser pays' rule that creates significant costs risks. On the other hand, the substantive law on prospectus liability had been recently reformed, providing for damages in case of substantial errors in the prospectus and presuming reliance on that error somewhat similar to the US-style 'fraud on the market' theory.

Based on these provisions, a growing number of citizens filed prospectus liability claims against Deutsche Telekom, claiming that the prospectus was wrong, in particular with regard to the real estate valuation, and also arguing that the VoiceStream takeover should have been announced in the prospectus. A large number of these cases were filed through attorney Andreas Tilp, who worked from a small office in a southern German village. Before the Telekom case, Tilp had worked on cases in commodities trading, representing private investors against banks. In the fall of 2000, Tilp appeared in a TV interview and argued that Deutsche Telekom could be sued for prospectus liability. From that day, the

[2] Interview with Manfred Krug in German magazine Der Stern, 30 January 2007.

[3] This prohibition was later eased by the German legislature after a Constitutional Court ruling: Bundesverfassungsgericht, 12 December 2006, Neue Juristische Wochenschrift (NJW) 2007, 979.

plaintiffs kept approaching him and other attorneys. Not only was Deutsche Telekom sued, but also the German federal government and a state-owned German bank that acted as an intermediary, as well as Deutsche Bank and Goldman Sachs which had advised Deutsche Telekom during the IPO.

To avoid the significant cost risks in private litigation, the private plaintiffs and their counsel used an insurance device that many risk-averse German households subscribe to and that is typically used for workplace and neighbourhood quarrels, for traffic accidents and substandard plumbing: a legal expenses insurance, which covers the risks of future litigation in exchange for a monthly fee. The affected insurance companies soon realized the potential costs of these suits and some denied coverage, but lost the battle in May 2003 when the Federal Court (Bundesgerichtshof) ruled that an insurance contract clause which exempted 'legal interests in the area of the law of commercial companies' from insurance coverage only applied to entrepreneurial commercial activities, not to the acquisition of securities in the context of private retirement savings and a connected prospectus liability claim.[4]

Under German law, a claim becomes time-barred after a certain period prescribed by law, unless the plaintiff files a court action. As Deutsche Telekom refused to enter into any agreements that would waive these rules during a period of ongoing negotiations, every claimant who wanted to secure his or her chances for recovery had to sue quickly. The number of suits filed with the Regional Court (Landgericht) in Frankfurt rose to about 1,700 cases in 2003, representing more than 15,000 individual plaintiffs. Due to legal rules on jurisdiction, all the cases relating to the third tranche of Telekom shares arrived on the desk of Judge Meinrad Wösthoff, who quickly realized that these cases alone would keep him busy for over ten years, not counting his normal caseload of ordinary commercial cases that kept coming in.

Wösthoff did his best to structure the Telekom cases on Excel spreadsheets. His plan was to litigate certain test cases first, while staying all others. But there was no rule in the German Code of Civil Procedure that would permit such a procedure. On the contrary, the German Constitutional Court ruled in 2004 that the right to a fair trial would be violated if any of the Telekom actions were intentionally put on hold.[5]

On top of these legal issues, the German court system was *de facto* not capable of dealing with the masses of Telekom cases. In a press release,

---

[4] Bundesgerichtshof, 21 May 2003, Versicherungsrecht (VersR) 2003, 1122.

[5] Bundesverfassungsgericht, 27 July 2004, NJW 2004, 3320.

the President of the Regional Court in Frankfurt explained to the public why the cases did not move forward:

> At the end of May [2004], there was a deadline for the plaintiffs to send in certain details regarding their claims. On the last days of May, the plaintiffs' attorneys (630 different firms) sent in hundreds of requests for an extension of this deadline. The fax machines of the court ran day and night; one broke down. The court employees have to take every fax, put it in the respective file and give it a page number by hand (there were two special rooms for the more than 1,000 files). Every single file had to be physically brought into the judge's office, so that he could decide whether the deadline extension should be granted. He writes his decision into the files by hand. The files are then brought back into the other office room, where an employee transfers the decision into the computer system, prints out the decision and sends it by mail to the affected parties.[6]

This was a cry for help, directed at the federal government in Berlin. There, at the Ministry of Justice, work had already begun on a legislative solution to the Telekom problem: the Capital Markets Model Case Act (KapMuG).

THE CREATION OF THE KAPMUG

The KapMuG passed swiftly through the parliamentary proceedings and came into force on 1 November 2005. At the time it was sometimes called the *lex Telekom*, as its clear objective was to enable the court system to deal with the Telekom cases in a structured fashion. The basic concepts of the KapMuG followed Judge Wösthoff's original plan of picking out a test case: from the multitude of plaintiffs, a 'model plaintiff' is designated who then litigates the common issues of law and fact in a 'model procedure', in which all other plaintiffs are only ancillary participants. This procedure is then transferred from the lower court (Landgericht) to the Appellate Court (Oberlandesgericht) and is supposed to end with a 'model decision' on these common issues, which is then handed down again to the lower court. The model decision is binding on the lower court and on all participants, and the individual cases can then be resolved on that common basis.

---

[6] Press release of the Regional Court Frankfurt am Main, 8 June 2004 [translation by author].

The KapMuG's focus to ensure that certain common factual or legal questions would be resolved with a final decision for all plaintiffs is a clear reference to the Telekom case. At the time the statute was passed, it was expected that the validity of Telekom's original assessment of its real estate would be a major factual issue in the litigation, for which very expensive expert testimony would likely be necessary, as an expert would have to look at every single piece of property. Ultimately, such expert testimony was not deemed necessary by the Appellate Court, because the court held that even if Telekom's assessment needed to be corrected in 2001, the method used *ex ante* in the prospectus had been in accordance with the law. This was later confirmed by the Federal Court.[7]

In addition to presenting a solution to the Telekom problem, in 2005 the KapMuG was presented by the German government as the German alternative to securities class actions. The KapMuG was supposed to not only provide more effective court proceedings in mass securities cases, but also to increase access to justice for investors, contribute to a stricter enforcement of the capital market laws and finally, make Germany a more attractive venue for transnational securities litigation.[8]

RELATION TO PROCEEDINGS IN THE UNITED STATES

The last argument was obviously directed at the United States (US) securities class action, which at the time dealt with many transnational cases. In the Telekom situation, a US class action had already been filed in 2001, based on the same facts as the German actions. The US action was certified as a class action in 2002, went into discovery in 2003 and was resolved by settlement in early 2005.[9] Under the settlement, Telekom paid $120 million, including a fee for the plaintiffs' lawyers in the amount of 28 percent of the settlement fund. This amount was later recovered by Telekom in a German proceeding based on corporate law arguments against its former majority shareholder, the Federal Republic

---

7 Bundesgerichtshof, 21 October 2014, NJW 2015, 236, 242.

8 Bundestags-Drucksache 15/5091, p. 16 et seq.

9 *In re Deutsche Telekom AG Securities Litigation*, U.S. District Ct., S.D.N.Y., Civil Action no. 00-CV-9475 (NRB).

of Germany.[10] In that litigation, Telekom claimed that it had spent more than €17 million on defense lawyers' fees in the US class action.[11]

Faced with the differences in procedural law between the US and Germany, the plaintiff lawyers in the German case applied for discovery assistance to the US courts under 28 U.S.C. § 1782, seeking access to documents produced by Deutsche Telekom in the US class action. The German Federal government filed a statement with the District Court in New York to the effect that access to these documents would possibly 'jeopardize German sovereign rights' and interfere with the criminal investigation by the Public Prosecutor in Bonn. Based on this letter and on comity considerations, the US District Court denied access to these documents.[12]

THE *DEUTSCHE TELEKOM* CASE BEFORE THE HIGHER GERMAN COURTS

From the Individual Cases to the Model Procedure

After the KapMuG entered into force on 1 November 2005, the plaintiffs in the Telekom case applied for a model procedure regarding the alleged errors in the prospectus. Under the KapMuG, it is the task of the lower court to decide on the admissibility of these motions and on the content of the model procedure, which was to be distilled from the many motions made by individual plaintiffs in their individual cases, represented by many different attorneys. This was a tedious process, and it took Judge Wösthoff until July 2006 to complete it and formulate the exact program for the model procedure. According to the KapMuG, the case was then transferred to the Appellate Court in Frankfurt am Main, which then

---

[10] Bundesgerichtshof, 31 May 2011, NJW 2011, 2719. After this judgment, the state-owned bank Kreditanstalt für Wiederaufbau paid €96 million to Deutsche Telekom AG and another €20 million to Deutsche Telekom's D&O insurer who had paid that amount to Deutsche Telekom, *see* the annual report of Deutsche Telekom AG 2012, p. 14.

[11] Bundesgerichtshof, ibid. With respect to the economics of the legal profession, it is interesting to note that the defense lawyers' non-contingent fees amount to about 18 percent of the settlement value, in relation to 28 percent on the plaintiffs' side as a fully contingent fee.

[12] Upheld by the Court of Appeals in *Schmitz et al. v. Bernstein Liebhard & Lifshitz et. al.*, 376 F. 3d 79 (2nd Cir. 2004).

appointed Bruno Kiefer, the plaintiff with the highest amount in controversy (Kiefer claimed more than €1 million in damages), as the model plaintiff, represented by his attorney Andreas Tilp.

The trial before the Appellate Court did not start until April 2008. One reason for this further delay was the KapMuG's two-level-system: only the model procedure is brought before the Appellate Court, the original procedure remains at the lower court. The KapMuG requires the lower court to explicitly stay proceedings in every case in order to wait for the outcome of the model procedure. The decision to stay a case had to be made separately in each case, particularly since the defendant Deutsche Telekom argued in every single case that this case should not be stayed as it could be decided on other (individualized) grounds that were not covered by the model procedure. Judge Wösthoff had to take each of the over 1,000 files into his hands again and decide on the stay of the procedure in view of the defendant's arguments.

Another cause for further delay was the KapMuG's rule on the introduction of new evidence: whenever the plaintiffs brought forward new arguments—in particular new alleged errors in the prospectus, as they tried to cover every possible error—the KapMuG of 2005 stipulated that the lower court should decide whether the trial plan for the model procedure should be extended to these new issues. Although there was some logic to this—after all, it was the lower court that had the original files and thus could assess best whether the new issue was really relevant for all of the original cases—it led to a game of ping-pong in which the case files went back and forth between the lower court and the Appellate Court.

Another issue was the participation of all the original plaintiffs. Under the KapMuG, they were represented by the model plaintiff and could not leave the model procedure unless they agreed to give up their claim completely. There was no alternative to the model procedure: plaintiffs had no right to opt out and pursue individual litigation as class members do in the US. The reason for this feature of the KapMuG was to prevent the litigation from drifting into different strands or sub-groups. On the other hand, mandatory participation in the model procedure had to conform with the German constitutional right to a fair trial. The Appellate Court solved this problem pragmatically by setting up a password-protected website for all participants in the case. All documents were published on this website, to dramatically reduce the amount of copied paper. At the same time, as all participants had access to all documents through the website, the constitutional requirements with regard to fundamental procedural rights were satisfied. This solution was later codified in the KapMuG reform of 2012 and is mandatory today.

The Model Procedure Before the Appellate Court in Frankfurt am Main

When the oral hearing before the Appellate Court finally began in April 2008, the presiding judge was Christian Dittrich, an experienced judge who had decided countless cases involving financial institutions in Frankfurt. Dittrich held the first hearing not in the court building, but in a local assembly hall in order to create more room for the many expected participants and spectators. It turned out that the large hall was unnecessary, and later hearings were held in the courthouse again. Nevertheless, there was significant media coverage, in particular when Telekom's former CEO Ron Sommer was called to the witness stand. Sommer had resigned from his CEO job at Deutsche Telekom in July 2002, after the stock price had fallen to €10. He had received a severance payment from Deutsche Telekom in the amount of €11.6 million.

The media also focused on Andreas Tilp as the outspoken representative of the plaintiffs. But other plaintiff lawyers also appeared on TV, in particular Klaus Rotter, who had competed with Tilp to become the lead lawyer on the plaintiffs' side. Today, Rotter and Tilp are probably the leading plaintiff-oriented law firms in Germany in capital market cases.

Judge Dittrich's goal was to finish the case before his retirement, which according to German law would be after his 65th birthday in 2009. Very early in the trial, Dittrich and his two colleagues on the bench made it clear that they were not convinced of the plaintiffs' allegation regarding the valuation of Telekom's real estate. In Dittrich's view, Deutsche Telekom had used a legally valid method to obtain the combined real estate value, so that the actual value of the assets at the time was irrelevant. Under this theory, there was no need for the originally expected, and very expensive expert testimony on the actual property value.

But Judge Dittrich partially accepted the plaintiffs' arguments with regard to the VoiceStream acquisition: if this risky acquisition had in fact been planned before the shares were issued (which was denied by the defendant), this should have been mentioned in the prospectus. It was therefore necessary to hear witnesses on this factual issue. As the relevant witnesses lived in the US, the Frankfurt Appellate Court travelled to the US in April 2009 and heard testimony on the VoiceStream acquisition. As the taking of evidence in a foreign country or the summoning of witnesses from a foreign country could have raised delicate public international law issues between Germany and the US, these hearings took place in the German Consulate offices in San Francisco and New York. This procedure is explicitly allowed under the Hague Convention of 1970 on the Taking of Evidence Abroad in Civil and Commercial Matters, to which both Germany and the US are parties. The result of the interrogations was that the Appellate Court was not convinced that there had been sufficiently specific preparations or plans regarding the Voice-Stream takeover, so that no mention in the prospectus was mandated by German law.[13]

As the plaintiffs realized that they might lose on these important aspects, they kept searching for additional material that could prove errors in the prospectus. The admission of these new issues into the model procedure required further decisions by the lower court. Judge Wösthoff granted several motions to extend the coverage of the model procedure and, in late 2009, it became clear that Judge Dittrich's plan to finish the case before his retirement would not work. In November 2009, the last oral hearing under Judge Dittrich's presidency was held and the case was stayed when Dittrich went into retirement on New Year's Day of 2010.

Fortunately, German procedural law allowed the replacement of the presiding judge, even in an ongoing case, so the results achieved up to now were not lost. Nevertheless, a new presiding judge at the Appellate Court had to be found. As this was a prestigious position, an internal quarrel broke out at the Court which even included legal actions by judges who were competing for the position. In April 2010, Birgitta Schier-Ammann came out victorious and was appointed as the new presiding judge for the 23rd Senate of the Appellate Court that was handling the Telekom case. She took her time to get acquainted with the case files and ordered the next oral hearing to be held in December 2010, more than a year after the last hearing.

At the December 2010 hearing, it became clear that Judge Schier-Ammann—assisted by her colleague Judge Rathmann, who had already been the lead rapporteur on the case under Judge Dittrich—was both well prepared and determined to bring the case to an end. Like Dittrich before her, she expressed serious doubts about most of the plaintiffs' arguments. And again, the reaction of the plaintiffs was to produce more material on alleged errors in the prospectus. The lower court needed time to decide on these motions. Several oral hearings were cancelled and postponed during 2011. The final oral hearing before the Appellate Court in Frankfurt was in January 2012. Reacting to public criticism on the duration of the procedure, Judge Schier-Ammann made an unusual

[13] OLG Frankfurt, model decision of 16 May 2012, 23 Kap 1/06, p. 87 et seq.

statement when she opened the hearing, explaining to the public that the many delays were not the fault of the courts, but were the result of a complicated procedure ordered by the law.

Finally: A (First) Decision

On 16 May 2012, more than 11 years after the first actions in the case were filed, the Appellate Court handed down the 'model decision'. Over 246 pages, the Court dealt with the plaintiffs' factual and legal allegations, only to come to the conclusion that there were no errors in the prospectus.[14]

This result is in contrast to a criminal investigation that had been undertaken by the Public Prosecutor in Bonn (where Telekom is headquartered) from 2000 to 2005. The Prosecutor's office had examined whether there was a crime of 'fraudulent accounting' with regard to the balance sheets published before the share emissions. Those proceedings were ended without a formal trial, on the basis of § 153a of the German Code of Criminal Procedure that allows the Public Prosecutor to quit prosecution if the suspect pays a voluntary fine. In 2005, Deutsche Telekom paid a fine of €5 million for charitable purposes and the affected six directors paid between €20,000 and €250,000 each. Under § 153a, such a voluntary fine can be proposed by the Prosecutor's office according to their discretion if payment of the fine would 'eliminate the public interest in criminal prosecution'. Originally designed for lesser offenses, today this provision is frequently used by prosecutors and courts to efficiently end large-scale criminal cases in complicated commercial matters.

However, the provision of § 153a is to be used only if the Public Prosecutor is convinced that there was a criminal offense—otherwise there would be no reason to ask the suspect for the payment of the fine. Accordingly, the Public Prosecutor noted in his press release in 2005 that he was convinced that there had been fraudulent accounting by Deutsche Telekom's management.[15]

Not surprisingly, the private plaintiffs in the Telekom litigation had tried to use this statement to support their theory of false balance sheets and misleading statements in the prospectus. They did not succeed on this basis, as the Frankfurt Appellate Court said that even if there had

---

[14] OLG Frankfurt, model decision of 16 May 2012, 23 Kap 1/06.

[15] Handelsblatt, 2 June 2005. The relevant passages from the prosecutor's files are quoted in Tilp, 2009. For an abbreviated English version of this article from the plaintiff lawyers' perspective, *see* Tilp & Roth, 2014.

been such a conviction by the Public Prosecutor, it would not be binding on a civil court.[16]

In this respect, the Court's model decision is—notwithstanding its paper weight—surprisingly lean in its reasoning. The Court also makes very clear that it is only presenting a legal solution and not a moral judgment on the whole Telekom story. This is most clearly expressed in the parts of the decision dealing with the marketing campaign that was organized by Telekom in 2000. Even though the marketing activities—including the famous Manfred Krug TV commercials—were directed at the ordinary citizen who might not be able to read a prospectus or a balance sheet with sufficient knowledge to understand its implications, this did not change the legal requirements for the prospectus which are based on the assumption that the investor has basic accounting knowledge or is at least well-advised in this respect. According to the Court, the prospectus 'is not directed at the ignorant investor'.[17]

Plaintiffs Win Before the Federal Court of Justice

Based on these and other contested issues, the plaintiffs appealed to the Bundesgerichtshof, the highest Federal Court in civil matters in Germany. It took the Federal Court another two years to decide this appeal. According to the procedural rules, this was an appeal on issues of law only, so there was no re-hearing of witnesses or other factual issues. There was also no oral argument, only a battle of papers in which the parties filed new briefs and the Federal Court judges reviewed the extensive documents that the procedure had produced before the Frankfurt Appellate Court.

Again, the presiding judge was close to retirement: presiding Judge Ulrich Wiechers would retire in November 2014, but had promised his colleagues that he would not leave them with a legacy of unfinished work. He succeeded. Ten days before his retirement, the Federal Court decided on the appeal by reversing the Appellate Court's decision and remanding it to the Appellate Court for further proceedings.[18]

This 2014 decision by the Federal Court confirmed the Appellate Court's view—that the Telekom prospectus was without a legally relevant error—on most counts, in particular on the real estate valuation issue. But the Federal Court found one relevant error: Deutsche Telekom AG had a substantial share in a US telecommunications company (Sprint

---

16 OLG Frankfurt, supra, note 14, pp. 133–135.

17 Ibid., p. 235.

18 Bundesgerichtshof, 21 October 2014, NJW 2015, 236.

Corp) and had reassigned that share to a subsidiary company within the Telekom group. In the annual report that was part of the prospectus, Deutsche Telekom AG had claimed that this 'sale' of the Sprint shares within the Telekom group had resulted in a profit of €8.2 billion. The Federal Court argued that this was a misleading statement as the actual risk of a loss in value of these shares remained within the Telekom group so that the stated profit would not necessarily be a lasting one.[19]

With this decision, the Telekom case has reached a new stage. It is now determined that the prospectus was wrong, although only on one count, but that is legally sufficient to create a prospectus liability claim for the investors. According to German procedural law, the case should now go back to the Frankfurt Appellate Court to determine issues of causality and negligence. During the whole year of 2015, the case files were still kept at the Federal Court in Karlsruhe, because there was an issue with lawyers' fees to be decided. The lawyer who worked on the appeal argued that he should receive the statutory fees in view of the whole group of plaintiffs, while the other side claims that the fee should be calculated only with regard to the individual plaintiff who had filed the appeal. The Appellate Court in Frankfurt has indicated to the parties that it will not continue the proceedings until the truckloads of files are returned to Frankfurt. It is therefore not likely that the next hearing in Frankfurt will be scheduled before the spring of 2016.

Notwithstanding these further delays, the situation for the plaintiffs has significantly improved. The applicable prospectus liability provisions assume liability where a prospectus error is found, unless the defendant can prove that he did not act with gross negligence in relation to the error or that the error did not influence the market price of the shares.[20] The onus of proof is therefore on the defendant now, so that remaining factual uncertainties would result in a judgment against the defendant.

In this procedural posture, one would normally expect the defendant to be willing to settle. However, this would require a change in strategy. During the first 13 years of the case, from 2001 to 2014, the defense lawyers always used a very strict defense strategy arguing that Deutsche Telekom never did anything wrong. Whether they will now switch to a more cooperative strategy and reach settlements with the plaintiffs remains to be seen. A further problem is that the KapMuG of 2005—which is still used in the Telekom case—allows for a binding settlement only if every single plaintiff agrees to it, which is highly unlikely in

[19] Ibid., p. 247.

[20] § 46 Börsengesetz (Stock Exchange Act) in the applicable version.

practice. A possible solution could therefore be a voluntary offer by Deutsche Telekom, but it is unclear how many plaintiffs would accept such an offer.

THE LEGACY OF THE *DEUTSCHE TELEKOM* CASE

Regardless of the specific results of the Telekom case, one can already draw tentative conclusions with respect to the social and historic relevance of the case. These relate to the emergence of mass litigation as an item on Germany's political agenda, the development of a sophisticated plaintiffs' bar and negative consequences on the shareholder culture in Germany.

Mass Litigation on the Political Agenda

The most obvious result of the Telekom case is that the issue of mass litigation has been on the political agenda in Germany from the inception of the KapMuG in 2005 until now. The KapMuG was originally limited to five years as it was regarded to be an experimental law. Besides the Telekom case, about a dozen other KapMuG cases were started in the early years of the KapMuG, and some of them progressed more quickly and smoothly. One KapMuG case even went up to the European Court of Justice regarding issues of substantive European capital market law and led to important developments in this area.[21]

The Federal Ministry of Justice commissioned a study in 2009 to evaluate the KapMuG.[22] In 2010, the original KapMuG was extended for two years in order to gain time for discussion. Finally, a new version of the KapMuG entered into force in 2012, which was not effective for the Telekom case but only for future KapMuG cases. This new law brought some technical improvements designed to speed up the proceedings. Furthermore, the 2012 KapMuG introduced two significant changes. One facilitates an amicable solution by introducing a court-approved settlement that becomes binding on every participant in the model procedure unless he or she opts out. This was proposed in the evaluation study with reference to the law on mass settlements in the Netherlands. However, in contrast to the Dutch solution, even the court-approved settlement under

---

[21] European Court of Justice, 28 June 2012, *Geltl v. Daimler*, case C-19/11, NJW 2012, 2787.

[22] Halfmeier, Rott & Feess, 2010. For an economic view on the KapMuG *see* Halfmeier & Feess, 2014.

the new KapMuG is binding only on those claimants who have filed a formal action and are thus participants in the model procedure. It does not have a general *res iudicata* effect on every possible claimant, as comparable settlements in the Netherlands or in the US may have.

A second major addition to the KapMuG in 2012 was the introduction of a 'registration' of claims with the court. A claimant who has not filed a regular action may now register his or her claim for a small fee if the claim is based on the same factual context as the existing model procedure. The registration does not create a risk of adverse costs, so the threshold to register is rather low. However, the claim registration does not lead to participation in the KapMuG procedure. The only effect of the registration is that the limitation period for the registered claim is eliminated. As limitation periods play an important role in German capital market law, this is seen by plaintiff attorneys as a possible step towards including more claimants in future procedures. Until 2015, this instrument has not been used much.

In 2012, the German legislator explicitly rejected an evolution from the sector-specific KapMuG into a more general instrument of collective litigation. The argument here was that the new law is not yet sufficiently tested and therefore needs another evaluation period of eight years, until 2020.[23] The opposition party *The Greens* later submitted a bill to German parliament that would have transformed the KapMuG into an opt-in group action not limited to capital market law.[24] Although this bill was rejected by the majority in parliament, the Ministry of Justice has indicated that it is working on a new proposal for 2016 which would use elements of the KapMuG for a new instrument of collective litigation. This means that collective litigation will remain an issue in Germany, and the existing KapMuG of 2012 may not be the end of the story.

A Plaintiffs' Bar

A second notable development is not a direct consequence from the Telekom case but is strongly connected with it. Unlike 20 years ago, Germany today has sophisticated and effective plaintiffs' law firms in the area of securities law. The law firms of Andreas Tilp and Klaus Rotter—to mention only two of the most prominent—are not comparable in size to US plaintiff firms, but for European standards, they are of significant manpower and are recognized today as an accepted part of the

---

23 Bundestagsdrucksache 17/8799, p. 14.

24 Bundestagsdrucksache 18/1464.

legal landscape. Both have succeeded in controversial cases and have helped to create significant new case law in the area of investor protection. They have managed to attract not only private investors as clients, but also large institutional investors who are now litigating securities cases. Losses suffered by investment funds are no longer simply accepted, rather institutional investors now take their fiduciary duties towards their members seriously and try to recover such losses if possible with the help of specialized law firms.[25]

Nevertheless, the economics for the plaintiff bar in Germany are still challenging. Andreas Tilp claims that he is losing money on the Telekom case while the case has dragged on, year after year, as he works for a fixed fee. The vehicle of legal expenses insurance that drove the Telekom case is no longer used, as all insurance companies have now changed their policies to specifically exclude disputes relating to investments.[26] With contingency fees outlawed to a large extent, most plaintiff lawyers resort to cooperation with third party litigation financing companies, or to other models that tend to circumvent the prohibition on contingency fees. A case such as the Telekom litigation—with thousands of small claimants—has not been brought again and is hard to imagine under today's circumstances. But what remains from the Telekom case, and the KapMuG legislation that arose from it, is that securities litigation is not necessarily a nuisance initiated by unqualified lawyers desperately searching for business, but that there are significant and serious social issues at stake that can be legitimately discussed in a rational, legal setting.

On the defense side, there has always been sophistication and no public insinuation that lawyers would be in it 'only for the money'. But even here, the Telekom case has highlighted certain trends. One is the creation of special litigation departments in well-established commercial law firms—litigation departments were uncommon in German law firms even in the 1990s—or even the emergence of boutique firms specializing in litigation.

The best example here is Bernd-Wilhelm Schmitz, the leading lawyer on the defense side who has represented Telekom since the beginning of the case. While the Telekom case went on, Schmitz moved from the international law firm Clifford Chance to Latham & Watkins, taking his Telekom litigation business with him, and then in 2009 he co-founded his

---

[25] *See* for example OLG München, 15 December 2014, Kap 3/10 (Hypo Real Estate case).

[26] *See* for example § 3 (2) (f) of the conditions ARB 2012 of ADVOCARD legal expenses insurance.

own boutique firm Schmitz & Partner, successfully specializing in national and international litigation and arbitration. His very strict strategy in the Telekom case—to deny any settlement and fight every single allegation by the plaintiffs—proved successful at least up until the model decision of 2012 that was in favor of Telekom. Now it may need to be revised after the pro-plaintiffs judgment by the Federal Court.

While in the 1990s there may have been a certain asymmetry in German lawyers' culture between more sophisticated (and well-paid) commercial lawyers and—allegedly—less competent and less successful lawyers on the plaintiff side, now this has changed to some extent as plaintiff law firms are also seen as competent and may even be regarded by some well-qualified law graduates as desirable places to work. There are still huge economic differences between the large commercial law firms on one side and plaintiff firms on the other side, but the evolving common ground is illustrated by a press release issued in 2012 by a formerly unknown coalition between the law firms of Tilp and Rotter together with the well-respected commercial law firms of Gleiss Lutz and Sernetz Schäfer. These four firms from 'both sides' apparently saw themselves as leaders in their field—collective litigation—and argued together against a restriction of the possibility of an appeal in KapMuG cases that was originally planned by the government during the KapMuG reform of 2012. They were successful in protecting their common interests and the KapMuG remained unchanged in this respect.

Frustration Regarding Shareholders' Culture in Germany

As one moves further away from the legal landscape into general German society, the effects of the Telekom case become more of a matter of speculation. One aspect seems to be the failure of the government and other actors to create a 'shareholders' culture' (Aktienkultur) in Germany. The financing of corporations in Germany was traditionally not established by way of shares spread over a large group of citizens, but rather through loans from banks, while the shares remained in the hands of a few very wealthy families or other corporations, sometimes with reciprocal ownership. The Telekom IPO was part of a strategy to change this situation, driven by several factors, such as the general de-regulation of the economy, individualization of retirement savings and also a financial interest on the side of the State as the seller of the shares.

In today's view, the Telekom IPO can be regarded as a huge mistake for approximately a million people. It is important to realize that the 15,000 plaintiffs in the Telekom litigation are only a small fraction of the number of citizens who had bought Telekom shares and who simply swallowed their losses—which means that the whole project of distributing shares to the general public has been discredited to a large extent. If we add to that the apparent failure of the German legal system to help the affected citizens in recovering their losses—even assuming that there will be some progress after the Federal Court's decision—this must have a negative effect on their willingness to become a shareholder in the future. The numbers seem to confirm this: the percentage of citizens in Germany who held shares in 2014 was not much higher than in the 1990s, and is very low in an international comparison.[27] Commentators from business circles explicitly draw a link between the catastrophic results of the Telekom IPO and the minimal interest in the stock market from German private investors.[28] Many ordinary citizens seem to feel powerless against an apparently overwhelming wall of accountants and lawyers erected by the State and the large corporations supported by it.

Such frustration with the stock market and with the lack of investor protection is detrimental both for the individual and for society. For the individual and his or her retirement savings, investing in the stock market is—at least in the long run—probably superior in comparison to a savings account. In the current environment of low interest rates, private investors may miss investment opportunities by disregarding the stock market. For the economy, a broad base of shareholders may reduce the costs of capital for companies. Most importantly, a society in which a large part of the population feels insufficiently protected by the legal system risks alienation and resentment against legal and democratic institutions.[29] One can therefore only hope that the Telekom case will act as a slow but steady catalyst towards more effective access to justice and shareholder protection in Germany.

---

[27] The percentage of direct stockholders among the German population was around 6 percent in the 1990s, compared to 18 percent in the United Kingdom and 21 percent in the United States. In Germany, this figure rose up to almost 10 percent in 2001, and later fell back to the 1990s level of about 6 percent, where it remains until today, according to statistics published by the Deutsches Aktien-Institut in 2015.

[28] *See* for example Gottschalck, 2013.

[29] See for example the self-published book by Philipp, 2006. Philipp is one of the lesser known, but active plaintiff lawyers in the Deutsche Telekom case. In his book, he tries to show that Deutsche Telekom and the Federal government deceived the public into buying the shares and speculates that this is all part of a giant conspiracy designed to rob the German working man of his earnings. Philipp also regularly writes in publications and blogs of the extreme right.

REFERENCES

Felix Bergmeister, *Kapitalanleger-Musterverfahrensgesetz (KapMuG)* (Mohr Siebeck 2009)

Stephen Choi & Linda Silberman, *Transnational Litigation and Global Securities Class Actions Lawsuits*, (2009) University of Wisconsin Law Review 465

Arne Gottschalck, *Wer von der Dax-Hausse profitiert*, Manager Magazin, 13 December 2013

Axel Halfmeier, Peter Rott & Eberhard Feess, *Kollektiver Rechtsschutz im Kapitalmarktrecht* (Frankfurt School Verlag 2010)

Axel Halfmeier & Eberhard Feess, *The German Capital Markets Model Case Act (KapMuG): A European Role Model for Increasing the Efficiency of Capital Markets? Analysis and Suggestions for Reform*, (2014) European Journal of Finance, 20(4)

Wolfgang Philipp, *Die Telekom-Ballade, Wegweiser in eine andere Republik* (AT Edition 2006)

Andreas Tilp, Das Kapitalanleger-Musterverfahrensgesetz: Stresstest für den Telekom-prozess, in *Festschrift für Achim Krämer* (De Gruyter 2009)

Andreas Tilp & Thomas Roth, The German Capital Market Model Proceedings Act as Illustrated by the Example of the Frankfurt Deutsche Telekom Claims, in Willem van Boom & Gerhard Wagner (eds.), *Mass Torts in Europe: Cases and Reflections* (De Gruyter 2014)

14. The L&H case: Belgium's internet bubble story[1]

Stefaan Voet

SUMMARY

Most Belgian mass claim cases from the last ten years have one common feature: they were criminal cases and were brought before a criminal court.[2] Contrary to common law jurisdictions, the victim of a Belgian criminal case is not absent from the criminal trial. He or she is a formal party to the proceedings and has standing to plead. With respect to his or her civil claim, the victim can piggyback on the evidence brought forward by the Public Prosecutor in order to prove a civil fault. The victims only have to prove individual causation and their damages.

The Belgian Lernout & Hauspie (L&H) case was one of the largest corporate scandals in European history. L&H had developed advanced Automatic Speech Recognition software and persuaded thousands of people to invest in the company. Some invested all their savings. However, L&H went downhill as quickly as it shot uphill. Allegations of fictitious clients, artificially inflated revenue, forgery, insider trading, abuse of confidence and other similar charges led to the bankruptcy of the company and a criminal investigation. Ultimately, 21 individuals and companies were sued before the Criminal Court of Appeal in Ghent. During the trial, more than 15,000 victims filed civil claims. Three years later the Court issued its ruling. L&H's founding fathers and most former

---

1 This chapter is based on the review of publicly available court documents, media reports and ten interviews (conducted between February and April 2011) with lawyers and others involved in the Lernout & Hauspie case. These were defense lawyers and lawyers acting on behalf of duped shareholders and associations representing them.

2 Since September 2014, Belgium has a consumer class action (*see* Voet, 2015). The procedure only applies to consumer disputes. Mass accidents and securities cases, like the L&H case, fall outside its scope.

directors were convicted. The deep-pocket defendants Dexia Bank and KPMG, respectively L&H's bank and statutory auditor, were acquitted. The civil claims were pending at the time this book went to press.

The L&H story illustrates what happens on the ground to mass claims in a regime where civil claims piggyback on criminal justice proceedings. The L&H case shows that in criminal mass cases most victims rely on associations to file their civil claims. In the absence of a collective litigation procedure, all claimants were required to come forward individually. Most (approximately 85 percent) gave a mandate to a consumer or minority shareholder association to represent them. These associations, some of which joined forces because of the scale of the case, mainly served as communicators with the civil claimants and as claims administrators, allowing the lawyers to focus exclusively on the legal issues. One association that was involved in the case from the beginning played an active fact-finding role. A few associations, which commentators compared to 'aggressive' American class action lawyers, were so vigorous in defending the interests of the civil claimants that they dominated the proceedings, in the eyes of some hindering the primarily criminal purpose of the trial.

In contrast to the individual defendants, the deep-pocketed corporate defendants (Dexia and KPMG) had more financial resources to master the case and especially the bulk of civil claims: they set up large teams of lawyers and paralegals, digitized the 400,000-page criminal file and developed tailor-made software in order to produce briefs for all 15,000 piggybacking victims to rebut the latter's claims. Because L&H also had a second headquarters in the United States (US), some class action procedures against Dexia and KPMG were brought there. Until these were ultimately settled, there was extensive sharing of information between the Belgian and US lawyers of Dexia and KPMG. To defend their clients in US courts, the US lawyers wanted information about the criminal investigation to use in pre-trial discovery. To defend their clients in the Court of Appeal in Ghent, the Belgian lawyers wanted information that L&H had disclosed to the US SEC during the latter's regulatory investigation.

The Public Prosecutor lacked the means and legal knowledge to deal with the complex L&H case. He largely relied on the investigative report drafted by one of the associations. The decision to indict so many people and companies considerably complicated the case, suggesting that this was a major strategic error on the Public Prosecutor's part. The Court of Appeal also had difficulty managing the case. Although it organized the orderly course of the proceedings, for example by providing a suitable infrastructure, commentators generally perceived that during the proceedings the Court was much too passive. Out of fear of violating the due process rights of the parties in this convoluted case, the Court was reluctant to actively manage and steer the proceedings.

RISE AND DOWNFALL OF L&H

In 1987, Jo Lernout, Pol Hauspie and Nico Willaert founded Lernout & Hauspie Speech Products (L&H), a speech recognition technology company based in Ypres, located in the province of West Flanders in Belgium. L&H had developed advanced Automatic Speech Recognition (ASR) software. ASR can be defined as the independent, computer-driven transcription of spoken language into readable text in real time. It allows a computer to identify the words that a person speaks into a microphone or telephone and convert it to written text. L&H had developed, or at least claimed to have developed, ASR software with a high reliability rate.

By the second half of the 1990s, in the middle of the internet bubble era, L&H blossomed. Because of this success and because Lernout and Hauspie were 'one of them', many working and middle-class families and pensioners from the greater area of Ypres invested in L&H. Some used all their savings. The company opened a second headquarters in the US and, after acquiring multiple companies worldwide in the field of speech recognition technology it went public on the US Nasdaq and the Brussels Easdaq in 1995. At its peak, L&H had a market capitalization of almost $10 billion. The site where L&H had its headquarters was called Flanders Language Valley, mimicking Silicon Valley.

At the end of the 1990s, L&H went downhill. It all started with some articles in the Wall Street Journal in early 1999. Journalists discovered that in one year, the revenue of L&H's subsidiary in South Korea had increased from $300,000 to $143 million and that L&H used fictitious clients, so-called Language Development Companies (LDCs) that were created by L&H itself, to artificially inflate revenue. The accounting methodologies that L&H applied were also criticized. As a consequence of these allegations, L&H shares plummeted.

To quiet the controversy, Lernout and Hauspie resigned, CEO Gaston Bastiaens left, and L&H's audit committee ordered an internal audit by New York law firm Bryan Cave and the auditors of Arthur Andersen. Unfortunately, these measures could not turn the tide. As time went on, L&H's Nasdaq and Easdaq quotations were suspended. In the US, L&H filed for Chapter 11 bankruptcy protection and the SEC started an investigation. In Belgium, a rescue operation by a new CEO failed. On 24 October 2001, the Commercial Court in Ypres declared L&H bankrupt and appointed five liquidators. In that same year, ScanSoft (now Massachussets Nuance Communications Inc.) bought all L&H technologies. At the time this book went to press, the bankruptcy proceedings were still pending.

CRIMINAL INVESTIGATION AND TRIAL

While L&H's business was unraveling, the aforementioned allegations triggered a criminal investigation by the Public Prosecutor and the examining magistrate in Ypres. During this investigation many deceived shareholders lodged a complaint with the examining magistrate against L&H and its managers. Ultimately, 21 individuals and companies were indicted, including the founding fathers of L&H (Lernout, Hauspie and Willaert), the former CEO (Bastiaens) and CFO, the members of the audit committee, multiple (former) directors, the company lawyers, the LDC intermediaries, KPMG (the statutory auditor of L&H) and one of its partners (William Van Aerde), and Dexia Bank (the banker) and its Corporate Banking director. The counts included forgery, emission fraud, price manipulation, violation of accounting rules, insider trading, abuse of company resources, money laundering and abuse of confidence.

Because one of the accused was a lawyer who was also a substitute judge in the Commercial Court in Ypres, the proceedings were immediately conducted before a three-judge panel of the Court of Appeal in Ghent, and not before the Court of First Instance in Ypres, as is required by Belgian law when a substitute judge is indicted. As a result, all 20 other defendants were tried in first and last instance before the Court of Appeal in Ghent. Some lawyers claimed that the prosecutors deliberately indicted a substitute judge to be able to bring the immense case before the Court of Appeal immediately, thereby avoiding a time-consuming repetition of the case before an appellate court.[3] Some defense lawyers found this very problematic, because they lost an opportunity for consideration of law and facts by multiple courts. Ultimately, the indicted substitute judge was acquitted.

On 21 May 2007, the criminal trial commenced. It was an event without an equal, with a 400,000-page criminal file, 15,414 civil claimants claiming

---

[3] Criminal (and civil) appellate proceedings in Belgium are a full re-trial of the issues of law and fact.

a total of (at least) €177 million, 61 hearing days spread over two years, 20 months of deliberation and a judgment of 2,100 pages.[4]

OUTCOME

On 20 September 2010, almost three-and-a-half years after the trial commenced, the Court of Appeal in Ghent ruled on the case. Its decision addressed a complex web of questions related to L&H's financial practices and the roles of multiple parties.

What is Revenue?

At the heart of the L&H case was the question: what is revenue? According to Belgian law, revenue is the amount of money coming from the sale of goods or the delivery of services, in the context of a regular business practice, after deducting the allowed discounts. The law does not offer a detailed framework for recognizing revenue. Each company can draw up its own rules. The central question in the L&H case was whether the company's revenue accounting was lawful.

Because of its Nasdaq quotation, L&H used the US GAAP—the Generally Accepted Accounting Principles—as a frame of reference, specifically Statement of Position (SOP) 97-2 US GAAP on Software Revenue Recognition. Based on this SOP, L&H adopted a rule stipulating that amounts coming from the sale of software licenses could be booked as revenue in its profit and loss account, as part of the annual report, when specific conditions were met. One of these conditions was that L&H could have no unfulfilled contractual obligations to the other party from whom it was booking revenue.

The Relationship Between L&H and the 'Language Development Companies'

In its decision, the Court of Appeal held not only that the general accounting rules were applied improperly, but that they were applied fraudulently. In the Court's view, L&H concluded fictional license agreements with the so-called LDCs for the sole purpose of booking the

---

[4] The judgment (in Dutch) was published on the website of the Court of Appeal in Ghent, available at http://www.juridat.be/beroep/gent/index.htm.

royalties paid by those LDCs to L&H as revenue in the annual report, thereby artificially inflating the assets of the company and misleading investors.

The licensing agreements between L&H and the LDCs were framed to enable L&H to book the royalties stipulated by the agreements as revenue. The Court ruled that this approach complied with the law. However, it held that in practice L&H violated the law because the evidence indicated that a key condition—that L&H have no unfilled contractual obligations to the LDCs when the license agreements were concluded—was not met.

Fraud

Based on its reading of the facts, the Court ruled that the initial license agreements deliberately omitted key factors in order to allow L&H to (illegally) book LDC royalties immediately as revenue. In addition, it held that the provision in the contracts that stated 'this agreement has been negotiated by the parties', was inaccurate because the content of the license agreements was imposed on the LDCs by L&H, and also as some of the LDCs had only just been established at the time the agreements were signed, it was not possible that there could have been negotiations. Finally, the Court held that all license agreements drafted from May 1999 onwards were completely fraudulent as they were drafted solely to artificially generate revenue, and that L&H's annual reports were fraudulent because they reported illusory royalties as revenue. However, it acquitted the company itself of criminal liability on the grounds that its officers and administrators were uninformed of these machinations.

Other Defendants

The Public Prosecutor sued both KPMG, the statutory auditor of L&H, and one of its partners (William Van Aerde). The Court acquitted both of intentional crimes on the grounds that they were given inaccurate data to audit by L&H management. However, Van Aerde was convicted of non-intentional negligence on the grounds that he did not act as a careful and reasonable auditor, since in the context of the financial audit, there were data about the recognition of revenue that he could have investigated that might have had an influence on his opinion about the annual assets.

L&H was financed by Artesia Bank, which merged with Dexia Bank in 2002. In June 1999, Artesia Bank had provided Lernout, Hauspie and Willaert with a personal loan of $20 million, knowing that this money would be used to finance the royalties the LDCs had to pay to L&H. The Court acquitted Dexia and its Corporate Banking director of wrongdoing on the grounds that it was not proven beyond a reasonable doubt that the bank knew that those royalties were illegally recognized as revenue by L&H.

By acquitting KPMG and Dexia, the Court eliminated the possibility of the civil claimants collecting substantial compensation, but this did not provoke a societal outcry. The reasoning of the Court (regarding the criminal liability) was viewed as sound and appropriately independent from the civil consequences.[5]

Lernout, Hauspie and Willaert were each given sentences of five years, including three years in custody and two years on probation. They were each ordered to pay a fine of approximately $33,000. Bastiaens, the former CEO of L&H, was sentenced to five years (two years in custody and three years on probation) and ordered to pay a fine of approximately $6,500. Smaller fines were imposed on other defendants. Van Aerde, the KPMG partner, was given a probationary sentence and ordered to pay a fine of approximately $3,300. All defendants who were found guilty were also ordered to pay the costs of the criminal procedure amounting to approximately $1,275,000.

Immediately after the decision, six convicted defendants appealed the decision before the Belgian Supreme Court (the Court of Cassation). Under Belgian law, the Supreme Court only reviews whether the lower court (in this case, the Court of Appeal in Ghent) applied the law correctly; it does not make factual findings. In its decision of 29 November 2011, the Supreme Court dismissed the appeal.[6]

An automatic consequence of the conviction of some of the defendants is that the Court has to deal with the bulk of civil claims, even though the deep-pocket defendants have been acquitted. At the time of this publication, the civil claims against the convicted defendants were still pending. In May 2014, the Court announced that the first hearing will take place in November 2016. A final decision on the civil claims is to be expected in 2017 or early 2018.

---

[5] Belgian criminal judges will not acquit defendants in order to do away with the civil claims. The criminal and civil issues are decided independently from each other. If a judge made his criminal decision dependent on the outcome (that is the fact that he will not have to deal with the civil claims), his decision would be reversed in appeal or quashed by the Supreme Court.

[6] Court of Cassation, 29 November 2011, P.10.1766.N/1, available at http://jure.juridat.just.fgov.be/pdfapp/download_blob?idpdf=F-20111129-1 (in French).

PIGGYBACKING CIVIL CLAIMANTS

In order to fully understand the civil aspect of the L&H case, it is important to explain the role of the victim in a Belgian criminal trial. In most common law systems, the victim is absent in a criminal trial. He or she may be called as a witness, but is not a formal party to the criminal proceedings. The victim cannot claim his or her damages during the criminal trial, but may do so in a separate civil case. In Belgium the role of the victim is different.[7] The victim is a formal party to the criminal proceedings, along with the Public Prosecutor and the defendant. In most cases, victims will file their civil claim during the criminal proceedings. After the judge has dealt with the criminal aspect of the case, and has convicted the defendant, the judge will rule upon the victims' civil claims. There is no jury in Belgian court proceedings, criminal or civil. If the judge acquits the defendant of all criminal charges, he or she will not rule upon the civil claims. In that situation, the victim can initiate a civil case based on another cause of action, for example negligence if the defendant was acquitted of fraud. The gain for the victim in filing a claim during the criminal proceedings is that he or she can piggyback on the evidence brought forward by the Public Prosecutor to prove a civil fault: if the judge convicts the defendant, the victim only has to prove his or her damages and causation. This is what happened in the L&H case: 15,414 deceived shareholders filed their civil claims during the criminal trial and piggybacked on the evidence brought forward by the Public Prosecutor.

A victim can freely choose not to piggyback on the criminal case, but to immediately initiate a civil case which will be heard by a civil judge. However, where a concurrent criminal case against the same defendant is pending, the civil judge will have to suspend the civil case until the criminal judge has ruled on the criminal case.

It is also possible for a victim to use both tracks: filing his or her civil claim during the criminal proceedings and piggybacking on the Public Prosecutor on the one hand, and initiating a separate civil case on the other hand. This is done frequently in big cases because the statute of limitation for filing a civil claim could run out as the criminal case proceeds. This happened in the L&H case. Besides claiming their damages in the criminal case, most victims, represented by associations, also initiated civil cases before the Commercial Court in Ypres, which

---

[7] *See* section 4 of the Preliminary Title of the Belgian Code of Criminal Procedure.

under law were suspended awaiting the outcome of the criminal case before the Court of Appeal in Ghent.

CIVIL CLAIMANTS AND REPRESENTATION BY ASSOCIATIONS

Procedural Options for Mass Claims in Belgium

Belgian law has no provision for a representative action for civil claims that piggy-backed on criminal proceedings. This means that in a criminal case all civil claimants have to come forward individually. In the L&H case *each* of the approximately 15,000 deceived shareholders had to file their own civil claim.

There were two groups of L&H civil claimants: non-shareholders (for example banks, insurance companies and the L&H liquidators) and shareholders. The latter included four subgroups, each of which proceeded differently:

(1) there were 2,347 shareholders who acted *pro se*;
(2) there were 467 shareholders who each had their own lawyer;
(3) there were groups of shareholders represented by a single lawyer or law firm (for example the group Verstraeten with 234 shareholders represented by one lawyer from Ghent (Michael Verstraeten)); and
(4) there were shareholders backed by associations.

The two biggest groups represented by associations were 'Spaarverlies/Dolor' with 1,589 shareholders and 'Deminor/Test-Aankoop' with 13,575 shareholders. Spaarverlies/Dolor is a non-profit consumer organization offering information and legal assistance to victims of mass harms. Deminor is a commercial company specializing in representing minority shareholders in listed and non-listed companies. Test-Aankoop is Belgium's largest consumer organization. Most associations used the technique of party representation, which enables a natural or legal person (the representative) to represent a group of individuals if he or she received an explicit mandate from each individual member of the group.

The difference between the Spaarverlies/Dolor group and the Deminor/Test-Aankoop group is that the members of the former only gave a mandate to the lawyer appointed by the association, while the members of the latter gave a mandate to the association and to the lawyer appointed by the association. One of the reasons for this was that Deminor was involved in the case from the beginning and had initiated civil proceedings to sue L&H on behalf of multiple shareholders before the criminal investigation commenced.

Deminor and Test-Aankoop teamed up to represent individual shareholders because Test-Aankoop did not have the legal knowledge to deal with the case. Of the 13,575 shareholders they both represented, approximately 4,000 were Test-Aankoop members.[8] In the criminal proceedings the Deminor/Test-Aankoop shareholders were represented by DLA Piper, a Brussels law firm associated with the US-based international law firm of the same name. Deminor was responsible for the legal part of the case and worked together with the law firm. Test-Aankoop was responsible for the logistics and the processing of all individual files, including the Deminor files. For these purposes, Test-Aankoop hired temporary personnel. The Spaarverlies/Dolor shareholders were represented by SQ Law, a Brussels law firm that did all the legal and administrative work with little involvement from the association.

Different associations used different criteria to retain clients. One association only wanted to act on behalf of *bona fide* victims: those shareholders who bought L&H stock before the SEC investigation and widespread publicity about the fraud. This association wanted to strike a balance between the quality and quantity of claims it represented. Shareholders who did not meet these criteria could join another association that did not impose such strict standards.[9] These associations were less critical and did not judge the merits of each individual shareholder before agreeing to represent them.

The Role of the Associations

The civil claimants and the representing and/or backing associations particularly focused on KPMG and Dexia, because they had deep-pockets. If the Court were to order compensation for the civil claimants, this would have to come from KPMG and Dexia, since from the beginning it was clear that the other individual defendants had no financial means to pay compensation.

---

[8] Initially, 8,000 duped shareholders contacted Test-Aankoop. Half of them were filtered out. Approximately 20,000 shareholders contacted Deminor. After selection, only half of them were retained.

[9] For example, one lawyer (backed by an association) admitted that 25 percent of his clients had been rejected by an association that imposed such a criterion.

With the exception of the Deminor/Test-Aankoop collaboration, there were no formal contacts before or during the trial between the associations, the lawyers and the Public Prosecutor, for example to align strategies or to make agreements with respect to the orderly evolution of the proceedings. Each association and law firm handled the case in its own way, and more importantly with its own resources.

Before and during the criminal trial the associations played three roles. Firstly, they communicated with the victims about the case, using email, newsletters, telephone helpdesks and similar means. One lawyer required his clients to have an email address for the purpose of communicating with them; if a client did not have email, the lawyer planned to charge the client for every letter he had to send. In the end, that was not necessary. Secondly, the associations administered the claims, which was a huge undertaking. And thirdly, one association also played an important role as fact finder. This association analyzed all annual reports of L&H, SEC filings, newspaper articles and so on and drafted its own investigative research report.

In a normal criminal trial, the victims plead first. They can file and explain their civil claim. Next, the Public Prosecutor and the defendants plead their arguments. In the L&H case the Court decided at one point to completely separate the criminal from the civil aspect of the case. Several parties attributed this decision at least in part to the aggressive role some of the associations played. From the Belgian legal perspective, the L&H case was primarily a criminal case in which the Court had to decide if the defendants had violated the law. On a secondary level, and only after its criminal decision, the Court had to deal with the civil aspect of the case, in which the associations, representing a multitude of deceived shareholders, played a key role. But for some of the associations, the L&H case was at least as much, if not primarily, a civil case. These associations started with the civil aspect of the case immediately, from the beginning of the trial, by promptly and vigorously attacking KPMG and Dexia. In doing so, they dominated the proceedings so much that they were perceived as hindering the criminal trial, which eventually led the Court to split up the criminal and civil aspects of the case, fearing it was starting to act more as a civil court then a criminal court. One person compared these associations with what he described as 'aggressive' American class action lawyers.

The Role of the Defendants

L&H itself played a dual role during the proceedings. On the one hand, it was prosecuted by the Public Prosecutor. On the other hand, L&H was also a claimant with a substantial civil claim against some of the defendants, including the previous managers and directors. Because of that double role, it had two representatives. The Commercial Court in Ypres appointed a curator *ad hoc*, whose exclusive mission it was to defend the company. The company was also represented by its liquidators who filed a claim of €744 million, the total amount of debts of the company, acting on behalf of all the creditors of L&H. Only two of the five liquidators actually engaged in the proceedings.

With respect to the other defendants, a distinction has to be made between the individuals and the companies. The latter, KPMG and Dexia, were able to master the case more easily because they had more financial resources. Immediately after the Bryan Cave report, KPMG set up a taskforce composed of lawyers and auditors that investigated all information revealed by this report, including *inter alia* the deception of KPMG by L&H management. Because of that internal investigation, KPMG was able to prepare its strategies and defense in the criminal trial. Moreover, KPMG had the means to digitize all relevant documents, not only internal documents and correspondence, but also parts of the criminal file. The same was true for Dexia. Once Dexia was targeted during the Public Prosecutor's investigation, it set up a team of eight criminal and civil lawyers to act on its behalf. For the Dexia lawyers it was more difficult to reconstruct the facts because they inherited an inadequate file from Artesia Bank (which Dexia had acquired) that had originally provided loans to L&H's principals.

The defendants not only had to rebut the indictments of the Public Prosecutor, they also had to reply to the claims of the approximately 15,000 civil claimants. Only KPMG and Dexia were able to do so thoroughly. For example, KPMG wrote several briefs adding up to 2,500 pages on the criminal aspect of the case and wrote briefs rejecting all of the civil claims. The way it produced those briefs is remarkable. After analyzing all civil claims, KPMG came up with about 15 arguments to reject every claim. These arguments were written down in one general brief. In addition to this general brief, KPMG generated a brief for each claimant in which it responded to his or her claim. KPMG designed tailor-made software for these purposes. After a thorough analysis by a team of lawyers, and inserting the data of all individual claimants,[10] the computer generated an individual brief for each civil claimant with one or more arguments refuting his or her claim.

Dexia established a team of 24 lawyers and paralegals that worked for six months to screen, systematize and analyze all individual claims. The actual work was divided between its lead law firm and the bank. The law firm identified relevant criteria and associated each criterion with a legal argument.[11] Also by using a tailor-made software program, the employees of the bank analyzed every civil claim and linked it to one of the criteria the law firm had established.[12] The law firm supervised this process by carrying out spot-checks. Based on that analysis, the bank and its lawyers generated a brief for each claimant. An exception was made for complicated and large claims, which were exclusively analyzed by the law firm. The bank set a threshold and ordered the law firm to analyze every claim above that threshold itself. Several civil claimant lawyers noted that some of the defense lawyers, although they had electronic versions of all of their arguments and briefs, overloaded the other parties with paper versions and refused to give them an electronic version. The huge efforts of the lead defendants illustrate the cost inefficiencies of proceeding on a case-by-case basis in large-scale mass litigation. However, they also suggest the value of individuation to deep-pocketed defendants when it comes to merits determination.

The lawyers for the individual defendants, who had less financial resources, made the best of what they had. Most of them were individual lawyers not belonging to big law firms. They managed the L&H case alone or with some assistants. They only focused on the criminal aspect of the case. One defense lawyer admitted that he had only one aim in the L&H case: making sure his client did not go to prison. All the rest was of minor importance. For most of these lawyers, managing the criminal aspects of the case was achievable because just like KPMG and Dexia, they had been involved from the beginning and had followed the

---

[10] For example when and where the civil claimant bought L&H stock, the price he or she paid, the kind of damages he or she was claiming, and so on.

[11] Examples of those criteria are: can the civil claimant be identified? Does the civil claimant produce sufficient evidence to prove he or she was an L&H shareholder? The latter criterion was sometimes difficult because it depended on the interpretation of the employee of the bank. For one employee a piece of evidence was unreadable. Another employee made more effort in reading and analyzing the same evidence.

[12] For each civil claim the employees of the bank received a list with all of the criteria. The employees had to cross a box on the list.

evolution of the case and relied on the development of the criminal file. Other lawyers who got involved at a later stage had to be more creative. One lawyer filtered the criminal file of 400,000 pages and looked only for the most important pieces of information: expert reports, summaries, all the statements of his clients, all the documents referred to in those statements and the statements of the key players in the case. He only analyzed these specific documents, which still numbered about 100,000 pages. Another defense lawyer had some assistants simply read the entire file and make summaries.

Unlike the indicted companies, the individual defendants paid little if any attention to the civil claimants. One defense lawyer said whether his client would be fined €1 million, €10 million, or €100 million, it would be useless putting any effort and energy in rebutting the civil claims, since he had no money. Another defense lawyer replied to the civil claims orally with two basic arguments:

(1) the shareholders accepted a risk when buying L&H stock, and
(2) they could have sold the stock, which most of them did not do, meaning that they speculated.

PUBLIC PROSECUTOR

The overall evaluation by the parties of the performance of the Public Prosecutor's Office was mixed. Some findings indicate that the Public Prosecutor lacked the means and legal and technical knowledge to deal with this convoluted case. At one point during the investigation, it was decided to transfer the case from Ypres to Ghent and to replace the examining magistrate in the Court of First Instance in Ypres with a senior and more experienced examining magistrate in the Court of Appeal in Ghent.

Many of the parties criticized the fact that the Public Prosecutor not only decided very late in the investigation who to indict, but also indicted too many individuals and companies, out of fear of forgetting somebody. This was considered a major strategic error, as it complicated things. Some lawyers indicated that the Public Prosecutor would have been better off prosecuting a smaller number of defendants, instead of a horde of individuals and companies.

Finally, several parties pointed out that the Public Prosecutor took full advantage of the comprehensive investigation that one of the associations, acting on behalf of duped shareholders, had carried out, because the

Public Prosecutor was not able to do it himself. Several defendants considered this inappropriate.[13]

FUNDING AND FINANCING

How were the associations paid? One association did not charge anything, partially out of guilt, because in the 1990s they had advised their members to buy L&H stock. The members of that association paid an annual €150 contribution. They were not charged an extra fee for the L&H case. The legal support in the case was offered as a free service to the members. The only condition the association imposed was that their members had to retain their membership until the end of the proceedings, which made it a perfect excuse to work on customer relations. Based on previous experiences, other associations charged a fixed sum of €25, €50 or €100, *pro rato* the number of shares they had, or charged a fixed sum based on the damages suffered. Exceptions were made for institutional investors, with whom special agreements were made. All associations used a success fee, usually 10 percent. The associations working together with a law firm were charged on an hourly basis or on a lump sum basis.

One lawyer, representing a large group of shareholders, offered three possibilities to his clients. They could choose an hourly rate, a contingency fee remuneration or pay a lump sum with a success fee. In the end, most clients opted for the third possibility. The second possibility is remarkable, since contingency fees are strictly prohibited in Belgium, on the grounds that they violate public order and are incompatible with attorneys' professional ethics.[14]

JUDICIAL MANAGEMENT

Before the Trial

First, there was the problem of the 400,000-page criminal file that was put together by the Public Prosecutor and the examining magistrate. During a criminal investigation the defendants and the civil claimants cannot order a copy of the file. Only at certain points in the proceedings can they read the file by going to the courthouse and reading it there. In

---

[13] One defense lawyer even suggested that the indictement of KPMG and Dexia was a reward by the Public Prosecutor for the association concerned.

[14] *See* section 446*ter* of the Belgian Judicial Code.

the L&H case, some law firms had to send two or three interns to the courthouse for weeks to read and take notes. At one point, the examining magistrate in the Court of Appeal in Ghent decided to give parties nearly permanent and unlimited access to the criminal file to fully guarantee their due process rights. He also decided to digitize the criminal file by making an electronic version. The reactions were mixed. The lawyers for the individual defendants were happy with this. Some lawyers for some company defendants did not really use it, because the quality was bad or they had done their own digitization, something the other lawyers could not afford. An advantage of the digital version was that it contained a useful search engine. A disadvantage was the limited access. One needed a special device to log in and each lawyer only received two licenses to do so.

Shortly before the trial, the Public Prosecutor and the examining magistrate organized an informal gathering with all of the parties. During this meeting the state of affairs of the case was shared and information was provided on the use of the digital version of the criminal file. This was particularly important for the defendants and their lawyers, who were indicted in the final phase of the investigation and who did not have enough time to plow through the entire file. Other lawyers regretted that this preliminary meeting, which was quite unique, was not used more effectively for arranging the practical organization of the forthcoming trial.

During the Trial

During the trial, the Court had to organize the infrastructure for 15,000 civil claimants to file their civil claim. To administer this, the Court did three things. Firstly, it temporarily moved to a conference center, because even the biggest courtroom in the Court of Appeal building in Ghent was too small. Secondly, for the individual shareholders who were not represented by an association or lawyer, the Court set up stands outside the courtroom with ten to 15 clerks. The clerks had prepared completion forms that could be filled out. They also told people which documents they had to submit. Most of the lawyers considered this totally unacceptable, because it violated the impartiality of the Court.[15] Thirdly, the Court

[15] For example, the completion form contained this sentence: *'I claim … euros, and … euros interests.'* For most lawyers the addition of the interest-phrase was improper, because the Court could not suggest to civil claimants that they should claim interest. The form also contained a list with all of the defendants. The civil claimants had to check a box next to the name of the

allowed civil claimants to file their claim past the regular deadline. In a normal criminal case, civil claimants have to come forward at the beginning of the trial, before the opening statement of the Public Prosecutor and the oral pleadings. In the L&H case, the Court made an exception and allowed civil claimants to come forward after the oral pleadings had begun, which frustrated the orderly evolution of the trial.

The general perception was that during the proceedings the Court acted professionally but was much too passive. There was little interaction with the lawyers and the other parties. Most lawyers attributed this to the Court's fear of violating the due process rights of the parties in this high profile case. Therefore, the Court allowed parties to plead and write as much as they wanted, which sometimes frustrated the orderly evolution of the trial. Only after a while did the Court adjust the procedural calendar by reducing the number of hearings. The perception of other parties, who were acquitted, was different. They believed the Court struck a good balance between the interests of the parties, their due process rights and the desire to deal with the case within a reasonable time.

Some parties observed that in the early stages of the trial, some associations and lawyers tried to pressgang additional clients that were not yet represented by an association or lawyer. Moreover, these same associations were perceived as lacking integrity because they simply copied the legal arguments of other associations. It was noted that this behavior was not restrained by the Court, again out of fear of violating due process rights. The same was true with respect to personal attacks by some parties on the Court and the Belgian political establishment that was considered partially culpable for the L&H fiasco. Those attacks occasionally derailed the proceedings because the Court did not intervene.

With respect to the piggybacking victims in the criminal case, it has to be underlined that normally the criminal and civil aspect of the case are tried and judged at the same time. After hearing the civil claimants, the Public Prosecutor and the defendants on the criminal and civil issues, the judge will deliberate on the case. The judge decides everything in one single judgment. Because in the L&H case it was going to take too much time for the civil claimants to take up positions, the Court made an exception and, on 29 September 2008, decided to split the criminal and civil aspect of the case. It would first deal with the criminal aspect of the

---

defendant from whom they wanted to claim money. It was noted that the clerks advised people to check all of the boxes.

case and render a criminal judgment. Depending on the outcome, the Court would allow the continuation of the case with respect to the civil claims, and would later render a second civil judgment. The Court ruled that the intervention of the civil claimants would take so much time that it could infringe on the right to have the case dealt with within a reasonable time. In a worst case scenario, it could even lead to the prescription of the case.

US CLASS ACTIONS

In the US, the SEC investigation, the bankruptcy of L&H, and especially the indictment of KPMG and Dexia in Belgium triggered multiple class actions, mainly before the District Court of Massachusetts.[16] Two cases are worth mentioning. In the first case, a class action was filed on behalf of all investors who bought L&H shares on the Nasdaq Stock Exchange. Ultimately, this case was settled with KPMG and Dexia. There was a KPMG Settlement, providing a fund of approximately $115 million, and a Dexia Settlement, providing a fund of $60 million. One of the Belgian lawyers, who had not been involved in the class action proceedings, regretted these settlements. If there had not been a settlement in the US, there would have been more discovery, which would have had a major impact in the gathering of evidence in the Belgian criminal investigation and trial. After these settlements, a second class action was initiated, this time on behalf of all investors that bought L&H stock on the Easdaq Stock Exchange. Ultimately, this case was dismissed under the US doctrine of *forum non conveniens*.

During the criminal trial the class action proceedings were not mentioned, with one exception. One civil claimant lawyer asked the Court to order the American class action lawyers of Dexia and KPMG to submit their files, because these could contain relevant information for the criminal trial. Not surprisingly, the Court refused to do so, by ruling that it was sufficiently informed by the voluminous criminal file to make a decision on the merits of the case.

During the pre-trial phase, there was extensive interaction and sharing of information between the Belgian and the US lawyers of Dexia and KPMG. There was an ongoing data flow between Belgium and the US, sometimes up to 500 emails a day. Because of the discovery pressure in

---

[16] *In re Lernout & Hauspie Sec. Litig.*, 138 F. Supp. 2d 39 (D. Mass. 2001); *In re* Lernout & Hauspie Sec. Litig., 208 F. Supp. 2d 74 (D. Mass. 2002) and *Warlop v. Lernout*, 473 F. Supp. 2d 260 (D. Mass. 2007).

the US, the Americans especially wanted information about the criminal investigation in Belgium. Some Belgian lawyers confirmed that the US class action proceedings were in fact a reaction to the indictment of KPMG and Dexia in Belgium.[17] In the other direction, the Belgians especially wanted information from the Americans about how the SEC proceedings in the US worked and what specific information L&H disclosed to the SEC. This data flow stopped when a class action settlement was reached in the US.

LESSONS

One of the consumer associations derived three lessons from the L&H case:

(1) The case made clear that it is difficult to handle and administer mass cases on one's own. One has to work together and join forces with legal specialists.
(2) The case exposed the inadequate IT system the association used to administer a multitude of individual cases. After the case, the system was enhanced.
(3) The association learnt something about its members' loyalty to the association, because even after the deep-pocketed KPMG and Dexia were acquitted, the victims it had represented retained their confidence and loyalty in the association.

One defense lawyer stated that the L&H case illustrated that civil claimants have no place in a criminal trial. They should be excluded, so the criminal trial can focus solely on the question of whether the defendants have violated the law. As in most common law countries, civil claimants should initiate separate civil lawsuits. A civil claimant lawyer defended the opposite view: the civil claimant in a criminal trial is neglected, and sometimes ignored. He made a plea for a renewed and more active role of the civil claimant in a criminal trial.

Most of the L&H lawyers argued for a procedural device in criminal cases that could deal with a mass of civil claimants: test cases, class actions or a tool similar to the Dutch Collective Settlements Act. Some

---

[17] Which can be proven by the fact that the class action proceedings were initiated a couple of days after the indictment. Moreover, the complaint was a copy of the indictment.

lawyers referred to specific class action techniques, for example sub-classing which would have allowed the L&H civil claimants to be divided into different groups. One lawyer argued that this would make handling mass claims more manageable. Other lawyers emphasized the importance of being able to close a deal with all civil claimants, offering finality and closure for the defendants. In the L&H case, it was theoretically possible to reach a global settlement with the shareholders that were represented by one lawyer or association because there was one contact point. It was impossible to do this with the shareholders who each had their own lawyer or with the shareholders who acted *pro se*.

If there were to be class actions, most of the lawyers, and even the associations, objected to giving exclusive standing to associations. The fact that some associations behaved badly (for example hindering the criminal aspect of the trial by vigorously focusing from the beginning on the civil aspect and the press-ganging of clients) without any intervention from the Court, probably explains this. It was emphasized that any representative should be screened carefully and should be appointed by the Court, whether this is an association or individual. Some lawyers referred to the US Private Securities Litigation Reform Act that establishes a rebuttable presumption in securities class actions that the person having the largest financial interest in the relief sought by the class is the most adequate class representative. The question was raised whether one could give standing to the Public Prosecutor to not only act on behalf of society, but also on behalf of the civil claimants. Some rejected this idea because it could lead to conflicts of interests, for example when a civil claimant committed a crime himself (for example forgery of documents, which apparently occurred in the L&H case) or when a defendant is a civil claimant too (for example the company L&H).

Finally, some lawyers indicated that Belgian lawyers' ethics rules are not adapted for mass litigation. Contrary to some of the associations, the lawyers could not actively recruit clients through the media because of ethical restrictions. Suggestions were made to allow lawyers to advertise more freely in mass cases so they could canvass large groups of clients more easily. In 2010, the Dutch Section of the Brussels Bar Association adopted ethical rules on collective procedures, making it easier for attorneys in Brussels to canvass large groups of clients.

REFERENCES

Stefaan Voet, *Consumer Collective Redress in Belgium: Class Actions to the Rescue?*, (2015) 16(1) European Business Organization Law Review 121

15. Parallel public and private responses: The Buncefield explosion

Naomi Creutzfeldt and Christopher Hodges*

OVERVIEW

The largest peacetime explosion in Europe occurred on 10 December 2005 at a major oil storage facility at Buncefield, north of London, when one of the tanks was mistakenly over-filled, causing a vapor cloud that exploded. The tank had two forms of control, both of which failed. Three principal legal consequences followed. Firstly, damage claims were made by the 3,379 individuals, seven local authorities and 754 businesses affected. Secondly, the government established a committee of inquiry to establish the causes of the incident, whether the public regulatory agencies had done their jobs, what lessons could be learned, and what changes should be made to the regulatory system and requirements on authorities and operators. Thirdly, the regulatory authorities' statutory investigations led to prosecutions, convictions and major fines for several operators and service companies. Although independent of each other, these three consequences proceeded largely in parallel and in practice interacted significantly with each other.

This chapter does three things. First, it examines how the damage claims were processed through the courts. It finds, surprisingly, that although the English courts have a mass claim procedure, the Group Litigation Order (GLO), judges declined to invoke that procedure as being unnecessary and instead processed different groups of domestic

* The authors are grateful to the following for agreeing to be interviewed: The Hon Mr Justice David Steel, Bob Woodward of HSE, Paul Wyatt of the Environment Agency, Nick Young of Davies Arnold Cooper, Nick Thomas of Kennedys, Simon Joyston-Bechal and Richard Dickman of Pinsent Masons, Des Collins of Collins Solicitors, Belinda Schofield of CMS Cameron McKenna. The authors are solely responsible for all statements of interpretation and opinion.

property and commercial damage cases by relying on the English courts' inherent case management powers. Those powers gave sufficient flexibility for judges and lawyers to make procedural management decisions, albeit within the framework of the Civil Procedure Rules, which importantly require parties and lawyers to seek to resolve issues by negotiated settlement. As a result, the vast majority of claims were agreed by parties bilaterally, and insurers and their lawyers played a major role in such resolutions. Further, managerial control was passed on to the most appropriate court at different stages, involving a series of four judges who each brought a high level of specialisation to give authoritative management and determination, depending on the key issue to be resolved (first, general case management, then a matter of construction of a commercial contract, then property issues and finally costs). Matters were disposed of effectively within five years.

Merely looking at the compensation claims gives an inadequate picture of what occurred. It is sometimes claimed that enforcement of civil law provides a deterrent effect. In England, that claim is not widely accepted (Ison, 1967; Elliott & Street, 1968; Atiyah, 1970; DeWees, Duff & Trebilcock, 1996; Cane, 1997; Cane, 2013) and behavioural aspects are addressed by a large corpus of public regulatory law, enforced by public enforcement authorities. The second purpose of this chapter, therefore, is to give an overview of the regulatory and enforcement steps that were taken in response to the Buncefield explosion. Not only were such matters important in their own right (the authorities brought a series of prosecutions that resulted in convictions and the imposition of large fines on the companies involved), but the progress of the civil damages litigation referred to above and the public proceedings were closely interlinked, and affected each other, in both helpful and unhelpful ways.

The importance of this case provoked an official review of what lessons should be learned for the safety and risk management requirements imposed under regulatory law, and whether the public authorities had adequately supervised the companies and the site. This process led to a large number of changes to regulatory requirements, with little criticism of the authorities. Thirdly, therefore, this chapter briefly notes how the review process was carried out through a formal public procedure. The conclusion is that matters of behavior and compensation were addressed by separate public and private law mechanisms within the English legal system.

THE INCIDENT

The Explosion and Fire

A major oil storage facility exists at Buncefield, Hemel Hempstead, north of London, close to the M1 motorway. It contains storage tanks used by a number of oil companies, including Total, Chevron, BP and Shell. It receives petrol, aviation fuel and diesel through three pipelines, for storage in overground storage tanks before being piped elsewhere, including to Heathrow and Gatwick airports.

The operator of the key tanks was Hertfordshire Oil Storage Limited (HOSL), a joint venture between Total UK Limited (60 percent ownership) and Chevron Limited (40 percent). HOSL was under the day-to-day management of Total UK Limited.

On the night of Saturday 10 December 2005, one of the tanks was being filled with petrol.[1] The tank had two forms of level control: a gauge that enabled the employees to monitor the filling operation, and an independent high-level switch (IHLS), which was meant to close down operations automatically if the tank was overfilled. The first gauge stuck and the IHLS was inoperable. The control room staff was therefore unaware that the tank was filling to a dangerous level. Three hundred tonnes (250,000 litres) of fuel overflowed from the tank, and a vapor cloud formed, which ignited, causing a massive explosion (measuring 2.4 on the Richter scale and heard 200 km away) and a fire that lasted five days. The authorities' report found that there were as many as fifteen root causes of the incident, notably:[2]

> The gauge had stuck intermittently after the tank had been serviced in August 2005. However, neither site management nor the contractors who maintained the systems responded effectively to its obvious unreliability. The IHLS needed a padlock to retain its check lever in a working position. However, the switch supplier did not communicate this critical point to the installer and maintenance contractor or the site operator. Because of this lack of understanding, the padlock was not fitted.
>
> Having failed to contain the petrol, there was reliance on a bund retaining wall around the tank (secondary containment) and a system of drains and

---

[1] See the statement of facts in *Buncefield: Why did it happen? The underlying causes of the explosion and fire at the Buncefield oil storage depot, Hemel Hempstead, Hertfordshire on 11 December 2005* (The Competent Authority, 2011).

[2] Ibid.

catchment areas (tertiary containment) to ensure that liquids could not be released to the environment. Both forms of containment failed. Pollutants from fuel and firefighting liquids leaked from the bund, flowed off site and entered the groundwater. These containment systems were inadequately designed and maintained.

The Damage Caused

Damage caused fell into various categories. Firstly, although no-one died in the blast, over 40 people were 'physically injured', two on the site suffering serious injuries. Secondly, all 600 businesses on the adjacent industrial estate, employing about 16,500 people, suffered 'some property damage and/or business disruption'. The incident was reported to have cost firms more than £70 million.[3] The premises of 20 businesses employing 600 people were destroyed and the premises of another 60 businesses employing 3,800 people were heavily damaged and unusable.[4]

Thirdly, damage and disruption was also caused to 'residential properties' outside the perimeter of the depot. Dacorum Borough Council said 2,000 homes were evacuated during the fire and the M1 motorway was closed. A survey of 761 private householders in the area surrounding Buncefield suggested that 76 percent had experienced some damage. This mainly comprised broken glass, damaged roofs, window and door frames, and cracks in walls and ceilings. The majority of households were able to claim against their insurance for damage, but at the time of the publication of this book some claims are yet to be settled and repairs to some homes have still not been completed.[5] As time progressed, some households reported new and further damage. The contamination close to the site did not affect drinking water supplies but the long-term possibility of pollution remains.

The total sums claimed in compensation are shown in Table 15.1. The 2012 estimate of total quantifiable costs arising from the Buncefield incident came close to £1 billion, summarised in Table 15.2.[6]

---

[3] Study by the East of England Development Agency, noted at *Buncefield explosion: One year on.*

[4] *Color Quest Limited and Others v Total Downstream UK plc and Others*, judgment of Mr Justice David Steel, [2009] EWHC 540 (Comm), 20 March 2009.

[5] One year on, two families remained in temporary local authority accommodation while an estimated three families were likely to be spending a second Christmas in a hotel. See *Buncefield Standards Task Group Final Report 2008.*

[6] *Buncefield Standards Task Group Final Report 2008.*

Table 15.1 Estimated total value of claims

Claimant type	*No. of claims*	*Estimated £ million*
Business		
inside site perimeter	5	£103
outside site perimeter	749	£488
Subtotal business	754	£591
Individuals	3,379	£30
Local authorities	7	£4
Totals	4,140	£625

Table 15.2 Summary of the overall costs of the Buncefield incident by main category

Sector	*Cost (£ million)*
Site operators (compensation claims)	£625
Aviation	£245
Competent authority and Government response	£15
Emergency response	£7
Environmental impact (drinking water)	£2
Total	£894

GROUP LITIGATION IN ENGLAND AND WALES

The legal system in England and Wales is the originator of common law legal systems worldwide. Its traditional style is adversarial, with parties exchanging pleadings and evidence—all relevant evidential documents (discovery) and the reports of each side's experts—followed by an adversarial trial before a judge (almost no civil cases have a jury). The traditional approach was radically reformed in 1999 by Lord Woolf, in response to concerns that costs were too high and disproportionate to sums in dispute.[7] The 1999 Civil Procedure Rules were based on the premise that since almost all cases are settled, the procedure and the

[7] Lord Woolf, *Access to Justice: Final Report* (HMSO, 1996).

courts should encourage settlement, rather than focusing on facilitating a trial. Thus, parties are required to observe pre-action protocols that are aimed at a voluntary exchange of relevant information and to make reasonable attempts to negotiate or mediate, to settle cases as swiftly and efficiently as possible. Some limitations were made in the extent of discovery, and the use of fewer expert witnesses, to reduce unnecessary costs, although these had less impact on large litigation cases. As ongoing problems continued to be experienced, especially in relation to the level of costs (Dwyer, 2009), further changes were made from around 2013 pursuant to Lord Justice Jackson's review, including giving judges costs management powers (Legal Aid, Sentencing and Punishment of Offenders Act 2012; Jackson, 2009; Jackson, 2010).

Large or commercial civil cases are commenced in the High Court and are allocated to specialist Divisions. Cases might typically be initially managed by procedural judges called Masters, possibly acting closely with assigned judges. The Divisions relevant to this chapter are the Commercial Court and the Technology and Construction Court (TCC). Costs orders might be made by judges, but more detailed costs work and assessment of bills and awards is usually done by Costs Judges.

Some mass claims have appeared in the courts stretching back at least 40 years. They have not been particularly frequent and the incidence of cases is closely linked to the availability of funding for claimant lawyers, and whether the costs rules encourage or discourage expensive and sometimes speculative litigation. A series of mass product liability cases was brought during the 1980s and 1990s, in which, in the absence of a formal effective class action rule, the courts fell back on their inherent common law authority to manage cases. This pragmatic approach was a success and led to the development of a body of practice that was crystallised into the GLO procedure in the 1999 Woolf rules.[8] In outline, an application is made to the Lord Chief Justice for a GLO to be made on the basis that there exist multiple similar cases that it would be effective and efficient to manage together. Under a GLO, all cases within the courts system that fall within the defined parameters set out in the GLO are transferred to be managed by a single judge or team of judges. The judges have significant discretion over case management decisions and there are usually master sets of pleadings for the generic aspects of the cases, supplemented by individual pleadings or schedules for non-generic matters. Single or integrated teams of lawyers are appointed to represent the group. Complex cost-sharing arrangements are usually

[8] Hodges, 2001.

entered into between group claimants, which cover sharing generic costs and liability when people join or leave the group. The case management approach to litigation was pioneered in the early multi-party cases to a significant extent, and was effectively applied to all types of litigation under the Woolf rules, so the approach is now firmly enshrined in litigation practice.

THE CIVIL CLAIMS

The Parties and the Claims: Organising the Groups

The first problem facing both householder claimants and the oil company defendants was one of organising their representation. The company side was complicated by the existence of various joint ventures and trust arrangements. A series of special arrangements had to be negotiated in order to overcome conflicts and to simplify representation in the litigation.

Four oil companies who owned pipelines agreed on terms of reference, under which a litigation committee would instruct a single firm (Pinsent Masons LLP) to represent them, including a procedure for resolving conflicts from which Chevron and Total were excluded.

Despite the 60/40 ownership split of Total and Chevron in HOSL, there was no operating agreement between the companies. HOSL had few assets and played little active role in the litigation. The central legal issue was whether the operator was HOSL or Total. Chevron issued an application against Total under section 459 of the Companies Act over the way that HOSL had been run. That claim was settled fairly quickly and a committee was appointed to run the litigation jointly.

In view of the potential for conflict between Total and Chevron, the oil companies appointed a respected insurance executive to look after the position of HOSL and it was agreed that one firm would represent HOSL, in addition to Total. Total and Chevron had complex insurance arrangements for different layers of cover and the insurers maintained a degree of oversight through their lawyers. There was no public knowledge of HOSL or of who owned it, so the brand damage to Total and Chevron, and claimants' leverage on those companies or on HOSL, was limited.

The claimant group was diverse and involved over 100 groups (Boylan, Frances & Briery, 2009) and around 3,300 claims filed by individuals and companies, or their insurers. Claims differed widely in size: around 250 individual claims involved a total claim value of £20 million each, and 2,754 claims were for less than £10,000.

A number of local solicitors' firms were initially instructed to represent householders. One firm, Collins, made particularly effective use of the media and attempted to try to form a steering committee of firms. Since many of the solicitors were not convinced that there was sufficient evidence that anyone had done anything wrong, virtually all householders were subsequently represented by Collins.

Many claims were settled by parties' insurers, who then brought subrogated claims against the owners or operators of the tank in question, divertingly named the Buncefield Property Insurance Group (BUNPIG). A consensus was reached that it would make sense for a single firm (Kennedys) to represent the interests of all insurers, in the names of the 'neighbours' of the site.[9] Kennedys benefited from having the gravity and freedom of action in being sole lead claimant, and not being subject to detailed control by a committee of insurers, although regular written reports were sent to a steering committee of around 40 insurers and there was a monthly meeting involving six of them. Kennedys persuaded every insurer that they would act for and fund *all* liability claims, whether they were subrogated or not, and this avoided splintering of representation. One consequence of this was that a claimant who was uninsured would be less likely to make an individual claim since he would have to fund it, and this approach forestalled those who would otherwise have 'tried it on'.

Strategic Decisions

The oil companies made a policy decision at the start that they would respond pro-actively and invite claimants to come forward, rather than fight all the way. This policy had been adopted with success in the major Lloyd's litigation of a decade earlier (Wakinshaw, 2001). The oil companies were also influenced by wanting to be seen to respond by 'doing the right thing' in the eyes of the Competent Authority (CA), since they had to deal with the twin fronts of regulatory investigation/enforcement and compensation claims.

The explosion occurred shortly before Christmas, so the impact on local people was significant. Loss adjusters Crawford were instructed to

[9] The 'grown up manner' in which other leading insurance law firms stood back and did not seek involvement was notable: some were later retained to prove quantum and to handle inward claims by insureds.

provide assistance to householders and to settle all direct claims as quickly as possible. Kennedys liaised closely with the loss adjusters at this stage.

The insurers decided fairly quickly that they would pursue recovery from Total of the subrogated claims paid out to insureds as claimants, rather than as defendants. Kennedys issued proceedings quickly, and effectively took control of running the litigation instead of Collins. They decided to sue Total only, and not Chevron, since it suited the insurer claimants that the two oil companies were to argue liability between themselves, which could produce useful discovery that might not otherwise have been available.

All claimants sued Total and HOSL, so indemnity issues between those two companies were of little consequence. Total brought in Chevron as a Part 20 (indemnity) defendant, and also made Part 20 claims against TAV (which manufactured the safety switch that failed) and Motherwell Control Systems (which installed and maintained the systems; it soon went into administration and played little further part).

Chronology of the Litigation

Lawyers for the leading claimant groups began to send letters claiming liability. Liability was initially denied because, for some weeks, the cause of the explosion was unknown. In previous large disasters, gossip usually circulated quickly about what the cause was, but here evidence from the investigation by the CA was crucial.

Collins applied for a GLO on 25 January 2006, with a statement of case that was a single page (unusually brief). All parties were summoned by the Senior Master of the Queen's Bench Division of the High Court, Master Turner, to a Case Management Conference (CMC) in March 2006. The GLO application was adjourned to the next CMC, but a general structure was established for the civil claims. It was ordered that all claims were to be issued in or transferred to the High Court. The judiciary thereafter controlled the progress of the proceedings—and pressured the parties to negotiate directly—through a series of CMCs.

The oil companies told Master Turner that they would deal with claims and report monthly to the Court on progress. The vast majority of the 3,300 claims were insured. As a first stage, it was necessary for the first party claims against insurers to be settled, before the subrogated claims by insurers against the oil companies could be dealt with. The oil companies established a Joint Claims Committee, which met every three weeks for four years, comprising representatives from Total, Chevron and their lawyers, which operated under the badge of HOSL. The members appointed one loss adjuster to act for HOSL in investigating the site and preparing loss reports.

In October 2006, HOSL and Total said they would pay all personal injury claims, as if liability was not in issue. This was in fact regarded by Collins as a problem for almost all householders, since they also had property claims that still had to be pursued. The defendants required receipts for all expenditure.

At the next CMC in October 2006, Master Turner decided against proceeding under a GLO and instead continued the 'overseen structured settlement' process. He divided claims into categories by size of claim and made various orders for service of further schedules of special damage and agreement on a panel of joint medical experts. Kennedys emerged as the leading firm driving the commercial claims, and an order was made that all parties should cooperate with that firm to develop General Particulars of Claim that would include standard specified items. Kennedys would maintain a Register of parties. Claims should be issued by 12 April 2007.

Master Turner ordered HOSL to mediate with the householders. Collins were ordered to file individual schedules of loss by the claimants by March 2007, and there was a mediation in March 2007, which was unsuccessful.

The parties reported at the CMC in June 2007. Master Turner adopted a firm interventionist approach over whether parties were seriously discussing settlement or not, and ordered all to write to him to confirm what progress had been made towards structured settlement of the claims.

Shell had decided to break away and had issued a claim in the Commercial Court, since its claim was primarily the consequential loss from being unable to supply fuel to its airline customers. That claim was essentially for economic loss, not claimable in negligence, and the Court of Appeal held that Shell was entitled to claim as beneficial owner. An appeal to the Supreme Court was settled before judgment.

It was clear that three main issues were emerging, which were primarily commercial:

(1) Whether the defendants (essentially HOSL) had liability to the claimants. A major element in this involved whether loss was foreseeable.
(2) The dispute between Total and Chevron over whether liability should be 100 percent that of Total, or split between them 60:40. It turned on two factors: interpretation of the legal agreements between the companies and on the actions of the controller, and whether there was vicarious liability.

(3) The claims by Total for a contribution or indemnity against TAV and Motherwell.

In mid-2007, the remaining parties to the commercial litigation concluded that the Queen's Bench Division of the High Court was not the right venue and agreed to transfer cases to the Commercial Court, where Mr Justice David Steel took over the management of all cases.

At a CMC in July 2007, David Steel J kept up the pressure for update reports on those 'outside the fence' (householders and some businesses) involved in the structured settlement process, and also decided that there would be a trial of preliminary issues in the 'inside the fence' cases (commercial companies located within the site) to be identified at the next CMC. He gave directions for standard disclosure of documents, negotiations on electronic inspection, expert evidence and witness statements. Certain disclosure issues were pursued and decided by a separate judge. The documents produced clarified many facts, and shortly afterwards, five months before trial, Total admitted negligence by their employee.

HOSL took the position that damage outside the site (further than 451 metres from the tank) was unforeseeable. This created a division of claimants into those 'inside the fence' or outside. The 'insiders' included most commercial claimants but excluded almost all householders. The costs risk to the householders facing the prospect of fighting a 13-week trial, with cost exposure estimated at £30 million,[10] was a major concern for them and Collins.

At the CMC in April 2008, David Steel J, faced with 'a cast of thousands', rationalised who was to appear at the trial in October 2008 to ensure that it would be manageable and costs contained. The judge strongly encouraged parties to collaborate and save costs, and made clear that some named parties (including the National Police Information Authority, whose national computer had been damaged) would not otherwise be awarded their costs of participation in the forthcoming trial and its preparations.[11] Subsequently, various groups shared work between their lawyers.

[10] Indemnity costs were awarded up to 23 May 2008 (when liability was admitted), on the basis that they had known from January 2006 what happened and that either HOSL or Total had been operationally negligent, so they just had to decide who had to pay.

[11] *In Re The Buncefield Litigation*, Order of Mr Justice David Steel, 7 April 2008, para 25.

The Commercial Court has long and extensive experience of handling big cases and has a reputation for demonstrating a degree of flexibility that is greater than in some other courts. However, concern over costs and delays had led to a series of recommendations over the adoption of further innovations in procedure, and the Buncefield case became the first and paradigm case to test new techniques.[12] The judge adopted an interventionist style of management and issued lengthy directions. In general, almost all lawyers involved considered that the new techniques worked well.

The first task was for the judge to determine which issues he had to decide. He again declined a GLO and progressed the cases as managed litigation. Instead of the parties sequentially exchanging pleadings, the legal teams had to fill out a large matrix document, which identified what the issues were, and on which each party filled in what their position was in relation to each issue, similar to a technique used in construction disputes (where it is known as a 'Scott schedule'). This identified how the various claims should best be managed so as to support both settlements and court determination of key issues in the most efficient manner.

In the disclosure exercise, 1.7 million documents were processed in six months. The parties were also required to produce witness statements (setting out evidence and not arguments) that were headed with the individual issue to which the statement was speaking. A detailed timetable was set for preparations for trial of all unsettled claims and for the trial itself, which was set for 12 weeks starting in December. Pinsent Masons drew up a large spreadsheet that stated which witnesses the parties were going to call and cross-examine, and apportioned time for each issue, witness, expert and counsel, as estimated by each team. The parties were required to produce timetables for the trial. The judge then required them to reduce the requested timetable by 20 percent, and gave them 80 percent of what they had asked for: nobody complained about this. In fact, the evidence stages of the trial were finished early, which enabled an adjournment period to be used for counsel to prepare their final speeches, which, possibly as a result, also finished early.

At the Pre-Trial Review and various other hearings in September 2008, some parties were forced to justify continuing to appear on their own. Summary judgment was given on the negligence issue.

---

[12] *Report and Recommendations of the Commercial Court Long Trials Working Party* (Judiciary of England and Wales, 2007).

Much of the trial was dominated by the fight between Total and its joint-venture partner Chevron over liability for the bill: or, in technical terms, to what extent Total was responsible for HOSL. TAV settled the third-party claim against it on the first day. On the third day, Total gave up the foreseeability argument. The other parties went away, except for some arguments towards the end of the trial over *Rylands v Fletcher* liability[13] and whether there was a claim in public nuisance. The judgment was delivered on 29 March 2009[14] and held that:

(1) The operator was Total and not HOSL. Total failed to discharge the burden of establishing that HOSL was responsible for the negligence of the supervisor. The Court also found there was a further contributory fault consequent on the failure of Total's head office staff to promulgate an adequate system for preventing the overfilling of a tank. This reflected the absence of any written tank filling procedures for use in the control room, even following a 'near miss' in August 2003. In the result there was a lack of careful monitoring of filling operations and an improper reliance on alarms.
(2) Total was not entitled to recover a contractual indemnity from HOSL or Chevron in respect of all or any part of the claim. Total appealed the first instance decision in the third-party claim that Chevron should not contribute 40 percent, but lost, and the Supreme Court declined to hear the case.
(3) Shell could not recover for consequential loss in its own name. Shell appealed and won its point in the Court of Appeal. Total then appealed but the issue was settled before the Supreme Court hearing.

After the trial, the claims that had not been settled went their separate ways for quantum to be dealt with. Determination of quantum in 140 individual large claims was transferred from the Commercial Court to the TCC, where they were all dealt with by Ramsey J. The claimants complained of four years of delay and asked the TCC for an immediate trial. Sensing that the claimants were not yet able to produce their evidence on quantum of their claims, the defendants accepted that request. Total asked for disclosure in every case, in order to be able to settle claims. The judge gave generic directions in every case, that there should be pleadings and (which was innovative) at the same time service

---

[13] This imposes strict liability for the escape of dangerous materials onto another's property.

[14] *Buncefield litigation* [2009] EWHC 540 (Comm).

of supporting documentation. The claims were divided into four batches (easy to complex) and a trial window for each was allocated, together with directions for timing of disclosure and the experts' reports. Generic CMCs were held every month.

Ramsey J managed the process under a tight timetable, which pressured the parties to settle cases. The parties opened every communication channel in order to reach agreements: adjuster-to-adjuster, lawyer-to-adjuster, lawyer-to-lawyer, independents. None of the 140 claims went to trial. The defendants concluded that some claims might have been overpaid, but there was a significant saving in resources and reserves.

Costs Issues

The company claimants did not share costs of representation, but did agree to divide up tasks so as to reduce overall costs. HOSL reached pragmatic agreements on costs with Kennedys, but not with Collins.

All of Collins' 275 clients entered into privately-funded arrangements, mostly conditional fee agreements (CFAs), except that about eight of those clients were on legal aid from the start until they converted to CFAs.[15] Under a CFA, Collins bears the cash flow financial responsibility, but is entitled to recover a success fee on a successful outcome. The clients also entered into complicated cost-sharing agreements between themselves. Collins appears to have suffered a significant reduction in fees paid by the defendants: an initial bill submitted in 2009 claimed £14.9 million costs (including a success fee of £14,000), which was later reduced to £1.7 million (including a success fee of £180,000). The arguments on how much the defendants would pay lasted into 2012, and were finally settled confidentially.

THE REGULATORY INVESTIGATION AND ENFORCEMENT PROCEEDINGS

The Competent Authority

European Union Member States have harmonised legislation regulating the control systems for major industrial hazards.[16] This establishes

[15] The legal aid contract arrangements were terminated in 2001, after which the Legal Services Commission put the case out to tender, which was won by another firm. However, the eight clients preferred to stay with Collins on a CFA.

[16] Directive 82/501/EEC, as amended.

extensive requirements on EU Member States and site operators. One of the requirements on every Member State is to have a Competent Authority (CA). Under the United Kingdom implementing legislation,[17] the CA for England & Wales[18] is the Environment Agency (EA) and the Health and Safety Executive (HSE) acting jointly. Operators of major hazard sites were subject to detailed requirements, including making safety reports and forwarding them to the CA. The authorities operated a procedure for inspecting and monitoring operators and sites, divided into a top tier of approximately 500 sites and a lower tier of approximately 5,000 sites.

The Public Oversight Response

The incident attracted extensive media coverage and hence political attention, in response to which an independent investigation board, the Buncefield Major Incident Investigation Board (MIIB),[19] was established to perform, in the public interest, a thorough, timely and cost-effective investigation and analysis of what had occurred and how the operational and legal systems had worked. The MIIB published a sequence of Reports, which included a large number of recommendations, and also formed a useful source of evidence for the civil damages actions. The MIIB scrutiny and oversight process was regarded by the HSE and EA as having been 'a great success'.

The Regulatory Response

The CA established a Panel to determine whether anyone had done anything wrong in the authorities' management of the site before the incident. That scrutiny drew a number of conclusions and was considered and actioned by the authorities internally, but was not published until after completion of the criminal process.[20]

In addition, the CA was obliged to carry out its statutory functions as normal. An HSE Investigation Manager was appointed for the incident, who supervised an investigation team of up to 250 people at its peak,

---

[17] The Control of Major Accident Hazards Regulations 1999 (COMAH).

[18] Different arrangements apply in Scotland and Northern Ireland.

[19] The Board was chaired by Lord Newton of Braintree and comprised senior HSE and EA staff (none of whom had any previous involvement with Buncefield or COMAH) and a number of independents, especially academics. It had a public supervisory role, acting under the mantra 'We are there for the public'.

[20] *Buncefield: Why did it happen?*, supra note 1.

with a range of technical and legal expertise, as well as independent experts. Their task was to find out what went wrong and to institute criminal enforcement if there had been any criminal activity. The EA also responded to the environmental aspects of the incident at time. Hence, the HSE in general dealt with the retrospective aspects (cause) and the EA with the prospective aspects (consequences).

Various other agencies were also involved. For example, there was an issue over decisions on whether, or at what distance, vulnerable sites like hospitals and schools should be built in relation to sites that have major hazards. This was essentially a local matter that required a balanced decision from Local Authorities under the Land Use Planning legislation. At Buncefield, an industrial estate had been allowed to expand over 40 years and to end up as a direct neighbour to the oil depot.

The authorities' primary concern was with systems. They were operating within and applying the pre-existing legal framework. Under the Control of Major Accident Hazards Regulations 1999 (COMAH), the EA were looking at whether 'Operators' had taken 'all measures necessary'. A key legal provision was whether individuals had taken 'reasonable care'. The officials regarded the legal provisions as broadly satisfactory, on the basis that the phrase 'reasonable care' is broad enough to cover all the required activities and issues.

The CA and its component authorities published a series of Reports throughout the investigation, to provide transparency and an opportunity for public dialogue.[21] The public dissemination of information was subject to the legal constraints that information or opinions that might be likely to prejudice any subsequent prosecutions should not be made public. Accordingly, some information was not published until after the conclusion of the prosecution appeal process.[22]

Prosecutions

The CA prosecuted five companies for various offences and on 16 July 2010 the Criminal Court imposed fines totalling £9.5 million:

---

[21] Available at http://www.hse.gov.uk/comah/buncefield/oneyear.htm.

[22] Public access to documents can now be achieved under the Freedom of Information Act and a separate provision in the Environment Act, and could have been available earlier but was subject to the exemption of not prejudicing ongoing criminal prosecutions.

(1) Total UK Ltd pleaded guilty to three offences and was fined £3.6 million (£3 million for safety; £600,000 for pollution) and ordered to pay costs of £2.6 million.
(2) The supply company British Pipeline Agency Ltd pleaded guilty to three offences and was fined £300,000 and ordered to pay costs of £480,000.
(3) Hertfordshire Oil Storage Ltd was found guilty of two offences and fined £1.45 million (£1million for safety; £450,000 for pollution) with costs of £1 million.
(4) TAV Engineering Ltd, which designed the crucial safety switch that failed, was found guilty of one offence, fined £1,000 and ordered to pay £500 costs.
(5) The installation and maintenance company Motherwell Control Systems 2003 Ltd was fined £1,000 and ordered to pay costs of £500 after being found guilty of one offence.[23]

Thus, HOSL, TAV and Motherwell pleaded not guilty but were found guilty. HOSL subsequently withdrew its appeal, which was based on the issue of whether it was the operator. The final appeal was by TAV, the switch manufacturer, which the Court of Appeal dismissed in January 2011.

When passing sentence on the defendants at St Albans Crown Court on 16 July 2010, Mr Justice Calvert-Smith commented that cost cutting per se was not put forward as a major feature of the prosecution case, but the failings had more to do with slackness, inefficiency and a more-or-less complacent approach to matters of safety.[24] The authorities noted that operating culture was a key factor:

> Cumulatively, these pressures created a culture where keeping the process operating was the primary focus and process safety did not get the attention, resources or priority that it required.

The Buncefield situation was highly unusual in that the civil compensation litigation made swift progress and was resolved before the regulatory cases. Decisions made in the civil cases hindered the administration of the regulatory enforcement process. Total conceded criminal responsibility on the basis that the operator had made a series of errors.

---

[23] Available at http://www.theengineer.co.uk/channels/process-engineering/buncefield-trial-ends-with-modest-fines-for-safety-and-pollution-offences/1003662.article#ixzz0zgVwBv9v.

[24] *Buncefield: Why did it happen?*, supra note 1.

However, HSE/EA did not accept this view and considered that there had been a fundamental systemic management failure, at the highest level. That was the basis on which the prosecution was put. The issue was who was the legal operator under the COMAH Regulations. In the civil case, David Steel J had found that the operator was Total, but the agencies thought differently. However, in view of the outcome of the civil case, procedural issues had to be dealt with in the criminal prosecution in the Crown Court over whether the judge's findings in the High Court should be binding on the Criminal Court. The position was resolved by the Court of Appeal, which decided that the civil findings were not binding, noted that the position was unclear as to who the operator was, and held that there were two legal criteria for deciding the position that should be applied by a jury in the criminal case. At the criminal trial, Total pleaded guilty but not as the operator, and HSOL were found by the jury to have been the operator.

Lessons Learnt for Future Behaviour

The MIIB and CA procedures together comprised both strategic and detailed reviews of the regulatory system and the roles and actions of the public authorities and the operators. The regulatory system was found to be a sound framework. Scrutiny of national arrangements is inherent in the European Union's legislative structure, both from the 'superior' dimension of the European Commission over the implementation and operation of EU legislation, and from a horizontal 'peer review' element amongst Member States. Such scrutiny is also constantly evolving.

The MIIB made 74 recommendations, all of which were officially accepted, public responses provided, and have been acted upon by HSE and EA. Lessons were learned about the supervision of operators and sites, and avoiding serious incidents such as this. Changes were implemented in the organisation, resource, priorities and the way the authorities investigate major cases. The EA and HSE felt that they had worked well together but could do better. Information was provided to operators to improve their understanding of risks and performance. Guidance has been issued and gaps in previous guidance have been filled, such as on containment policy.

After all prosecutions and appeals had been concluded, the CA issued a final Report on the causes of and lessons from the incident in February 2011.[25] The CA concluded that the incident did not have any unknown or

---

[25] Ibid.

new cause. The basic issues revolved around inadequate management systems, their operation in practice, and culture. The Foreword stated that the following actions had been taken:

> Since the incident, the Competent Authority, industry and trade unions have worked together to drive forward high standards at fuel storage sites. This has resulted in agreement on improved standards of safety and environmental protection for all UK sites storing large volumes of gasoline and to systematically upgrade sites to meet these standards, with progress monitored by the Competent Authority as part of its regulatory programmes. This work has also established a set of process safety leadership principles for top-level engagement in all businesses involved with significant risks to people and the environment—see www.hse.gov.uk/comah/buncefield/response.htm.
>
> The Competent Authority has also improved its approach to regulating onshore major hazards in the light of ten years of operating the COMAH regime including incidents such as Buncefield. More information on the Competent Authority's remodeling programme is at www.hse.gov.uk/comah/remodelling/index.htm.

CONCLUSIONS

A series of conclusions are suggested by this case study:

(1) The regulatory and compensation aspects of the Buncefield incident were dealt with separately by different actors and through different —public and private—systems and courts. It is normal practice in the United Kingdom, as in many other European states, that public scrutiny of the behaviour of the companies leading to administrative action and enforcement is dealt with by public agencies. Here, the HSE and EA investigated the events, instituted criminal prosecutions, and issued a series of public investigation reports and changes to the guidance and administrative requirements regulating control of similar sites. The civil courts dealt with the liability and compensation aspects alone, in accordance with British practice that court decisions in damages claims have little impact on defendants' future behaviour.

(2) This case illustrates how two features can succeed in processing complex compensation cases: flexible but clear managerial control by experienced judges, and a culture in which experienced lawyers aim at agreeing whatever issues can be agreed. The time taken to dispose of the cases, effectively six years with many claims being settled earlier, was remarkably short.

(3) The mechanism by which the judiciary managed the litigation procedures was based on acting on the basis of the courts' inherent jurisdiction to manage cases: no new or extra rules were required and, indeed, the GLO or any other pre-existing procedure was not invoked. All the actions remained separate and not formally joined or within any formal coordinated structure. It is arguable that the progress of the cases would have been largely similar to what occurred if a GLO had been invoked, save that final arguments over costs might have been curtailed. A GLO may be appropriate where there is a homogeneous group of individual claimants and a single defendant. But where there are disparate groupings of claimants and defendants, rationalisation and ingenuity are needed. The judges demonstrated flexibility on various formalities, such as the normal rules on pleadings and discovery. Instead, the parties were told to produce lists of the issues that arose.

(4) There were so many parties on both sides, and therefore so many lawyers, that the cases would have been unmanageable without significant rationalisation and managerial control over representation. Rationalising the many parties into smaller coordinated groups was achieved at various stages either spontaneously by the parties themselves, or as a result of pressure from the court. The lawyers had to respond to a series of complex situations through sophisticated matrix management, described by Nick Young of Davies Arnold Cooper as 'like eight-dimensional chess'.

(5) Judicial control at every stage was vested in a single judge or master, 'passing the ball'. At the start, all claims were managed by being listed before the Senior Master. After the main issues had crystallised, the case was transferred to the Commercial Court, and managed by a single judge, with a separate judge dealing with documentary privilege issues. After the central liability issues were resolved, the remaining 140 claims were transferred to the TCC, again managed by a single judge. Finally, costs issues were handed over to a single costs judge. This single managerial control afforded consistency and continuity. All four judges involved were experienced in handling multi-party cases.

(6) The lawyers were able to make swift progress towards settlement of many issues directly between the parties, strongly encouraged by the judiciary, for two reasons:

    (a) Almost all of the key lawyers were highly experienced. The management of major litigation requires considerable resource, in terms of personnel, IT systems, experience, imagination and strategic judgment. Only the leading commercial law firms possess all of these requirements. The local firms are notably effective in enlisting media support.

(b) The Civil Procedure Rules have required settlement and case management since their fundamental reform in 1999. The defendant oil companies made a clear policy decision at the start to adopt an orderly approach towards settlement, rather than an old-fashioned litigation approach, although the householder group might not have thought this. Negotiated settlements occurred between the commercial claimants and the defendants, assisted by pressure from the insurance sector and judges, from an early stage throughout the six years. Some settlements took longer than they might have done, partly as a result of a lower level of trust between the lawyers for the householders and the central defendants, and partly because the insurance claimants felt that the defendants took every point and then abandoned it at the last minute, thereby considerably increasing costs. Overall, there were interesting divergences of view over the opponents' tactics and approaches.

In contrast, the influence of insurers in reaching sensible, cost-effective solutions was significant. Insurers were ultimately behind the central defendants, many of the commercial claimants, and the property (but not personal injury) claims of householders.

(7) The judges identified the principal issues that they needed to decide, which impeded the parties reaching settlements. Those issues involved significant commercial consequences, of issues of apportionment of risk that could have been determined by contract in advance but were not, namely whether HOSL or Total was the operator, and how liability was shared between HOSL, Total and Chevron. Hence it was not surprising that judicial determination was needed.

A final tantalising observation may be made about how things might be different if a similar situation were to occur. Since 6 April 2010,[26] the EA has had power to impose civil sanctions, which may include a Restoration Notice requiring specified steps within a stated period to secure that the position is restored, so far as possible, to what it would have been if

---

[26] The Environmental Civil Sanctions (England) Order 2010/1157 and The Environmental Civil Sanctions (Miscellaneous Amendments) (England) Order 2010/1159.

no offence had been committed.[27] The EA may also accept Enforcement Undertakings, which will enable a person, who a regulator reasonably suspects of having committed an offence, to give an undertaking to a regulator to take one or more corrective actions set out in the undertaking.[28] A person may give a Third Party Undertaking to compensate persons affected by an offence, and the regulator if it accepts the undertaking must take it into account in determining the variable monetary penalty. Such powers are now regularly used, thereby avoiding the necessity for separate civil liability litigation.

REFERENCES

Patrick Atiyah, *Accidents, Compensation and the Law* (Cambridge University Press, 1st ed. 1970)

Patrick Boylan, Will Frances & Chris Briery, 'Counting the Total Cost', *New Law Journal*, 31 July 2009

Buncefield: Why did it happen? The underlying causes of the explosion and fire at the Buncefield oil storage depot, Hemel Hempstead, Hertfordshire on 11 December 2005 (The Competent Authority, 2011), available at http://www.hse.gov.uk/comah/buncefield/buncefield-report.pdf

Peter Cane, *The Anatomy of Tort Law* (Hart Publishing 1997)

Peter Cane, *Atiyah's Accidents, Compensation and the Law* (Cambridge University Press, 8th ed. 2013)

Don DeWees, David Duff & Michael Trebilcock, *Exploring the Domain of Accident Law. Taking the Facts Seriously* (Oxford University Press 1996)

Deirdre Dwyer (ed.), *The Civil Procedure Rules Ten Years On* (Oxford University Press 2009)

Derek Elliott and Harry Street, *Road Accidents* (Penguin Books 1968)

Christopher Hodges, *Multi-Party Actions* (Oxford University Press 2001)

Terence Ison, *The Forensic Lottery* (Staples Press 1967)

Rupert Jackson, *Review of Civil Litigation Costs: Preliminary Report* (TSO 2009)

Rupert Jackson, *Review of Civil Litigation Costs: Final Report* (TSO 2010)

Report and Recommendations of the Commercial Court Long Trials Working Party (Judiciary of England and Wales, 2007), available at https://www.judiciary.gov.uk/publications/long-trials-working-party-report/

Gary Wakinshaw, 'Lloyd's Litigation' in Christopher Hodges, *Multi-Party Actions* (Oxford University Press 2001)

Lord Woolf, *Access to Justice: Final Report* (HMSO 1996)

---

[27] Schedule 2 of the Order.

[28] Schedule 4 of the Order.

16. Public as private and private as public: MTBE litigation in the United States

Elizabeth Thornburg

INTRODUCTION

In the end, it is a question of governance: in modern society, who should make and enforce the rules? In the context of dispute resolution, the debate is often framed as a choice between 'public' legislatures and administrative agencies on the one hand and 'private' enforcement by litigants using the court system on the other. Even that description shows that the public and private labels are misleading, since courts themselves are public agencies staffed by government employees, applying laws created by government actors. In addition, multiple public agencies with different missions may make conflicting choices.

The 'public' label is an inadequate descriptor in another way in countries with multiple levels of government. Rules created by the central government and its courts may differ from those created at a different level—such as a US state government—by another set of legislatures, agencies and courts. Even municipalities may make decisions that create standards different from those made at higher levels. Yet all are forms of 'public' norm creation and enforcement.

The story becomes even more complicated when government entities become litigants, and especially when they are plaintiffs. While they sometimes act in a clearly governmental capacity, acting to enforce their laws, sometimes they are very much like private litigants, seeking compensation for their own damages.

One further wrinkle: the public norms themselves are sometimes deeply influenced by the private entities that can anticipate being affected by those rules. Legislatures are lobbied. Administrative agencies rely on data provided by regulated industries and are subject to 'agency capture'.

Judicial appointments and elections are influenced by campaign contributions and privately-financed issue advertising. And so the 'public' rules themselves may bear the thumbprints of private design.

Not surprisingly, situations involving claims of mass harm often involve these kinds of complex interactions of the public and private. Government enforcers and private litigants, at all levels of government, participate in the push and pull over levels of enforcement and claims for compensation. There is no clean line between public and private.

This case study focuses on one cluster of disputes in the US growing out of the use of a chemical called Methyl Tertiary Butyl Ether (MTBE) in gasoline. The use (or not) of this chemical had implications for air quality, drinking water quality, energy policy, agriculture policy and public health at national, state, and local levels. The chapter begins by introducing the factual underpinnings of the dispute and then turns to the evolving legal context in which the MTBE litigation played out. The case study of the court action itself follows. The chapter concludes by comparing the impact of agency and court actions, highlighting the most significant ways in which public and private roles blurred throughout the dispute.

THE CHEMICAL

MTBE is a gasoline additive with a complicated history. It was once thought to be a cheap, safe and environmentally friendly route to cleaner air. MTBE is one of several chemicals (the best known alternative being ethanol) that increase the level of oxygen in gasoline, which in turn promotes more efficient combustion and decreases the emission of harmful chemicals. MTBE was the favorite oxygenate of refiners for several reasons. They themselves, or their subsidiaries, were often the manufacturers of MTBE, and it is made from their own byproducts. It was also cost effective because it can be blended at the point of petroleum production and transported through gasoline pipelines.

Unfortunately, MTBE's benefits are directly related to its problems. Major parts of the national infrastructure, including both pipelines and underground storage tanks (USTs) are old, often leak, and are themselves inadequately regulated.[1] MTBE entered the water supply through overfill,

[1] For a discussion of industry involvement in limiting the regulation of USTs, *see* McGarity, 2004, 301–305.

spills and leaks through corroded USTs.[2] When gas mixes with soil, MTBE separates from the gas and reaches the groundwater before any other gasoline component and quickly dissolves—it is highly soluble in water, does not readily bind to soil particles, and resists natural biodegration. It is, in short, a very efficient water pollutant, and its chemical properties also make it difficult and expensive to clean up.

Everyone agrees that the presence of MTBE in the water supply, even in relatively small amounts (although there are disputes about how small), gives the water an extremely unpleasant taste and odor. Experts disagree, however, about the extent of the effects on human health from ingesting MTBE (especially because it becomes undrinkable at very low levels). The Environmental Protection Agency (EPA) has listed MTBE as a possible human carcinogen in high doses, but has not reached a conclusion about exposure to lower doses when the substance is swallowed rather than inhaled. The Energy Policy Act of 2005 contained a provision requiring a public health study, but that study had not been completed at the time of publication of this book.

THE LEGAL ENVIRONMENT

Federal Law

A few decisions at the federal level made it unlikely that either EPA action or private lawsuits based on federal law would become the basis for dealing with MTBE's impact on groundwater. First, the Comprehensive Environmental Response Compensation and Liability Act (CERCLA),[3] the law that would ordinarily have provided a right to sue for the cost of cleaning up environmental hazards, excludes petroleum products. This exclusion was born of political reality. CERLCA's proponents realized after the election of 1980 that if the Act was going to pass it would have to be enacted quickly, before the new Congress and President Reagan took office. Accomplishing that goal required defusing the objections of the oil and gas industry, and so petroleum products were omitted from the Act's citizen suit provisions (Pereira, 2004). Agency enforcement is also problematic: MTBE is included under CERCLA's definition of a hazardous

---

[2] *Id.*; *see also In re Methyl Tertiary Butyl Ether ('MTBE') Prods. Liab. Litig.*, 209 F.R.D. 323, 330 n.5 (S.D.N.Y. 2002) (hereinafter cited as MTBE MDL).

[3] 42 U.S.C. § 9659(a) (1).

substance,[4] but the EPA has expressed doubt about whether the MTBE clean-up can be done under CERCLA's authority.[5]

Further federal legislation—aimed at air rather than water pollution—makes the federal status of MTBE even murkier. When Congress considered amending the Clean Air Act (CAA) in the early 1990s to require higher oxygenate levels in the gas sold in areas with high levels of carbon monoxide or ozone, the resulting legislation made it possible to use MTBE as a gas additive. The debate made the political nature of the decision startlingly clear. Oil companies lobbied for a lower oxygen-content requirement that would allow the use of more MTBE and less ethanol. Farmers preferred the higher standard that would require the use of ethanol, often made from corn and other starch crops. The following remarks, from Congressional floor debates, are emblematic of the open competition between oil states and farm states:

> [Senator Grassley from Iowa, an agricultural state]: So who will really gain … ? The answer is obvious! Big oil!! Big oil will gain because those companies control … MTBE. [Instead, vote] to encourage the use of ethanol – a proven pollution fighter produced by American farmers, not big oil.
>
> [Senator Simpson from Wyoming, an oil state]: We often react to issues based on parochial concerns. Here is such a case. I find that I must support the amendment offered by my able colleague, the Senator from New Jersey. There are many small refiners in my State that produce MTBE … and a major corporation just announced they are planning to build a new MTBE plant in my State and that they will be making MTBE from natural gas … I also have farmers to represent and they would like to produce ethanol as well, but not on the same scale as the MTBE producers.[6]

The oil companies won the political fight and the CAA was amended to adopt an oxygenate level that permitted the use of MTBE. This decision was to become the basis for many of the oil companies' key claims in the later MTBE litigation:

(1) removal to federal court on the theory that they were acting under the direction of the federal government;
(2) the allegation that the state tort law on which plaintiffs relied was preempted by this federal law and resulting regulations;

---

[4] 42 U.S.C. § 9601(14); EPA Designation of Hazardous Substances, 40 CFR 302.4.

[5] Memo 9200.4-21 (14 May 1997), available at http://www.epa.gov/superfund/policy/remedy/pdfs/92-00421-s.pdf.

[6] 136 Cong. Rec. S 2290, 2295–96, 2299 (7 March 1990).

(3) the claim that even state tort law must incorporate the CAA's preference for clean air over other pollution issues; and
(4) the claim that the EPA rather than the courts was the proper venue to resolve questions about the use of MTBE in gasoline and any resulting groundwater contamination.

At the time when the oil companies were lobbying for greater use of MTBE, they were aware of its ability to contaminate groundwater through the combination of its chemical properties and the high incidence of leaks in the storage infrastructure. As early as 1980, well contamination was discovered in New Jersey and Maryland. A 1986 study from Maine had been widely circulated throughout the industry and various companies had knowledge of East Coast pollution. Some oil companies and industry legal advisors cautioned against promotion of MTBE, warning of the potential for liability for the groundwater clean-up. Documents introduced in early spill trials showed that Shell Oil engineers were aware of the problem; they made jokes about what 'MTBE' really stood for. 'Most Things Biodegrade Easier' was a favorite, as were 'Menace Threatening Our Bountiful Environment' and 'Money To Be Extracted'. This industry awareness, coupled with further allegations that the information was suppressed while lobbying Congress and the EPA, became the basis for plaintiffs' state-law claims of fraud and conspiracy.

In 1999, a Blue Ribbon Panel convened by the EPA considered the effects of MTBE and the trade-offs between cleaner air and contaminated water. The panel's report recommended a package of reforms including:

(1) stronger regulation of USTs;
(2) better monitoring of water quality;
(3) expanded federal resources for up-front funding of the MTBE clean-up;
(4) a substantial reduction in the use of MTBE; and
(5) a clarification of the CAA to specifically provide that states may regulate or eliminate the use of gasoline additives that pose a threat to drinking water supplies.

The panel also urged accelerated studies of the health effects of all oxygenates, including both MTBE and ethanol. It was years before any of the panel's recommendations made an impact, and some (notably tougher UST standards and health effect studies) have not yet been implemented.

Later efforts to authorize a federal claim by injured citizens through a different statute also ran aground. Although in 2000 the Clinton administration had drafted proposed rules to eliminate or limit the use of MTBE under the Toxic Substance Control Act (which would have both given the EPA more enforcement authority and made citizen suits available), those regulations were 'quietly shelved' by the Bush administration. Newspaper reports suggested that the decision to abort the proposal was influenced by pressure from the three largest MTBE producers.[7]

In short, at the federal level (both legislative and administrative) at least two forces prevented federal law from being a meaningful factor in remediating the impact of MTBE on drinking water. One was very much a 'public' factor: the competing demands of big picture policies on air quality, water quality, energy, agriculture and public health. The other influence was 'private'—extremely powerful businesses, acting in their own self-interest, were able to help mold the content of the law and its enforcement mechanisms.

State Law

State governments, in contrast, had preexisting laws that created causes of action in tort against those whose breach of a duty of care harmed certain foreseeable others. Most of this was common law—as decided by a judge—and enforced through private litigation rather than agency action.

State agencies, though, were among the first to notice an MTBE-related water pollution problem and to take action to advocate its removal from gasoline. As early as 1986, employees of the Maine Department of Environmental Protection documented the extent of MTBE contamination of groundwater, noted that the chemical moved faster and farther in groundwater than other contaminants and reported that MTBE is difficult to remediate. Water authorities in other New England and Mid-Atlantic states also detected high levels of MTBE in groundwater, and California authorities were quite proactive in both regulation and litigation. For example, in 1986 California voters passed Proposition 65 (officially, the Safe Drinking Water and Toxic Enforcement Act) which, among other things, prohibits the discharge of toxic chemicals into potential sources of

[7] Pereira (2004), citing Pete Yost: 'How Bush Reversed Effort to Ban Water Polluter; Critics Cry Foul, But Companies Say Chemical Makes Air Cleaner,' Chicago Sun-Times, 16 February 2004 at 22, available at http://www.purewatersystems.com/whats_hot%28feb04%29.php.

drinking water. It can be enforced by both government agencies and private citizens.

It is state common law, though, that has served as the primary vehicle to challenge MTBE pollution and to seek compensation on behalf of water users. Tort claims include public nuisance, private nuisance, negligence, fraud and trespass. Early litigation used these causes of action to seek compensation from the owners of identifiable sources of specific spills, but the game-changing legal theory was the claim that gasoline containing MTBE is a defective product, thus creating potential liability not only for specific gas stations or pipelines where leaks occur but also for all of the companies involved in the manufacture, distribution and sale of gasoline and MTBE.

Within the defective product claims lurk difficult decisions about the degree of direct involvement required to satisfy the element of causation. One problem arises due to the fact that leaks and spills often go undetected for long periods of time or have no obvious single source, and complex (and expensive) hydrological expert opinion is therefore required to trace particular spills to particular wells.

The more serious problem arises from the method of gasoline distribution in the United States. To oversimplify, MTBE and gas from different manufacturers are blended and mixed at various points in the distribution chain in an undifferentiated stream, so that in most cases it is impossible to tie any particular gallon of leaked or spilled gas to any particular refiner.

> [G]asoline is almost never produced exclusively by [a particular] company's refineries. Instead, the gasoline sold at each service station in a particular area is usually the same: a blend of a large number of refiners' products.

Further complications result from 'complex arrangements whereby the defendants trade, barter and otherwise exchange product for delivery throughout parts of the country'.[8] Because of this difficulty in connecting particular MTBE pollution to particular manufacturers, most of the plaintiffs' common law claims only work in states that recognize a theory of causation such as market-share liability, conspiracy, concert of action or other collective responsibility.

---

[8] *MTBE MDL*, 591 F. Supp.2d 259, 269–73 (S.D.N.Y. 2008).

Summary: The Regulatory Situation as Aggregate Litigation Approached

By the early 2000s, MTBE had been a major component of gasoline in high-air-pollution parts of the country for more than a decade, but it was increasingly clear that the chemical's use as a gasoline additive was under attack. Federal legislation had been repeatedly introduced to phase out its use (although it had not yet passed); the EPA had threatened to add it to the Toxic Substance Control Act. Beginning in 2000, based both on concerns about health and about the problems of taste and odor, states began to ban MTBE, require its phase-out, or place limits on the acceptable levels of MTBE in the water supply. Eventually about half the states enacted bans or imposed limits. Individual lawsuits arising out of identifiable leaks were becoming increasingly common. And pro-ethanol forces from farm states were continuing to exert political pressure for a switch to biofuels and away from MTBE. It is in this environment that mass litigation by hundreds of plaintiffs against scores of defendants took off.

THE LITIGATION

Early Claims

The earliest lawsuits alleging damages caused by MTBE in groundwater were individual claims based on specific spills. For example, in 1995 a suit was filed on behalf of residents of Wilmington, North Carolina after leaks at a Conoco station led to residents being warned not to drink their water. The Wilmington case resulted in a jury verdict and large settlement, but it did not focus specifically on MTBE. Other early lawsuits were filed against gasoline manufacturers and distributors alleged to have caused the contamination of drinking water in Alabama, California, North Carolina, New York, Illinois and Florida.

As MTBE was discovered in more and more communities, these and other suits—mostly structured as class actions—were filed by private well owners in state court based on state law claims. These private plaintiffs asserted legal theories like public nuisance that are based on community impact, and sought remedies not only for themselves but also for the community:

(1) testing of the water;
(2) remediation of the contamination; and

(3) monitoring of health effects of all persons affected by the MTBE contamination.

The defendants were many of the major players in the oil and gas industry—companies that are normally business rivals were co-defendants in the MTBE litigation because of their combined efforts to market MTBE-containing gas.[9] Because they generally find federal court more congenial than at least some state courts, the defendants removed the cases to federal court.

MTBE I

The federal forum, unlike state litigation, makes lawsuit coordination possible. On 9 November 2000, the Judicial Panel on Multidistrict Litigations consolidated and transferred all the MTBE cases to Judge Shira Scheindlin's court in the Southern District of New York for pre-trial management.[10] MDL treatment of the MTBE cases is extremely significant. As the statute intends, consolidation allows for more efficient coordination of discovery, settlement negotiations and preliminary motions, and the defendants hoped that the MDL would decrease total litigation costs. Lawyers on both sides, moreover, knew that consolidation made a huge strategic difference in another way: had the litigation proceeded as hundreds of separate cases in hundreds of separate courts, multiple judges would have made decisions about:

---

[9] Because different companies had different 'personalities', different litigation philosophies and different levels of commitment to MTBE, they did not always agree on strategy. So while they did manage to work together and leverage their combined resources to good effect, it would be a mistake to think of the defendants as a monolithic group. They were particularly resistant to disclosing information about market share. In the interest of clarity, however, and because most legal positions were shared by most defendants, this chapter will refer to 'defendants' collectively.

[10] The statute creating and empowering the Judicial Panel on Multidistrict Litigation, 28 U.S.C. §1407, provides for consolidation only for pretrial. If cases are not dismissed or settled, they eventually return to their original courts for trial. On questions governed by state law, the MDL judge must apply the law (including choice of law rules) of the state in which the action was filed in each case. Thus for the MTBE claims based on state substantive law, Judge Scheindlin must apply California law in the California cases, New York law in the New York cases, etc.

(1) the viability of the plaintiffs' legal theories, including the defective product theory;
(2) the certifiability of cases as state or even nationwide class actions;
(3) the availability of collective liability standards for causation; and
(4) the defendants' preemption and primary jurisdiction defenses.

With a consolidated case, on the other hand, a single judge makes all of these decisions that, as a practical matter, determine whether and how a case can continue. Who this hurts and who this helps depends on the conduct and rulings of the MDL judge.

In MTBE I, Judge Scheindlin actively managed the case and turned early attention to a handful of important motions. For the most part, she rejected motions to dismiss the claims on the pleadings.[11] She oversaw disputes about discovery and expert witnesses as the parties aimed toward the crucial decision about whether the case would proceed as a class action. The certification issue was decisive as a practical matter. All of the lawyers knew that, as individual lawsuits, the plaintiffs' claims had negative value because the cost of proving liability, especially causation, was close to or exceeded the value of the relief sought (Ratner, 2012, 804–805).

In July 2002, Judge Scheindlin refused to certify the class, finding too many factual and legal differences to make certification proper under any section of Rule 23. This decision made the cases uneconomical to litigate and the private well owner claims were voluntarily dismissed. One plaintiff-side attorney from MTBE I estimates that the collective cost to class counsel of litigating the case through the denial of class certification, including both hard costs and the value of attorney time, was approximately $5 million. The lack of a mechanism that would allow recovery of damages beyond the wells of individually-named plaintiffs thus doomed a privately-financed action, because there was no prospect of a fee shift (and not much of a cost shift) from the defendants to plaintiffs even if the plaintiffs prevailed.

MTBE II

The MDL got new life when a crucial change occurred: the plaintiffs challenging MTBE contamination in the second phase (MTBE II) were public and private water suppliers in 16 states in which the common law recognized a flexible theory of collective causation. The damage claim of

[11] *MTBE MDL*, 175 F. Supp. 2d 593 (S.D.N.Y. 2001), rejecting preemption claim.

an agency that supplies water to an entire community is potentially much larger than that of the owner of an individual well, and so the economics of bringing those claims is different. Contingent fee arrangements also decreased the risk of litigation from the perspective of the water suppliers. Trade groups also spread the word about the litigation and lawyers, and lawyers spoke at water industry conferences, resulting in more water suppliers being interested in becoming plaintiffs.

Many of these cases were filed in the fall of 2003—the timing was dictated by the threat posed by pending legislation. Congress was considering the Bush/Cheney energy bill, and it contained a 'safe harbor' provision—added by legislators from Texas—that would have eliminated claims based on the defective product theory, effectively insulating most defendants from all claims filed after 5 September 2003. (Eventually only two votes prevented the end of the filibuster that kept the final bill from a Senate vote and likely passage.)

The water suppliers sued under state common law asking the court to award damages and remediation. Because it can take a long time for leaking MTBE to make its way into water supplies, the plaintiffs included water suppliers who had not yet detected MTBE in their water as well as those who had high levels of contamination. They included state governments (such as California and New Hampshire) as well as municipal water districts and private water suppliers. Because water suppliers had to buy substitute water or clean up the contamination based on the foul taste and odor of contaminated water, the unresolved issue of MTBE's health effects was not crucial to these plaintiffs' claims.

The water supplier plaintiffs, for the most part, filed their claims in state court, once again suing all of the major players in the industry. The defendants once again removed the cases to federal court based in large part on a claim that the Clean Air Act effectively required them to use MTBE and so they were acting as federal agents. Some defendants also based their removal on bankruptcy jurisdiction (from the Texaco bankruptcy that had occurred for unrelated reasons), preemption, or on a claim that the defective product claim itself must incorporate CAA approval of MTBE, thus making even the state law claim a substantial federal question.

Having removed the cases, the defendants again urged the Judicial Panel on Multidistrict Litigation to consolidate the cases and to assign them to Judge Scheindlin because of her expertise as an MDL judge and because of the expertise she had acquired during MTBE I. They were happy with her refusal to certify the class and so liked their chances for favorable rulings as the case moved into its second phase. Most of the plaintiffs' attorneys also agreed that Judge Scheindlin would be an appropriate choice, because although she had refused certification she was expected to be less sympathetic to the defendants' preemption and causation arguments on the merits. The Panel agreed to the parties' request, and so Judge Scheindlin once again found herself overseeing the pretrial processing of a large number of MTBE cases.

The defendants raised the usual common law responses to the state tort law claims: denials, as well as the affirmative defenses of contributory negligence, assumption of risk and statute of limitations. Based on the difficult causation issues embedded in the defective product claims, the defendants moved to dismiss any claims relying on 'alternative' causation theories. They also challenged the standing of the plaintiffs who had yet to detect MTBE in their water supply.

More significantly, the defendants asserted two defenses that are particularly relevant to the role of different levels of government and to what we mean by 'public' enforcement of legal norms. First, the defendants claimed that because Congress and the EPA (federal level) clearly anticipated that MTBE would be used to meet the vast majority of the gas oxygenate requirements created by the Clean Air Act, common law causes of action seeking to impose liability for the use of MTBE in gasoline (state law) are preempted. Some claimed that federal law expressly preempts non-identical state law controls (express preemption); more relied on a theory of 'conflict preemption'—that state and federal law are inconsistent and compliance with both is impossible or that state law thwarts federal goals. Should a preemption theory prevail, there would be little left of the plaintiffs' claims because the federal permission to use MTBE to help attain cleaner air would eliminate the ability of the state governments to enforce more general laws intended to protect their citizens from the effects of harmful products or even specific groundwater regulation.

Second, the defendants made the argument of the doctrine of primary jurisdiction; primary jurisdiction applies to issues falling within the realm of special administrative expertise. In this case, it was a claim that the court should put the litigation on hold and refer the issue of MTBE contamination to the EPA. This argument, in effect, emphasized that federal administrative agency treatment was preferable to private litigation.[12]

Judge Scheindlin accepted the 'federal agent' removal claim and rejected the primary jurisdiction argument, finding the nature of the

---

[12] Some defendants also moved to dismiss based on an additional defense relying on the federal provisions: an argument that the plaintiffs' claims were non-justiciable political questions.

dispute to be well within normal judicial competencies. The combination of those rulings allowed her to keep jurisdiction of the MDL (because the cases were properly in federal court) and continue with the case (because no deferral to the EPA was required).

Faced with hundreds of suits against numerous defendants, involving both common and individual issues, she used her case management skills to keep the enormous dispute moving forward. The plaintiffs' Steering Committee and Liaison Counsel were identified. Discovery management was put in place, designating four actions as 'focus cases' and otherwise staying discovery except for information relevant to all cases. The court held regular conferences, issued numerous case management orders and also ruled on a number of potentially dispositive motions. For the most part, Judge Scheindlin rejected claims that the cases should be dismissed based on either the preemption defenses or on objections to the collective causation theories; these decisions kept the cases alive and preparing for so-called 'bellwether' trials (trials of a small number of cases sampled from the mass in order to provide information about how juries are likely to rule in future cases). While efforts to structure a bellwether trial that would definitively resolve some issues through the use of collateral estoppel were unsuccessful, the judge and lawyers nonetheless hoped that the results of the trials could help assign value to cases and promote settlement.

In some senses the litigation was extremely contentious—virtually every viable defense on the merits was asserted, motions to reconsider and motions to certify appeals followed each significant ruling and procedural decisions (including discovery issues) were hotly disputed. In other senses the litigation was conducted in a professional and cooperative spirit; both sides were represented by firms with extensive experience in mass tort litigation who respected each other's understanding of the stakes and the legal and strategic moves in the case. Contested merits motions, discovery disputes and preparation for bellwether trials ran parallel with more cooperative activity and, eventually, settlement negotiations.

The Settlement

As the case developed and facts emerged, the court ruled on significant merits motions. Each set of lawyers was able to assess the strengths and weaknesses of its clients' positions and a range of settlement possibilities became clearer. By 2007–2008, a number of things had happened that moved the parties toward settlement:

(1) About half of US states had banned or limited the use of MTBE in gasoline.
(2) The Energy Policy Act of 2005 once again failed to include a legislative 'safe harbor' provision insulating the industry from MTBE litigation. It also replaced the CAA's oxygenated gasoline requirement with a renewable fuels plan, which in effect chose ethanol over MTBE. Because an oxygenate was no longer required by law, this put refiners at a higher liability risk if they continued to use MTBE. Effectively, the use of MTBE in US gasoline was over and so discussions could focus on the consequences of past events.
(3) Courts were rejecting defense arguments that relied on the dominance of federal over state law:
  (a) The Second Circuit rejected the defendants' federal agent removal and substantial federal question arguments, paving the way for some of the cases to be remanded to state court.
  (b) The Second Circuit rejected the defendants' express preemption argument, diminishing the possibility that that single issue would knock out all of the litigation. The court also noted with approval Judge Scheindlin's order denying defendants' motion for summary judgment on the conflict preemption defense.
(4) Judge Scheindlin denied the motion to dismiss based on the causation issues, finding various theories under which several of the states might allow the plaintiffs to prevail without being able to trace particular contamination of particular wells to particular manufacturers.
(5) The bellwether well trials in the focus cases were fast approaching.

The combined effect of these decisions created incentives to settle for both sides. The plaintiffs' claims survived, but they were still faced with the enormous challenge (and enormous expense) of proving causation even under the more flexible standards. Multiple differing state standards on allowable levels of MTBE created additional complications. And there was still a possibility that the preemption or causation rulings would be reversed on appeal or that a judgment could be reversed for lack of subject matter jurisdiction. The defendants, having failed to get a legislated 'safe harbor' through Congress, had reason to find a way to put MTBE claims behind them. With the extent of MTBE pollution closer to a known quantity, and with future use of the chemical no longer a factor, a large-scale national solution had a lot of appeal.

Given all of these forces, it is not surprising that the parties began exploring settlement in late 2006, or that Judge Scheindlin appointed a

Special Settlement Master in March 2007. At the same time that the lawyers were working feverishly to prepare for bellwether trials on the selected wells, they were also diligently discussing the contours of a possible global settlement. The complexity of the issues, the parties' differing positions and the need to get each party to individually agree to the settlement (attempts to agree to a class settlement failed) meant that the discussions took quite some time. An outline of settlement terms was drafted in December 2007 and the final agreement was signed in March 2008. Thirteen of the large oil companies agreed to pay $422 million to 153 public water systems in 17 states and also agreed, over the next 30 years, to pay 70 percent of the decontamination costs for wells owned or operated by the plaintiffs that became contaminated with MTBE in the future and required clean-up efforts. The settlement funds were to be allocated to the various water providers based on a complex list of factors relevant to the extent of contamination. Although MDL judges do not have to approve non-class settlements, state laws in California and Illinois protecting the settling defendants from future contribution claims led to a ruling on the fairness of some of the specific settlement amounts and Judge Scheindlin found them to be within the range of estimated median clean-up costs.[13]

Since the big 2008 mass settlement, many more claims have been settled. In addition, new cases have been filed, some cases have been returned to their original courts and others have been remanded to state court. New York City's claim against ExxonMobil did not settle, but instead it went to trial and resulted in a verdict for the plaintiffs in the amount of $104.7 million in compensatory damages (and a ruling that punitive damages were not available). That decision was affirmed by the Second Circuit, which also rejected Exxon's claim that state law was preempted by the federal Clean Air Act. In many of the new suits, it is the state itself that is the plaintiff, seeking damages for the cost of cleaning up the groundwater.

---

[13] The settlement was between these defendants and the plaintiffs in the cases brought by three prominent plaintiff firms. The biggest holdout on the defense side was ExxonMobil, which refused to participate in this settlement and which challenged a certification of its fairness under California and Illinois law. Many of the settlement terms and the controversy about the fairness certification are described in *MTBE MDL*, 578 F. Supp.2d 519 (S.D.N.Y. 2008).

LEGISLATIVE AND ADMINISTRATIVE PROPOSALS RETURN

Developments also continue on the 'public' front. In late 2011, the EPA proposed the first update of the regulations governing USTs since 1988, adding requirements for the structure, maintenance and monitoring of the leaking infrastructure. Industry opposition has slowed the rulemaking process, and the comment period was extended while meetings with storage tank owners continued, and as of June 2015, final regulations had not yet been put into effect.

The prospect of 'safe harbor' anti-litigation legislation also returned, although the focus has shifted to ethanol. For example, in the spring of 2012, legislation was introduced in the House and Senate that would protect products registered with the EPA under the Clean Air Act from litigation:

> [n]otwithstanding any Federal, State, or local law (including common law), no qualified product shall be considered to be a defective product.

In fact, the bill would have both prohibited future suits and eliminated pending ones, providing that new suits could not be filed and pending suits 'in any court of the United States or any State court ... shall be dismissed with prejudice'. The bill also would have explicitly overridden state authority to impose stricter requirements or additional liability for leaking underground storage tanks.

The National Conference of State Legislatures (NCSL) opposed the legislation in a way that highlighted the 'public vs. public' governance issue that pervades the MTBE dispute. In a letter to the House Judiciary Committee, the NCSL complained that the bill 'unnecessarily infringes on the common law police power of the states under which they protect the health, safety, and welfare of their constituents'. While the legislation did not pass, similar measures continue to be introduced.

THE IMPACT OF PUBLIC AND PRIVATE PROCESSES

Remedies

While the 'public vs. private' debate is about governance, it is also about results. How did the legislative, administrative and judicial processes, alone or in combination, affect the development and enforcement of the law and the remedies available to parties who claim to have been harmed? In the MTBE situation, there was little dispute that the gas additive had made it into the groundwater and had or would make some water undrinkable. What was disputed was what to do about that: between the oil and gas industry, the federal government, the state governments, local water providers and individual water users, who was going to bear the cost of the clean-up or of living with water that was at best unpalatable and possibly a health risk?

Eventually, federal legislation put an end to MTBE use as a gas additive in the United States. As to past harm, those affected by MTBE got differing results. In some parts of the country, there has been neither 'public' nor 'private' action, because neither federal law nor state tort law provides a remedy. Even in states where the law is more favorable, results are mixed. Those worst off were individual well owners. Federal law did not provide a cause of action. State law claims for relief may have been theoretically available but individual well pollution generated only negative value claims: the cost of proving liability was likely to equal or exceed the amount of damages recoverable. For them, the lack of an administrative remedy and lack of a mechanism for collective action meant that they received little or nothing. They themselves bore the cost of the clean-up or decreased property value or fear of disease. Their lawyers bore the large out-of-pocket costs of the unsuccessful MTBE I litigation.

The water providers who were the plaintiffs in MTBE II fared better. Those who became part of the multidistrict litigation and settlement recovered substantial sums. These payments, especially after subtracting litigation costs and attorney's fees, may not have covered the entire cost of the actual clean-up and the purchase of substitute water, but nevertheless provided some relief. In at least some cases, a clean-up of the water sources has occurred. The suppliers also have some protection against the continued impact, if any, of the MTBE already in the system, thanks to the settling defendants' promise to pay a substantial portion of the cost of newly-occurring contamination for 30 years. Some of the water providers (notably New York City) who went to trial rather than settling have also won judgments for damages, although they incurred greater litigation costs and suffered continuing delays in payment.

In all, then, the costs of MTBE groundwater pollution have been borne by a combination of private individuals, state and local agencies, and members of the oil and gas industry. Because federal law did little to regulate petroleum-related ground pollution, did not list MTBE under the Toxic Substance Control Act, did not complete a study of the human health effects of MTBE and relied on property owners to monitor leaks in underground storage tanks, federal contributions toward the clean-up of

MTBE pollution was comparatively low. However, Congress and the EPA incurred substantial costs in the process of considering legislation and rules, and the federal court system devoted enormous resources of time and money to hosting the MDL.

The defendants who genuinely believe that the Clean Air Act forced them to use MTBE, who find collective causation theories to be bogus, and who believe that energy and environmental regulation should be done only at the federal level may feel themselves ill used by the combination of litigation and settlement costs. The suits were undoubtedly extremely expensive for all of the parties and settlement sums were in the multi-millions. On the other hand, the total national cost of the MTBE clean-up has been estimated as high as many billions of dollars, and more than one source indicated that a settlement in the hundreds of millions was not a large sum for a combination of oil companies to pay.

Public and Private Processes

It is harder to say what combination of public and private enforcement brought about this result. One major factor was the MTBE damage itself. The longer MTBE was used in gasoline, the more leaks spread to more water supplies. This caused damage to water users and suppliers who had to spend extra money to acquire drinkable water through new supplies or the clean-up of existing ones, and they were anxious to be reimbursed.

What was the impact of litigation? It was the only process that provided any remedy to those whose water was affected by MTBE, shifting some of the cost from water drinkers to the oil companies. (It also ultimately provided a profit for the sophisticated plaintiffs-side law firms involved in MTBE II, a reward for undertaking the risk of litigation and fronting the costs of investigation and enforcement.)

Litigation also had some effect on the existence and timing of MTBE-related legislation. It exposed holes in the legal infrastructure at the federal level, encouraging states to regulate at their own level. It added to the level of publicity surrounding the MTBE problem, adding momentum to calls for regulation. (Both sides, in fact, had dueling websites putting their own spin on the MTBE situation.) One federal legislative impact is the recurring—but so far unsuccessful—effort to use federal law to eliminate MTBE litigation entirely. Political maneuvering at the federal level also demonstrates that potential liability in the MTBE litigation was one of the variables affecting whether the industry could continue to profit from using MTBE and what kind of legislation was desired by gasoline manufacturers and retailers.

The impact of 'public' enforcement on water quality was a mixed bag. Its initial impact was strongest as an effect on the litigation. State regulation may have modified tort claim standards of care, although its relevance was disputed and the standards were quite varied. Lawyers involved with the litigation itself described the EPA as largely irrelevant, except that the Clean Air Act may have preempted state law and thus eliminated much of the litigation. As to direct impact, while the federal CAA contained an oxygenate mandate, state regulation did not end the use of MTBE. Not until the Energy Policy Act of 2005 changed that calculus did continuing use of the chemical cease to be a factor, and even then the continued risk of lawsuit-based liability was part of the cost-benefit analysis.

CONCLUSION

In an ideal world, it might make sense to only regulate environmental policy at a national level, and to do it through prospective regulation that prevents rather than remedies harm. National regulation would allow uniformity in national markets and for the balancing of the big-picture of the interests of air quality, water quality, energy use, national defense, agriculture and public health. A fast and inexpensive mechanism to fund the water clean-up and reimburse water users might in theory work faster than litigation and decrease transaction costs. This is not, however, an ideal world. The regulation (or the lack thereof) of MTBE has been described as a 'poster child for regulatory failure'.[14] Federal legislation and regulation was weakened by the influence of private groups. State legislation came long after the damage was done, and did not provide an effective mechanism for remediation. It did affect incentives going forward, but in an inconsistent patchwork framework, challengeable as prohibited by federal law. Powerful parties pushed for an end to liability rather than for a more efficient dispute resolution system.

That left 'private' litigation and the court system—retrospective enforcement through a shifting of the cost of the clean-up—accomplished through local 'public' agencies filing lawsuits to recover their own damages. Whether aggregate litigation was available made a big difference in the course and scope of this private enforcement. Without a class action, small private claims were too expensive to pursue. On the other hand, the availability of coordinated multidistrict litigation created a

[14] McGarity, 2004, 282.

different kind of national uniformity, substituting federal procedure for a variety of state processes, decreasing litigation cost, and encouraging large-scale negotiation and settlement. Consolidation also raised the stakes: decisions by one judge, as a practical matter, had enormous impact on both substantive and procedural advantages and disadvantages. Acting as the decision-maker in a collection of private enforcement actions, applying a combination of legislative, regulatory and court-made principles, the MDL judge presided over a process of information gathering, negotiation and prospective rule creation that resembled regulation as much as litigation.

What is public and what is private and which should we choose? In this litigation at least, it's the wrong question.

REFERENCES

Thomas McGarity, *MTBE: A Precautionary Tale*, (2004) 28 Harvard Environmental Law Review 281

Cesar Pereira, Comment, *Protecting The 'Underground Seas': A case for protecting and creating claims against oil companies for Methyl Tertiary Butyl Ether (MTBE) groundwater contamination*, (2004) 12 University of Baltimore Journal of Environmental Law 1

Morris Ratner, *A New Model of Plaintiffs' Class Action Attorneys*, (2012) 31 The Review of Litigation 757

Justin Scheck, *Water Gun*, The Recorder, 27 January 2005

United States Government Accountability Office, Report to Congressional Requesters, GAO-11-254, *Safe Drinking Water Act: EPA Should Improve Implementation of Requirements on Whether to Regulate Additional Contaminants* (May 2011), available at http://www.gao.gov/assets/320/318967.pdf

17. Self-interested gatekeeping? Clashes between public and private enforcers in two Chilean class actions

Agustin Barroilhet

INTRODUCTION

Many scholars believe that using public agencies to control the flood of private lawsuits is a creative way to enact regulatory regimes that benefit from both the impetus of private enforcement and the accountability of public enforcement (Stephenson, 2005). In the context of class actions, this idea implies broadening the standing required to file class actions to multiple private parties while granting the Office of the Attorney General or other public agencies 'the power to oversee and manage private litigation efforts' (Engstrom, 2013, 616). However, the idea of bringing public accountability to class actions by the means of public agencies might be defeated by public agencies' self-interested behavior. As most sophisticated class counsel in Chile have found, in the absence of clear and workable rules to coordinate public and private enforcement, public agencies can use their discretionary powers and preeminent position to prey on private enforcers, effectively hijacking their cases or settlements for short-term political gains. The two cases presented in this chapter illustrate this. They describe how the Servicio Nacional del Consumidor (SERNAC), the Chilean consumer protection agency, hijacked cases and took credit for redressing the consumers for their losses, knowing that the defendants' willingness to compensate the consumers was the result of the efforts of private enforcers. The backdrop of the cases reveals an 'insecure' agency driven by self-interest that shunned competing private enforcers who threatened to displace it in its perceived role as the most effective defender of the consumers' rights in the country.

THE CHILEAN CLASS ACTION PROCEDURE

Chilean class actions are, in general, opt-out 'class-issue actions' which aim to declare the liability of the defendant with *erga omnes* effects, similar to those existing in Brazil (Gidi, 2003, 359). If the defendant is found liable, class members can come forward to prove their class membership and damages in individual cases or in an aggregated stage before the same court that heard the case. However, if the defendant knows class members, and their damages can be determined without additional information, the class action procedure authorizes the judge to order the defendant to redress the consumers directly without any additional proceedings. In these cases, which are the most common in the Chilean class action litigation practice, class actions work as full opt-out class actions for damages (Barroilhet, 2012).

Opt-out class actions for damages are considered attractive for private enforcers because they increase the value of the case and, hence, potential attorneys' fees. Yet, Chilean class action litigation shows substantially more public enforcement, almost no cases are initiated by sophisticated private enforcers and a few definitive judgments. To a great extent, this is owed to very strict statutory provisions designed to prevent a flood of private litigation. The Chilean class action procedure:

(1) sets barriers against early settlements;
(2) limits the ability of class counsel to monopolize the device;
(3) sets unclear rules for the judge to set attorneys' fees;
(4) prohibits fluid recovery mechanisms for small-value cases; and
(5) prohibits the imposition of trebled damages or punitive interest that could be used to leverage settlements (Barroilhet, 2012).

These circumstances not only make class actions risky as a for-profit enterprise but also places them at a relative disadvantage when compared to individual procedures and joinders that can target the same abuses on a smaller scale or to administrative actions that can also be used to curtail abusive practices (Barroilhet, 2012, 311 (n. 131)).

However, there is a more definitive reason why class actions have not spurred sophisticated private litigation, especially after the La Polar case of 2011, described later. This reason concerns SERNAC. The Chilean class action procedure grants SERNAC broad gatekeeping powers over private enforcement. The agency has to be notified *ex officio*, or by initiative of the court, of any class action filed in the country, and it can become a party at any stage of any class action case. Furthermore, if the agency is not a party to a case, it has to be notified, again *ex officio*, of any attempt by the parties to withdraw the class complaint, and can choose to continue cases on behalf of absent members of the class, even if the class counsel settles it for her direct clients (Barroilhet, 2012, 294).

All the previous prerogatives—added to SERNAC's position as the most prominent consumer defender in the country in decades—give the agency effective control over private litigation, as the Chilean class action statute intended. Yet, they also give the agency a highly extractive power over private enforcement. The mere threat of using these powers allows it, in the best scenario, to push for more prosecutorial efforts, more compensation, or a better balance between paying redress to class members and attorney's fees. Sadly for legal entrepreneurs, in the worst scenario, these powers also allow the agency to simply take over the best private cases and settlements for political gain, regardless of the need for its intervention and the harm caused to private enforcers.

THE VTR CASE

The VTR case comprises two related court cases: an individual case filed before the class action and the class action itself. The latter was one of the first class actions in the country and the only one that actually put money into the consumers' pockets in the first five years of class actions' existence, even though formally the defendants won in court. This brief account will describe the participation of both the legal entrepreneur behind the case and of SERNAC, inside and outside the courthouse.

The case started when Matías Cortés, an attorney with experience in litigating class actions in the United States, received a call from a former neighbor who saw him in the media talking about class actions. The neighbor had a complaint against his TV cable company, Metropolis-Intercom (MI), regarding a technical service support charge called Soporte servicio técnico (SST) that cost a bit less than a dollar a month that was not on his contract and that he had never agreed to pay. The neighbor told Cortés that MI's explanation for the SST charge was that it was insurance to cover the company technicians' fee in case the service failed within his house and that he had received a letter offering him an opportunity to opt out of the charge, something he failed to do. Cortés saw immediately that MI had violated several norms of Chilean consumer law, most importantly the one that says explicitly 'silence does not constitute acceptance in case of the consumers' contractual relations'.[1]

[1] *See* LAW NO. 19496, Art. 3(a).

Cortés saw Metropolis as an attractive target to institute the class action procedure, but, for strategic reasons described below, he decided to invest his time by trying his neighbor's case individually.

The neighbor's case, tried in a local police court (*Juzgado de Policía Local)*, went according to Cortés' plans. MI, used to dealing with small claims on a daily basis, put a junior in-house lawyer in charge of the case. As expected, this lawyer did not notice that the complaint, drafted by Cortés but filed by the plaintiff to avoid raising early alarms, was framed to force the judge to address key legal issues that would be relevant to the class action Cortés was planning. In his ruling, the judge declared the SST charge to be illegal and an evident violation of the Consumer Law.[2] Moreover, he awarded the neighbor contractual damages for the full amount of the SST charge for five years, which is the usual limitation period for contractual obligations in Chile, and ordered VTR—the company that bought Metropolis while the case was being adjudicated—to pay approximately $400 to the State coffers as penalty, which was about seven times the amount of compensation.

In November 2005, with this judgment in hand, Cortés started to draft the class complaint and presented it to a consumer association called Asociación Nacional de Usuarios de la Seguridad Social (ANADEUS, the National Association of Users of the Social Security Services) that was listed in SERNAC's official record of consumer associations with standing to file class actions. The complaint was simple. It told the story of the SST charge and how Metropolis sent letters inviting the consumers to reject the charge and took their silence as consent. It also described the neighbor's case, in which the company's behavior was proven to be abusive. The latter was quoted often, citing the company's defense arguments, such as the recognition of the 'involuntary error' and the company's invitation to the plaintiff 'to approach the company's consumer satisfaction department for reimbursement of the charge'. The complaint also described events that happened after the case. It claimed that after the judgment in the neighbor's case, VTR deliberately renamed the SST charge Garantía de Mantención (Maintenance Guarantee), to avoid liability associated with the SST charge. Furthermore, the complaint described how VTR discounted the charge to former Metropolis clients who bought VTR's additional services. In conclusion, the complaint asked for reimbursement of the SST charge to all VTR clients,

---

2 *See* 3er Juzgado de Policía Local de las Condes (3rd J. Pol. Las Condes) [3rd Local Policing Court Las Condes], 17 de octubre de 2005, rol de la causa 35172-2005.

which the complaint valued at 2,359,800,000 Chilean pesos (approximately \$4.8 million), the suppression of the illegal charge and, pressing the interpretation of a provision in the Consumer Law that preexisted class actions, any fines that the judge desired to impose for 'each' individual case within the class.

Cortés did not file the case immediately after ANADEUS' assembly approved it. First, emulating the practice of some American plaintiff lawyers and knowing how protracted is the civil litigation in Chile, he contacted VTR executives and their lawyers to negotiate an agreement.

The first contact between the parties was disastrous. VTR's law firm, which was among the most prominent and well-regarded in the country, considered Cortés an aggressive newcomer with an opportunistic claim. The firm convinced VTR executives that it would easily deal with the case and the company refused to engage in negotiations.

Secure that his claim was justified and invigorated by VTR's reaction, Cortés filed the complaint with the court on 18 January 2006. Again he did not serve it to VTR immediately.[3] Instead, he gave VTR's lawyers one more chance to resolve the issue outside the court. To press his case, he told them that if he served the complaint, he was not going to be able to control what the judge and SERNAC would do with the case and that they were risking huge penalties if the judge applied the generic fine of the Consumer Law for each case in the class as the judge did in the neighbor's case. VTR's lawyers responded to this second contact by asking for time to consult with their client. More than a week went by without an answer before Cortés decided to service the class action complaint.

In the meantime, VTR's lawyers used the time they obtained from Cortés wisely. They had a former SERNAC official on their team who had been hired amidst the class action debate precisely to defend corporate clients. Using him as a liaison, they contacted SERNAC, which until then, had been silent and likely unaware of the case. The defense and SERNAC met at least once before the class actions complaint was served and apparently reached an informal agreement that has never been disclosed to the public. Soon after the meeting and ten days after Cortés' filing, SERNAC issued a press release announcing:

---

[3] The case was assigned to the 25vo Juzgado Civil de Santuago (25 J. Civ. Stgo.) [25th Civil Court of Santiago], 'Asociación de Consumidores con V.T.R.', rol de la causa 973-2006.

> Following its constant role of overseer of the protection of consumer interests, SERNAC communicates the following proposal of solution offered by VTR to all its clients: ...[4]

The solutions that VTR offered and SERNAC endorsed were that the company would hire Ernst & Young to audit all its billing procedures and identify those clients who had paid the SST charge. As compensation for those clients, VTR offered a direct discount on its services or a promotional discount on the company's new products. The press release concluded saying:

> SERNAC recognizes VTR's collaboration and good will in this case, considering the company has adopted all the adequate measures to protect [former] Metropolis' clients.

To informed observers, this was a case of an agency selling the resolution of class members' claims in exchange for discount coupons, a practice widely decried in the United States when used by private class action attorneys.[5]

VTR's bold move and SERNAC's response took Cortés by surprise. Realizing his mistake in giving VTR the chance to meet with SERNAC and not going public with the case earlier, he tried to regain control by servicing the complaint and neutralizing the agency. To do so, he asked representatives of ANADEUS to parley with SERNAC. This tactic seemed to work because SERNAC later rejected VTR's requests to appear in the case and ANADEUS received SERNAC-distributed public funding for all the projects the association presented to the agency that year. Yet, the damage was done. At least in public opinion, it was SERNAC and not Cortés who set in motion the redress scheme that VTR had offered.

However, not everything was lost. The class action procedure in Chile was new to Cortés and to everybody else, and it allowed a lot of room for interpretation, one of which favored Cortés. The civil judge in charge of the case decided that the ten-day period to answer the class complaint

---

[4] Translation by the author. *See* SERNAC, Agenda Noticiosa, 27 January 2006.

[5] *Id.* Even though collective mediations were not in place in 2005, SERNAC's deal with VTR contained two elements that became common in the agency's collective mediations: first, the presence of a well-respected auditor in charge of determining the extent of the abuse against consumers that would shield SERNAC from future consumers' claims, and second, compensation in the form of discounts or other non-cash equivalents.

mandated by the statute meant continuous days, including non-working days. Hence, she ruled VTR's answer to the complaint untimely by two days and, showing strict adherence to civil procedure that forces judges to rule against the absent party unless the public interest is at stake, she declared the class action admissible for the collective interest of the consumers.[6] This judgment saved this case from going through the admissibility stage that would so dramatically delay other similar cases (Barroilhet, 2014, 5).

VTR's lawyers panicked in the face of this admissibility judgment and their animosity towards Matías Cortés grew. At the time, only a few commentators and practitioners had noticed that the generic fines of the Consumer Law, buried in an article that was not modified by the class action, could be applied to class actions on the aggregate. If the judge in the case applied the fines to each member in the class as the Local Policing Court had done in the neighbor's case, the company could lose up to $32 million. Fines had to be avoided at all costs. And they were; VTR's lawyers appealed immediately and hired Davor Harasic, a law professor of the University of Chile who was renowned as one of the best litigators in the country.

Under Harasic's influence, VTR's defense strategy changed dramatically. Instead of using formal arguments against the admissibility judgment, the company decided to inhibit the substantial cause of action by redressing the harm completely, and to focus its attack on the class counsel and his relation to the consumer association that acted as plaintiff. To implement the plan, VTR first changed the compensation it had offered SERNAC to cash returns in the form of cashiers' checks that would be available in the company's stores for all consumers who, according to Ernst & Young, had suffered the SST charge. This action allowed the company to present as a defense in the Court of Appeals that it had redressed all consumers by issuing the checks that were no longer in its possession. Secondly, it asked SERNAC to get involved but this time the agency declined to take an active role and only handed the defense a new letter confirming what was already stated in the January 2006 press release in which the agency supported the company. Thirdly, VTR crafted its allegations over Cortés's behavior as class counsel arguing that he had not serviced the complaint immediately and that he had induced ANADEUS to file the class action complaint, something the

---

[6] *See* 25vo Juzgado Civil de Santiago (25 J. Civ. Stgo.) [25th Civil Court of Santiago], 10 de marzo de 2006, causa rol 973-2006, 'Asociación de Usuarios con V.T.R.'. *See* also El Mercurio, 2006.

consumer association would never have done on its own because its declared mission was to protect clients of health-related providers and not users of cable companies like VTR. According to Harasic, if the Court believed that the company had acted in good faith and did everything it could to resolve the abuses, something that SERNAC's involvement would help to establish, and also believed in Cortés's bad faith and profit motivation, it would kick the case out on any formal ground it could find.

Harasic's predictions were correct. The First Room of the Court of Appeals of Santiago delivered its brief judgment on VTR's appeal against the admissibility on 6 June 2006. The ruling was 2-1 against the plaintiffs. In the judgment, the majority argued that the period to answer the class action complaint was ten business days, an interpretation that has been reversed in subsequent cases. Then, having cleared the way for a replacement judgment, the majority accepted VTR's argument that ANADEUS was acting out of the scope of its intended mission and therefore it could not have a legitimate interest, and therefore, legitimate standing, to file a class action against a telecommunications' company. Having established this point, the Court refused to address other issues and declared the class action inadmissible.[7]

Encouraged by the minority vote in the Court of Appeals,[8] Cortés tried an extraordinary appeal to the Supreme Court to clarify some interpretations of the class action procedure, in particular, the Court of Appeals' restrictive interpretation of the consumer associations' class action standing, even though he knew that VTR's compensation, endorsed by SERNAC and certified by Ernst & Young, had effectively killed his case. The Supreme Court, having no motivation other than granting Cortés his fees or monitoring the implementation of the redress plan already supervised by a respected firm of auditors and SERNAC, ruled in December 2007, with minor alterations, that the Court of Appeals was

---

7 *See* Corte de Apelaciones de Santiago (C. Apel. Stgo) [Court of Appeals of Santiago], 6 de junio de 2006, rol de la causa 1904-2006, Asociación de Usuarios con V.T.R.'.

8 *Id.* The minority vote, delivered by a law professor acting as *abogado integrante* (prominent lawyers or professors that sit in the court when there are not enough judges to conform a room) explained that the case fitted perfectly with the purpose of class actions in other jurisdictions and that ANADEUS had standing to pursue the case because the law only required the entity who filed the claim to be registered as a consumer association.

right.[9] This ruling ended the VTR Case, the only case in the first five years of the class actions' existence that delivered cash compensation to the consumers and no fees for the lawyer who had worked on it for more than two years.

LA POLAR CASE

The La Polar case is by far the largest and most complex class action ever filed in Chile and will certainly be featured in Chilean textbooks on Finance, Consumer Law and Corporate Governance in years to come.[10] This brief account of the case will be limited to SERNAC's participation in the case and the agency's relationship with the legal entrepreneur who stepped in its way.

Like most cases since SERNAC consolidated its position as the only relevant enforcer of class actions, the case started with a collective mediation (Barroilhet 2012, 309). The collective mediation was triggered by 123 consumers' claims against La Polar, a Chilean department store, that were recorded on SERNAC consumers' claims webpage. The claims revealed a consistent practice of La Polar's financial branch: inflating debts in arrears by adding special interest and 'renegotiation' fees which would clear them only to be renegotiated again, month by month, for years, without the consumers ever knowing about it. Some of the consumers also claimed that La Polar reported the balances resulting from the invalid renegotiations to credit bureaus which ruined their credit-scores.

The collective mediation procedure started in August 2010 and arrived quickly at a 'communicable' agreement. La Polar promised SERNAC that it was going to reverse the renegotiations for the 321 known cases (the original 123 plus others that appeared during the mediation), and that it was going to compensate clients for the cost of claiming in the form of coupons euphemistically called in the agreement 'exchanges for future purchases'. As in the VTR Case, SERNAC traded its standing for discount coupons for the consumers.

---

[9] *See* Corte Suprema (C. Sup.) [Supreme Court], 17 de diciembre de 2007, rol de la causa 3542-2006, 'ANADEU A.C. con V.T.R.'.

[10] After a year the case had triggered more than 500 criminal prosecutions, a criminal case with more than 20,000 pages of documents and ten imprisonments, more than $6 million in administrative fines and more than 2,600 press releases. The case ultimately affected approximately 900,000 consumers, which is about 5 percent of the country's population. *See* LaSegunda.com, 2012.

However, La Polar did not keep its promises. According to SERNAC's own database and a follow-up audit performed in April 2011, La Polar did not reverse the invalid debt renegotiations in most of the 321 claims, and furthermore, persisted in the practice of unilaterally 'renegotiating' debts in arrears, which increased the number of claims to more than 800, according to SERNAC's internal report. Following what SERNAC's claims is its usual practice after a failed collective mediation, the agency filed a class action on behalf of La Polar clients' collective interest in May 2011.

The news about the class action did not produce a shocked reaction from the consumers or the stock market, where La Polar has been publicly traded since 2003. For the public it was just another of SERNAC's class actions which had become frequent. The turmoil started two weeks later when La Polar's board of directors met to familiarize themselves with SERNAC's class action complaint and the extent of the renegotiated accounts. Immediately after the meeting, the board informed the market that the company had to increase its provision for delinquent credits by more than $325 million.[11]

As everybody found out on the morning of 9 June 2011, La Polar had been silently but persistently hiding its delinquent credits for eight years using a twisted interpretation of a mandate it obtained from the consumers to liquidate their debts. Immediately after the information was released to the market, the stock fell 42 percent before transactions were blocked. Days later, the estimation of La Polar's financial fraud had doubled, which led the stock to fall another 63 percent and reporters to start calling this case 'one of the biggest financial scandals of Chile's 20-year economic boom' (Barrionuevo, 2011).

It would be inaccurate to credit SERNAC or the consumers for the scandal that followed, however. La Polar's consumers were poor and difficult to locate and their damages could not be easily assessed, thus the agency did not know the extent of La Polar's abuses when it filed its class action. What drove the La Polar scandal was the fraud on stockholders, including institutional investors, pension funds and thousands of wealthy private investors. Unlike other Chilean companies that are clearly controlled by a single economic group or family, La Polar's

[11] See *Hecho Esencial* (Current report containing a relevant material event, equivalent to the United States' 8K Form (4.02) of SEC) de 9 de Junio de 2011 de La Polar S.A. a *Superintendente de Valores y Seguros*. The $325 million additional provisions required by La Polar were approximately 35 percent of the company's market cap that day.

diversified ownership only increased the scandal because it was unclear who might save the company and if it could remain financially viable.

As weeks went by, the anxiety the case produced only grew. The market was eager for information and anyone who said or did anything regarding La Polar got press. An endless parade of Public Prosecutors, administrative officials from several agencies, including the banking agency and the stock exchange agency, SERNAC, the Minister of Interior and the President himself, along with seemingly every politician in the country, appeared day after day to give their opinion and announce some kind of measure against the company. The consequences of these announcements are still ongoing. Two weeks after La Polar's board of directors' initial press release, the seven top executives of the company were in jail. Three weeks later, the board that had issued the initial press release was completely removed and almost every agency that had a remote connection with the case started administrative procedures. A month later, Congress triggered special investigations against all the administrative agencies that could have prevented the fraud. Among these was SERNAC, which was blamed for not taking sufficient action and for engaging in a useless collective mediation that ended in a coupon settlement that allowed La Polar to continue its abuses for a year after the first cases came to light.

Things started to untangle, at least on the stockholder front, when the main stakeholders, large creditors and pension funds gathered in an emergency meeting and decided to take over the company to try to save it. To do this they called on César Barros, a skillful executive who had obtained unprecedented cooperation from the government a few years before when a crisis hit the salmon industry.

Barros set his strategy in motion as soon as he assumed the presidency of La Polar. He needed time to make the company viable and thus tried to delay every possible administrative and legal action by convincing stakeholders that their interests would be preserved. He told investors he would turn La Polar into a new and profitable company in the long run and that anyone ever involved in the abuse either had been or would be fired, and that all guilty parties would be prosecuted. He informed the administrative agencies that the company would cooperate with every prosecution, including putting at their disposal all company records. He openly acknowledged to the general public that La Polar was an 'icon of corporate abuse' and that the fraud was 'the biggest financial cover-up in the history of the country'. Finally, he declared that the goal of La Polar's new leadership was to preserve the more than 7,000 jobs the company provided and eventually to recover the losses for the investors, emphasizing that if SERNAC's class action went forward, the company would go bankrupt and the 900,000 potentially affected consumers—the company's own estimate—would not be redressed. This cleverly gave the impression that all these consumers needed to be compensated, when in fact only a fraction of that number would turn out to be creditors of La Polar. However, by increasing instead of decreasing the size of the conflict and by shifting the blame to the group of executives that were already being prosecuted, Barros was able to relieve pressure on the company and soften the administrative measures against it (Emol.com, 2011; Emol-.com, 2012).

In the meantime, on the class action front, instead of untangling, things were becoming more complex. To start with, SERNAC was overwhelmed. The media turmoil mobilized more than 30,000 of La Polar's customers who contacted the agency claiming compensation. This represented the largest group the agency had ever handled for a class action. Also, the political opposition was pressing for monetary compensation and accused SERNAC of being inefficient and lax with La Polar in the past. All this pressure pushed the agency to press for immediate monetary compensation without having established a legally formed class or a proper mechanism to monitor its development. The results on the ground were disastrous. Seizing the opportunity to step in, La Polar started to 'regularize' the affected consumers, which in practice meant that many uneducated consumers ended up with the prior agreed-upon renegotiations. SERNAC quickly stopped inviting the consumers to approach La Polar and the episode became part of the class procedure against the company.

To make things worse for SERNAC, right after it filed its class action in May 2011, a consumer NGO called *Fundación Chile Ciudadano* represented by Tomás Fabres joined the case with one client and then started a public campaign inviting the consumers to join the case as well.[12]

It took the agency some time to understand why anybody would invest in attracting consumers to join a case in an opt-out system where—according to the law—they did not need representation if the case was declared admissible. The answer became evident a few weeks later when Fabres, taking advantage of SERNAC's hesitation between prosecuting

[12] One of the contradictions of the Chilean class action procedure is that, even if it is an opt-out system, consumers can join the case as parties with their own lawyers. *See* Barroilhet, 2012, 289 (f. 49). *Fundación Chile Ciudadano* was not a newcomer on the consumer protection scene. The NGO had acted with SERNAC in 2007 to stop abusive practices from cemeteries, in a case also led by Fabres.

La Polar at all costs or preserving jobs, and having acquired a considerable number of individual clients, asked the judge to be named the class counsel.

For the judge, the decision regarding the class counsel was an easy one. On one side there was an agency that initiated the case but seemed trapped in political turmoil and was not actively inviting the consumers to come forward, something that could become crucial if the case reached a compensation stage. And on the other side there was an energetic lawyer who upheld his aggressive speech against the company in every forum and was by then the attorney for three consumer associations and more than 1,000 individual clients who had come to *Fundación Chile Ciudadano* seeking legal representation. Three months after the complaint had been filed by SERNAC and right after it was declared admissible in August 2011, Fabres became the class counsel.

Fabres' nomination as class counsel dismayed SERNAC. The agency could not allow itself to be relegated to a secondary position in its own case and quickly tried to regain traction by establishing alliances with other consumer associations that were not represented by Fabres and by promising the public it would prosecute La Polar even if it meant that the company would go bankrupt. It also invited the consumers to keep filing claims in its online database, something the agency had previously considered unnecessary after the case was admitted. However, no matter how hard SERNAC tried, the Court of Appeals did not reverse the civil judge's decision to allow the case to move forward with Fabres as class counsel

In Fabres' hands the case took a different direction. He let SERNAC continue to handle the courtroom work, something the agency was forced to do anyway because it involved the officers' administrative responsibility. In the meantime, he focused on getting La Polar to settle the case. For him the value of being the class counsel was not to be able to litigate the case, but to have the power to end it through a settlement. While continuing to attack La Polar publicly, he decided to also attack the company on two judicial fronts parallel to the class action. First, he started handing his most grievous individual cases to other lawyers for them to try for a profit, using the individual procedure of the Consumer Law which allows the plaintiffs to claim moral damages and the full amount of the generic fines of the Consumer Law. Allegedly, these cases belonged to the class action, but the accumulation procedure is cumbersome and thus is not enforced. Fabres wanted to show La Polar that individual cases were harmful in the pursuit of leveraging a global settlement. Second, he tried to stifle La Polar financially by filing motions for provisional remedies and injunctions that would prevent the company from negotiating its consumer credits with the factoring industry.

Fabres' strategies were partially successful. In the months after he took over the case, several individual cases ended with exorbitant moral damages for the consumers even in cases in which, after adjustments, the consumers remained as debtors of the company. Also, the injunction was granted at least once for all his clients and he was planning on trying it again to extend its scope to the universe of cases that, according to La Polar, could potentially include more than 900,000 affected consumers. Chile has no formal discovery procedure and at that time nobody other than La Polar knew how many consumers were affected by the re-negotiations and what the financial status of the company was. Hence all the information provided by Barros to inhibit administrative actions against La Polar was new information that Fabres could use to support injunctions against the company. In this way, Fabres turned Barros' heretofore-successful media strategy against the company on the judicial front.

Fabres' intervention was pivotal in La Polar's decision to settle the case. His aggressive strategy was an ongoing threat to La Polar that was harming the ability of La Polar's current leadership to present the company as a victim of its former executives in order to soften administrative actions against it. It was also hindering the company's efforts to encapsulate the conflict and keep it out of the media so that it could still attract new investors. If Barros and his team wanted to raise the capital that the company needed to survive, the contingency that the case produced needed to be limited by a settlement. Fabres understood this fact well and this is why keeping the case alive in the media in a more aggressive way than SERNAC was key to his strategy.

Not surprisingly, once La Polar decided to negotiate, it did not approach Fabres but instead approached SERNAC, the agency that had initiated the case and that could better shield the agreement from the consumers' dissatisfaction. The agency had taken over other cases in the past, such as the VTR case described earlier, so there was no reason for La Polar to think that the agency would reject its approaches. However SERNAC did that several times. According to a former official, the agency was 'ideologically blocked' against La Polar. To be fair to SERNAC, it had tried approaching La Polar twice before in the collective mediation and in the voluntary compensation scheme at the beginning of the case, and both attempts had backfired, legally and politically. Also, SERNAC's officials did not feel they could settle a case in which a private foundation's attorney was the class counsel. This blockade forced

Barros' team to try the only alternative they had: approach the more flexible private counterpart that Fabres represented.

Fabres was receptive to La Polar's approach, but cleverly, the company only agreed to start negotiating a formal settlement with the class counsel if he could bring the gatekeeper-agency onboard. Yet, following what had been a prickly relation between the agency and the legal entrepreneur throughout the case, SERNAC declined to meet with him. Believing that he had La Polar at his mercy, Fabres then tried to approach SERNAC through seasoned politicians that could exert some pressure on the agency. These individuals told Fabres that he could move on with the settlement negotiations because the agency was going to be forced to accept the settlement as long as it was fair and included certain minimal compensation.

Fabres and La Polar engaged in negotiations for weeks between March and April 2012. They agreed on an elaborate compensation scheme that, first, reversed all the fraudulent renegotiations, special interest charges, renegotiation fees, fines and collection fees, to the moment in time before the first renegotiation for each consumer. Once the original debts were determined, a special interest rate, lower than the average market rate, would be applied and the total would be brought to their present value. The debts calculated in this fashion would then be reduced by the consumers' actual payments, also at their present value. Once these sums were established, the consumers would be sorted into different sub-classes, depending on whether they ended up being debtors or creditors of La Polar. Creditors would be compensated with the full amount in cash, and debtors would be given 24 months to pay at an additional 20 percent discounted rate if they paid within six months. The parties estimated that 143,000 clients would be creditors for a total of $27 million, and another 851,000 would remain debtors. The agreement included a fund of approximately $200,000 for special cases, and granted *Fundación Chile Ciudadano* approximately $1.8 million for expenses, which included monitoring costs, litigation costs, and Fabres and his team attorneys' fees, all conditional on the shareholders' approval of an increase in the company's capital and—off the record—on SERNAC's acquiescence. The latter was required because La Polar didn't want to risk SERNAC using its gatekeeping powers to continue the case after the settlement, something they believed the agency might do, given its relation with Fabres and the potential shortcomings of the settlement.

During the time Fabres and La Polar were negotiating, SERNAC remained reluctant to meet with La Polar. Yet, the politicians with influence over SERNAC that Fabres had approached were clever and would not allow SERNAC to be weakened while under their watch. Their advice to SERNAC officials was straightforward: if Fabres already had a settlement, settling was going to be inevitable and the agency's only option was to better Fabres' settlement.

However straightforward the politicians' 'recommendation', SERNAC's officials remained reluctant to approach La Polar. The agency needed one last push to action and this push was the comprehensive settlement of La Polar with *Fundación Chile Ciudadano* leaked to SERNAC by La Polar as soon as it was drafted. With the threat of this settlement becoming public, which was a requirement of the stock market's regulation, SERNAC first secured the agreement of the securities regulatory agency to temporarily delay disclosure and then negotiated its own settlement in less than ten days. As advised by the savvy politicians, the agency made improvements to the agreement that Fabres and La Polar had drafted; it asked for 36 months instead of 24 for the debtors to repay their debts, increased the discount for debtors from 20 to 30 percent if they paid within the six months, and added a $30 bonus payable in cash to the consumer-creditors' subclass and deducted from consumer-debtors' debts. The $30 bonus, which did not appear on Fabres' agreement had a clear origin. The text of SERNAC's agreements was explicit:

> This proposal does not involve in any way attorney's fees for the plaintiffs, which should be not considered surrendered, but transferred to the consumers affected and as a part of their compensations agreed upon in this proposal.[13]

SERNAC's choice of words had clear intentions: to gain distance from Fabres and his ilk and to provide a basis to shame Fabres for being profit-motivated once the competing agreements came to light. This was revealed in a later press release in which SERNAC presented itself as an efficient and powerful agency that protected all without seeking a profit (El Mercurio, 2012).

SERNAC's agreement caught Fabres off guard. Knowing Cortés' experience in the VTR case, he anticipated that SERNAC could try to

---

[13] Translation by the author from the original text:

'Esta propuesta de conciliación no conlleva en forma alguna el pago de costas judiciales para la parte demandante, las que para todos los efectos no se entenderán renunciadas sino que traspasadas en beneficio de los consumidores afectados e incorporadas a los montos acordados en el marco de ésta propuesta de conciliación.' *See* Agreement La Polar-SERNAC, informed by *Hecho Esencial de 22 de Mayo de 2012 de La Polar a Superintendente de Valores y Seguros.*

settle the case before he did. If that were the case, he was prepared to defend his position as class counsel and press for a better deal. Yet, he had not expected La Polar to offer the agency a parallel agreement that included compensation for the absent members of the class that he believed he represented. However this was exactly what happened.[14] On 22 May 2012, La Polar informed the market in separate letters to the *Superintendente de Valor y Seguros*, the securities regulator, that it had reached an agreement with *Fundación Chile Ciudadano*—which included expenses and attorneys' fees for Fabres—and a separate agreement with SERNAC that included a $30 bonus for the consumers and no expenses or attorney's fees. Having reached these two agreements but not knowing which would ultimately prevail, the management team focused on raising capital for the 'New La Polar'. That day La Polar's shares spiked by 5.71 percent (Estrategia, 2012).

At that point the judge's path was unclear. Was she going to favor her chosen class counsel and his agreement or was she going to accept SERNAC's competing agreement? The doubt caused Fabres to rush to the court to show *Fundación Chile Ciudadano*'s agreement in the hope that this would keep him in control of the case. However, this proved a fatal mistake. The judge interpreted the presentation as a settlement proposal for the class action procedure and rejected it. According to her ruling, the case could not be settled until the period of 20 days to opt-out, after the news media invited the consumers to do so, had expired. Furthermore, she expressed her desire to have both SERNAC and the class counsel agree on a global solution and that the solution should not be conditional on the shareholders' approval.[15] This ruling gave SERNAC the opportunity to withhold its agreement and save it from the same fate (Cooperativa.cl, 2012). Moreover, it gave both SERNAC and La Polar

---

[14] SERNAC justified the inclusion of the absent members of the class in its agreement on a textual interpretation of the judge's rectifying ruling over her nomination of Fabres as class counsel. In the ruling, the judge said that Fabres was the common procurator for 'all natural persons, consumer associations that had become parties or will become parties in the case, with the sole exception of SERNAC' (translation by the author). According to SERNAC's interpretation, absent members of the class 'were not parties', therefore their representation remained with the agency. *See* the rectification, Primer Juzgado Civil de Santiago (J. Civ. Stgo) [First Civil Court of Santiago], 6 de Septiembre de 2011, rol de la causa 12105-2011, 'Servicio Nacional del Consumidor con Inversiones C.S.G.S.A.'.

[15] *See* Primer Juzgado Civil de Santiago (J. Civ. Stgo) [First Civil Court of Santiago], 30 de Mayo de 2012, rol de la causa 12105-2011, 'Servicio Nacional del Consumidor con Inversiones C.S.G.S.A.' §3, 5.

confidence that the judge was going to uphold a future settlement that was not conditional upon the shareholders' approval and that Fabres, disallowed by SERNAC's media strategy, the press and several consumer associations because of what they considered exorbitant expenses and because of the 'opportunistic-by-comparison' and failed agreement, was going to be excluded if he did not collaborate in the settlement that they were going to negotiate.

The judge's rulings on Fabre's team presentation triggered a new round of negotiations that started in August 2012 and this led to a new agreement that, once approved by the shareholders' extraordinary meeting, was presented to her in the mandatory conciliation hearing that the class action procedure requires after the opt-out period had expired. This time the class counsel, who was fighting privately for the expenses relegated to a secondary role, concurred with everything that SERNAC's agreement contained. The judge accepted the agreement in December 2012.[16]

Up until now *Fundación Chile Ciudadano* and their attorney have only received a small portion of the expenses and fees that were advanced to them the day they signed the agreement which the judge later rejected as a settlement. The La Polar case is still ongoing at the time of this book's publication, and probably will be for several more years as the parties try to figure out how to implement the agreement and deal with other problems that arose later. One thing is certain though—after the agreement was approved, La Polar effectively limited the contingency of new injunctions and the potential fines. Investors reacted happily with a 4.1 percent increase in the price of shares that day.

ASSESSMENT OF SERNAC'S BEHAVIOR IN THESE CASES

Class actions are complex legal transplants. Depending on how a class action procedure is designed and implemented, it may fit smoothly into a jurisdiction's legal regime or it may (inadvertently or not) create contradictory rules or loopholes that create opportunities for judges to craft additional rules and for lawyers to shape outcomes to their own ends (Hensler, 2016).

---

[16] *See* resolution approving the SERNAC's agreement in Primer Juzgado Civil de Santiago (J. Civ. Stgo) [First Civil Court of Santiago], 10 de Diciembre de 2012, rol de la causa 12105-2011, 'Servicio Nacional del Consumidor con Inversiones C.S.G.S.A.'.

In the VTR case, the Consumer Law's fines that were enacted prior to the class action procedure that Cortés used to pressure the company produced such an opening. If the judges had decided that these fines were applicable to each case on a class basis, they would have created a huge incentive for the defendants to avoid judgments and to settle their cases (Fernandez, 2008, 2). This uncertainty, later clarified by the majority of the courts as being in favor of applying one fine for the whole class, prevented other plaintiffs from using it. In the La Polar case, the loopholes were the Consumer Law's individual procedures that were never fully coordinated with the class action and the provisional remedies and injunctions of the Code of Civil Procedure that are applicable to all procedures unless expressly prohibited, which Fabres used to stifle La Polar. The need to clear out these contingencies, added to the size of the case and media pressure, led the company to agree to the compensation that the plaintiffs were demanding.

The previous circumstances explain why—in a country where class actions were designed to be a ritualistic procedure in the hands of the agency that lobbied for them—sophisticated private attorneys became involved. But they cannot explain SERNAC's behavior in the cases. To understand that, it is necessary to understand SERNAC's normal intervention—that is, when there are no sophisticated private attorneys exploiting loopholes against a future or existing defendant.

In the normal scenario, what corporations want from SERNAC is clear: SERNAC's involvement gives the defendants the highest value for their money (or their coupons) once they have decided to redress the consumers. The agency carries a well-respected name and has fought enough sincere battles with corporations to shield agreements from public criticism. Even if it did not have gatekeeping powers, settling with SERNAC or getting its stamp of approval will be the dominant strategy for the defendants whenever possible.

Whether the agency demands enough from the culpable defendants—indeed whether it even possesses the technical capacity or tools to press the defendants for more when it considers the defendants' offer insufficient—is another matter. First, the agency is understaffed and has not developed a particularly sophisticated expertise in negotiations or class action litigation. Second, the director of the agency has little political incentive to expedite the litigation because definitive judgments will almost always take longer than the director's term of office. The average litigation lasts well beyond four years, and the director's term is usually the same as the president who appointed him or her, which is four years. Also compensation for small-value claims and the imposition of ridiculous fines is hardly an attractive announcement to make years after the complaint. This explains why SERNAC rarely files class actions immediately but instead deploys collective mediations, a form of 'understanding' in which the agency temporarily trades its prerogative to sue for some forms of redress that are often favorable to corporations when compared to potential exposure in individual cases. These collective mediations allow the agency to claim or 'communicate' that it has obtained redress for the consumers which helps it to preserve its most valuable asset: its public image.

Compared with the scenario just described, the extraordinary cases presented in this chapter were tremendous opportunities for SERNAC. They offered the chance to obtain the immediate and substantive results that the agency seeks in each of its cases, but that are rarely possible given the weak legal tools at its disposal and the 'unwritten' rule against pushing the boundaries of interpretation as the private attorneys were able to do in these cases.

The question that remains, however, is why SERNAC knowingly took credit that was not its due for bringing the defendants to their knees when it could have limited itself to monitoring the fairness of the settlement agreements. The answer involves several cultural and institutional aspects of SERNAC.

On the cultural side, SERNAC is full of faithful zealots and advocates of consumer rights. Many of them are frustrated because they know they have blunt weapons and little space to use them creatively (that is, in ways unforeseen by Congress and the government) against what they consider to be widespread abuses. Fueling this frustration is the fact that they are often sidelined by more powerful agencies like the telecommunications or banking agencies that, unlike SERNAC, have rule-making and adjudication powers and constantly engage with potential defendants. Thus, when corporations are (or expect to be) sued in large class actions and come knocking on SERNAC's door to offer more serious compensations than the agency would normally obtain in its collective mediations, the temptation to respond, ignoring whoever pushed them to the doorstep, is enormous. And it also seems righteous for SERNAC's officials, who believe corporations should come to them to repent and offer their penitence. These officials see themselves as abnegated public servants who, unlike the private enforcers, have committed to fulfill the sacred mission of protecting the consumers' interests.

On the institutional side, SERNAC competes with other agencies for influence and relevance within the administration, and with private enforcers for its public image. Its advantages in this competition are its constant presence in the media and its undisputed position as an uncompromising consumer defender that can provide the best possible compensation within a period when it still matters, politically speaking. If private enforcers surpass SERNAC in the media, like Fabres clearly did in the La Polar case, or if courts and class actions start to be perceived as the institutions where the consumers can find substantive and timely relief, as could have happened if VTR had been sentenced by the courts, then SERNAC would become largely irrelevant within the administration and more likely to be sidelined by other agencies.

To be fair, SERNAC has done much for the consumers in Chile. In particular, it has provided a powerful balance against other agencies' practices that more often than not prefer to ignore the consumers' statutory rights or look the other way when the consumers are not able to voice their claims strongly enough. SERNAC performs this task silently and informally through meetings and phone calls to avoid creating turmoil inside the government to which it belongs and to which it is politically bound. Yet, the cases in this chapter show that SERNAC's agency comes at a cost. SERNAC's power to perform this balancing task rests on SERNAC's matchlessness when it comes to defending the consumers. This balancing power is likely to decrease if consumer associations or charismatic individuals displace SERNAC. This issue was most clearly seen in the La Polar case, where Fabres' litigious strategy forcefully displaced SERNAC's leadership in the mass media and threatened its status as the country's strongest protector of the consumers.

CONCLUSION

While using agencies to control private enforcement might be an attractive idea to get the benefits of private enforcement and the accountability of public enforcement, giving these agencies preeminence and gatekeeping powers might not be enough to strike the desired balance. Public agencies have their own problems as enforcers and if not forced to coordinate with private enforcement, they might prey on them instead of directing their efforts against the corporate defendants. Contextual factors that might explain this harmful behavior are:

(1) the relative chance of success of non-coordinated public enforcement when compared to sophisticated private enforcement;
(2) the independence and the status of the public agency in charge of controlling class actions' private enforcement; and
(3) the importance of class actions in the agency's toolkit and its closeness to the agency's institutional mission.

Together, they provide for the following: in a country where class actions are a cumbersome procedure offering little chance of success unless some loophole is exploited, a politically-bound agency with few other powers which lives in competition with other agencies, cannot risk being displaced by aggressive private class action enforcers who threaten to supplant it in the fulfillment of its perceived institutional mission.

REFERENCES

Alexei Barrionuevo, *Abuses by Credit Issuers in Chile and Brazil Snare Consumers*, The New York Times, 23 July 2011

Agustin Barroilhet, *Class Actions in Chile*, (2012) 18 Law and Business Review of the Americas 275

David Freeman Engstrom, *Agencies as Litigation Gatekeepers*, (2013) 123 Yale Law Journal 616

Gonzalo Fernandez, *Class Actions: Are They an Effective Access to Justice Tool?* (2008) presentation IBA Association Pro Bono Conference, Buenos Aires, Argentina

Antonio Gidi, *Class Actions in Brazil—A Model for Civil Law Countries*, (2003) 51 American Journal of Comparative Law 311

Martin Gubbin, *Chile*, Country report, (2014) available at www.globalclassactions.stanford.edu

Deborah Hensler, *Introduction*, (2016) Ch. 1, this book

Matthew Stephenson, *Public Regulation of Private Enforcement: The Case for Expanding the Role of Administrative Agencies*, (2005) 91 Virginia Law Review 93

***

A un año del terremoto La Polar: Casi 500 querellas, 10 formalizados, multas por $2.851 millones, 2.600 notas de prensa / *A year since the La Polar earthquake: Almost 500 prosecutions, 10 indicted, fines for over $2.851, 2600 press notes*, LaSegunda.com, 18 May 2012

Acuerdo entre La Polar con el Sernac y clientes está supeditado al éxito del aumento de capital / Agreement between La Polar and SERNAC is conditioned to the approval of a capital increase, Estrategia, 24 May 2012

Acuerdo entre Sernac y La Polar incorporará 800 millones que se le pagarían a Fundación de Fabres / Agreement between Sernac and La Polar included 800 million pesos ($1.8 million) that would be paid to Fabres' foundation, El Mercurio, 1 June 2012, available at http://diario.elmercurio.com/detalle/index.asp?id={efd925a5-a694-4bcd-826a-655eebc6fe68}

Anadeus visita Sernac / Anadeus visits SERNAC

SERNAC, Agenda Noticiosa, 6 February 2006

Presidente de la compañía: La Polar hizo el maquillaje más grande de una empresa en Chile / President of the company: La Polar made the biggest cover-up of a company in Chile, Emol.com, 27 October 2011

Presidente de La Polar: Si la empresa quiebra no hay plata para pagar la multa/ President of La Polar: If the company goes bankrupt there will no money to pay the fines, Emol.com, 18 January 2012

Revés de VTR en demanda colectiva de usuarios/VTR suffers drawback in class action, El Mercurio, 15 March 2006

Sernac modificará acuerdo con La Polar para evitar rechazo de la Justicia/ SERNAC will modify the agreement with La Polar to avoid justice's rejection, Cooperativa.cl, 1 June 2012

VTR: Anuncia solución a consumidores/VTR announces solution to consumers SERNAC, Agenda Noticiosa, 27 January 2006

PART V

Conclusion

18. Class actions in context

Deborah R. Hensler

INTRODUCTION

Legal scholars who write about class actions, group litigation and other collective litigation focus on statutes and rules. Public policy-makers who debate adopting collective procedures focus on consequences. Neither scholars nor policy-makers typically pay much attention to the circumstances that give rise to the mass claims that the procedures address, the cultural values and institutions that shape beliefs about when people and businesses should be compensated for losses, the economic arrangements that facilitate or deter litigation and the politics that shape decisions about who will be responsible for paying compensation to whom and how much.

The case study research reported in this book highlights the importance of these contextual variables for understanding the functions collective litigation plays in different legal regimes and polities and the roles of parties, lawyers, judges, politicians and civil society in shaping litigation. By juxtaposing the stories of how collective litigation arose and evolved in different contexts, it is possible to discern both the common features of different jurisdictions' collective litigation processes and the importance of regime-specific characteristics in determining the outcomes of collective litigation. Close observation of class actions and non-representative group procedures reveals a more complicated picture of the challenges mass claims present than is typically suggested by the debates over the adoption of collective litigation procedures.

Qualitative studies of a small number of mass litigations leave many empirical questions unanswered. How many such lawsuits are there? What types of injuries are most (and least) likely to lead to mass litigation? How are the benefits and costs of various forms of collective litigation distributed? The answers to such questions await quantitative research. But the rich narratives about litigation in diverse legal, cultural, economic and political circumstances presented in this book offer lessons for policy-makers and suggest avenues for future scholarship. This chapter discusses both, and ends with an epilogue about the process of conducting collaborative comparative research.

LESSONS FOR POLICYMAKERS

When it Comes to Efficiency, Collective Litigation Procedures are Not Created Equal

When the resolution of a common issue such as the application of the relevant liability rule has a dispositive effect on many claims that arose under the same factual circumstances, it seems sensible from an efficiency standpoint to resolve that issue once for all claims. However, it is possible to design a collective litigation procedure that introduces so much complexity into litigation that it outweighs savings due to aggregation. It is also possible to implement a collective litigation procedure in a way that preserves so much of the individualization that is traditional in ordinary litigation that the potential gains from aggregation are unrealized.

The Deutsche Telekom securities litigation (Chapter 13) illustrates this lesson. The 'model case' procedure (KapMuG) developed to speed the litigation specifies an appellate process that has resulted in multiple trips up and down the court ladder to resolve key issues. The result is that the case lingers on at the time of this writing, more than ten years after its inception. Moreover, although the procedure provided for decision-making on a single 'model case', judges were required to record the decision in the model case in the hundreds of individual case files that were registered as part of the proceeding, defeating some of the benefits of aggregation.

In contrast, the US multi-district litigation procedure (MDL), another form of group proceeding, is used efficiently in US federal courts, as illustrated by the Toyota unintended acceleration litigation and the litigation arising from the British Petroleum oil spill (Chapter 5). US judges assigned to oversee an MDL issue decisions on pleadings, discovery and summary judgment motions that apply by law to all the individual claims that have been consolidated for pretrial management. No individual record-keeping is required to implement the intent of the legislators who enacted the MDL statute. Only final decisions on the merits are reserved for individual judgment.

However, sometimes ad hoc processes may prove more efficient than special collective procedures. The English property damage litigation that arose as a result of the Buncefield explosion (Chapter 15) illustrates this lesson. Over time some English judges and lawyers have decided that in some circumstances judicial case management is more efficient than the English group litigation procedure (GLO) that bears some resemblance to the German and American group proceedings.

In contrast to all these group litigation approaches, class action procedures create a single lawsuit. Absent class members' opt-in or opt-out, decisions typically must be made within a limited time period, minimizing uncertainty about who is bound by these decisions. However, as illustrated in the case study of the Royal Dutch Shell securities litigation (Chapter 8), class actions may require extensive—and expensive—notice campaigns that introduce an element into collective litigation that is not present in group litigation procedures or judicial case management. Not all class actions proceed swiftly. (However, none of the class actions described in this book took as long as the Deutsche Telekom proceeding.)

Efficient dispute resolution—whether within or outside the court—can come at the price of accuracy, as illustrated in the British Petroleum litigation (Chapter 5). The private Gulf Claims Facility paid over $6 billion to more than 169 000 claimants in less than two years. But the potential of 'easy money' attracted thousands of fraudulent claims as well as many honest claims that would likely not have survived formal legal tests had they been litigated, increasing the total compensation paid by the facility.

Designing aggregative procedures that achieve an optimal balance between efficiency and accuracy is hard. Optimal design may not be possible because of legal rules that require or prohibit certain procedural options. Moreover, an aggregative procedure that makes sense on paper may not achieve its desired goals in practice. Whether a procedure will achieve the balance its designers sought depends on how it is implemented by those charged with doing so and how those it is intended to serve respond to it. The responses of both groups are shaped not merely by formal legal rules but also by culture, economic incentives and politics.

Effective implementation of aggregative procedures depends critically on judges' perceptions of their role: where judges pro-actively manage cases—often termed 'case management'—the procedures are more likely to be implemented effectively. Adopting case management techniques may require a shift in judicial culture and specialized training.

Mass Media Set the Stage for Mass Claims

Law students are taught that substantive legal doctrine determines who has a claim against whom and for what, and procedural rules determine how a justiciable claim will be litigated. But when mass losses or injuries occur, mass media often clamor for investigation and draw (sometimes hasty) judgments about causation and fault that encourage litigation and compensation, even when the claims do not satisfy exacting legal standards. Available evidence suggests that protracted media attention to mass injuries and losses and the oft-times dramatic responses to these spur litigation. The influence of a particular procedural mechanism on claiming behavior pales beside the effects of mass media.

The effects of media on mass claiming are not limited to certain types of jurisdiction or particular types of loss. In the trans-national Royal Dutch Shell securities litigation (Chapter 8) and the US Toyota unintended acceleration litigation (Chapter 5) persistent reporting may have contributed to quicker corporate responses to management failures and more vigorous regulatory investigations. In the Toyota case these in turn encouraged thousands of complaints to the regulatory agency. In the English Buncefield explosion, media coverage contributed to quick corporate acceptance of responsibility for losses (Chapter 15). National media coverage of contamination in the Gulf of Mexico following the BP oil spill increased public attention to the spill and likely contributed to President Obama's decision to press the company's CEO to set up a $20 billion compensation fund (Chapter 5). The Chilean La Polar case (Chapter 17) generated 2,000 newspaper articles and occupied the national political agenda for three weeks, ultimately moving the Minister of Interior to issue a call to compensate consumers. The involvement of a media celebrity in a public relations campaign to encourage ordinary German citizens to purchase Deutsche Telekom shares may have contributed to investors' perception that they were owed compensation when the share price collapsed (Chapter 13).

Notwithstanding the importance of crisis management and media relations to parties and lawyers engaged in mass litigation, no law school offers courses in this topic; nor has it attracted serious legal academic attention. But the role of media in shaping mass litigation has drawn the attention of large corporations that are most frequently the targets of such litigation, and the large law firms that usually represent them, many of which have created formal crisis-management practice groups. Smaller firms that represent plaintiffs exclusively in jurisdictions that have divided bars are unlikely to have the resources to deploy the full range of strategies that public relations firms and law firms offer corporate clients. But the most experienced plaintiff firms, especially in the United States (US), have a sophisticated understanding of how media coverage shapes government responses to mass injuries and losses, and they use this knowledge to shape the litigation environment.

Judges are the least comfortable with the media firestorms that frequently accompany mass litigation. Formally judges are presumed to be 'above the fray' and most strive to maintain their distance from media representatives. Whether and to what extent judicial decision-making is responsive to media portrayals of mass claims and mass litigation is unknown.

Mass Claims Incentivize Legal Adaptation

There is an extensive literature on societal responses to mass injury victims. Survivors of terrorist attacks and natural disasters tug on the public's sympathies, which often leads to an outpouring of relief aid from private and public sources. Key to arousing public sympathy is the perception that the survivors' injuries and losses were a result of bad luck or someone else's incompetence or malfeasance rather than the survivors' own behavior. When the circumstances surrounding the injury are ambiguous, survivors are less likely to be perceived as 'victims' and more likely to be seen as unworthy to receive aid and left to fend for themselves. When mass injuries lead to protracted and disputatious compensation processes, those who were at first viewed as worthy victims may come to be seen as greedy supplicants or perhaps fraudsters (Barrett, 2005; Dauber, 2003–2004; Tugend, 2013).

Whether claiming is seen as righteous or exploitative is culturally determined. Today, even in capitalist societies, there seems to be a tendency to favor redress for ordinary people—'mom and pop' investors, pensioners, middle- and lower-income consumers and small-business owners—who have suffered losses in their dealings with large corporations, even when the terms of the transactions between such citizens and corporations arguably do not justify legal redress. However, sympathy for individuals who may not have understood the terms of a contract they entered into does not necessarily extend to providing collective redress to a class of similarly situated individuals. In part as a result, the litigation described in this book did not always—or even often—lead to formal legal victories. However, the litigation sometimes encouraged doctrinal changes and procedural innovations that tilted the legal regime towards the claimants. Moreover, as lawyers became more familiar with mass litigation, some began to change the way they practice law. In some instances, these changes may have shifted the course of subsequent litigation.

The Vie d'Or litigation (Chapter 6) offers a vivid example of the potential of sympathetic claimants to shift legal norms. The 11,000 Dutch consumers who lost their investments and life insurance policies when

Vie d'Or was declared insolvent were relatively affluent. But because they were mainly independent contractors and small business owners, they lacked the safety net afforded to government and corporate employees. As the insolvency litigation ground on, their plight attracted media and ultimately political attention. The Public Prosecutor was permitted to file a request for an inquiry into Vie d'Or's affairs with the Enterprise Chamber of the Amsterdam Court of Appeal, even though normally only company shareholders can file such requests. The public Insurance Regulator established and funded a special purpose foundation to represent the Vie d'Or claimants' interest in the litigation, the first time in the Netherlands that a public agency took such a step. Although the Dutch State contested its liability for the lax regulation that contributed to the fall of Vie d'Or all the way up to the Supreme Court and formally resisted public pressure to contribute to a settlement fund, behind the scenes the government eventually helped facilitate a collective settlement of the claims. Out of concern for its public image, the industry trade association contributed to the settlement fund, even though it was not a party to the litigation.

Germany's group litigation procedure (KapMuG) was adopted specifically to expedite the resolution of claims for financial loss filed by thousands of ordinary citizens who had been encouraged to buy shares in the newly privatized Deutsche Telekom company in an era when it is was uncommon for middle class Germans to invest on the stock exchange (Chapter 13). When the shareholders turned to their legal expenses insurance policies to cover their litigation costs, their insurers argued that the policies' language excluded their claims. Rejecting the insurers' argument, the Court ruled that the exclusive contract language the insurers relied on did not apply when the claims at issue alleged prospectus liability in the context of retirement savings—which fit precisely the circumstances of the Deutsche Telekom shareholders. Although the KapMuG was primarily intended to assist the courts in dealing with the flood of claims that followed the ruling on legal expenses insurance, over the longer term the new procedure came to be seen as helping to assure access to court for investors. To guarantee that all of the claimants whose cases were registered in the model case proceeding were accorded their constitutional right to participate in the trial of their claims, the Deutsche Telekom court created a password-protected on-line database—a first for German courts—that allowed all claimants to access court documents, a procedure that was subsequently incorporated in the KapMuG when it was revised and extended in 2012.

The $20 billion settlement fund established by BP to compensate property owners and commercial fisherman for loss of income due to contamination from the Gulf oil spill (Chapter 5) was less a consequence of legal doctrine than a result of political pressure on behalf of those who suffered losses, most of whom were small business owners and independent operators. Although BP was liable for damages under the Oil Pollution Act, the statutory cap on damages was a mere $75 million. Although BP might have chosen to establish a compensation fund as an alternative to litigation under other circumstances, it is unlikely that the company would have moved so swiftly and so generously—or that President Obama would have pressed them to do so—were it not for the characteristics of those who had suffered losses. The special claim to compensation that Gulf residents (arguably) had was invoked in an eloquent White House address by President Obama.

Lawyers also change their practices in response to mass litigation. Until recently, firms specializing in representing plaintiffs were uncommon in civil law jurisdictions. Now that has begun to change. A Dutch lawyer who represented the special purpose foundation established to consummate the trans-border settlement negotiated by Royal Dutch Shell and US plaintiff lawyers left his former law firm to establish a new firm modeled along the lines of a US plaintiff law firm. Firms specializing in mass litigation played a prominent role in the Belgian L&H securities litigation (Chapter 14) and the German Deutsche Telekom litigation (Chapter 13). In Chile an entrepreneurial lawyer came forward to prosecute the consumer class action against La Polar (Chapter 17).

Agency Problems are Inherent in All Forms of Collective Litigation—and More Complicated than Generally Recognized

All litigation involving represented parties carries with it the potential for 'principal-agent' problems: the possibility of conflicts of interest between a lawyer and her client stemming from the fact that the lawyer's incentives are not perfectly aligned with the client's (Hay, 1997; Mnookin, 1993). Class actions have traditionally been viewed as presenting a higher risk of such problems (Coffee, 2000), indeed such a high risk that some believe class actions should be prohibited altogether. Some who support class actions in principle favor assigning the class representative role to specially-selected associations thought to be better at protecting the class' interests, or prohibiting certain types of class actions that are thought to be particularly prone to principal-agent problems, such as cases where each class member's monetary claim is very small.

Some critics of class actions prefer group litigation procedures in which each claimant is individually represented for resolving mass claims, believing that these procedures mitigate agency problems. However, the case studies illustrate that agency problems exist in all forms of collective litigation, not just class actions, and that the nature of these problems is more complicated than generally recognized.

At first glance, the Israeli securities class action *Shemesh v. Reichart* (Chapter 10) illustrates the paradigmatic principal-agent problem: a lawyer who pursues his own goal to the detriment of his class-member clients. In that long-running case, the class counsel refused to drop an appeal of a trial court ruling in favor of two defendants, notwithstanding the fact that the appellate litigation prevented class members from collecting compensation that had been extended to them in prior settlements with other defendants. But the principal-agent story in *Shemesh* had an unusual twist: by continuing to litigate, the lawyer not only delayed the payment of settlement funds to the class members for many years, he also delayed payment of his own fees and expenses. The class obtained a bit more in total compensation as a result of the protracted litigation but the class counsel himself arguably would have been better off financially if he had dropped his appeal. Asked by the researcher why he persevered with the case for such a long time, the lawyer asserted that he saw it as a duty to vindicate the class's claims against the non-settling defendants.

The Royal Dutch Shell case study (Chapter 8) illustrates one of the dangers of principal-agent problems in class actions: defendants may be able to play off entrepreneurial class action lawyers against each other in ways that may benefit the defendant more than the class members. The Royal Dutch Shell case was initially litigated in US federal court, even though the putative class comprised investors from all over the world. As required by the Securities Litigation Reform Act, the trial court judge appointed two pension funds as representative plaintiffs that together had the largest financial stakes in the litigation, and these funds' lawyers became class counsel. The effect of the appointment was to exclude law firms hired by other class members from becoming class counsel—and potentially earning very handsome fees. Objecting on principle to the notion of resolving the claims of non-US investors in a US court and seeking to limit the total amount required to resolve all claims, Shell's general counsel and its outside defense counsel negotiated a settlement of the non-US claims with one of the law firms that had been shut out of the class counsel role, and used the Netherlands settlement class procedure to resolve all of the non-US claims in the Amsterdam Court of Appeal. The result was to sharply reduce the value of the class action that was proceeding in the US court and hence the expected value of the class counsel's fees. The non-US investors were represented in the Amsterdam court by a special purpose foundation, whose lawyer was paid on an hourly basis. However, the US firm with which Shell negotiated the Dutch foreign investors' settlement received fees according to what they would have received for representing a US class in US courts. Because of uncertainty at the time as to whether the US court would retain jurisdiction over the non-US claims, it is not clear whether the foreign investors were better or worse off as a result of Shell striking this deal, but it clearly benefited the US law firm that lost the competition to be class counsel in the US class action

The Dutch Vie d'Or case (Chapter 6) and the Chilean La Polar case (Chapter 17) demonstrate that agency problems are not eliminated by laws favoring social associations or public agencies as class representatives. Perhaps because of concerns about the resources that would have been required to play a role in the litigation, the Dutch national consumer association did not come forward to represent the purchasers of Vie d'Or life insurance policies after the insurer became insolvent. Instead it fell to the public Insurance Regulator to appoint a special purpose foundation to represent the policy-holders and to fund the foundation. Concerned that their relationship with the Regulator might compromise its independence, the Foundation's board revised its articles of association to sever its relationship with the Regulator, a move the Regulator initially resisted. The history of the Vie d'Or Foundation suggests that its commitment to its independence stemmed more from the personal characteristics of its board members than from the special rules on class representation in the Netherlands.

Chile's class action law confers authority to bring class actions and also to intervene in class actions brought by private lawyers on SERNAC, the national consumer protection agency. The intent of this structure is to guard against perceived agency problems in private class actions. In the La Polar case, SERNAC used its power to negotiate a better settlement on behalf of the company's consumers than had been negotiated by a private lawyer who was appointed as class counsel. But SERNAC's efforts came in response to the private lawyer vigorously pursuing recompense for the class members, after SERNAC had presided over a mediation that produced scant benefits for the consumers who had been charged illegal fees. SERNAC's belated effort to strike a better deal for consumers seems to have been motivated by a desire to protect its own reputation as the Chilean consumers' champion. And by negotiating the settlement that was ultimately approved by the court, SERNAC denied the private lawyer the fees for his efforts—which had arguably set the stage for SERNAC's success—and in the long run may have disincentivized private lawyers from bringing class actions.

The BP oil spill case (Chapter 5) presented unusual principal-agent problems. The lawyers who brought a class action for economic loss on behalf of Gulf property owners and commercial fisherman charged Kenneth Feinberg, appointed by BP to administer the Gulf Claims Facility, with having a conflict of interest because he was handsomely compensated for his time and efforts by BP. Because Feinberg had previously administered similar claims facilities *pro bono* and became a national hero for his stewardship of the 9/11 Victims' Compensation Fund, the class action lawyers felt that the oil spill claimants needed to be put on notice that in this instance Feinberg was working for BP, which arguably gave him an incentive to offer less compensation than he might have if he were serving *pro bono*. Concerns about Feinberg's independence did not prevent more than 169,000 gulf residents and businesses from accepting compensation from the fund. However, the claims facility was ultimately replaced by a settlement fund established as a result of settling the parallel class action and Feinberg's position was terminated.

As is common in mass money damage class actions, the BP oil spill class members' interests were potentially adverse to each other: if BP set a cap on the compensation it was willing to pay to resolve the class action, whatever amounts were paid to some class members would leave less to be paid to others. US Supreme Court decisions have held that certification is usually inappropriate in such situations; at a minimum, the Court held that when class members have adverse interests, the trial judge should require that the class be divided into sub-classes, each with its own lawyer. However, the judge who presided over the BP class action did not require sub-classing. Concern that perceived conflicts within the economic class might derail certification and judicial approval of their negotiated settlement likely contributed to BP's agreement to an uncapped fund. Arguably when a fund is uncapped one class member's recompense has no effect on others'.

Having argued in favor of the proposed settlement at the district court, BP quickly reversed course when the amounts paid out by the fund administrator—whose appointment the company had supported—proved larger than BP had expected. Although formally a court officer (as the court retained jurisdiction), in practice the fund administrator was (like Feinberg) an agent of BP, as he was distributing their corporate funds. BP's attempts to undo the settlement terms and fire the fund administrator were turned away by the appellate courts on the grounds that the multinational corporation had been well represented during the settlement negotiations and must have understood the consequences of the settlement's terms.

In Canada (Chapter 11), the two case studies illustrate the conflicts of interest that can arise when lawyers' fees are contingent on the class' success and are deducted from the common fund to be distributed to the class. In the Atlas securities case, the judge rejected class counsel's fee request on the basis that it was too high relative to the outcome achieved for the class and ordered that a greater proportion of the settlement fund be paid to the class. Although the decision inured to the financial benefit of the class, lawyers for the class nevertheless appealed the ruling in an effort to promote their own financial self-interest. In the *Hislop* pension benefit case, the government defendant successfully argued that class counsel's contingency fee could not be deducted from the trial judgment as a result of pension law designed to protect pensioners from creditors. The legal maneuver created a conflict between counsel and the class members, forcing the attorneys to take collection proceedings against their clients, and causing one Crown lawyer interviewed for this book to opine that class actions create inherent conflicts of interest between lawyers and individual claimants.

To date, analysis of agency problems has been limited to those posed by the lawyer-class relationship in regimes that grant standing to class members. Scholarship on agency issues when standing is limited to ad hoc or pre-existing associations or government officials is sorely needed. Without such analysis, debates over standing rules for class actions will continue to rely on ideology and untested empirical assumptions.

Legal Financing Shapes Collective Litigation

In most societies, even those with the most plaintiff-friendly legal doctrine, when bad things happen to people their first thought is not about bringing a lawsuit against someone. Although the specter of a flood of frivolous litigation has been raised in virtually every jurisdiction that has debated adopting a class action procedure, the available evidence in the jurisdictions with the longest experience with class actions—the US, Australia, Canada and Brazil—does not support such fears. There are a variety of factors that militate against victims bringing suit, including victims' failure to recognize their legal rights, lack of information about how to access the courts and lack of disputatiousness. Perhaps most important though is perceived litigation cost.

Because of differences in legal financing rules, the expected costs of individual litigation differ substantially across jurisdictions. How legal financing rules affect the cost of collective litigation depends on how the financing rules intersect with the features of the collective litigation procedure (Chapter 7). In many jurisdictions that have adopted class actions, legal financing rules constrain their use, in some instances all but eliminating claimants' ability to use the procedure. If a representative plaintiff has to pay the class counsel on an hourly basis and also bear the risk of adverse costs, few individuals or associations are likely to step forward to play this role. The unattractiveness of the class representative role will be exacerbated if class members are under no obligation to contribute to legal expenses if the class prevails, a classic 'free rider' problem. Where the class counsel is allowed to represent the class on a 'no win, no pay' basis, thereby freeing the representative plaintiff from laying out funds, there may be few law firms that are able to front the costs of class litigation.

The case studies reflect two responses to addressing these obstacles. In Canada and the US, judges have crafted special fee rules for class actions that reward lawyers for assuming litigation risk and eliminate the 'free rider' problem. Judges calculate the fee amount either as a percentage of the compensation fund created when plaintiffs prevail in a damages class action or by totaling hourly fees and adding a premium (the 'multiplier') to reflect the lawyers' risk and quality of representation. Under equitable fund doctrine, class members all contribute proportionally to the lawyers' fee award, so there is no 'free rider' problem. In the US, class action fee rules facilitated the Toyota brake litigation in which the judge awarded class counsel $227 million in fees and expenses (Chapter 5). In Brazil, the new Consumer Code that shifted fees from class action plaintiffs helped facilitate the consumer association's lawsuit against tobacco manufacturers (Chapter 3).

In jurisdictions where legislatures and judges have been more wary of changing the conventional fee rules, lawyers and others have responded with 'work-arounds'. In Australia, third-party funders emerged to pay lawyer fees while the litigation is ongoing and assume the risk of adverse costs; as a result the opt-out class action modeled on the US procedure was converted to an opt-in procedure, a move that was ultimately endorsed by the High Court (Chapter 9). The acceptance of 'closed classes' in the Australian regime also addresses the 'free rider' problem. In Canada, two provinces adopted public funds to provide up-front litigation costs and guarantee adverse costs; the public funds are replenished by taking a share of monetary awards in successful class actions (Chapter 11). In the Royal Dutch Shell transnational securities class action litigated in the US and the Netherlands, the lawyers adopted a different kind of 'work-around': with the Amsterdam Court of Appeal's consent, US lawyers were paid on a 'percentage of fund' basis (as they would have been in a US court) for their contribution to settling the non-US claims, even though Dutch lawyers are not permitted by their professional responsibility rules to charge contingency fees (Chapter 8).

The development of special fee rules and institutional 'work-arounds' to address the constraints legal fees impose on class actions is another example of legal adaptation in response to mass claims pressure. Once rules and practices change for mass claims, the changes may migrate to other areas of law. Like the representative class action, third-party litigation funding is a legal transplant. Since its inception in Australia, litigation funding has spread to Europe and North America, where it has rapidly become a feature of general commercial litigation outside the collective litigation domain.

Litigation and Regulation are Symbiotically Related

As resistance to the adoption of class actions outside the US has diminished, one legal norm remains potent: the belief that private class actions (and private litigation generally) should not become an ancillary mechanism for enforcing market regulations. Although the 'private attorney general' theory—the notion that an important function of private litigation is to deter illegal behavior—is deeply entrenched in US legal scholarship and is also recognized in Australian and Canadian jurisprudence, it is fiercely contested in countries that have a long tradition of relying on public law enforcement. The public policy debate as well as some continental legal scholarship set litigation and regulation in opposition to each other. The case studies challenge this framing of an oppositional relationship between private litigation and public regulatory enforcement. In mass claims circumstances, criminal investigation, public agency enforcement actions and private damage litigation often proceed in parallel and influence each other.

In some of the cases described in this book, private litigation or the threat thereof incentivized government investigations. The Toyota brake litigation (Chapter 5) provided grist for media reports of automobile accidents allegedly traceable to brake design, which in turn gave rise to an extensive investigation by the US National Highway and Transportation Safety Administration and a high-profile congressional investigation. The Gulf oil spill class action (Chapter 5) was part of a complex web of public investigations by the US Congress, federal regulatory agencies and a bi-partisan Presidential Commission; criminal and civil enforcement actions by the US Department of Justice; damages litigation by state and local government entities and private corporations that sought compensation for clean-up costs; and lawsuits by private property owners, small businesses and independent contractors that claimed loss of income due to the spill. Proceeding in parallel with each other, these processes inevitably influenced each other.

Sometimes litigation described in this book contributed to the adoption of stricter regulatory standards. Regulatory reform in the face of litigation may reflect, in part, the desire of public regulators to protect their scope of authority and, ultimately, their institutional power. The Gulf oil spill, and subsequent public investigations and litigation, dramatically increased the legislative and executive branches' attention to the regulatory oversight mechanisms whose failure was determined to have contributed to the oil rig explosion. As a consequence, the pre-spill regulatory agency was eliminated and a new agency was established in its place. The Vie d'Or life insurance company insolvency litigation (Chapter 6) led to stricter regulation of life insurance products even as the State prevailed at the Supreme Court on its claim that consumers' losses were not attributable to lax regulation by the public Insurance Regulator. US litigation by private and public actors over contamination of water supplies by the gasoline additive MTBE contributed to changes in state regulations and federal law that ultimately eliminated the use of the gasoline additive, despite continuing fierce opposition from its manufacturers (Chapter 16). The Australian securities regulation agency, ASIC, played a novel role in class action litigation when it ruled on an interim basis that the litigation financing arrangement that the lawyer and class members had entered into with a third-party funder was not, as the defendant had charged, a violation of the federal Corporations Act. Later the relevant Minister introduced changes in regulation that made this clarification permanent (Chapter 9).

When they addressed the circumstances of mass claims, regulatory agencies and courts did not always arrive at consistent outcomes. To some this may reflect the failure of one or the other branch of government. But criminal prosecution, regulatory enforcement and private litigation respond to different incentives. The German Deutsche Telekom case study offers an interesting example of this. While the 'model case' proceeding was ongoing in the regional court, the public prosecutor was conducting a criminal investigation of Deutsche Telekom. That investigation ended without an indictment; however, both Deutsche Telekom and several of its directors paid substantial fines amounting to €5 million for the company. Although described as voluntary and paid to charities rather than the State, under German law such payments are considered an appropriate strategy for efficiently resolving large-scale criminal cases in complicated commercial matters, but should only be requested when the Public Prosecutor believes that a crime has been committed (Chapter 13). The prosecutor's assessment, however, was not matched by the High Court's ruling in the model proceeding many years later, which rejected most of the plaintiff's claims that Deutsche Telekom had violated securities regulations.

The Belgian L&H securities fraud case (Chapter 14) illustrates the complete melding of criminal and civil actions. At the time that the L&H case unfolded, the primary way for investors to claim redress was to 'piggy-back' their claims on the criminal case brought by the State. The judge's determination that 'deep pocket' corporate defendants were not criminally liable for the fraud meant that only the investors' claims against the criminally liable but judgment-proof individual defendants remained viable. Under Belgian law, it was left for the criminal judge to decide these civil claims after he issued judgment in the criminal case.

Collective Litigation Challenges Power Structures

Legal regimes reflect the distribution of power within societies. If large corporations hold sway, substantive legal doctrine will likely reflect their perceived interests. If worker organizations command political support, the law will grant employees protections they may not enjoy in societies where these organizations are less politically powerful. If civil society organizations skillfully mobilize their supporters, the law will be more likely to reflect their concerns. In sum, substantive legal doctrine in every jurisdiction reflects a balancing of interests that matches the jurisdiction's political power distribution.

In ordinary litigation, less powerful litigants are generally at a disadvantage (Galanter, 1974). By providing mechanisms for mobilizing the less powerful in a society, collective litigation procedures have the potential to disrupt the power structure. The fear that collective procedures will disrupt the economic, political and social status quo powers much of the opposition to adopting class actions outside the US as well as the efforts to restrict class certification within the US.

The Taiwanese class action brought by parking lot attendants against the Taipei municipal government (Chapter 4), the Brazilian class actions against tobacco corporations (Chapter 3) and the Canadian class action that sought recognition of gay partners' rights (Chapter 11) all provide different examples of the ways in which parties may use collective litigation to challenge the status quo. As private contractors, the Taiwanese workers were disfavored in comparison to public employees and struggled to unionize at time when the Taiwanese government was hostile to unions. The workers were ultimately able to organize and their new union engaged in a variety of public activities to improve the workers' economic situation, including bringing a class action for back pay. The dollar value of individual workers' claims was too small to justify individual litigation but when combined in a class action their total value was large enough that the municipality fiercely contested the litigation. Ultimately the workers won their case. But perhaps as a result, the union officials who led the fight lost their jobs—illustrating that it can also be dangerous to use class actions to take on powerful institutions.

Brazilian law has long permitted certain types of collective litigation. However, the corporate community viewed the 1990 adoption of a new consumer code as ushering in a new era for consumer class actions, which corporations fiercely resisted. Their fears were justified when an anti-smoking consumer association filed a class action against the Brazilian subsidiaries of multinational tobacco corporations. Not surprisingly, the tobacco industry vigorously contested the association's suit. Aided by provisions of the new consumer code that lowered their financial risk, the consumer association persevered and eventually prevailed on the merits. The plaintiff's victory was short-lived; years of appellate litigation followed from which the tobacco manufacturers emerged largely victorious. But by attracting media attention and civil society support (including financial support), the consumer association's class action sustained and empowered the political campaign against tobacco not just in Brazil but in other South American countries as well.

Litigation by gay rights groups in the 1990s led to a ruling by the Canadian Supreme Court that defining 'spouse' to apply solely to heterosexual partners for purposes of statutory benefit schemes was a violation of the Canadian Charter of Rights and Freedoms and subsequently led to amendments to pertinent statutes to bring them into compliance with the ruling (Chapter 11). However, the amendments to the statute that governs Canada's national pension plan denied retroactive compensation for the payment denials that the Court held violated the Charter. The financial consequences for Canadians who had lost same-sex partners to HIV-AIDS were substantial. Individual suits challenging the retroactivity provisions would have allowed the State to settle a few claims without redressing the losses of hundreds of similarly situated people, an attractive outcome for the State given its potential financial liability. To secure redress for all of those who had lost their same-sex partners, the national AIDS organization decided to file a class action. The class ultimately won a partial victory securing about eight years of pension payment arrears.

Process Outcomes Often Turn on Personalities as Well as Law

Historians have long debated the extent to which the outcomes of historical events turn on individuals: the 'great man in history' hypothesis. Would the American colonies have succeeded in their revolt against the British and their subsequent constitutional union without the influence of George Washington? What would the post-revolutionary era in France have looked like without Napoleon? Would the Soviet Union have crumbled if Mikhail Gorbachev had not appeared on the political scene? Although not of the same significance as these great turning points in history, litigation also has its heroes (and villains). Just as institutions help shape mass litigation, individuals do so as well. Their roles in turn are shaped by their unique personalities and experiences.

The role of individuals *qua* individuals was illustrated in several of the litigations described in this book. Mario Albanese, one of the three co-founders of the anti-tobacco consumer association that was established for the purpose of bringing class actions against the Brazilian tobacco industry, became an anti-smoking activist when his father died of smoking-related coronary disease in the 1950s (Chapter 3). José Rosemberg, another of the co-founders, was a physician who published the first Latin American research on nicotine dependency in the 1970s; he was the first Latin American awarded the prestigious World Health Organization medal on Smoking and Health.

When British Petroleum acceded to President Obama's request to establish a multi-billion fund to compensate Gulf Coast property owners and business operators for their losses due to its oil spill, the company's executives quickly turned to Kenneth Feinberg to head the fund (Chapter 5). Feinberg brought broad experience in designing and administering compensation funds, political savvy that served him well in dealing with the many private and public institutions that were engaged in addressing the aftermath of the spill and a reputation for dealing compassionately with victims that he had earned in the aftermath of the 9/11 terrorist attacks. It seems unlikely that a differently positioned individual would have been able to pay out more than $6 billion to some 220,000 claimants in less than two years.

The special purpose foundation established and funded by the Insurance Regulator to represent the interests of Vie d'Or's policy-holders in the insolvency litigation might easily have simply done the regulator's bidding, perhaps to the detriment of the policy-holders (see Chapter 6). Those familiar with the litigation attributed the persistent advocacy of the Foundation's board, which extended to suing the Regulator, to its chair Jaap van Rijn, a former bank executive who was widely respected for his integrity and acumen. When Van Rijn retired from the board, his successor took up the torch on behalf of the policy-holders. With his singular leadership, Van Rijn had not only developed a legal strategy that served the policy-holders well but established a board culture that persisted through the protracted litigation.

Rami Ben-Nathan became the lead counsel in *Shemesh v. Reichart*, one of Israel's first securities class actions, after a district court judge conditioned certification in part on the representative plaintiff securing an experienced commercial litigator to act on behalf of the class (see Chapter 10). Ben-Nathan pursued an aggressive strategy that led to protracted litigation that was arguably not in his own financial interest. Through the rulings in Shemesh, Ben-Nathan helped shape Israeli class action law.

George Hislop played a heroic role in the Canadian litigation before the High Court on behalf of Canadians who had lost their gay partners to HIV-AIDS but were denied the survivor benefits that the national government afforded to survivors of heterosexual marriages (Chapter 11). A gay rights activist, Hislop came forward to represent a class of survivors at a time when many homosexuals were wary of disclosing their sexual identity. Hislop was advised by his lawyer that by agreeing to serve as class representative he was giving up a likely possibility of settling individually with the government. Agreeing to serve as class representative also put Hislop at risk of adverse costs if the class—which was taking on the federal government—did not prevail. Hislop died before the landmark case was finally decided.

The Globalization of Law Shapes Mass Litigation

With the exception of the Royal Dutch Shell litigation (Chapter 8), all of the litigation described in this book was 'domestic', meaning that the claims arose in a single country and were prosecuted on behalf of that country's citizens and against either its government or a corporate entity headquartered or doing business in that country. Notwithstanding these formal legal facts, several of these litigations had an extra-national legal dimension. US investors brought class actions against the Belgian L&H (Chapter 14) and the German Deutsche Telekom (Chapter 13) in federal courts in the US, based on the same facts that gave rise to the litigation in Belgium and Germany. The US Securities Exchange Commission (SEC) investigated L&H. Relying on a provision of the US civil code, the German plaintiff lawyers tried unsuccessfully to obtain documents that had been produced by Deutsche Telekom for the US litigation for use in the German litigation. Relying on The Hague Convention on the Taking of Evidence Abroad, German trial court judges traveled to New York and San Francisco to conduct hearings with fact witnesses in Germany's consulate offices.

Even where legal action did not take place in multiple jurisdictions, an increasingly globalized legal system informally helped shape domestic litigation. The young Israeli lawyer who advised Shemesh to file a class action (who was a son of a friend) had studied for an LLM degree at New York University Law School where he had been exposed to US class action jurisprudence (Chapter 10). The lawyers for the Brazilian tobacco company defendants were advised by lawyers for British American Tobacco and Philip Morris International who were well versed in defending smokers' suits in other jurisdictions, including the US (Chapter 3). Shell's Swiss General Counsel had developed a sophisticated understanding of US plaintiff lawyers' litigation practices and strategies as General Counsel of ABB, whose US subsidiary was a prime target of long-running asbestos litigation in the US. Matías Cortés, the lawyer for the consumers in the Chilean VTR case had studied US class action law and worked with American class action lawyers. The English High Court judge who closely managed the Buncefield damages litigation is a frequent participant in international legal conferences where judges share their experiences managing complex litigation (Chapter 15). The English CEO of British Petroleum met with President Obama to discuss compensating US victims of the oil spill and the Japanese CEO of Toyota appeared before Congress to testify about Toyota's safety program and apologize for deficits in the company's quality control program (Chapter 5).

Whether it is because mass injuries or losses spill over borders, or because defendants are multi-national, or because judges and lawyers are now participants in a global legal system who are educated together, confer together and read each other's scholarship, practitioner guides and judicial opinions, mass litigation is increasingly global. The globalization of class actions is a symptom of this broader globalization of the legal system, as well as a contributor to it.

There is No One Size Fits All Response to Mass Claims

Although we can draw general lessons from comparative analysis of collective litigation procedures in different jurisdictions, the diverse experiences reported in this book indicate that there are many possible responses to mass injuries, mass financial losses and mass claims. The qualitative research approach does not provide the evidence that would be necessary to determine whether some responses are universally better than others in terms of efficiency or fairness. Indeed, different participants in the legal system might apply different metrics to measure efficiency or fairness and would likely assign different priorities to these and other values by which they might assess dispute resolution procedures.

The comparative case studies suggest that the same procedure might produce different results in different factual circumstances both within a single jurisdiction and across jurisdictions. This is especially true with regard to class actions, which have only recently been transplanted to many of the jurisdictions represented in this book, and which are a better fit in some of these jurisdictions than others. A final lesson to be drawn from this comparative research is that what appear to be the same procedures when reviewing statutes and rules are likely to be implemented differently in different legal contexts and to achieve different outcomes, for all the reasons discussed in this chapter.

FUTURE SCHOLARSHIP

Most of the procedures discussed in this book are quite new to their jurisdictions and few have been subjected to empirical analyses. Legal scholarship in most parts of the world focuses on doctrinal analysis that considers philosophical underpinnings of legal norms and the logic that connects statutes, codes, judicial decisions and procedural rules. How law affects behavior is left to conjecture. Empirical legal scholars view doctrinal scholarship as the foundation for legal analysis, not its endpoint. Contemporary behavioral studies in economics and cognitive and social psychology demonstrate that many human intuitions are not supported by factual evidence. Because law is ultimately a tool for regulating human behavior, it is dangerous to proceed with legal development and law reform on the basis of untested hypotheses.

Both qualitative and quantitative methods can be deployed to test hypotheses about how substantive legal doctrine and procedural law operate in practice. Quantitative methods, often considered the hallmark of empiricism, collate information collected in a standardized fashion from or about large populations. Because such data collection is expensive and time-consuming, often the data is collected from representative samples of the population of interest, using rigorous selection procedures. The use of statistical sampling techniques and standardized data collection allow inferences to be drawn from quantitative data using statistical modelling.

To understand how different collective litigation procedures are being used and with what effects, scholars should collect information on:

(1) the frequency of different types of collective litigation (for example, securities, anti-trust, workers' rights, consumer protection);
(2) the monetary damages alleged (if any);
(3) the time from filing to disposition;
(4) the parties' costs to litigate;
(5) the public costs (for example, judicial time);
(6) the litigation's outcomes; and
(7) the distribution of monetary remedies (if any) to class members.

As courts adopt information science technology (albeit slowly) to manage lawsuits, this data should become increasingly accessible to researchers.

The strength of quantitative analysis is that it allows inferences from the data collected to the population it represents. But the act of quantifying inevitably omits important information:

(1) What were the circumstances that gave rise to mass claims?
(2) Who came forward to organize or prosecute collective litigation?
(3) What were their goals?
(4) What conflicts of interest did they encounter?
(5) How did the litigation progress in the courts?
(6) What obstacles did plaintiffs and defendants encounter?
(7) How was the litigation financed?
(8) How did the form of financing affect the progress of the litigation?
(9) What approaches did judges and other court officials use to manage the litigation and encourage its resolution?
(10) Did the litigation encourage changes in substantive or procedural law?
(11) What was the relationship, if any, between the civil litigation and criminal prosecution or public regulatory action?

It is difficult to determine the answers to such questions using wholly quantitative methods. Qualitative case studies are the method of choice for investigation.

Typically, case studies are conducted within individual jurisdictions, to 'hold constant' the effects of substantive and procedural rules and other social, economic and political contextual variables. Confining case study research to individual jurisdictions, however, sacrifices the opportunity to understand how differences in legal regimes affect the uses and outcomes of similar substantive and procedural legal rules. Comparative case study research offers opportunities to investigate the consequences of different legal rules and norms in different social, economic and political contexts. Often comparative research also deepens our understanding of how legal rules operate within a single jurisdiction. For example, studying the consequences of collective litigation procedures in the Netherlands or Germany helps one to identify the critical features of US class action and group litigation practice. By developing and sharing case study findings over time, scholars can contribute important insights into the operations and consequences of collective litigation in a variety of legal regimes.

EPILOGUE

Large-scale comparative research, both quantitative and qualitative, requires significant investments of time and financial resources. Often such studies are funded by contracts and grants secured by scholars at one or a few institutions and directed by principal investigators using a 'top-down' approach. This project evolved in a different fashion. The 14 scholars who participated in this project came together serendipitously as a result of meeting at conferences and professional networking. Although established legal scholars, most had not previously conducted empirical social science research on law. Some were at first somewhat surprised at the notion of learning about their country's collective litigation procedures by conducting qualitative interviews. (Many of the lawyers they interviewed were similarly surprised to be approached for information.) What united the participants was an interest in developing a better understanding of how collective litigation procedures were being implemented in their jurisdictions.

In the absence of a contract or grant requiring 'deliverables', the study evolved organically. Progress depended critically on electronic communication as ideas, research protocols, book outlines and ultimately draft chapters were shared using email, cloud storage and video conferencing. Progress was also facilitated by the establishment of an 'international research collaborative' under the auspices of the American Law & Society Association and by meetings at a series of international conferences on the globalization of class actions, co-sponsored by Stanford Law School, the Oxford Centre for Socio-Legal Studies, Tilburg University, Australian National University and Florida International University.

The research project has spawned a variety of other initiatives. The project's participants have invited each other to speak at national conferences and to give guest lectures at their own institutions, to co-author articles and to co-teach courses on comparative class actions. In the process it has created a model for global scholarship. But perhaps most importantly it has created a set of warm friendships among people of different nationalities, generations, ideologies and training that will hopefully endure beyond the completion of this book.

REFERENCES

Greg Barrett, *Relief Workers Worried about Donation Fatigue*, The Times Picayune, 14 October 2005

John Coffee, *Class Action Accountability: Reconciling Exit, Voice, and Loyalty in Representative Litigation*, (2000) 100 Columbia Law Review 370

Michele Dauber, *The War of 1812, September 11th, and the Politics of Compensation*, (2003–2004) 53 DePaul Law Review 289

Marc Galanter, *Why the 'Haves' Come Out Ahead: Speculations on the Limits of Legal Change*, (1974) 9 Law & Society Review 95

Bruce Hay, *Contingent Fees, Principal-Agent Problems, and the Settlement of Litigation*, (1997) 23 William Mitchell Law Review 43

Robert Mnookin, *Why Negotiations Fail: An Exploration of Barriers to the Resolution of Conflict*, (1993) 8 Ohio State Journal of Dispute Resolution 235

Alina Tugend, *After a Tragedy, Calculating the Best Ways That People Can Help*, The New York Times, 31 May 2013, available at http://www.nytimes.com/2013/06/01/your-money/contemplating-effective-relief-actions-when-tragedies-occur.html?_r=0

Index

'opt-in' jurisdictions 8